About the CD-ROM

DISC CONTENTS   The CD-ROM supplied with this book offers a collection of utilities, graphics and sound files, authoring tools, and even a book! Some of the software runs on the PC, some runs on the MAC, and some of the programs have versions that run on both MAC and PC. In all cases except for the sound files, the software cannot be used for commercial purposes. There are several very useful shareware programs for both the MAC and the PC and, of course, if you use these, please pay the registration fees and get involved in the upgrade programs. You can also look at the back of the book for discount or upgrade offer coupons. The following is a brief overview of what is on the disc:

- Compton's New Media has supplied a multimedia book called **The Healing Foods Cookbook.** This will run on DOS, Macintosh, and Windows.
- Macromedia's exciting **Authorware** program is supplied in both MAC and PC versions. The only limitation is the size of the project, but you can create small files.
- The award-winning **Fractal Design Painter** is supplied in both PC and MAC formats. While you cannot save or print your projects, all other functionality is included.
- Corel Systems has provided **clip art** and some of their award-winning art.
- Laser Resources has provided limited versions of two of their products for Windows, **Barron's Profiles of American Colleges** and **Harry's Story Disk and Coloring Book.**
- ARIDI Computer Graphics has supplied a collection from their **Initial Caps** decorative fonts CD-ROM on the Mac.
- There are a number of **sound files** in the sounds directory on the CD-ROM.

The shareware for the PC includes:

- **Multimedia Maker** and **Multimedia Workshop** to help develop good multimedia applications; the **.WAV manipulation program**; and **CDLDOS**, the cache for CD-ROMs.

The shareware for the MAC includes:

- **Metamorphosis,** the morphing program; **Craig's Audio Player** which plays CD audio discs; **CDAudio,** a HyperCard stack that plays audio CDs; and **CD Programs**, which reads files created by Apple's CD Audio player.

For more information about these programs, see About the Disc in the Preface to the book.

SYSTEM REQUIREMENTS This CD-ROM contains software for both the Macintosh and IBM PC compatible computers. Much of the IBM PC software requires Microsoft Windows version 3.1, a mouse, and a VGA monitor. A sound card is required for some of the PC software.

WARNING: BEFORE OPENING THE DISC PACKAGE, CAREFULLY READ THE TERMS AND CONDITIONS OF THE CD-ROM WARRANTY BELOW.

Disc Warranty

This software is protected by both United States copyright law and international copyright treaty provision. You must treat this software just like a book, except that you may copy it into a computer to be used and you may make archival copies of the software for the sole purpose of backing up our software and protecting your investment from loss. By saying, "just like a book," Osborne/McGraw-Hill means, for example, that this software may be used by any number of people and may be freely moved from one computer location to another, so long as there is no possibility of its being used at one location or on one computer while it is being used at another. Just as a book cannot be read by two different people in two different places at the same time, neither can the software be used by two different people in two different places at the same time (unless, of course, Osborne's copyright is being violated).

Limited Warranty

Osborne/McGraw-Hill warrants the physical compact disc enclosed herein to be free of defects in materials and workmanship for a period of sixty days from the purchase date. If Osborne/McGraw-Hill receives written notification within the warranty period of defects in materials or workmanship, and such notification is determined by Osborne/McGraw-Hill to be correct, Osborne/McGraw-Hill will replace the defective disc.

The entire and exclusive liability and remedy for breach of this Limited Warranty shall be limited to replacement of defective disc and shall not include or extend to any claim for or right to cover any other damages, including but not limited to, loss of profit, data, or use of the software, or special, incidental, or consequential damages or other similar claims, even if Osborne/McGraw-Hill has been specifically advised of the possibility of such damages. In no event will Osborne/McGraw-Hill's liability for any damages to you or any other person ever exceed the lower of the suggested list price or actual price paid for the license to use the software, regardless of any form of the claim.

OSBORNE, A DIVISION OF McGRAW-HILL, INC., SPECIFICALLY DISCLAIMS ALL OTHER WARRANTIES, EXPRESS OR IMPLIED, INCLUDING BUT NOT LIMITED TO, ANY IMPLIED WARRANTY OF MERCHANTABILITY OR FITNESS FOR A PARTICULAR PURPOSE. Specifically, Osborne/McGraw-Hill makes no representation or warranty that the software is fit for any particular purpose, and any implied warranty of merchantability is limited to the sixty-day duration of the Limited Warranty covering the physical disc only (and not the software), and is otherwise expressly and specifically disclaimed.

This limited warranty gives you specific legal rights; you may have others which may vary from state to state. Some states do not allow the exclusion of incidental or consequential damages, or the limitation on how long an implied warranty lasts, so some of the above may not apply to you.

The Byte Guide to CD-ROM

Michael Nadeau

Osborne **McGraw-Hill**

Berkeley New York St. Louis San Francisco
Auckland Bogotá Hamburg London Madrid
Mexico City Milan Montreal New Delhi Panama City
Paris São Paulo Singapore Sydney
Tokyo Toronto

Osborne **McGraw-Hill**
2600 Tenth Street
Berkeley, California 94710
U.S.A.

For information on translations or book distributors outside of the U.S.A., please write to Osborne **McGraw-Hill** at the above address.

The BYTE Guide to CD-ROM

Copyright © 1994 by McGraw-Hill, Inc. All rights reserved. Printed in the United States of America. Except as permitted under the Copyright Act of 1976, no part of this publication may be reproduced or distributed in any form or by any means, or stored in a database or retrieval system, without the prior written permission of the publisher, with the exception that the program listings may be entered, stored, and executed in a computer system, but they may not be reproduced for publication.

1234567890 DOC 9987654

ISBN 0-07-881982-2

Information has been obtained by Osborne **McGraw-Hill** from sources believed to be reliable. However, because of the possibility of human or mechanical error by our sources, Osborne **McGraw-Hill**, or others, Osborne **McGraw-Hill** does not guarantee the accuracy, adequacy, or completeness of any information and is not responsible for any errors or omissions or the results obtained from use of such information.

For my family: Lynne, Julie, and Claire.

CONTENTS

ACKNOWLEDGMENTS   xi

PREFACE   xv

CHAPTER 1   INTRODUCTION TO CD-ROM   1

- PORTABLE AND SAFE ■ THE MEDIUM SPREADS THE MESSAGE ■ FUN AND GAMES LEADING THE WAY ■ "NINETY PERCENT OF EVERYTHING IS CRAP" ■ STANDARDS AND PLATFORMS ■ THE INFORMATION GAP ■ THE FUTURE OF CD-ROMS

CHAPTER 2   WHAT IS A CD-ROM?   17

- IT'S ALL OPTICAL ■ COMPOSITION OF A CD-ROM

CHAPTER 3   CD-ROM STANDARDS   45

- WHAT'S IN IT FOR YOU ■ STANDARDS AT ALL LEVELS ■ THE COLOR BOOKS ■ MEETING PLATFORM REQUIREMENTS ■ PROPRIETARY FORMATS

CHAPTER 4   CD-ROM Hardware   79

- COMPUTER-BASED PLAYERS ■ PHILIPS' CD-I: THE "I" IS FOR "INTERACTIVE" ■ PORTABLE PLAYERS ■ CD-ROM MAVERICKS: PROPRIETARY TV-BASED PLAYERS ■ CD-RECORDABLE: FOR THE PUBLISHER IN YOU ■ THE SOUL OF A CD-ROM DRIVE

CHAPTER5 5   DO-IT-YOURSELF CD-ROM   121

- BEFORE YOU BEGIN ■ INSTALLING AN INTERNAL CD-ROM DRIVE ■ INSTALLING EXTERNAL DRIVES ■ THE MAC MAKES IT EASY ■ SOUPED-UP CD-ROM ■ TROUBLESHOOTING YOUR CD-ROM DRIVE ■ CARE AND FEEDING OF DISCS AND DRIVES

CONTENTS

CHAPTER 6 MAKING THE MOST OF CD-ROM SOFTWARE   155

■ THINGS YOU SHOULD KNOW ■ ART AND MUSIC: APPRECIATE AND LEARN ■ BUSINESS SOFTWARE ON CD-ROM ■ CD-ROMS FOR YOUNG FOLK ■ CLIPS, CLIPS, AND MORE CLIPS ■ DIGGING FOR DATA ■ EDUCATION: SLIMMER PICKINGS SO FAR ■ BEST SELLERS ON DISC ■ ALL WORK AND NO PLAY... ■ SPORTS SPECIALS AND HOBBY HELPERS ■ HOME IS WHERE THE CD-ROM IS ■ PERIODICALS ON DISC ■ DISCS FOR SOFTWARE JUNKIES ■ IN TRAINING ■ SPECIAL PROJECTS

CHAPTER 7 CD-ROM PUBLISHING: GETTING STARTED   209

■ WHY PUBLISH ON CD-ROM? ■ HOW TO CREATE A CD-ROM ■ DO-IT-YOURSELF VERSUS SERVICE BUREAUS ■ MARKETING AND DISTRIBUTING YOUR CD-ROM

CHAPTER 8 USING CD-ROM ON A NETWORK   237

■ SERVER-BASED LANS ■ PEER-BASED LANS ■ WRITABLE SYSTEMS

CHAPTER 9 THE FUTURE OF CD-ROM   257

■ SOFTWARE CHALLENGES ■ HARDWARE NEEDS TO GET BETTER ■ THE UBIQUITOUS CD-ROM ■ THE DATA HIGHWAY: ROUTE 66 WAS NEVER LIKE THIS ■ AN ENDING, A BEGINNING

APPENDIX A GLOSSARY   273

CONTENTS

APPENDIX B VENDOR RESOURCE GUIDE — 293

■ ACCESSORIES ■ BUSINESS APPLICATIONS ON CD ■ CD-ROM-PUBLISHED PERIODICALS ■ CONSUMER CD-ROM SOFTWARE ■ DATABASES, DIRECTORIES, AND OTHER REFERENCES ■ DEMO SOFTWARE ■ DEVELOPER PROGRAMS AND ASSOCIATIONS ■ DEVELOPMENT TOOL VENDORS ■ DISTRIBUTORS ■ DRIVE VENDORS ■ EDUCATIONAL CDS ■ MARKET RESEARCH ■ MEDIA CLIPART ■ MEDIA SOURCES ■ MULTIMEDIA UPGRADE KIT VENDORS ■ NETWORKING PRODUCTS ■ PHOTO CD PROCESSING ■ PORTABLE COMPUTERS WITH CD-ROM DRIVES ■ PRESENTATION SOFTWARE ■ PROCESSOR UPGRADES ■ PUBLISHING SERVICES ■ RETRIEVAL SOFTWARE VENDORS ■ SCSI PRODUCTS ■ SECURITY SOFTWARE VENDORS ■ SHAREWARE ■ SHOWS AND CONFERENCES ■ SOUND PRODUCT VENDORS ■ SYSTEM INTEGRATORS ■ TRAINING CD-ROMS ■ TV-BASED PLAYERS ■ UTILITIES ■ VIDEO HARDWARE/SOFTWARE VENDORS

INDEX — 377

Acknowledgments

Special thanks go to four people who contributed significantly to this book. Jeff Sengstack co-authored Chapter 7. He is a former television news reporter and anchorman who is now a video producer and freelance writer living near Portland, Oregon. He is currently developing a series of travel oriented CD-ROMs. Ed Perratore of *BYTE* Magazine's New York office co-authored the material for Chapter 8. Friend and neighbor Mark Reynolds did much of the research and legwork for Chapter 5. A major debt of gratitude is also owed to Becky Lockwood Grossman at Silverplatter Information for lending her CD-ROM troubleshooting expertise to Chapter 5.

My wife, Lynne, and daughters, Julie and Claire, contributed not only their patience and support, but their expertise as well. Lynne helped critique educational titles, while Julie and Claire provided their views on the latest children's titles.

Bruce Levy at the National Software Testing Laboratory helped fill in the technical holes in my original manuscript. The editorial staff at Osborne/McGraw-Hill provided their enthusiasm and expertise in shaping the book; their help and support have made this a much better guide. Their names won't appear elsewhere in this book, so I'll list them here: Editor-in-Chief Jeff Pepper, Associate Editor Vicki Van Ausdall, Editorial Assistant Alexa Maddox, Project Editor Claire Splan, and Illustrators Lance Ravella and Marla Shelasky.

I am grateful, too, to Editor-in-Chief Dennis Allen and Executive Editor Rich Friedman of *BYTE* for their encouragement. Rick Grehan, the technical director of the *BYTE* Lab, helped me gain a better understanding of SCSI, and Senior Technical Editor and world-class Mac guru Tom Thompson provided his Apple expertise.

Many people in the CD-ROM community helped me with this book. Particular thanks go to Creative Labs and Apple Computer for loaning the equipment needed to make this guide possible. I would also like to thank Harry Lakerveld, Director of Philips Interactive Media Systems, for his time and perspective on the CD-ROM industry. Mr. Lakerveld is a true pioneer in the industry, having played a major role in the development of the laser videodisc, CD-I, and CD-ROM. Finally, I'd like to thank all the following people who gave their opinion and advice, and who arranged interviews and evaluation copies of CD-ROM titles:

John Albee, IBM; *Debra Armstrong*, MicroSolutions; *James Baker*, Music Factory; *Mike Bell*, Corel Corp.; *Mike Bilous*, Chinon; *Scott Blum*, Pinnacle Micro; *Judy Bolger*, Scenario; *Rich Bowers*, Optical Publishing Association; *Kathleen Burke*, Broderbund; *Susan Cashen*, Sony Electronic Publishing; *Norman Clark*, Plum Productions; *Jeff Croson*, 7th Level; *Graeme Devine*, Trilobyte; *Mike Duffy*, The Software Toolworks; *David Elliot*, Cohn & Wolfe; *Paul Evans*, IBM Multimedia Publishing Studio; *Christine Ferrusi*, Brodeur & Partners; *Bill Fiesterman*, New Media Magic; *Rick Fisher*, Sony Electronic Publishing; *Christa Freeman*, IBM Multimedia Publishing Studio; *Rolland S. Going*, The Terpin Group; *Sherri Grand*, Technology Solutions; *Andy Gregory*, BRS; *Brad Grob*, Baker & Taylor Software; *Bill Harlow*, Philips Interactive Media; *Michael Harrigan*, Eastman Kodak; *Jeneane Harter*, The Software Toolworks; *Larry Hayes*, Media Vision; *Robert J. Headrick*, Nimbus Information Systems; *Bob Helfant*, Laser Resources; *Gary Hornbuckle*, Apple Computer; *Kathy Howell*, IBM Software Manufacturing Co.; *Kathleen Hunter*, Dataware; *Bob Hurley*, Sony Electronic Publishing; *Dave Iverson*, 3M Corp.; *Tom Johnston*, Microsoft; *David Kalstrom*, Plasmon Data Systems; *Rose Kearsley*, Novell; *Chris Kitze*, Aris Entertainment; *Rich Kreuger*, Meridian Data; *Rob Landeros*, Trilobyte; *Eric Larsen*, Planet Productions; *Robert Lindsay*, Acculogic; *Tony Magoulas*, Tandy; *Andy Marken*, Marken Communications; *Paul McAfee*, Eastman Kodak; *Dean McCrea*, Planet Productions; *Hal W. McLenon*, Eastman Kodak; *Ray Moore*, OCP International; *Jack Moran*, JVC; *Kurt Mueller*, Dataware; *Daniel M. Murphy*, Sony Corp. of America; *Felix Nemirovsky*, Plextor; *Jennifer Nielson*, Pinnacle Micro; *Dirk Peters*, Sony Electronics; *Eric Pozzo*, Creative Multimedia; *Nancy Pressel*, Intel Corp.; *Theresa Pulido*, Creative Labs; *Jim Riggs*, Verbatim; *Bob Ryan*, BYTE; *Julie Schwerin*, InfoTech; *Laury Scott*, Atari; *Jim Sciales*, Pezzano & Co.; *Danny Spell*, Disctronics; *Jim Swenson*, New Media Magic; *Masayoshi Takahashi*, Plextor; *Robert Tatar*, Plextor; *Jorge Thiry*, BRS;

Karen Thomas, Thomas PR; *Dan Urbas*, The Newlin Company; *Marija van Hooren*, Philips Interactive Media Systems; *Manny Vera*, Sony Electronics; *Ray Vicenzo*, Pezzano & Co.; *Keri Walker*, Apple Computer; *Linda Wolfe*, Commodore Business Machines; *Robert Woodruff*, Foundation Solutions; *Chen Chi Yuan*, Creative Multimedia.

Preface

It's not easy coming to grips with a new technology. As the "Outland" comic strip on this page illustrates, people tend to feel either exhilarated about the promises of the technology or totally bewildered. Whichever way you feel about CD-ROM, *The BYTE Guide to CD-ROM* can help you get the greatest possible benefit from using CD-ROM applications. It will tell you what the technology can and—more importantly—cannot do.

©1993, The Washington Post Writer's Group. Reprinted with permission.

HOW TO USE THIS BOOK

This book is arranged so that each chapter builds on the other. You can think of each section as parts of a house. The nuts-and-bolts information on standards and how CD-ROM hardware and software works is the foundation (Chapters 2, 4, and 5). The how-to tutorials on installation, troubleshooting, networking, and do-it-yourself publishing (Chapters 3, 7, and 8) are the framework for the house. The section on CD-ROM applications (Chapter 6) provides the furnishings.

You can read only those chapters that most interest you if you wish. Not everyone will use CD-ROM on a network or publish their own discs, for example. The chapters are also designed so that you easily get the information that is most important to you. Each chapter begins with the basics, and then progresses to more technical material. The text is further segmented by subheadings.

You can decide which parts of each chapter to read with a quick scan. If you are already a computer wiz, you can skip the sections about computer hardware platforms. If you don't yet own a computer or CD-ROM player, you might want to read only the non-technical portions of the book to get a sense of what platform is right for you.

The most technical portions of each chapter are marked with an "Under the Hood" symbol, shown below:

You don't need to be an engineer or programmer to understand the "Under the Hood" sections, but you can easily skip them if you have no interest in the nuts-and-bolts discussions. I recommend that you read as much as you can. Understanding the capabilities of the hardware, the media, and the applications will help you make better purchasing decisions. To get the best possible video playback, for example, requires that you know something about your system's hardware and the various standards used to execute the software.

Other symbols indicate helpful tips, cautions, or trivia, as shown below.

Preface **xvii**

As with any technology, CD-ROM has its own vocabulary. New terms are defined in text as they come up, but if you skipped or forgot the meaning of a term, you can find it in the glossary (Appendix A).

The information provided in this book was up to date at the time of writing. The CD-ROM industry is moving very rapidly, however. While the basic descriptions of standards and hardware should remain relevant for the foreseeable future, new or revised products are constantly appearing. Appendix B is a Vendor Resource Guide. You can contact the companies listed there for the latest information about their products.

ABOUT THE DISC

The disc included with this book contains a wide sampling of CD-ROM applications for both MS-DOS/Windows and Macintosh computers. Our purpose in supplying the disc is to give you an idea of what makes a good application, what multimedia development tools are all about, and finally to supply useful utilities and files to help you in your work with CD-ROMs. A special note of thanks to Laser Resources for putting together the CD for the book.

Some of the programs are shareware. There is a MAC shareware folder and a PC shareware directory on the disc. Each of these programs has a registration fee associated with their use. If you find that you will be using the programs, you need to follow the instructions in the program to register. Otherwise, the programs are free for your use. There is a restriction, however, in that all of the files except for the sound files cannot be used for commercial purposes. The programs in this book are not copyrighted by Osborne/McGraw-Hill but are copyrighted by the original publisher. Osborne/McGraw-Hill is making them available so that readers may gain from their inclusion. Make sure you look through the coupons in the back of this book for discounts and upgrades of these products.

The CD-ROM in the book can be read by either a PC or a MAC. For the most part, the PC files are in directories and the Mac files are in folders. A description of each program follows:

Compton's New Media's The Healing Foods Cookbook   This multimedia book is unique for a couple of reasons. First, it represents state of the art multimedia book production. Second, it utilizes Compton's new MOST technology which allows the code to run on DOS, Macintosh, and Windows formats. Be sure to read README2 to get started with The Healing Foods Cookbook.

Macromedia's Authorware   Macromedia has come to the forefront of producers of multimedia development tools. The disc contains both MAC and Windows versions of Macromedia's exciting Authorware program. Authorware is the premier program for creating courseware and training modules. Be sure to read README1 to get started with Authorware. The program in this book is the "Working Model." Its only limitation is that you can create files containing up to 50 icons for small applications. This program requires 4MB of RAM. If you need the complete documentation for the Authorware Working Model, please call 1-800-945-9357.

Fractal Design Painter   The award-winning Fractal Design Painter is supplied in both PC and MAC formats. Painter is a remarkably flexible and fun program that allows you to paint like a real artist. If you have trouble getting started, you can import graphics and use them to trace out your project. While you cannot save or print your projects, all other functionality is included.

Corel Systems Clip Art   Corel Systems has provided some of their enormous clip art collection made available on CD-ROM. In addition, Corel runs an annual contest and some of their award-winning art is on the disc.

Laser Resources Applications   We have also included demonstration versions of two of Laser Resources' Windows products, Barron's Profiles of American Colleges and Harry's Story Disk and Coloring Book. The latter is a collection of stories and printable coloring book pages.

ARIDI Initial Caps   ARIDI Computer Graphics has supplied us with a collection from their Initial Caps decorative fonts CD-ROM on the Mac. These files may be displayed with any standard graphics package.

Sounds   There are a number of sound files in the sounds directory on the disc. Some are just funny sounds, others are MIDI clips from classical music.

PC Shareware   The shareware for the PC includes Multimedia Maker and Multimedia Workshop to help develop good multimedia applications; the .WAV manipulation program; and CDLDOS, the cache for CD ROMs.

Macintosh Shareware The shareware for the MAC includes: Metamorphosis, a morphing tool created in France but containing documents in English and sample files with instructions; Craig's Audio Player, which plays CD audio discs under the MAC; CDAudio, a HyperCard stack that plays audio CDs, along with documentation and XCMDs so that users can create their own stacks; and finally, CD Programs which reads files created by Apple's CD Audio player so that you can include the names of the songs on specific CDs. Like CDAudio, users can create their own stacks.

Many of the programs on this disk include documentation. Unfortunately, it wasn't always possible to get the manufacturer's documentation for the software. We apologize for the inconvenience but felt that the undocumented or partially documented programs were simple enough so that their inclusion on the book was an asset. We hope that the CD-ROM and the book together will give you a strong sense of this rapidly changing technology.

CHAPTER 1

INTRODUCTION TO CD-ROM

What began more than a dozen years ago as a better way to play your favorite tunes has emerged as the most important media device since the Gutenberg press. The compact disc is now a powerful tool for distributing and enhancing all types of information inexpensively. You can find, understand, and enjoy that information better than with any other medium—print or electronic.

CD-ROM (Compact Disc Read-Only Memory) is a unique medium. Made mostly of aluminum and plastic, it is a version of the familiar audio CD that has been modified for use with a desktop computer or with a player that attaches to your TV, as shown in Figure 1-1.

A typical 4.72-inch CD-ROM holds about 680 megabytes of information. That's equivalent to roughly 500 copies of this book. But if all CD-ROM had going for it was capacity, it would be pretty ho-hum technology. The most exciting features of CD-ROM are its ability to play a wide repertoire of material, its size, and its durability. If it can be *digitized*—converted to electronic form—you'll find it somewhere on a CD-ROM:

- ▶ Music
- ▶ Directories
- ▶ Books
- ▶ Periodicals
- ▶ Computer applications

2 BYTE Guide to CD-ROM

Chapter 1

FIGURE 1-1
A typical TV-based CD-ROM player

- Games
- Educational material
- Movies

A CD-ROM can play all this and more because both the medium and many of its players are designed for *multimedia*. In the context of CD-ROM, multimedia is the ability to play different types of data simultaneously. From the perspective of the viewer, multimedia is the delivery or presentation of information using multiple modes of communication. These communication modes, or data types, are

- Text: up to 680 million characters
- Video: up to 74 minutes of movies or other video

Introduction to CD-ROM 3
Chapter 1

- Sound: up to 18 hours—everything from your basic beep to professionally produced music
- Graphics: thousands of charts, computer renderings, and other static visual elements
- Animation: thousands of graphics with movement

Software—the program code that tells the computer to perform specific tasks—is the final data type. You can run a program from a CD-ROM on your computer just as you could run it from a hard or floppy disk drive. Not all CD-ROMs have executable software on them; many are just collections of items, such as video clips, sound clips, or graphics files, that require a separate program to access them. Most CD-ROMs, however, are built around software that coordinates all the different elements on the disc and presents a user interface from which you access the content.

GETTING THE SEMANTICS STRAIGHT

Throughout the book, you will see the terms CD-ROM, audio CD, CD-R, CD-I, drive, and player. Here's what each one means in the context of this book.

- *CD-ROMs* are the read-only, noninteractive discs used in computers and some TV-based players. However, this book also uses the term to refer to the overall family of nonaudio compact disc products and technologies.
- *Audio CD* refers specifically to products or technologies associated with producing digital audio on compact disc.
- *CD-R* refers to all *Compact Disc Recordable* products and technologies. It is sometimes referred to as CD-WO (Compact Disc Write-Once).
- *CD-I* is specific to Philips' *Compact Disc Interactive* products and technologies.
- A *drive* is the basic hardware unit that reads a disc. It can be part of a standalone player or installed in a computer.
- A *player* is a standalone device that either has its own display or attaches to a TV, or sometimes a computer. It generally has its own little computer inside to execute and display the software on the disc.

Chapter 1

PORTABLE AND SAFE

Only 1.2 mm thick, a CD-ROM is surprisingly tough. Its durability enhances the disc's portability. Not only is a CD-ROM much more resistant to damage than other media, such as a floppy disk, there is no chance that you will ever accidentally overwrite any information on a CD-ROM or infect it with a *virus*—program code designed to damage or alter other programs or data. (It is possible, however, for a virus to be introduced during the manufacturing process.) Furthermore, it is impossible for a CD-ROM drive to experience a head crash; it has no mechanical read hardware to fail and damage the medium.

Why is a CD-ROM so tough? First, the aluminum surface that actually holds the data is protected on one side by a layer of plastic and on the other by a special coating. Second, a CD-ROM player reads information optically using laser light. To read a CD-ROM, a player bounces a laser light off the spinning disc's aluminum layer and measures the light's reflection. The pattern produced by these measurements represents the digital form of the information recorded on the disc—the ubiquitous 1's and 0's that make up all digitized information. If the laser read mechanism fails, your data is still safe on the CD-ROM.

Since you can only read a CD-ROM—recording is possible only with special discs and equipment—you cannot accidentally erase or overwrite anything on it. For the same reason, it is impossible for anyone to plant a virus on your CD-ROM after it is produced.

On top of it all, CD-ROMs are cheap to produce and to use. It costs only a few dollars per disc to duplicate a CD-ROM title in quantity. Publishing an equivalent amount of data would require nearly 400,000 print pages or over 470 1.44-megabyte floppy disks. Needless to say, both options would be a tad more expensive. A bare-bones CD-ROM drive for a computer now costs well under $200. A TV-based player costs between $400 and $800. This is well within the means of most households and businesses.

THE MEDIUM SPREADS THE MESSAGE

Distributing text, video, sound, and all the other previously mentioned data types in electronic form is not new. The CD-ROM makes it possible for

Chapter 1

information providers to deliver their wares more cheaply, more portably, and with greater flexibility than ever before. The best, albeit cliched, analogy is the Gutenberg press. At first, the Gutenberg press did not inspire the production of new information. Thousands of monks were already painstakingly recording the knowledge of the day with pen and ink.

What the Gutenberg press did was allow mass production of existing works. It not only allowed wider distribution of books, it allowed anyone who could afford a press to print books. At first, these early publishers just reproduced the monks' work. Eventually, the more creative press owners entered the information producing business as well. This caused no end of worry and complaint among the monks and their bosses, who saw themselves losing their franchise. Civilization benefited greatly, as knowledge and literacy spread with the availability and variety of books.

CD-ROM technology, too, is distributing information and the ability to produce information. You can set yourself up to be a CD-ROM publisher for the price of a good used car—about $8000 including all the hardware and software. Publishing CD-ROMs is not quite as simple as buying a used car, but owning and running a modern printing press is well beyond the means of all but a few people—latter day monks who have not fully realized the threat CD-ROM publishing poses to their livelihood.

Even the best printing presses cannot match the versatility that CD-ROM publishing offers. Some CD-ROM publishing companies produce families of discs that include books, directories, and movies—all using the same basic equipment and software. And while desktop publishing software and a good laser printer will let you effectively produce small runs of newsletters and other simple publications, that combination is not practical for any size run of content-intensive publications such as large catalogs or directories. No printing press or laser printer can yet imbed video or sound on paper.

FUN AND GAMES LEADING THE WAY

The first CDs played only music and, rarely, some limited video. This was enough, however, to condemn millions of LP record players to yard sales and land fills. CD-ROM is vastly more versatile than audio CD and more threatening to other entertainment appliances such as your VCR, TV, and game boxes such as Nintendo and Sega. Don't worry, these providers of leisure and

CRITICAL MASS

Philips and Sony invented the compact disc in 1980 and began producing audio CD players two years later. The CD-ROM has been around since 1983 as a specification and since 1985 as a product, but until recently sales of CD-ROM drives and software have been slow. According to the Optical Publishing Association, an estimated 5.8 million computers in the United States had CD-ROM drives in 1993, double the number from 1992. TV-based players now number over a million, according to the market research firm InfoTech. The number of CD-ROM titles rose by 30 percent in 1993 to over 3500, based on listings in *CD-ROMs in Print 1993* (Meckler Publishing, Westport, CT, 1993).

So why is it that these devices have caught on only in the last couple of years? A diversity of good new titles, particularly in the areas of entertainment and education, are making CD-ROM players a must-have option for desktop computers. The fact that players have become faster, less expensive, and able to play more formats is icing on the cake.

One upshot of this trend is that CD-ROM players and computers are improving to accommodate CD-ROM-based multimedia software. CD-ROM drives and high-quality sound and video capability are well on their way to becoming standard features on desktop computers. Companies such as Apple Computer, Gateway 2000, and Tandy sell mainstream desktop PCs that come standard with CD-ROM drives. TV-based players, too, are getting sophisticated graphics and faster processing engines to drive the latest software.

Best of all, prices are rapidly falling. At this writing, you could buy a fully equipped multimedia PC for about $2000—several hundred dollars less than the cost of a plain-vanilla PC just eight months before.

escapism won't disappear like the record player. Many manufacturers have decided to offer their own CD-ROM-based products rather than resist. This explains the recent flood of CD-ROM products for use with TVs and game systems, such as Sega CD, Atari Jaguar, and Tandy VIS.

Just as it was with TV, entertainment has been a key driving force behind the upsurge in CD-ROM player sales over the last couple of years. Developers are starting to learn how to make the best use of the CD-ROM medium, and consumers are responding by increasing their purchases.

A whole generation of game players brought up on Nintendo machines and home computers is responding to what CD-ROM can deliver. Killing aliens or fighting your way out of dungeons is a lot more exciting when you can interact with the characters, for instance. Replacing low-resolution graphics and cheesy sound effects with full-motion video and a high-quality soundtrack are other compelling reasons to play games from CD-ROM.

"I GOT IT FOR THE KIDS"

If you or someone you know recently purchased a CD-ROM player and claimed, "I bought it for the kids," you're not alone. While this refrain has probably caused a lot of spousal eye-rolling, it is the justification used in many households.

Kids are growing up in a digital age, and anyone who has watched them interact with a computer or Nintendo player knows that it soon becomes second nature to them. In fact, getting kids interested in more traditional forms of entertainment—reading or playing a musical instrument—is difficult once they've developed a digital habit.

Why limit tomorrow's generation to "Super Mario Brothers" when CD-ROM titles are just as interesting, but educational as well? You can choose from dozens of creative, well-produced CD-ROM titles that:

- ▶ Encourage reading
- ▶ Teach foreign languages
- ▶ Show how to play a musical instrument
- ▶ Describe what the age of dinosaurs was like
- ▶ Teach geography

CD-ROM'S LITTLE SECRET

It is well known in the CD-ROM industry that many of the so-called early adopters of the technology used it to distribute and view erotica—pornography to some. Trade magazines are full of advertisements for adult CD-ROMs, some proclaiming their use of "wife-proof labels." These usually contain digitized photos or graphics of semi- and unclad women; some have video. A perennial CD-ROM best-seller is "Virtual Valerie."

Chapter 1

It is amazing that this genre has been so popular, given that for a fraction of the cost of a CD-ROM you can get the same thing on the newsstand or at the video store. Yet many people believe that the vendors of adult titles were a key factor in building the installed base of CD-ROM players. This parallels what happened in the early years of the VCR. Though sales of adult titles are still strong, their overall market share has been declining.

THE PRICE IS RIGHT

Though some highly specialized CD-ROM databases can cost thousands of dollars, most consumer and business titles are remarkably affordable. You can buy an entire encyclopedia with sound clips, animation, *hypertext links* (which let you jump directly from one related piece of information to another), and other features for a few hundred dollars. Your kids will beg you to let them use it. Or you can spend as little as $20 on a collection of shareware items such as games, business software, video and sound clips, and clip art. *Shareware* is software and other files that you can try out before purchasing. If you like something, you either send in the requested fee or pay what you think it is worth. Chapter 6 lists some good examples of shareware.

Top-quality children's titles cost from $40 to $100. Games are about the same. Vendors of business applications want to encourage the use of CD-ROM because it is cheaper for them to send one disc rather than a handful of floppies. Therefore, you rarely pay a premium when you buy a business application on CD-ROM. The exception is when a software publisher uses the CD-ROM to add value—including a tutorial on disc, for instance.

"NINETY PERCENT OF EVERYTHING IS CRAP"

Sadly, science-fiction author Theodore Sturgeon's observation holds true for CD-ROM titles. Some CD-ROM publishers are merely reproducing existing works on CD-ROM without thought to how the medium can add value. Some go to the other extreme and bury information in too many multimedia bells and whistles.

For every "Encarta 94," by Microsoft—a wonderful multimedia encyclopedia—or "Just Grandma and Me," by Broderbund—a clever multimedia translation of a best-selling children's book—there are too many duds that fail because the creators made classic CD-ROM publishing mistakes.

The most common mistake is viewing the CD-ROM as a big bucket to be filled with whatever is handy. Size doesn't always matter when it comes to producing quality CD-ROM software. It is relatively easy to put, say, the entire works of Shakespeare on a CD-ROM, graft on software to search text, and maybe build a few links among different sections, and think you have a great CD-ROM product. Chances are that the developer gave little or no thought to whether Shakespeare scholars need yet another collection of his works or whether they built the searching and linking capabilities appropriately for the intended audience.

If you first study the needs of those scholars, then you are in a position to intelligently add value by leveraging what the CD-ROM offers. Let's assume that the scholars need a collection of Shakespeare's work as a teaching tool. You might add some sound clips of readings of Shakespeare, some video clips of his plays, some recorded commentary by leading literary critics, and mold the mix into a tightly integrated whole. Now you are beginning to grasp what it means to publish on CD-ROM. You must have a clear, original vision of what you want to do and how the CD-ROM can help you accomplish it.

STANDARDS AND PLATFORMS

Frustrating for consumers and producers of CD-ROMs alike is the number of different formats and platforms for CD-ROMs. *Format* standards deal with media and player issues of how information is stored on a CD-ROM and how a player reads it. Audio CD players, for example, locate data differently from CD-ROM.

The *platform* refers to the hardware and software interface through which you access the information. An Apple Macintosh and its System 7 graphical interface are an example of a platform; the Multimedia PC (MPC) computers based on Microsoft Windows are another. MPC is a specification produced by the Multimedia Marketing Council that defines the requirements of a multimedia-ready Windows PC in terms of:

▶ Sound capability
▶ Video capability
▶ CD-ROM drive type
▶ System memory
▶ Size of the hard disk drive
▶ System processor type

Chapter 3 has more information on the MPC standard. System 7 already supports CD-ROM and multimedia, so it needs no MPC-like standard. OS/2 also has its own multimedia standard.

What the different format standards mean to you is that you need to be aware of which ones your platform and drive can handle. This means knowing the specifications of both. Chapters 3 and 5 will help you determine how well your system matches up to each standard.

What makes life difficult for developers is that they must increasingly make their CD-ROM titles compatible with a range of standards and platforms. This makes the development process more complex and expensive. The good news is that the latest standards tend to be compatible with previous ones. Unfortunately, it takes time to build an installed base of CD-ROM players compatible with those new standards. New cross-platform development tools are making it easier to produce CD-ROM that can run on a number of popular platforms.

Users suffer the most. Some platforms are more consistent about how they implement the various standards, however. If you use a Macintosh, for example, you can be fairly sure that the CD-ROM will work as expected as long as it's labeled for the Mac. For Windows PCs, however, you have to first know a lot more about what's inside your computer: Is your CD-ROM drive MPC-compatible? Do you have the appropriate sound card? Can your graphics card handle video? Even if you've bought an MPC system, it might not be up to the latest specification of the standard.

Most of these standards are set by the industry, which has been generally good about following them. Others, such as the International Standards Organization (ISO) 9660 standard, have become more formalized. ISO 9660 deals only with the file system—the manner in which information is indexed on the disc—and most other standards accommodate it. For this reason, CD-ROM players on incompatible platforms can often read which files are on the disc even though they cannot play them.

The major format standards are referred to by color.

Red Book   Red Book was established in 1980 and covers audio CD; all subsequent standards incorporate it in some way. This is why you can play audio CDs on your CD-ROM drive. Red Book is optimized for audio; for example, where a CD-ROM can locate portions of a block of data, audio CDs locate only the beginning of a block, or song.

Yellow Book   Yellow Book was released in 1985 by the ISO. It establishes the physical format for how information is stored and indexed on CD-ROM discs. Yellow Book created a media standard for text and graphics information. As with Red Book, most subsequent standards can read Yellow Book discs.

In 1989, Yellow Book was extended with the CD-ROM XA (eXtended Architecture) standard. CD-ROM XA is very significant in that it serves as a bridge to other standards such as CD-Interactive (CD-I), Philips' TV-based format for interactive media, and Photo CD, Eastman Kodak's CD-based digital photo storage media. CD-ROM XA drives can read these formats, and vice versa, though they won't be able to execute software specific to the respective operating systems of each platform. A developer can, however, choose to support multiple operating systems on one disc. XA-compatible drives were slow to appear at first, but most of the CD-ROM drives sold today are XA-compliant.

Green Book   Green Book appeared in 1988. CD-I is based on Green Book, and Photo CD uses part of it. Green Book defines not just the media, but the entire hardware and software system, including CPU, operating system, memory, and audio and video compression methods. This standard allows for tighter integration of audio/visual and textual data so that everything plays more in synchronization.

Orange Book   Orange Book is the standard for recordable media—also called CD-Recordable (CD-R) or CD Write-Once (CD-WO). Orange Book forms the basis for Photo CD, and it accommodates multisession recording. Photo CD is Kodak's recordable system for placing photographic images on CD-ROM. *Multisession* means that you don't have to record the entire disc at once; instead you can do it incrementally. Recordable media and players have opened a door of opportunity for CD-ROM publishers and in-house production staffs by dramatically lowering the entry fee. CD-ROM mastering systems were in the $50,000 range before CD-R came into being. Now you can buy a CD-R drive for under $4000.

ISO 9660 defines the CD-ROM file system, which supports Microsoft's MS-DOS and Apple Macintosh. An update—a replacement, actually—to ISO 9660, called the Frankfurt specification, will probably be accepted by the time you read this. It will create a standard file system that supports Orange Book.

Beyond the media and players are the system or platform standards such as Microsoft Windows, Apple Macintosh, or Unix. Although the CD-ROM standards might cross platforms, the software through which you interact with the CD-ROMs must still be compatible with the computer system or TV player on which it is running. Chapter 3 describes these and other standards and platforms in detail.

THE INFORMATION GAP

CD-ROMs have potential for bridging what's been called the "information gap" between computer-literate and computer-ignorant people. The concern is that people who are proficient with computers will increasingly have social and professional advantages over those who are not, essentially creating a two-class information society.

CD-ROM technology has a long way to go before it can perform in this role—a wide and confusing selection of devices to read CD-ROMs is available. Some work with a computer, others attach to your TV, and some are simply dedicated CD-ROM players.

The key issues for widespread use are accessibility and ease of use. The more consumer-oriented players attach to your TV and have the best interfaces; they are simpler and coach the user along. Graphical user interfaces (GUIs), such as Windows or Apple System 7, are more complex, but a dedicated novice can still learn how to use them. At the other end of the spectrum are the text-based reference CD-ROMs. Though some have reasonably good interfaces, many are arcane and intimidating to novice users.

Information seekers who are intimidated by computers or otherwise feel they have no need for them have several options with CD-ROM technology. All of these options, however, have yet to meet their full potential. First, you can hook up a CD-I-based device such as the new 3DO player, Philips CD-I, or the Tandy VIS (Visual Information System) to your TV. Most of these products are not wedded to a computer interface and are the easiest to use. Titles for these systems are heavy on entertainment and education, but the software base is expanding.

Another alternative is to buy a standalone CD player such as the Sony MMCD Player. It is little more intimidating than an audio CD player and is simple to use. You also have the option of hooking it up to a TV. However, selection of software is limited at this time and will continue to be so until sales of these units reach a level that encourages developers to produce software in that format.

The best solution might be to go to the library. Libraries long ago embraced CD-ROM technology as a cost-effective means to serve a wide range of information needs. Most large libraries will have CD-ROM stations; patrons can either use them themselves or ask a librarian to retrieve the needed information. Unfortunately, the selection of CD-ROMs at a given library is often limited to only the most general references.

ONLINE SERVICES COMPETE AND COMPLEMENT

Many libraries got into CD-ROMs in part to control costs. Previously, they had been providing *online data retrieval*, where they connect via telephone to a service such as Dialog or CompuServe. These services store vast amounts of reference data at a central location and usually charge for both the time spent using the service and for the actual retrieval of data. Online search and retrieval costs are unpredictable by nature. If a librarian knows the most often requested types of information, he or she can order the appropriate CD-ROMs at a fixed cost and save money.

At present, a much greater body of information resides in the centralized databases of these services than on published CD-ROMs. Online advocates claim that some day you will be able to tap into the knowledge of the world from your computer or telephone. This is a nice concept, and online searches are sometimes better than polling a CD-ROM.

The reality today, however, is that it is often difficult to locate the information you want online, and when you find it, it is usually expensive to download. Searching online is a notoriously arcane procedure; it can sometimes be like writing computer code. Unless you know exactly how to phrase your query, you will likely access a lot of information that is irrelevant to your needs. (See Chapter 6 for more information on data search and retrieval.)

So, even if all the world's knowledge were online (it isn't), finding the specific item you need is like looking for a book in a library that doesn't use the Dewey decimal system. You are forced to go through the service's "librarian," and you'd better be prepared to ask your questions in precisely the manner in which they are expected.

CD-ROMs present the opportunity to package information so that it is targeted at the people who need it. No Dewey decimal system for CD-ROMs exists, either. But you are dealing with a more focused data set to begin with, and you aren't charged for time wasted on inefficient searches.

APPLICATIONS EXPLOSION

The most interesting software in the world today is being produced on CD-ROM. Developers have scaled the medium's learning curve, and consumers are beginning to see the benefits. Here are some examples of what to expect:

- **Microsoft's "Encarta 94"** Microsoft started with the *Funk & Wagnalls New Encyclopedia* and added about 7 hours of sound clips (including wildlife, music, and speeches) and over 100 animations. Microsoft spent a great deal of time testing the product for usability. The effort paid off.

- **Broderbund Software's "Just Grandma and Me"** Based on the popular children's book by Mercer Mayer, this interactive title is a joy for kids and adults alike. You can choose to read the story with its animations and sound effects, or you can explore the pictures onscreen with the mouse. Clicking on the items you see often has surprising and humorous effects. It's also a great tool for teaching reading skills to young children.

- **Interactive Ventures/Sony Electronic Publishing's "Mayo Clinic Family Health Book"** A high-tech Dr. Spock for the whole family. Find a reference to what ails you fast. Some of the accompanying photos are not for the squeamish, however.

- **Washington Post Co.'s "Newsweek Interactive"** This is a well-conceived implementation of a news magazine on CD-ROM. Most of the material was created specifically for this publication, sold as a quarterly on a subscription basis. It uses video well, and allows you to go to historical data for background.

THE FUTURE OF CD-ROMS

The title of this book is misleading. The book isn't really about compact discs or the CD-ROM players themselves. It's about content: how you can use it and how you can produce it. CD-ROM-based content can inform, educate, and entertain in ways never before possible. If the previous sentence reminds you of the promises made when TV was introduced, it's no coincidence.

As it has been with TV, the qualities that CD-ROMs bring to distributing information and to entertaining will not always be exclusive to the technology. In fact, everything that a CD-ROM can deliver today can be delivered on other media or over a communications network—just not as well. Today's CD-ROM users are early adopters riding the wave of a longer-term trend that will fundamentally change how you seek, gather, and analyze information; how you spend your leisure time; and how you educate your children.

Content delivery is changing from the traditional linear text-and-picture-on-paper medium to a nonlinear, free-form, multimedia environment. The old way forces you to adapt to how the information is presented; the new medium adapts to the way you absorb information.

In a few years, CD-ROMs and the players will likely be different—smaller with higher capacity is always a good bet. Ultimately, the CD-ROM will be eliminated as the middleman of content delivery. You will get the data, software, entertainment program, literature, and so on that you need transmitted by fiber-optic cable or the airwaves directly to your TV or computer.

This is the dream of the *Data Highway,* a national fiber-optic network of immense capacity that will piggyback on the existing phone and cable TV networks. When will this happen? No one really knows, but guesses range from 5 to 10 years or more. Due to the complexities involved in building the infrastructure, not to mention a viable industry of content producers, it's safest to assume that this will happen later rather than sooner.

In the meantime, it's nice to know that you can get a jump on your neighbors, your coworkers, or your competitors today by taking advantage of what CD-ROM technology has to offer.

CHAPTER 2

WHAT IS A CD-ROM?

The great value of CD-ROM is its use as a delivery vehicle for information, entertainment software, educational programs, and business applications. Think of it much as you do the pages in this book, the telephone line from which you download remote data, a VCR tape, or the floppy disk on which your last computer application came. CD-ROM is a unique publishing medium designed to deliver all types of content electronically, be it text, graphics, video, software, or sound.

Features that make the CD-ROM a good delivery vehicle are

- ▶ Large capacity
- ▶ Ability to hold and play back multiple data types concurrently
- ▶ Durability and stability
- ▶ Small size/portability
- ▶ Low cost
- ▶ The large, growing installed base of CD-ROM players

You might find other media that match or even exceed CD-ROM in any one or two areas, but nothing else provides this mix of features.

In itself, the CD-ROM's 600-megabyte-plus capacity is not that startling compared to most other media. Hard disk drives, for example, can now hold in the *gigabyte* (1000 megabytes) range. The CD-ROM not only holds all common data types, but allows them to be played back in a synchronized fashion at near real time. For example, a training CD-ROM might simultaneously show text and a demonstration video while playing a soundtrack. Even though each type of data is coming from different locations on the CD-ROM, all play in rhythm with one another and at close to natural speed, or *real time*.

Cost and portability are related. Duplicating what a CD-ROM can hold on other media such as paper or floppy disks would be much more expensive. Mastering a CD-ROM might cost a few thousand dollars, but replication costs per disc can get below two dollars in large quantities. It is also more cumbersome to carry and use those other media.

Imagine what it would be like if your job required that you carry around the equivalent of an encyclopedia every day. For some people, that analogy is all too real. Airline mechanics, technicians on submarines, or even the clerk at your local auto parts shop rely on volume after volume of printed manuals and parts lists to perform their tasks.

One half-ounce CD-ROM can replace hundreds of pounds of paper. To understand how it does this, you need to look at how a CD-ROM is made and how data is recorded on it.

CD-ROM MYTHS VERSUS REALITY

Although CD-ROMs have been available for over eight years, they are not well understood by many people. Here are some common misconceptions (myths) about CD-ROM along with the reality.

MYTH: Using CD-ROMs saves hard disk space.

Most CD-ROMs load files on your hard disk drive that allow you to access the disc's information. This can be as little as 100,000 to 200,000 kilobytes or as high as several megabytes. CD-ROMs might also use your hard disk drive as a temporary storage area during run time. For example, a game might save pointers to where you left off or high scores to disk.

MYTH: CD-ROMs will last forever.

While more stable than other media, most CD-ROMs are rated for only 10 to 15 years of use before the aluminum data layer begins to deteriorate. While with care, that estimate might be conservative, you should not count on more than that, especially if the disc contains important information. Some special discs are rated to hold data for up to 100 years.

What Is a CD-ROM?   19
Chapter 2

MYTH: CD-ROMs will play even if severely scratched or dirty.

Light scratches and some dust usually aren't a problem, but a scratch can destroy a disc and dirt can interfere with the player's ability to read a disc.

MYTH: CD-ROMs are all the same.

Data can be recorded on CD-ROMs in many different formats, some of which require their own type of player. You need to make sure that you buy discs in a format that your player can read.

MYTH: Recording on a CD-ROM requires going to an outside service.

You can buy recordable CD drives now for under $4000. They use a special type of disc, but do-it-yourself CD-ROM recording is here.

MYTH: CD-ROMs are expensive.

Early uses of CD-ROM usually involved placing collections of highly specialized textual data that were sold for very high prices. Most consumer and business applications on CD-ROM today are priced competitively with floppy-based software products.

IT'S ALL OPTICAL

CD-ROMs, audio CDs, and their relatives are *optical* media, which refers to the fact that the data is stored and read using light—laser light. To record data on a disc, a laser is used to burn a specific pattern into the surface of the media. To read that recorded data, the laser in your CD-ROM player, which is different from the recording laser, scans that surface to detect the pattern.

Laser light has unique properties. Unlike magnetic media, such as floppy drives or tape, optical devices have no mechanical read or write head. Figure 2-1 shows schematically how a laser reads a CD-ROM, and it shows a hard disk drive's read head.

The laser is aimed perpendicular to the disc's surface, deflected by a mirror through two lenses onto the disc. A photodetector then measures the reflected light. This eliminates or lessens a number of problems: First, the laser

Chapter 2

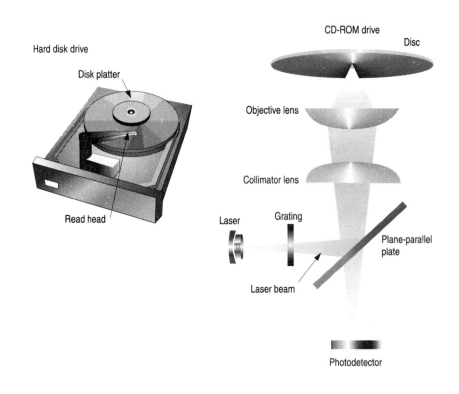

FIGURE 2-1
A hard disk drive and a CD-ROM drive read data in different ways

cannot damage the media or the information on it if the laser mechanism fails. During a read, the laser light simply bounces off the reflective surface of the CD-ROM and does not burn it. The laser mechanism is relatively far from the disc—1 millimeter. By comparison, the mechanical head of a hard disk drive is 2000 times closer.

Also, because it is not mechanical, laser light can be very narrowly focused on tiny, discrete areas of the CD-ROM, so a small surface area can store a great deal of information. By reducing the size of the laser beam during both the recording and the reading of a disc, it is possible to increase the *density* (amount of data in a given area of disc) even further. Although work is under way to do just that, the task still presents some technical and practical problems. For example, a smaller beam might require a special type of laser. Also, your current CD-ROM player could not read these denser discs, so compatibility would be sacrificed for the greater density.

USING CD-ROM AS A STORAGE MEDIUM

All optical media allow random access to data, as opposed to sequential access, which is found on magnetic tape. *Random access* is much faster than sequential access because it lets you go directly to the location of the desired information. In contrast, a tape drive, which uses *sequential access*, must first scan the areas of a tape that precede the requested data.

Most optical media are used for *archival storage*—for old or rarely used network files, documents, system backup, and so on—because of their high capacity and stable, reliable storage characteristics. Optical technology is inherently more stable than magnetic devices because it has no mechanical read head to "crash" and destroy the medium, and the optical medium itself is less delicate. It is less prone to physical damage and is not affected by magnetic fields. Furthermore, write-once optical devices pose no risk of accidentally erasing or overwriting important information.

Slow read and write performance compared to hard disk drives makes most optical technology less practical as a computer's primary storage medium—one that holds the system and application files that you use all the time. The fastest CD-ROM drive, for instance, might find a piece of information in 140 milliseconds; a fast hard disk drive might find it in as little as 12 milliseconds. This speed disparity is exacerbated when the CD-ROM drive has to locate and read many small files.

However, CD-ROMs don't usually serve well as a backup storage medium, either. Expense is one factor. CD-Recordable (CD-R) drive prices start at $4000, while a tape backup drive might cost only a few hundred dollars. The bigger problem is simply the difficulty of recording directly on a CD-ROM.

You have two choices if you want to place your backup data on a CD-ROM: Send your data to a mastering service for conversion to CD-ROM, or buy a CD-R system and record your own discs. Both options are expensive and time-consuming compared to tape or other writable optical media. The CD-R recording process might require that you record the entire disc in a single session. This means you must maintain a sustained data transfer rate of 300 kilobytes per second (Kbps). To do that, you must have a controlled environment with a fast hard disk drive. Pulling the data directly off a network to disc, for instance, risks interrupting the flow and forcing you to start over with a new disc.

At present, only in cases that require a highly stable digital medium for long-term (10 years or more) storage of very important data do you find CD-ROMs used for archival storage. This might change, however. Companies such as Pinnacle Micro and JVC are developing software and hardware that allow a CD-R drive to perform as a backup device. The Pinnacle software, called RCD-PC Backup, makes use of the company's multisession RCD 200 CD-R drive. Rather than record an entire disc at once, this system can update the disc incrementally until it is full. You can schedule backups on your network much as you would for a tape backup system. It is still faster and cheaper to record backup data to tape, but products like Pinnacle's are just the first step for CD-ROM as a backup technology. As more people use CD-ROM for backup, prices will drop and performance will improve.

CD-ROM does have one other feature that makes it a potentially appealing backup medium. You can place the system files as well as the data files on the archival disc. This has the advantage of guaranteeing that you will always be able to access the archived data. For example, you might be using a version of the computer's operating system that cannot read the files that were recorded several years before using an earlier, incompatible version. With the system files on disc, you can run your computer using the older operating system and ensure file compatibility. You cannot easily execute system files from a backup tape.

WHY NOT FASTER?

CD-ROM trades access speed for capacity. Part of the reason is in how the CD-ROM is structured. Unlike a hard disk drive, which has concentric tracks, a CD-ROM's tracks are spiral, as shown here:

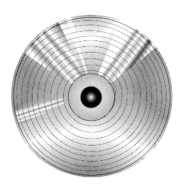

Consequently, the player must vary the speed at which it spins the disc to maintain a constant rotation speed. This is called *constant linear velocity (CLV)*, and it poses some technical hurdles to creating faster CD-ROM drives.

A CD-ROM drive reads a disc starting at the innermost track. Inner tracks are shorter than outer tracks, so the CD-ROM drive must spin a disc faster as it reads outward to cover the greater distance at the same read rate. The range for most drives is 200 to 530 revolutions per minute.

One way to make a faster drive is to increase the rotation speed of the disc. The faster you spin a disc, however, the finer the tolerances to synchronize all the components of the read mechanism become, especially if that spin must constantly vary. Also, because the read mechanism must respond more quickly to a faster spinning disc, it needs a larger, stronger servo motor to control the focus of the laser onto the disc.

If the spiral tracks are a barrier to higher performance, then why use them? The spiral pattern allows tracks to be variable in length, and it is a more efficient way to store data. But it is not the most efficient track arrangement for speedy access. The spiral pattern is an artifact from the audio CD, which required only limited random access of data.

The method used by hard disk drives, *constant angular velocity (CAV)*, is much faster at getting data off a medium. Figure 2-2 shows how a hard disk is structured. Its tracks are concentric, which allows the drive to spin the disk platter at a constant rate. Furthermore, the disk is divided into pie-shaped sectors. Data is addressed by track and sector. Finding a specific piece of data is a relatively simple matter of instructing the drive head to go directly to the proper track and sector.

A CD-ROM addresses data using a minute:second:sector scheme. This method is slower than the track and sector addressing used on hard disk drives. The drive focuses the laser to the approximate location, adjusts the spin rate of the disc to find the address information, and then accesses the specific sector.

A typical CD-ROM drive has a transfer rate of 150Kbps. *Double-speed* CD-ROM drives are, appropriately, about twice as fast. NEC recently introduced a family of triple-speed drives, called the MultiSpin 3X series, with a claimed transfer rate of 450Kbps. Until recently, the fastest CD-ROM players—referred to as *quad-speed*—were available only in large, external boxes. It was only at the end of 1993 that quad-speed drives small enough to fit inside a PC were available.

Quad-speed drives from vendors such as Pioneer and Plextor provide a transfer rate as high as 600Kbps. Most multimedia applications demand a transfer rate of at least 300Kbps, which is what double-speed drives provide.

Chapter 2

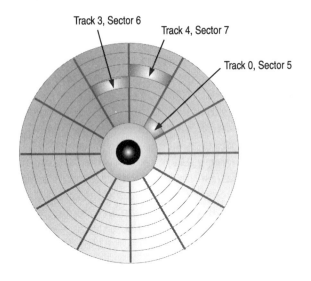

FIGURE 2-2
Structure of a hard disk

These faster-speed drives are technically compatible with all existing CD-ROM software, but the higher spin rate can pose problems. A triple- or quad-speed drive might not be able to read a poorly recorded disc at the fastest rate. Production flaws become magnified as the disc spins faster, making it a lot harder for the laser to pick up the information. To compensate, most high-speed drives will kick down to lower spin rates until they can read the disc. This points out the need for disc replicators to raise the bar on production quality to accommodate faster drives.

The demands of multimedia applications will continue to force improvements in both the CD-ROM media and the players. This means that there might always be a better player or version of your favorite CD-ROM title to lust after. Thanks to the established standards for CD-ROM format, however, the odds are good that subsequent improvements will maintain compatibility with the titles you have now.

FOR INTERNAL CORPORATE USE

You don't have to be in the business of selling CD-ROM-based software and information to take advantage of CD-R technology. Many companies find it useful to produce CD-ROMs for internal use. For example, rather than print continuous updates on product specification sheets, price lists, or market information, a company can produce a few CD-ROMs with the complete information quarterly, monthly, or whenever they want.

CD-ROM excels at getting large amounts of important, time-sensitive data like this to a few people when they most need it. It is easy for a company to justify the cost of a CD-R recorder if it means, say, that the sales force gets market data on its competitors a week earlier. And because CD-ROM is durable and small, it can be shipped in an overnight letter envelope with little fear of damage.

A few creative professionals are producing presentations and then recording them to a CD disc, complete with graphics, sound, and video. If you can create a presentation on your computer, it's not much harder to record it to a CD disc. All you need is the equipment and software, which Chapter 7 will describe in detail. Just flashing the disc in the meeting before popping it into the player is enough to make a good impression.

CD-ROM AS AN EXTENSION OF AUDIO CD

There is no difference in the basic principles of how information is stored and retrieved between CD-ROM and audio CD. CD-ROM is, in fact, just an extension of the audio CD, or CD Digital Audio (CD-DA), format. This format is defined by the Red Book standard. Although primarily for audio, the specification does permit limited use of graphics.

When the CD industry agreed to follow the Red Book specification in 1982, few people expected that the compact disc could become an important peripheral for a computer. Although CD-ROMs existed then, they were used in highly specialized applications. The IBM PC, after all, had yet to appear, and most of the early computer users were just beginning to discover the wonders of floppy disks. However, it was clear that CD-ROM needed its own standard to accommodate the requirements of the computer environment and the various types of data it processes.

Subsequently, the industry leaders created standards to define how different data types are recorded and organized on the media, the specifications of the CD-ROM drives, and the minimum overall system configurations. They all, however, incorporate the original Red Book standard. As a result, you can play audio CDs on virtually any CD-ROM drive, but most audio CD players will play only sound from a CD-ROM or nothing at all. Chapter 3 describes these standards in detail.

OTHER OPTICAL MEDIA

If the place where you work has a lot of computers or a network, chances are you'll find an optical device of some sort there. Other optical media include

▶ WORM (write once, read many)

▶ MO (magneto-optical)

▶ Videodisc

All these media share the disc shape of the CD-ROM. However, they come in varying sizes and with their own way of storing and reading information. The following table lists the basic features of each type of device, as well as the applications for which each is commonly used.

Optical Media	Maximum Capacity	Recordable?	Applications
Audio CD	601MB	No	Entertainment
CD-ROM	650MB*	No	Data and software distribution, entertainment, education
CD-Recordable	650MB*	Yes	CD-ROM mastering, limited archival storage
Magneto-optical	2Gb	Yes	Archival storage, potential for primary storage
WORM	1.3Gb	Yes	Archival storage

*Assuming a 330,000-sector disc with error-correction

These devices also share a common ancestor, the laser videodisc. Invented in 1970, the laser videodisc was intended as an add-on to the TV. It was to perform essentially the same function that VCR tapes do today: allow you to watch movies and other entertainment that you bought or rented in the comfort of your own home.

There are some obvious and not-so-obvious differences between the laser videodisc and CD-ROM. The videodisc is bigger—12 inches (sometimes 8 inches) versus 4.72 inches for the CD-ROM and as small as 2.5 inches for magneto-optical. A more subtle difference is in how the videodisc stores information. It can use both sides of the disc for data, and it stores that data in analog, rather than digital, form.

Several different, incompatible videodisc systems fought it out in the 1970s, but the format that prevailed was RCA's LaserVision. In the meantime,

What Is a CD-ROM? 27
Chapter 2

having so many different systems on the market caused confusion among consumers and wasted a lot of development effort among the vendors. Out of the mess, however, rose the beginning of today's audio CD and CD-ROM standards.

Philips and Sony, who own the significant patents on both audio CD and CD-ROM, agreed on an audio optical standard that was eventually accepted by most of the hardware and software manufacturers. When the audio CD debuted in 1982, consumers could be reasonably confident of compatibility among the different players and music titles. The success of this standard—Red Book—encouraged the industry to do the same when CD-ROM was being developed.

DIGITAL VERSUS ANALOG

Text, sound, and video as you perceive them are analog in nature. *Analog*, as defined by the *IBM Dictionary of Computing*, pertains to data that consists of continuously variable physical qualities. This is contrasted to *digital* data, which consists of discrete digits. Computers and CD-ROM drive electronics are digital. They deal with all types of data that have been converted into a binary, numerical representation—1's and 0's.

Each 1 or 0 is a bit. Eight bits equal 1 byte. A byte has 256 possible combinations, each one able to represent a unique piece of information, such as a letter of the alphabet. Stringing bytes together allows much more complex representations, which can be the letters of a sentence, the image of a person's face, or the sound vibrations that make up a song.

Available in Different Sizes

Cited CD-ROM capacity varies from 527MB to 742MB depending on a number of factors, one of which is whether a disc uses 270,000 or 333,000 sectors. A standard CD-ROM has a 60-minute spiral (the same as an audio CD), with 270,000 sectors and up to 99 tracks. (Tracks are *logical entities*, meaning that there is no physical beginning and end to a given track. The length of a track varies depending on how the data is organized. For example, a single song is usually considered a single track on an audio CD.) It is possible to produce a 74-minute disc, however, by using the outer 5 millimeters of the disc. Normally, this area is not used because it is the hardest to record on and to keep clean.

Also important is how the capacity is calculated. If the disc contains all error-corrected data, then it can hold only 2048 bytes per sector. This means that a 270,000-sector disc can hold 552,960,000 bytes. Divided by 1K (1024 bytes), this comes to 540MB, though some manufacturers divide by 1000 and call it 552MB. The most accepted way to figure the capacity, however, is to divide the number of bytes by 1MB (1,048,576 bytes). This results in a true capacity of 527MB of error-corrected data—650MB for a 333,000-sector CD-ROM, which holds 681,984,000 bytes.

An uncorrected sector can hold 2336 bytes of usable data. A 270,000-sector CD-ROM can hold 601MB of uncorrected data, and a 333,000-sector CD-ROM can hold 742MB. Of course, a CD-ROM doesn't have to hold its maximum capacity of data. Once recorded, however, it is impossible to add more data to it later.

From a user's perspective, this issue is moot. You can't write to a CD-ROM, so its capacity is important only in terms of what is already recorded on it. Where consumers have to be wary is with CD-R discs. All have the same maximum capacity of 742MB. Any claim of higher capacity is a misrepresentation of the numbers.

THE EVOLVING CD-ROM

CD-ROM technology has evolved into several related formats. These include the Sony MiniDisc and optical ROM (O-ROM), also called partial ROM (P-ROM).

Sony's MiniDisc is what its name implies, a small optical disc that looks something like a miniature version of a CD-ROM, or more like an audio CD. At 2.5 inches in diameter, the MiniDisc can hold 74 minutes of recorded music or 130MB of data. Sony markets it as a means to digitally record and play audio.

The MiniDisc is not technically a CD-ROM; it uses a modified magneto-optical recording and reading method. However, it records data using the CD-ROM Mode 2 format (explained in the later section, "Data Organization") and uses the same error-correction scheme as CD-ROM.

Last year, Sony announced that it would adapt the MiniDisc for computer data storage as an alternative to floppy disk drives. Sony calls the new format MD DATA, and it has some obvious advantages over floppies. It has greater capacity (140MB versus 1.44MB for a standard floppy) and is more durable, for example. MD DATA discs come in three variations: writable, read-only, and a hybrid version that is partially writable/partially read-only. All discs are readable on the same drive. The discs themselves are encased in a shuttered cartridge for protection.

Because MD DATA has its own file system, the discs are interchangeable among PCs, Macintoshes, and other supported platforms. Sony expects blank MD recordable discs to cost about $20. Read-only versions of the disc, called MD-ROMs, will target software publishing. They can be mass produced using the same premastering process as CD-ROMs. The hybrid MD DATA discs are aimed at interactive applications where you have an unalterable read-only core program and a rewritable space to record data.

MD DATA differs from conventional magneto-optical technology in two important ways. First, the drive can erase and rewrite data in a single pass; regular drives require two passes. Second, this direct-overwrite technology allows a greatly simplified optical head, thus reducing cost, size, and power consumption.

MD DATA isn't a replacement for CD-ROM because it offers only about one-fourth the storage capacity. It also won't replace hard disks because the data transfer rate is only 150Kpbs, the same as most CD-ROMs. But MD DATA could fill the need for a writable, removable storage medium. This is especially true for portable computers, where small size and large capacity are always highly valued. It might be particularly well suited for the Personal Digital Assistants (PDAs), such as the Apple Newton MessagePad. Standard CD-ROM drives are too big and consume too much power for these tiny handheld devices.

Partial-ROM (P-ROM) allows you to record some of the disc permanently—perhaps with an application—and use the remaining, rewritable portion for user files. The discs come in 3.5-inch form with a capacity of 128MB including ROM and rewritable areas. The rewritable portion is in a magneto-optical format, while the permanently recorded area conforms to CD-ROM standards. P-ROM has potential as a software distribution medium. P-ROM discs are available for Macintosh, MS-DOS, and Unix platforms.

Chapter 2

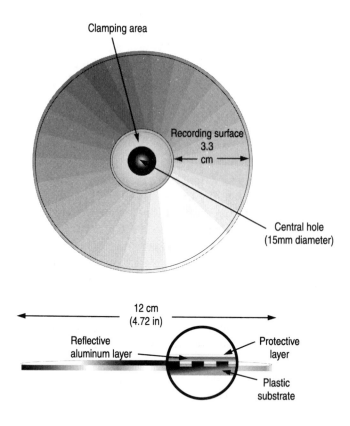

FIGURE 2-3
The three layers on a CD

COMPOSITION OF A CD-ROM

The CD-ROM is a 4.72-inch disc composed of three layers, as you can see in Figure 2-3. The first or top layer of the disc—the side with the label on it—is a lacquer coating that protects the reflective layer. The second, middle *reflective layer* is what actually holds the recorded data. For most CD-ROMs, this layer is made of aluminum and is only a few hundred angstroms thick (an *angstrom* is one ten-billionth of a meter). Covering the reflective layer is the bottom protective layer, or *substrate*, 1.2 mm-thick polycarbonate plastic that gives the disc form and rigidity. The label is silk-screened on the lacquer layer, and the laser reads the disc through the protective plastic layer.

CD-ROM media manufacturers can and do experiment with the materials used to make a CD-ROM, but not with its basic structure. Different materials are used for one of three reasons: to make the CD-ROM more durable, to make the CD-ROM recordable, or to allow greater density. With proper care, you can expect most CD-ROMs to last up to 15 years or more before the reflective layer begins to deteriorate (aluminum tends to oxidize over time). Some media suppliers use varying compositions and chemical treatments of the lacquer layer to enhance its protective qualities. Others might replace the plastic layer with a glass one. Some of these longer-lived discs are guaranteed for as long as 100 years.

THE RECORDABLE CD'S DIFFERENCE

CD-R discs use a gold-based reflective layer. Figure 2-4 shows that CD-R discs have a fourth layer between the reflective layer and the plastic substrate called the *dye recording layer*.

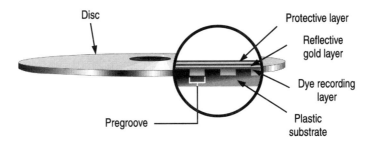

FIGURE 2-4

The four layers of a CD-R disc

Chapter 2

A preformed groove 600 nanometers (nm) wide and 100 nm deep serves as the track. (A *nanometer* is one-billionth of a meter.) During the recording process, the gold and dye layers become fused where the laser etches its pattern in the groove. The lasers used in CD-R drives are higher energy versions of the ones used in your CD-ROM player. Compare the CD-R laser mechanism in Figure 2-5 with that of the CD-ROM mechanism in Figure 2-1.

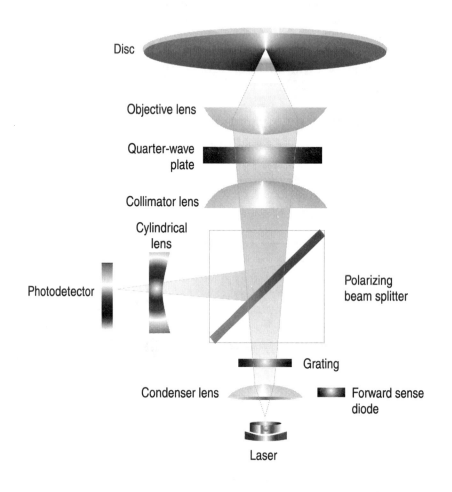

FIGURE 2-5

The CD-R laser mechanism

What Is a CD-ROM?

Chapter 2

Unlike a CD-ROM drive, the laser in a CD-R drive shoots straight at the disc. An additional *condenser lens* increases the laser's output, while the nearby *forward sense diode* measures the intensity of the laser. The *quarter-wave plate* rotates the beam's polarizing direction twice, so the reflected light takes a 90-degree turn to meet the photodetector.

The dye used in this recording layer must have special properties. First, it must match the reflectivity of the aluminum coating on standard CD-ROM discs. Second, the dye must react so that when the laser hits it, it becomes nonreflective. Finally, it must be able to withstand physical abuse, heat, and direct sunlight. Nevertheless, a CD-R disc is not as durable as a standard CD-ROM. It is more susceptible to all three of the hazards just mentioned. With careful handling, however, a CD-R disc might retain information even longer than an aluminum-based disc, since aluminum oxidizes over time and gold does not.

HOW CD-ROMS ARE DUPLICATED

Mass production of CD-ROMs is a complicated process with similarities to both photographic development and pressing vinyl LP records. The CD-ROM data is sent to a company that specializes in replicating CD-ROM. This data can be sent on nearly any digital media—tape, floppy or hard disk, WORM media, or even a CD-R disc—depending on the preferences of the replicator. The most common formats today are 8 mm Exabyte tape and CD-R. Almost every CD-ROM produced in quantity goes through the same basic process, though it varies from replicator to replicator.

The replicator first creates a master disc from the data. A mastering system uses a highly polished glass disc coated with a photosensitive chemical layer. A blue argon laser then photographically exposes in the areas that will later become the pits (described in the next section), which represent data.

This glass disc is now the glass master. To get the "die" used to actually press the CD-ROMs, the glass master is first coated with a reflective metal and then submerged in an electrolyte solution. An electrical current is applied to the solution, which causes metal to be deposited on the master.

When the metal reaches the right thickness (usually about 1/16th of an inch), the glass is removed and usually destroyed in the process. The remaining metal is called the *father*. The replicator repeats the process to create a *mother*. The replicator then makes one or more other dies, called *sons* or *daughters*, from the mother. The sons are the dies, or *stampers*, actually used to press the CD-ROMs.

Chapter 2

Some replicators, including 3M and Nimbus, make multiple stampers directly from the glass master as shown in Figure 2-6. The advantage to this simpler process is that it reduces the chances of errors being introduced by the replication process. Each step runs the risk of creating flaws that could manifest themselves on the disk.

The discs are formed using an injection mold process. After they are formed, machinery trims the rim of the disc and punches a center hole. Then the side of the disc with the pits is coated with aluminum and covered with the protective lacquer finish. Finally, the label is silk-screened onto the lacquer layer. Pressing each disc takes no more than 10 seconds.

Quality checks on both the physical and data integrity occur during the production process. The glass master is checked byte-to-byte against the original data. Each disc is laser-scanned after it is molded and the aluminum is applied to detect physical flaws. After the protective coating and labels are applied, a sampling of discs is compared byte-to-byte against the original data.

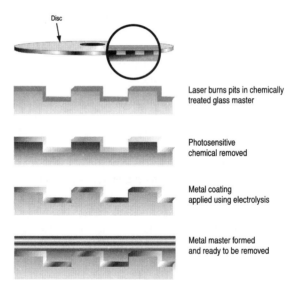

FIGURE 2-6

How a master is formed

CREATING PITS AND LANDS ON THE DISC

NOTE The material through the rest of the chapter is somewhat technical. If you are not interested in the physical makeup of a CD, you may just want to skim through "A Look at Error Correction" at the end of this chapter.

Data is recorded on a master or CD-R disc by burning little holes, or *pits*, into it with a laser. This laser differs from the one used to read a CD-ROM. Your CD-ROM player uses a low-power gallium arsenide laser and a photodetector, while a CD-R drive uses a higher power version of the same laser. Standard mastering uses a blue argon laser. The areas on the reflective layer surrounding the pits are called *lands*. Figure 2-7 shows how pits and lands would look on a disc if they were large enough for you to see.

Pits are so tiny—0.6 microns wide (a micron equals one-millionth of a meter), 0.12 microns deep, and 0.9 to 3.3 microns long—that the tiniest of contaminants can cause flaws in production. Consequently, CD-ROMs are

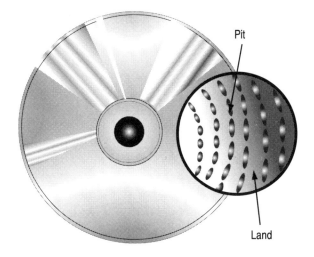

FIGURE 2-7
Pits and lands on a CD

produced in a clean-room environment where dust particles are limited to a few hundred per cubic meter.

The pits are arranged in a single spiral track, again much like a vinyl record. The first track is on the inside of the disc near the hub. The distance between tracks—called *pitch*—is 600 nm. Track density is 16,000 tracks per inch. The width of a human hair would cover about 50 tracks. The total track length on a CD-ROM is about 3 miles and can contain over 2 billion pits.

The laser in a CD-ROM player follows these tracks looking for transitions between pits and lands. It reads a transition as a 1, and no transition as a 0. The pattern of these 1's and 0's is the binary representation of the recorded data. The CD-ROM player electronics then convert this pattern into the appropriate graphics, text, or sound.

TRIVIA CDs and CD-ROMs are visually striking objects. Hold them to a light and you will see the colors of the rainbow. The reason you see these colors is that the plastic covering the tracks on a disc act as a prism, breaking natural light into its component reds, yellows, and blues.

HOW CD-ROMS STORE DATA

All CD-ROMs look the same, but how they store and index data can vary widely from type to type. Capacity can vary, for instance. And while the size of a physical sector is well established at 2352 bytes, the mode in which CD-ROMs are recorded can differ. Some modes, for instance, consist of all-user data, while others contain data that helps ensure data integrity.

Between the disc-level formatting and you is the *logical file format*, which creates a master listing of directories and files. The logical file format helps both you and your computer or player navigate the contents of a disc. Most CD-ROMs base their logical file format on the ISO 9660 standard, which is discussed in detail in Chapter 3.

The CD-ROM architecture starts with the Red Book audio CD standard. Audio CDs do not use ISO 9660, but they do have a table of contents on the first track of each disc that contains the location of each track. Audio CDs use a two-layer architecture: Layer 0 is the bit structure, and Layer 1 is the physical block structure. The *bit structure* defines how bits are formed into bytes.

The *physical block structure* defines how those bytes are organized. The minimum unit of data that an audio CD player can address, or locate, is a *block*—also called a *sector*. A sector consists of 98 frames, each of which is 24 bytes. A sector, therefore, equals 2352 bytes. The player reads the address in a time-based minute:second:sector format. For example, the start of a song on an audio CD might start 12 minutes, 36 seconds into a CD at sector number 56,700, assuming that the player is reading the sectors at a standard rate of 75 per second.

The CD-ROM Yellow Book standard adds two layers to the CD-DA architecture, keeping the same Red Book Layer 0 structure and modifying Layer 1. Layer 2 is the *logical sector structure,* and Layer 3 is the *logical file structure.*

Together, these structures form a logical format that defines a file system. It defines where to put addressing data on a disc, where to find file directories, and how that directory is structured.

The frame and sector organization for CD-ROM is the same as audio CD. However, CD-ROM drives need to access data randomly, so a different way to identify sectors is needed. To accomplish this, CD-ROM uses 12 sync bytes from each sector and 4 header bytes. The *sync bytes* identify the sector, and the *header* uses 3 bytes to give the physical address in a minute:second:sector format, and 1 byte to identify the mode in which the data is recorded. Using this identification scheme, your CD-ROM drive can go to any given sector on the disc as needed.

These blocks can be structured according to one of three modes. Each mode provides for some combination of user and auxiliary data, such as error detection code (EDC) and error correcting code (ECC). Mode 0 is all zeroes; this is used to represent blank areas—within a line drawing, for example.

Mode 1 stores 2048 bytes of user data per block plus 288 bytes of EDC and ECC code. This mode is for text and computer data, which are most susceptible to data errors; most CD-ROMs are recorded in Mode 1. Mode 2 blocks are entirely devoted to audio and video data and provide no error correction. The following table and Figure 2-8 summarize the content of each mode.

Mode	User Data	Auxiliary Data
0	Data field all zeroes or empty	Data field all zeroes
1	User data (2048 bytes)	EDC, ECC (288 bytes)
2	User data	User data (2336 bytes total)

The first track on a CD-ROM is always recorded in Mode 1 because it contains all the indexing information for the entire disc; if any of it were lost, portions of the disc would be unusable.

Discs with Red Book audio tracks recorded in Mode 2 are called *mixed-mode discs.* You can play these tracks of a mixed-mode disc on any audio CD player or CD-ROM drive.

38 BYTE Guide to CD-ROM

Chapter 2

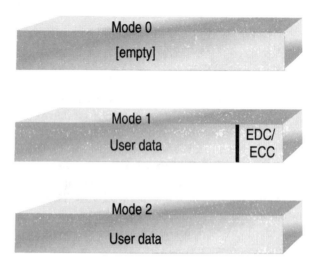

FIGURE 2-8
Modes on a CD-ROM

IT'S ALL DONE WITH LASERS AND MIRRORS

To read the CD-ROM, a CD-ROM player bounces a laser beam off the reflective layer's surface back through a lens to a photodetector that measures the difference in how far the light has traveled, or *wavelength*. The pit depth, also called the *bump height*, corresponds to about 1/4 the wavelength of the laser light. The laser overlaps the land and the pit, causing the light reflected from the land and the light reflected from the pit to be out of phase by about 1/4 of the wavelength, or 180 degrees. This difference results in the light from the pit canceling out the light from the land, and the read mechanism interprets this as a transition, or binary 1. No transition is a binary 0. Figure 2-9 shows what a transition looks like to the laser read mechanism.

Each bit of data requires about 300 nm of length along the spiral track. To synchronize the laser with the spinning disc, the length of pits and lands is limited to a specified range to ensure that transitions occur frequently enough for the CD-ROM player to clock itself. In fact, a CD-ROM stores bits using the same self-clocking scheme that many hard disk drives use, called RLL (run length limited). *Run length* refers to the distance between transitions.

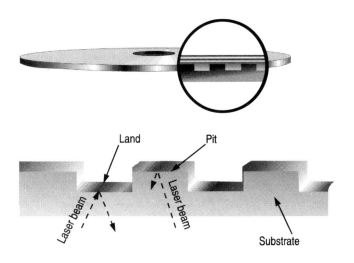

FIGURE 2-9
Light reflected to the photodetector

The player uses this clock to count the number of bits a pit or land represents, which is determined by its length. The minimum practical length of a pit or land is 3 bits, or 900 nm. The maximum is 11 bits (3300 nm). This makes it impossible to have two consecutive transitions (1 bits); you must have at least two and no more than ten 0 bits between 1 bits. Figure 2-10 should shed a little more light on this concept.

It is possible, though, that a byte (8 bits) of stored data might have combinations of 1's and 0's that violate the 3-bit minimum, and multiple bytes could create bit patterns that break the 11-bit maximum rule.

CD-ROMs, therefore, cannot use recorded data in the 8-bit format familiar to other forms of data storage. To compensate, the CD-ROM drive converts the 8-bit data bytes into 14-bit patterns called *channel bits*. This process is called Eight-to-Fourteen Modulation (EFM). A decoder in the CD-ROM drive electronics converts the 8-bit data into its corresponding 14-bit form using an internal look-up table.

Yet even using 14-bit bytes can result in back-to-back transitions if one of them ends in a 1 and is followed by another byte beginning with a 1. To avoid this problem, three merging bits are placed between bytes. The 8-bit bytes that make it to the computer therefore require 17 channel bits on the CD-ROM.

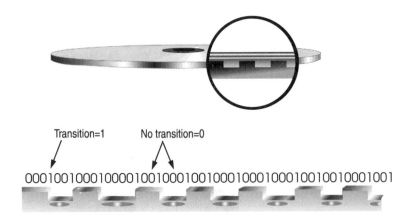

FIGURE 2-10

Transition pattern for pits and lands on a CD

Channel bits are read in 588-bit frames. The drive takes 27 of those bits to synchronize, or align, the laser. What remains are 33 bytes, each 17 bits long. From these bytes, 9 of the 17 bits are removed to form 8-bit bytes, which are required by the computer. One of the 33 bytes is a *subcode byte* that contains positional information, which goes to a special decoder. Of the other 32 bytes, 24 contain data and 8 are error correction code. The error correction bytes are discarded after the data is corrected or if no errors are found.

A Look at Error Correction

Both audio CDs and CD-ROM use error correction and detection schemes. These schemes are necessary even if the data on a CD-ROM was originally perfect. Dust, scratches, or other imperfections on the disc can interfere with the reading process.

With audio, a bad frame or block is unlikely to significantly degrade the play quality of the disc. Audio's estimated error rate translates to about one click in the music for every 86 days of continuous play. Believe it or not, this is not good enough for CD-ROM, where a bad frame or block could mean the loss of critical data.

An audio CD player's first line of defense against errors is called cross-interleaved Reed-Solomon code (CIRC). Developed specifically for CDs,

CIRC can detect and correct errors as large as 4000 bits. It is designed to handle sequences of errors, such as those caused by a scratch. CIRC resides in a decoder in the CD player circuitry. Using just CIRC, the error rate is roughly one error for every two discs.

If an audio CD player encounters a data error that its error correction circuitry cannot fix, it has three options: average or interpolate the data's value based on the data surrounding it, hold the previous value, or simply blank the data so you hear nothing. The duration of this silence would be so short that you would not be able to detect it.

Every byte must be correct for CD-ROM data, so CD-ROM drives cannot use these options. Instead, they correct bad bits by using a layered ECC (LECC) scheme—basically a two-dimensional version of CIRC. The LECC approach uses auxiliary data in each sector that the player can use to help find and fix errors. This auxiliary data is in the form of checksums created by the EDC/ECC code, and these checksums make up most of the 288 bytes set aside in each Mode 1 sector: 4 bytes are for error detection, 8 bytes are unused, and 276 bytes are the checksum bits.

A *checksum* is formed by summing the user data values placed in a grid both horizontally and vertically. After the player reads the data, it sums those numbers again to see if they match the checksums. If something doesn't add up, the decoder can find the error and come up with the correct value by looking at the difference between the wrong and the right checksum numbers (see Figure 2-11).

The error detection scheme that's built into your CD-ROM drive places the values within a given sector into a grid and then sums the values both horizontally and vertically. These checksums are recorded in each sector on the CD-ROM. To find an error, a CD-ROM drive re-sums the data after reading it and compares the checksums to those on the CD-ROM. If, say, the 8 in the top left cell was a 7, the EDC will pinpoint it by recognizing that the checksums in the top right and bottom left are off by one. The error must have occurred at the intersection of the row and column.

This example represents an ideal situation—one wrong bit. Multiple errors complicate matters. A technique called *cross-coding* deals with multiple errors by organizing the data in a grid, but it creates checksums diagonally as well, as Figure 2-12 shows.

By adding diagonally, layered EDC/ECC brings another set of checksums into play. When multiple errors within a sector occur, the diagonal checksums provide more reference points to pinpoint and correct them.

CIRC, EDC/ECC, and LECC are the standard means of encoding data for error detection and correction for all CD-ROMs. However, each CD-ROM

Chapter 2

8	1	7	5	3	4	5	5	6	44
4	7	6	5	5	2	1	1	2	33
3	3	4	4	7	8	9	1	2	41
5	7	4	6	8	3	5	7	2	47
1	3	7	1	3	5	9	8	2	39
4	6	7	3	4	4	5	6	9	48
8	8	7	1	1	2	4	6	5	42
4	3	2	1	7	8	3	4	6	38
5	6	6	6	7	1	1	3	3	38
42	44	50	32	45	37	42	41	37	

Horizontal checksums ↓ (top-right). Vertical checksums ← (bottom-right).

FIGURE 2-11
A table of horizontal and vertical checksums

drive maker is free to use its own method of interpreting that data to ensure accuracy. For this reason, it is possible for one drive to have a lower block error rate (BLER) than another.

The *block error rate (BLER)* is the measure that the industry uses to determine the quality of the error correction. It is expressed in terms of the number of errors per second. The acceptable BLER for a CD-ROM is 50 errors per second. At this rate, the error correction capability of the CD-ROM drive should be able to correct them without significantly slowing down the transfer rate. For perspective, a newly stamped disc averages about five errors per second.

As a result, you can expect one unrecoverable error in every 2000 discs you play. You pay a small price in some loss of speed in transferring data off the disc; creating, reading, and correcting the checksums takes processing time that would otherwise go to pumping data through the system. But in return you get data reliability unmatched by any other media.

What Is a CD-ROM? 43
Chapter 2

	8	5	17	19	20	24	41	42	40	
43	8	1	7	5	3	4	5	5	6	44	44
61	4	7	6	5	5	2	1	1	2	33	39
71	3	3	4	4	7	8	9	1	2	41	48
67	5	7	4	6	8	3	5	7	2	47	55
59	1	3	7	1	3	5	9	8	2	39	47
65	4	6	7	3	4	4	5	6	9	48	71
49	8	8	7	1	1	2	4	6	5	42	82
60	4	3	2	1	7	8	3	4	6	38	80
49	5	6	6	6	7	1	1	3	3	38	77
42	42	44	50	32	45	37	42	41	37		
	112	107	121	106	103	95	93	82	75		

Diagonal checksums

FIGURE 2-12
A table of diagonal checksums

The brains behind all this processing of data from the CD-ROM are the CD-ROM drive and the hardware platform. The drive contains not only the laser mechanism and motor to spin the disk, but considerable electronics to interpret and prepare the data for output to a computer or TV display. Chapter 4 describes the various types of drives and platforms and explains how they work.

CHAPTER 3

CD-ROM STANDARDS

Companies naturally feel a great urge to control any new technology they create. When the first personal computers appeared in the mid-1970s, each brand had its own operating system that required its own unique software (known as *proprietary* software). This put software developers at the mercy of the computer makers, who figured that since they built the hardware, they ought to be able to say what would and would not run on it.

Wrong! If the early years of the computer industry taught high-tech companies anything, it was the value of standards. Proprietary software stunted the growth of the software industry. No one wants to develop software for a platform with a small installed base, and back then every computer had a small installed base by today's standards. Furthermore, the lack of standards confuses consumers, especially those not technically astute enough to understand the differences among platforms.

It took the combined forces of IBM and Microsoft to create a de facto standard out of the PC and MS-DOS, and now, more PC compatibles are sold in a week than all the different early systems combined in all of 1979.

CD-ROM had a better start in life. The industry had already decided on a standard before the first disc was ever pressed. The companies that developed CD-ROM's ancestor, the laser videodisc, learned the standards lesson the hard way: incompatible videodisc players turned off consumers and retarded the growth of the market.

Philips and Sony, the two key developers of both the videodisc and CD-ROM, realized that a common CD-ROM format would enhance the technology's chances for success. While CD-ROM was in the early stages of development, the two companies cooperated to develop a standard, called Yellow Book, that would ensure that any disc would work on any player.

While this level of compatibility existed in the early years of CD-ROM, it is not necessarily true today. The industry still believes in standards, but technological advances have mandated the creation of new standards and extensions to Yellow Book. Depending on the type of application, these extensions may or may not be necessary. Within each application category, compatibility is still very high. There are, unfortunately, a few exceptions, which will be discussed later in this chapter.

WHAT'S IN IT FOR YOU

Consumers of CD-ROMs are the big winners when it comes to standards. The obvious payoff is compatibility. Within a given class of titles and platforms, you know that all the discs will work on all the players.

It is less obvious that standards save you money. Software producers, for instance, save money in development costs when they need to target only one or two platforms. Similarly, standardization increases the economies of scale on the hardware side; components common to all players become cheaper. These cost savings are passed on to you.

By creating one big market instead of a lot of little ones, standards encourage the best developers to produce titles. This increases both the level of choice and quality of discs.

Finally, standards take some of the risk out of innovation. Vendors know that as long as format compatibility remains, a ready-made applications base already exists, and people can take immediate advantage of enhancements. Innovation produces cheaper, faster, and smaller players, and it creates entirely new ways to use CD-ROM technology.

 We want to give you as complete an overview of the standards as possible in this chapter. Consequently, some of the material is more difficult than what you have seen up

Chapter 3

to this point, but we feel that users at all levels can benefit from these discussions.

STANDARDS AT ALL LEVELS

If you only had CD-ROM-specific standards to worry about, buying and using CD-ROM products would be very simple—no such luck. A disc may or may not work on your computer depending on the operating system you use, the type of video or sound hardware you have, or even the amount of memory or storage you have installed. As a result, other system-level standards exist to ensure that your computer can handle the demands placed on it by the material on a CD-ROM.

TV-based CD-I and CD-ROM products are more consistent within each specific implementation. For example, every CD-I disc will work in every CD-I player; every VIS disc will work in every VIS player. The vendors of the set-top boxes (a term often used to describe TV-based players) that play the CD-ROMs have standardized the hardware so that you don't have to worry about operating system incompatibilities or whether you have enough RAM.

You do run into another problem with some of these players, however. Although all meet the basic Red Book and Yellow Book specifications, a few use their own, proprietary enhancements. This means that titles designed for these systems will run properly only on those systems—full compatibility is lost.

Examples of these systems include Sony's MMCD (Multimedia CD) and 3DO players such as Panasonic's FZ-1 REAL 3DO Interactive Multiplayer, Commodore's CD32, Atari's Jaguar, Sega CD, and the Tandy VIS system. Chapter 4 will describe these players in detail.

THE COLOR BOOKS

The primary CD-ROM standards usually come with a color designation: Red Book, Yellow Book, Orange Book, Green Book, and so on. These were described briefly in Chapter 1. They cover the basics of how information is stored on a disc and how a player reads that information. Only the Green Book standard for CD-I (which is exclusive to Philips) specifies the entire system

48   BYTE Guide to CD-ROM

Chapter 3

from CPU to operating system. Table 3-1 lists the most popular players and the standards to which each conforms, and Figure 3-1 outlines how the standards relate to one another. Conforming to a given standard does not guarantee that the players will execute all software in that standard's format,

Player Type	Red Book	Yellow Book	CD-ROM XA	Green Book	White Book	Orange Book	ISO 9660
Audio CD	✔						
CD-ROM single session	✔	✔					✔
CD-ROM multi-session	✔	✔	✔		✔		✔
CD-I	✔		✔	✔	✔		✔
CD-R	✔	✔	✔			✔	✔
Photo CD	✔		✔	✔		✔	✔
CD-MO						✔	✔
Apple PowerCD	✔	✔					✔
Tandy VIS	✔	✔					✔
Sony MMCD	✔	✔	✔	✔	✔		✔
3DO				✔	✔		✔
Commodore CD32					✔		✔
SegaCD	✔						✔
Atari Jaguar	✔				✔		✔

TABLE 3-1

Players and Standards

CD-ROM Standards 49

Chapter 3

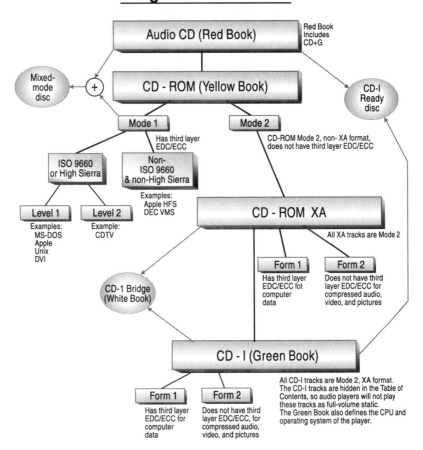

FIGURE 3-1
How the Color Book standards relate to one another (courtesy of Jim Fricks, Disc Manufacturing, Inc.)

however. It will be able to read the files, but executing the software requires that the operating systems be compatible, as well.

 Though the players and drives listed here conform to the indicated standards, they won't necessarily play every disc in those formats due to differences at the system level.

RED BOOK: AUDIO CD

The original specification for compact disc, Red Book, is the common thread that runs through all subsequent standards. Everyone supports Red Book. Its basic purpose is to define how digital audio information is stored and indexed on a disc.

When Philips and Sony proposed Red Book in 1980, audio CDs were seen almost exclusively as a means of recording and distributing music. Consequently, the specification is heavily slanted toward that purpose.

For instance, the Red Book logical file structure is relatively simple. It specifies that a disc can have up to 99 tracks arranged in a spiral. A table of contents on the first, innermost track contains the location of each track. The location is an address in the minute:second:sector form. In practice, each song is placed on its own track, and the addresses in the table of contents indicate the beginning of each song.

A standard audio CD uses a 60-minute spiral, although 74 minutes are possible by using the outer 5 mm of recordable area. This area is usually left blank due to the difficulty of recording on it, but CD-ROM software providers are starting to use it with some frequency. A standard audio CD player reads data at a rate of 150 kilobytes, or 75 sectors, per second.

Unlike a CD-ROM drive, an audio CD player reads a disc sequentially, following the spiral track and playing the audio in the order in which it is arranged. You must manually move to another song or another spot within the song that is playing by pressing a button. Red Book specifies that each track must begin with two seconds of blank data, in other words, silence. The break is used to locate the beginning of a song, which often resides on its own track.

Red Book specifies a two-layer architecture. Layer 0 is the bit structure; it defines the format for the 14-bit channel bits discussed in Chapter 2. Layer 1 is the physical block structure. A block, or sector, is the smallest amount of data that an audio CD player can address, or locate. A block is made of 98 frames, each of which equals 24 bytes. A block, therefore, contains 2352 bytes of data.

A CD player must read the digital audio code from a disc and convert it to an analog signal. Red Book says that this must happen at a sampling rate of 44.1KHz, or 44,100 samples per second. A sample, or *pulse*, is simply the amount of voltage applied at an instant in time to produce a sound. This rate covers virtually all of the audible frequencies. The term *CD quality* is often used to refer to a sampling rate of 44.1KHz.

Why 44.1KHz? The specification was developed by Sony. At the time, Sony was selling digital tape decks that sampled at that rate. The company simply decided to keep the sampling rate consistent across its product line, and 44.1KHz has been subsequently accepted by the industry as the standard.

Each sample is assigned one of 65,536 values. These values are placed on the CD in binary form represented by the transitions between pits and lands (discussed in Chapter 2), which are arranged on a spiral track.

To record analog sound on an audio CD, it is digitized using pulse code modulation (PCM). PCM matches samples against a predefined set of permitted values. It then codes the selected value as a series of pulses representing "on" or "off" (or the binary 0 or 1). The CD player circuitry then reads these pulses and converts them back to analog for you to hear.

Nearly all CD-ROM drives are capable of reading audio CDs. Your computer or player, however, needs software that will allow the system to play the music. Most CD-ROMs encode music according to their own format. The mixed-mode discs you read about in Chapter 2 use both CD-ROM and audio CD encoding. These discs place the computer data on the first track and audio data on the subsequent tracks.

Red Book originally defined a means of placing limited graphics on a CD. Compact Disc plus Graphics (CD+G) allows up to 20MB of graphics stored in subcode channels that are normally left blank. Because it allows only 6 bits of data per sector, these graphics are of low resolution and slow to read.

CD+G requires a special player and was never very popular. Nonetheless, players such as Commodore's CDTV, Philips CD-I, Sega CD, and Turbo Technologies' Turbo Duo with the CD accessory can read CD+G discs. Aiwa, a Sony company, has also recently introduced a small, portable CD+G player called the XP-80G. It looks like Sony's portable CD Walkman, but has sockets that allow you to connect it to a digital echo microphone and a television set.

Correcting Audio Errors

Audio data is more tolerant of lost bits of data, or more correctly, your hearing can either compensate for or not notice a few lost bits in the music. At worst, you might hear a little click; usually you hear nothing. Yet the player's circuitry must compensate for or correct any bad or missing bits of data.

Red Book provides what is called Level 1 error correction. Compared to later error-correcting schemes, Level 1 is not very sophisticated. It uses the CIRC (cross-interleaved Reed-Solomon code) method—explained in Chapter 2—and can correct 220 erroneous frames per block. In real-world terms, this means that after CIRC does its job, you can expect to hear one click due to uncorrected errors for every 86 days of continuous playing.

For large data errors that CIRC cannot correct, Red Book provides three means of compensating. It can interpolate, or average, the data using the values of the data before and after the bad section. It can hold the value of the data preceding the previous value. Or it can simply blank, or mute, the bad section. In any case, you are unlikely to notice the results.

YELLOW BOOK: CD-ROM

CD-ROM handles many types of data and must be able to access all of it randomly. Without the random-access ability, CD-ROM is no longer an interactive multimedia medium; you are forced to use the data in the order in which it is recorded, not in the order you want to use it.

To accommodate the multimedia, interactive nature of CD-ROM, the Yellow Book standard significantly extends the Red Book audio CD specification. This affects primarily how data is stored and indexed, and how errors are corrected.

Yellow Book, also known as ISO (International Standards Organization) 10149, defines only the physical properties of the disc: the pits and lands, their arrangement on the spiral tracks, the speed at which they are read, error correction, and sector size.

The specification also takes into account the different computer platforms that can use CD-ROM. Yellow Book supports several formats, such as Apple's HFS (Hierarchical File System, the native Macintosh hard disk drive format), Digital Equipment Corporation's VMS, and the ISO 9660 format described shortly.

The basic Yellow Book architecture breaks data into two types: Mode 1 and Mode 2. Mode 1 is for text and computer data and provides error detection code (EDC) and error correcting code (ECC) because data loss is much more critical with this type of data. Lose a byte of sound and your ear won't notice the difference; lose a byte representing, say, a decimal point, and you've got a potentially costly mistake. Most CD-ROMs are recorded in Mode 1 and use the ISO 9660 logical file format and structure.

Mode 2 is for audio and video and relies solely on CIRC for error correction. The first track, which contains vital indexing data for the entire disc, is always Mode 1. Mixed-mode discs record Red Book audio tracks in Mode 2, and CD-I and CD-ROM XA use Mode 2 to record audio and video data.

CD-ROM is a four-layer architecture. It uses the same Layer 0 as Red Book for the bit structure. The Yellow Book Layer 1 is, as with audio CD, the physical block structure, but modified to accommodate EDC and ECC.

CD-ROM Standards 53
Chapter 3

Layer 2 is the logical block structure. Although CD-ROM sector (or block) size is set at a specific length, file systems for some computers, for instance, might prefer a different-size sector. The logical block structure standardizes the increments to which the drive's contents can be referred. A few SCSI CD-ROM drives provide even more flexibility, allowing a block to appear any size, even smaller than the actual physical size. This accommodates certain software that requires sectors of a specific size.

Layer 3 is the logical file structure, which, as stated previously, is usually ISO 9660.

ISO 9660

The original Yellow Book specification did not adequately ensure compatibility among all discs and all players. The main missing ingredient was a standard file structure. This file structure would have to be the same whether you were using a Hitachi or Sony drive, or using a PC or a Mac.

To achieve this goal of an operating-system independent file structure, researchers and developers from many of the most important CD-ROM companies got together in 1985 to hash out the problem. The results of this meeting are known as the "High Sierra Standard," named after the hotel in Lake Tahoe, California, where the participants stayed.

Later, a somewhat modified version of this standard was formally accepted by the ISO and is now known as ISO 9660. The ISO is the parent organization of the American National Standards Institute (ANSI).

Both the ISO and ANSI review and establish standards based on the work of various committees. Committee members are primarily representatives from the specific industries affected by a given standards proposal.

ISO 9660 organizes CD-ROM sectors into logical records, and then arranges these records into files. Each set of files is called a *volume*, and a volume can span multiple discs. As long as a disc is formatted according to ISO 9660, file information is always in the same place. And any ISO 9660-compatible drive can read that information, whether it's in a Windows-based PC, a Mac, or a CD-I player.

Unfortunately, the ability to read that data isn't always the same as being able to run it on a given platform. While you will usually be able to get a directory that tells you what files are on an ISO 9660 CD-ROM, differences among the other components of the platform, such as the video or CPU, could prevent you from accessing or executing those files. For example, multimedia titles have program code that make use of the resources of a given computer platform. You can't expect a Mac to run Windows code, for example.

Chapter 3

ISO 9660 establishes a standard file system, much like the file system found in MS-DOS. It uses a hierarchical directory tree structure. These directories can be eight levels deep. The following illustration shows the ISO 9660 directory structure with four directories. Each directory can contain individual files.

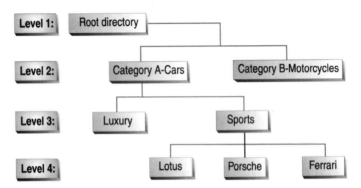

The data in the individual files is recorded contiguously near the directory information. This is contrary to what happens with a computer's hard disk drive, where a file can be stored in different locations anywhere throughout the disk. The advantage of storing this way is that it reduces *latency*—the time the read mechanism spends scanning the disc searching for the appropriate files. This scheme works for CD-ROM and not hard disk drives because CD-ROMs are recorded only once, so their structure is static.

The specification also establishes a few file attributes: directory file, ordinary file, and a timestamp. The ISO 9660 file-naming conventions allow for the eight-character-maximum file name, three-character file extension, and the optional version number. The specification was designed so that the file attributes could be expanded at a later date.

An ISO 9660 file name might appear like this:

FILENAME.EXT;2

As you can see, the specification calls for uppercase letters in the file name and extension. A couple of things in the file-naming convention can cause compatibility problems with some operating systems. Unix, for example, won't accept the semicolon in a file name. Developers get around these incompatibilities by creating code to make the appropriate conversions.

Two types of volume descriptors are allowed. The *primary volume descriptor* contains information on the characteristics of the file system data. For example, data indicating the location of the root directory information is in the primary volume descriptor. The size of the logical blocks is also part of the primary volume descriptor.

Since any type of file system can be placed on a CD-ROM—the Mac HFS, for example—ISO 9660 accommodates them. The primary volume descriptor must always be present, however. You can even produce a disc that uses both the host's native file format and ISO 9660. These are called *hybrid* CDs, and while they offer some cross-platform compatibility, they do limit each format to only half the disc.

A CD-ROM drive finds a specific ISO 9660 file in one of two ways. It can follow the directory tree structure until it comes to the needed file. This is how MS-DOS and Unix work. Alternatively, the drive can consult a precompiled table of paths showing the location of each file. The latter method is used on systems that do not have a native directory file structure.

Extended Yellow Book: CD-ROM XA

Proposed in 1989 by Philips, Sony, and Microsoft, CD-ROM XA is meant to improve the audio and video (or multimedia) capabilities of CD-ROM and to serve as a bridge between CD-ROM and CD-I. In fact, CD-ROM XA uses part of the Green Book standard, which you'll read about next. An XA-compatible drive can read standard Yellow Book CD-ROMs and CD-I discs, and some can even read partially recorded CD-R discs.

Until recently, XA-compatible drives were slow to come out because manufacturers were waiting for XA CD-ROMs to be available. Meanwhile, CD-ROM software developers were hesitant to create XA-compatible titles without an installed base of drives—the classic chicken-and-egg scenario. The benefits of XA and the success of Kodak's Photo CD, however, encouraged manufacturers to make XA-compliant drives. Some CD-ROM drives labeled as XA-ready will play XA discs with an XA-compatible controller.

CD-ROM XA uses a new Mode 2: Mode 2 XA, which is defined in the Green Book CD-I standard and has two forms. Form 1, like Yellow Book Mode 1, is for computer data that requires EDC/ECC. It uses the same sector format, in fact, except that the 8 bytes between the EDC and ECC sections are moved to between the header and user data. These 8 bytes now contain a subheader that tells the CD-ROM drive which form the sector uses. Form 2 also uses the 8-byte subheader, but leaves only 4 bytes for EDC. This leaves 2324 bytes left for video, audio, or graphics, which don't require as rigorous error detection and correction.

Chapter 3

Both forms can be interleaved on the same track. This means that a Form 1 sector can be followed by a Form 2 sector—remember, each sector contains information that tells what kind of form it is. Interleaving allows simultaneous playback of audio with video or text (see Figure 3-2).

CD-ROM XA audio data is usually *compressed*—the digital signals are put through an algorithm that encodes the data in a condensed form, thereby saving space on the disc. Compression requires additional hardware on a CD-ROM drive to decompress that data.

XA discs record audio in ADPCM (Adaptive Differential Pulse Code Modulation) format in Mode 2, as in Green Book. The difference is, of course, that XA discs are intended to play on a computer. ADPCM compresses sound by recording the differences in successive digital samples rather than the full values like PCM. This method requires as little as 1/16th the space of Red Book audio.

Thanks to ADPCM, XA discs can hold up to 18 hours of monaural audio. The downside is that not all XA controllers have ADPCM decoders (for decompression). This will likely change, however. Most sound cards used with multimedia PCs have ADPCM decompression capability, too.

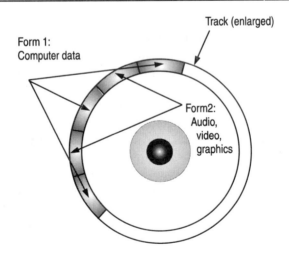

FIGURE 3-2

The CD-ROM XA format allows interleaving of sectors with computer data and sectors with audio, video, or graphics data.

CD-ROM Standards 57

Chapter 3

Some CD-ROM XA discs will play on CD-I drives if the drives conform to the CD-I operating system, which is CD-RTOS. These are called *bridge discs*, because they bridge the two formats. CD-ROM XA drives will play Photo CD discs, and if the XA drive supports multisession, it will even read partially recorded Photo CD discs.

GREEN BOOK: CD-I

Yellow Book and ISO 9660 created a standard that ensured basic compatibility among discs and players. They did not, however, account for CD-ROM's full potential—interactive multimedia, for instance.

Philips and Sony saw this potential in 1986, shortly after the CD-ROM appeared. In 1988, Philips put together the Green Book standard for CD-Interactive (CD-I). Green Book not only covers the disc format, but defines the hardware specifics of the player as well. This includes the CPU, memory, operating system, video and audio controllers, and compression methods for audio and video. A standard ensures that all CD-I discs play on all CD-I players, which are designed to connect to a TV and stereo system.

Not all TV-based players are CD-I. For now, only Philips makes CD-I players in the United States, but other vendors such as JVC, Matsushita, and Sony have announced that they will license the CD-I technology from Philips and produce players. Goldstar, Sony, and others are building them now, but only for sale in Asia. Sony recently introduced a portable CD-I player in Japan. Philips estimates that the installed base of CD-I players could reach 1 million worldwide in 1994. The following illustration shows a typical CD-I setup.

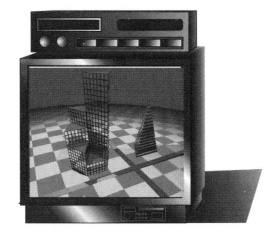

CD-I discs are identical to a standard CD-ROM in physical dimensions and capacity. The difference is that CD-I discs are meant to be played in real time. This means that sound, video, graphics, and text must be synchronized so that they play together in a smooth, realistic way.

To this end, Green Book defines the Mode 2 described in the preceding CD-ROM XA section. In short, each Green Book sector contains a subheader that tells the player what kind of data it holds. This permits interleaving, so that a sector of text can follow a sector of sound on the same track. Interleaving eliminates the need to jump from track to track for different types of data, allowing faster access and better synchronization.

The CD-I operating system is CD-RTOS (Compact Disc Real-Time Operating System). It is based on the OS-9 operating system developed by Microware. (OS-9 eventually became the official operating system of the Tandy Color Computer, and subsequent versions are popular in real-time applications.) The "real-time" part of CD-RTOS refers to its ability to synchronize the concurrent playback of audio, video, and other data.

CD-I video allows 16 million color variations. It specifies four planes of video. The background plane, for instance, can be a permanent image while the other planes overlay animation, video, or other images. Using the four-plane setup allows for more efficient use of memory.

Philips recently released Full Motion Video (FMV) as an add-in cartridge to a regular CD-I player. FMV is a CD-I video standard based on MPEG (Moving Picture Experts Group), a popular video compression scheme described later in this chapter. FMV will allow CD-I players to play full-screen, full-motion video (30 frames per second). With FMV, a CD-I system will be able to play feature-length movies up to 72 minutes in length. This limitation, and the fact that few CD-I movie titles exist, means that you don't have to throw out your VCR yet. Paramount Pictures, however, has announced that it will develop movies in CD-I format.

Green Book accommodates four types of sound qualities:

- CD-DA
- Hi-Fi
- Mid-Fi
- Speech

Three of these—Hi-Fi, Mid-Fi, and Speech—represent levels of ADPCM described in the CD-ROM XA section. CD-DA, of course, is Red Book audio. A CD-I disc can have multiple language commentary on up to 16 parallel audio tracks. This is useful particularly for internationally oriented training applications. With CD-I, the images can play without interruption while the audio switches from one language to another.

CD-I Ready

The CD-I Ready format is a standard that bridges CD-I and audio CD. It allows a disc containing both audio CD data and CD-I data to work on both types of players. On an audio player, you will only hear the Red Book audio; the player ignores the CD-I data. On a CD-I Ready player, you get both audio CD and CD-I capability. Standard CD-I players can't yet read the format.

To accomplish this feat, CD-I Ready discs make use of the track pre-gap that audio CDs use. This is about a 2-second gap placed between tracks to indicate the beginning and end of songs. CD-I Ready expands this gap to at least 180 seconds, which is enough space to place CD-I data in the XA version of Mode 2 using either or both forms.

A typical CD-I Ready application would be to enhance an audio CD with information about the songs it plays—liner notes, lyrics, and so on. On a CD-I Ready player, the CD-I data is loaded into and played from the system's memory while the music plays in Red Book audio mode. You see information about the song on the TV screen as the music plays.

WHITE BOOK: CD-I BRIDGE

White Book defines how CD-I data is recorded on CD-ROM XA discs. As its name implies, it represents a standard that allows discs to play on CD-ROM XA, CD-I systems, and recordable discs such as Photo CD.

A CD-I Bridge disc complies with both CD-ROM XA and CD-I formats. However, it can record data only in Mode 2 XA in either form, or in Red Book audio. It cannot be recorded in Mode 1.

The two most intriguing qualities of CD-I Bridge are that its discs work across a wide variety of players, and compatible players can read partially recorded discs. Most of the latest computer-based CD-ROM drives, all CD-I players, and stand-alone players based on the XA format, such as the Sony MMCD, can share CD-I Bridge discs.

The ability to read partially recorded discs is important to a wide range of CD-Recordable users. You can display your Photo CD pictures on any CD-I Bridge player, for instance. This is significant not just to home-based users, but also to the many graphic arts professionals who have embraced Photo CD, which is described later.

Video CD

The White Book format is also the basis for Video CD. Video CD is the use of film footage on compact disc. Using the MPEG video compression standard, a compact disc can store up to 74 minutes of full-screen, full-motion video—enough for feature-length films. Video CD is also referred to as the Karaoke CD Specification because one of the applications originally envisioned for Video CD was for use in video Karaoke systems.

Very few Video CD titles exist at this time, but the format is relatively new. More titles are expected to debut soon. You can play Video CD on any CD-I player equipped with the FMV module, or on any Windows or Mac equipped with an appropriate video board and a multisession CD-ROM drive. The Commodore CD32, Sony MMCD, and 3DO players are also Video CD capable.

ORANGE BOOK: CD-MAGNETO-OPTICAL AND CD-WRITE ONCE

The advent of recordable CD media is one of the most significant events in the history of publishing. It allows anyone with a few thousand dollars to own what amounts to a printing press. That printing press would be rather useless, however, if the discs you produced on it worked in only a few players. The Orange Book standard ensures that the discs you record will play on all the CD-ROM drives in Peoria.

Created in 1990 by—you guessed it—Philips and Sony, Orange Book defines the recordable media only. It has two parts: Part 1 deals with CD-MO (magneto-optical), which is not technically CD-ROMs but an increasingly important rewritable storage medium. Orange Book does not cover WORM (write once, read many) optical technology. Part 2 covers CD-R, also called CD-WO (Write Once). For the sake of consistency, the remainder of this book will use CD-R to indicate a recordable disc or drive.

MO has similarities to both CD-ROMs and hard disk drives. It is an optical disc that is recorded and read using a laser, but it can be written to many times. MO access speeds are starting to challenge the access speed of hard disks, with which it shares a concentric track structure. Concentric tracks eliminate the need for a variable rotation speed.

An MO drive records data by focusing a laser on a spot on the disc's surface. An electromagnet polarizes that spot from the other side of the disc. This changes the reflectivity of the spot, which the drive recognizes as a transition.

Some MO devices can be premastered to be partially read only. A CD-ROM drive can read those read-only areas. These partial read-only memory

(P-ROM) discs are useful in situations where you want to protect some data from erasure or overwriting, but where you also need rewrite capability on the same disc.

So, MO shares only a recording format with CD-R. The respective media and drives differ significantly, as do their intended use. Whereas MO is most often used as an archival storage device, CD-R is used more as a publishing tool.

Provided you are recording using a multisession drive, you can write to CD-R discs more than once—up to 99 times, which is the maximum number of tracks on a CD-ROM. You cannot, however, overwrite previously recorded information. The ability to append CD-R media is referred to as multisession. A multisession drive can read partially recorded discs, while a single session drive cannot.

CD-R media can be in one of four states:

▶ Unrecorded—blank

▶ Partially recorded but finalized

▶ Fully recorded

▶ Multisession

Standard CD-ROM drives can read only the fully recorded, or finalized, disc. You can, however, record under any of the standards—Red, Yellow, Green, Orange Books—depending on the variety of CD-R drive and recording software you use.

Before recording, the laser must be calibrated to the disc. Each blank CD-R disc has a program calibration area (PCA). The laser reads this area during a test run to perform the calibration.

Going outward from the PCA is the program memory area (PMA). The PMA contains track numbers with their starting and stopping addresses. The lead-in area follows, in which the CD-R drive will record the disc's table of contents once it is completely recorded. The lead-out area is placed at the end of the data to tell the player that there is no more data to read. The following illustration shows the PMA and lead-in and lead-out areas.

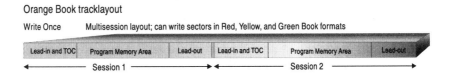

You can record all the data at once to a disc—the process is referred to as track-at-once. Or you can record incrementally—referred to as multisession. The *track-at-once* process writes the lead-out area and table of contents at the end of the session, and after that no more data can be recorded to a disc.

Multisession recording does this differently. It gives each recording session its own lead-in and lead-out areas, in essence creating a new volume each time. When the last session is recorded, the CD-R drive writes a table of contents. The difference between a single-session and a multisession CD-ROM drive, therefore, is the ability to read a disc that does not yet have a table of contents.

The Frankfurt Group

Orange Book does not explicitly cover multisession recording. In 1991, nine companies met in Frankfurt, Germany, to define a file organization for Orange Book to fill this gap, as well as to resolve several problems with ISO 9660. The group also wanted to provide the ability to extend the standard in the future—for instance, to support Windows NT. Whatever the group decided on, it had to be compatible with ISO 9660 as well.

Philips and Sony, of course, were part of the group, as were Digital Equipment Corporation (DEC), Kodak, Ricoh, Hewlett-Packard, Meridian Data, Sun Microsystems, and the Jet Propulsion Laboratory (a heavy user of CD-R). The nine became known as the Frankfurt Group.

Features that the group proposed include support for Unix files. Unix stores the information that a system needs for creating a directory with the data file as Extended Attribute Records, not with the directory records that ISO 9660 requires.

The Frankfurt Group proposal also has support for ISO 10646—a standard for using the different character sets of the world (English, Cyrillic, Chinese, and so on). Most importantly, though, it provides a means for a partially recorded disc to be read on a CD-ROM drive.

Here's how: ISO 9660 places the volume descriptor, which contains information about a disc's contents, on sector 16 of the first track. A CD-ROM drive always looks there to find the path and directory table that says where all files and directories are. Sector 16 can only be written once, so it is impossible to append a writable ISO 9660 disc.

The Frankfurt Group proposal allows volume descriptors on sector 16 of any track. A CD-R drive will leave track 1 blank until the disc is full. Then it will write a volume descriptor for the entire disc on track 1 using both Frankfurt and ISO 9660 formats (see the following illustration). Consequently,

CD-ROM Standards   Chapter 3

a Frankfurt recording drive must also be able to read the already-recorded volume descriptors before it can write track 1 (some CD-R drives are write-only). Multisession CD-ROM drives, therefore, look for volume descriptors on sector 16 of every track, while single-session drives do not.

Formally, the proposed standard is organized into four parts:

▶ Part 1 describes the notations and definitions that the standard uses.

▶ Part 2 describes the volume and boot recognition structures for compatibility with other standards.

▶ Part 3 describes volume and file descriptors. This also includes an improved extended attribute capability for Unix.

▶ Part 4 defines the different record types used.

A developer can implement each part independently or in any combination. For example, a developer can choose to create his or her own volume and file descriptors or rely on those used by the native operating system, such as MS-DOS or the Macintosh's System 7.

By the time you read this, the Frankfurt Group proposal should be a recognized international standard called ISO 13490. It has already been adopted by the European Computer Manufacturer's Association as ECMA 119.

Rock Ridge Extensions   The current way to get around ISO 9660's deficiencies in dealing with the Unix file structure is to use the Rock Ridge Extensions. The Rock Ridge Extensions, also known as the Rock Ridge Interchange Protocol Specification (RRIP), were proposed in July 1990, by a consortium of 16 companies, including DEC, Hewlett-Packard, Sun Microsystems, Santa Cruz Operation, and Silicon Graphics.

The group also developed the System Use Sharing Protocol (SUSP). SUSP also extends the ISO 9660 standard and enables multiple file system extensions to coexist on one disc. RRIP is built on top of the SUSP extension, and it allows POSIX (Portable Operating System Interface) files and directories to be recorded on CD-ROM without modification. For example, you don't have to shorten file and directory names. RRIP also permits Unix applications to execute directly from CD-ROM, rather than copying them to the hard disk drive.

RRIP and SUSP allow CD-ROM to use the complete Unix file system and directory structure, specifically according to X/Open and POSIX implementations. Most Unix CD-ROMs use Rock Ridge. The Frankfurt Group proposal, however, will eventually make these extensions superfluous.

Hybrid Disc: Kodak's Photo CD

In 1990, Kodak came up with one of the most creative and interesting uses of CD-ROM technology: Photo CD. The original concept was to create a consumer device that attaches to your TV and displays family photos. You would take pictures the same old way with your 35 mm camera, but in addition to 3-by-5-inch glossies, you can also get a Photo CD disc back from your friendly Kodak developer.

This is a great idea. A CD will hold up better than most prints over time, and seeing your shots on the tube is much more impressive than thumbing through a photo album. In truth, though, consumers have been slow to adopt Photo CD. The players cost $200 and up, but not everyone is ready for the technology. Graphic arts professionals, however, think Photo CD is the greatest thing since rubber cement.

For 50 cents to 3 dollars a shot, a designer can send out a standard roll of film and get back digitized images that he or she can immediately pop into a desktop publishing template on a computer. It's cheaper than scanning an image, and the image quality is often better. Just as important, it saves time as well.

Kodak further supports the graphic arts with its Kodak Picture Exchange. Announced in 1992, the Picture Exchange is an online database of Photo CD images. Sellers can place images on the Picture Exchange, and buyers can browse and purchase what they need.

You can play a Photo CD disc on Photo CD, CD-I, Apple PowerCD, Panasonic's FZ-1 REAL 3DO Interactive Multiplayer, or CD-ROM XA players. Photo CD players, however, are designed to read only audio CD and Photo CD discs. This cross-standard compatibility required its own format, which is based on Orange Book with some elements of Green Book. Kodak and Philips collaborated on this format, called the Hybrid Disc specification.

CD-ROM Standards 65
Chapter 3

The Photo CD development process records images on a CD-R-like disc in Mode 2, form 1 in accordance with CD-ROM XA and CD-I Bridge formats. Since you can put up to 100 images on a Photo CD disc, it will take several rolls of film to fill it. Each photo is placed on the disc in compressed form at about 3 to 6MB each. In uncompressed form they would require about 25MB each. Directory overhead consumes about 18MB for each session, reducing image count even further. Photo CD Master, designed for 35 mm consumer photography, does not support text files at this time. However, Photo CD Portfolio discs, designed for professional use, can contain text, graphics, audio, and menus. Each photo gets its own three-digit ID number, and each disc has its own four-digit ID number. This makes each image easier to find and catalog.

The basic Photo CD Master format supports image resolutions of up to 3072 by 2048 pixels. (A *pixel* is the smallest dot of light that a video screen can display.) This is far more than your TV or computer monitor can display, but the resolution is useful for producing photographic-quality output for use in, say, publishing applications. A high-end version, Pro Photo CD Master, supports resolutions up to 4000 by 6000 pixels, though only Kodak's Photo CD Access Plus, a software tool that you can use to view and manipulate Photo CD images, supports this resolution at this time.

In a nutshell, the Photo CD development process takes your roll of 35 mm film, develops it, and then digitizes the image. You can take your film to any Kodak authorized developer (Appendix B lists some of the larger ones). Photos you take with digital cameras must be converted to 35 mm format before they can be placed on a Photo CD Master disc. Pro Photo CD Master discs can take up to 4-by-5-inch film.

All Photo CD Master images are scanned in five resolutions:

- ▶ **Base/16** 192 by 128 pixels—used to display contact sheets
- ▶ **Base/4** 384 by 256 pixels—used for page layout positioning
- ▶ **Base** 768 by 512 pixels—for display on your TV
- ▶ **Base 4** 1536 by 1024 pixels—the resolution used for 3-by-5-inch and 5-by-7-inch prints
- ▶ **Base 16** 3072 by 2048 pixels—a proprietary Kodak format not used at this time

Each pixel is 24 bits deep; each bit represents a level of color for the pixel. The Base 4 resolution will support HDTV (high-definition TV) when it becomes available. HDTV is a proposed higher-resolution standard for TV displays. The Base 16 format is not practical for TV right now; the player would require a massive amount of memory and a fast processor in order to display those images. Kodak is just keeping the door open for compatibility with future resolutions, and making high resolution available for prepress and publishing.

On a computer, you can manipulate Photo CD images using most available image editing tools. You can crop, size, rotate, or alter the image itself. The Apple Macintosh has Photo CD support built into its QuickTime multimedia environment. QuickTime provides an image viewer that you can configure to your favorite image processing software. Microsoft Windows, on the other hand, does not directly support Photo CD, though many of the third-party Windows image processing software packages do. Likewise, most Unix image processing packages support Photo CD. Native OS/2 applications do not yet support Photo CD, but you can use Photo CD images through a DOS or Windows session running under OS/2.

If you want to print a reasonably good quality Photo CD image, you must have a good color printer. Dye-sublimation printers, which "burn" full-color images onto a special type of paper, provide near photo quality, but are very expensive—$3000 and up.

MEETING PLATFORM REQUIREMENTS

The Color Book standards work at a very low level—mostly in the world of how bits are stored on disc and read by players. At the high level—the level at which you interact with the contents of a disc—other standards come to bear. These are platform standards. They deal with the native operating systems and hardware of the host system.

Some stand-alone CD-ROM players are based on one or more of the Color Book standards, but they extend them to create their own environments. On the plus side, these players can add new features or extend existing capabilities. Unfortunately, this often comes at the expense of compatibility. Examples include Commodore's CD32, Panasonic's FZ-1 REAL 3DO Interactive Multiplayer, and Sony's MMCD. Turn to Chapter 4 for a full description of these devices.

Platform standards are more complicated when it comes to computers. Here, you must contend with different operating systems, graphics standards, memory and storage configurations, and sound capabilities. Just because a disc is labeled PC compatible does not mean it will necessarily run on your PC. You have to read the fine print to see exactly what kind of PC it requires.

First, each operating system supports CD-ROM and multimedia in different ways. Depending on the version you are using, your operating system might not support either; you must either upgrade or acquire the appropriate drivers—software that tells the operating system how to handle a specific component such as a CD-ROM drive. Even if your operating system does provide CD-ROM support, it does not guarantee that a given disc will work correctly. CD-ROMs, especially those with multimedia content, sometimes require greater support than the basic operating system and host hardware offer.

You might have to extend an operating system for greater video or audio support; this often entails upgrading your hardware as well. To confuse matters further, there can be several different standards for video or audio for a given platform.

The general trend is to build in CD-ROM and multimedia support to the point where you don't have to worry about it. Some platforms, such as the Apple Macintosh, are there now. Others, such as Windows-based PCs, are struggling to catch up.

APPLE SETS AN EXAMPLE

The Apple Macintosh is the one popular platform that has embraced CD-ROM to the point that it builds support into both the operating system and hardware. You rarely have to worry whether a Mac CD-ROM will run on your system as long as you use the System 7 operating system.

Most Macs sold today are also multimedia-ready with built-in sound and video capabilities. CD-ROM drives are standard on many Mac models. You won't have to upgrade your Mac to run multimedia discs.

QuickTime

Apple's QuickTime is a cross-platform multimedia development architecture. This software simplifies both production and distribution of multimedia because it is available on both the Mac and Windows platforms. You need only create one master version of the software for both platforms, where otherwise you would have to create separate versions for each. This saves a lot of work. Unfortunately, QuickTime for Windows has been slow to catch on, partly because Microsoft is pushing its own competing architecture, Video for Windows (described in a later section of the chapter).

The three main parts of QuickTime are the Movie Toolbox, the Image Compression Manager, and the Component Manager. The Movie Toolbox is just what its name says: a collection of utilities to help both amateur and professional developers incorporate QuickTime movies into any application.

The Image Compression Manager is a set of tools for compressing and decompressing images. Since CD-ROM drives are not fast enough to properly display uncompressed video or animation, compression algorithms are always a very important piece of any environment standard such as QuickTime. The Image Compression Manager can use a number of different compression methods. The Apple Photo Compressor uses the standard JPEG (Joint Photographic Experts Group) algorithm—a common compression scheme for photographic images. It achieves compression ratios of 5:1 to 100:1, depending on the type and size of the image.

The Apple Video Compressor uses a scheme that Apple developed for decompressing video movies. It uses *frame differencing*—a technique that removes parts of a frame that have not changed from the previous one. You can adjust the frame differencing to get faster or slower decompression. The faster the decompression, however, the lower the image quality.

QuickTime also provides the Apple Animation Compressor for graphics animation; the Apple Graphics Compressor, for maximum compression on still images; and the Apple Raw Compressor, which reduces image size by reducing the number of available colors.

Version 1.6 of QuickTime also supports Intel's Indeo compression standard. Indeo is a popular standard for compressing and decompressing video on Windows, and is described later.

The Component Manager acts like a socket into which you can plug various types of software to add or customize functionality. For example, you can use the Component Manager to select the type of compression you want to use, or to add a device driver.

Photo CD support is standard with QuickTime. It provides an image viewer configurable to your favorite image processing software. QuickTime makes Photo CD files appear to be Apple's standard PICT graphics files, which most image manipulation software can handle.

QuickTime for Windows extends Windows 3.1 to integrate compressed video, graphics, and sound in cross-platform format. It integrates Apple's video compression, which supports Windows MCI (Media Control Interface) and OLE (Object Linking and Embedding) 1.0. MCI support integrates QuickTime for Windows into authoring and presentation applications. OLE support allows you to integrate movies into business applications. If they like, developers can use custom compression/decompression, such as Intel's Indeo.

QuickTime for Windows supports the same movie format, video compression, user interface, and application programming interface as the Mac. It allows movies to play at up to 30 frames per second (fps) and up to 320 by 240 pixels.

MPC 2 SETS THE STANDARD FOR WINDOWS

Many popular PC-based CD-ROM titles are multimedia based. In fact, if you simply add a CD-ROM drive to a garden variety PC, you will be disappointed in the selection of titles that you can play. You need to be able to play video and professionally produced sound if you want to run the best CD-ROM software.

Multimedia features are not standard on most PCs. This would pose a risk of incompatibility among the different vendors' versions of what constitutes a multimedia PC. Fortunately, the PC industry foresaw this problem and formed the Multimedia PC Marketing Council, whose responsibility it is to establish standard minimum requirements for multimedia PCs.

The Multimedia PC (MPC) 1 standard was established in 1991 and set the following minimum requirements:

- 386SX CPU
- 2MB of RAM
- 3.5-inch, 1.44MB floppy disk drive
- 30MB hard disk drive
- CD-ROM drive with a 150Kbps transfer rate
- An 8-bit sound card with music synthesis capability
- VGA display and video card
- Two-button mouse
- Serial, parallel, MIDI, and joystick ports
- Microsoft Windows 3.0

In the short time since MPC 1 was introduced, the demands of the latest software on CD-ROM have outgrown the specification. In 1993, MPC 2 was announced, and it significantly upped the ante for an "official" multimedia PC. The new minimum requirements are

- 25MHz 486SX or compatible CPU

Chapter 3

- 4MB of RAM (8MB recommended)
- 3.5-inch, 1.44MB floppy disk drive
- 160MB hard disk drive
- XA-ready CD-ROM drive capable of 300Kbps
- 16-bit sound card with music synthesis capability
- VGA display and video card capable of 640 by 480 resolution with 65,536 colors
- Two-button mouse
- Serial, parallel, MIDI, and joystick ports
- Microsoft Windows 3.0 with multimedia extensions or Windows 3.1

In addition, MPC 2-compatible multimedia upgrade kits must provide the MPC 2-specified CD-ROM drive and audio, plus the MIDI capability, described later. MPC-compatible hardware and software will use the logo shown here:

MPC 2 makes a number of recommendations, as well, for nearly every category. The reason the recommendations are not requirements is to keep costs down. If vendors followed every MPC 2 recommendation, you could pay as much as $1000 more per system. The goal is to create a basic standard that meets the demands of the latest multimedia software without pricing the hardware beyond the reach of most consumers. Over time, as prices come down and performance goes up, you can expect to see these recommendations become requirements.

Keep in mind that MPC 2 specifies only the minimum requirements for a multimedia PC. When buying or upgrading to a multimedia PC, more is almost always better. Get as much memory and as much storage as you can afford. Software has been steadily demanding more and more of both; video and audio files take up a lot of space. You can also never have a PC that's too fast. Running multimedia software chews up a lot of processing power. So if you can't afford the fastest processor, make sure that the

PC has a socket to upgrade the CPU later. Don't forget graphics. Although you can run most multimedia software at the 640-by-480-pixel resolution specified by MPC 2, much of it allows you to use higher resolution modes. These modes, of course, give you a much richer, more attractive image.

The MPC 2 CD-ROM Drive

You can't use any old CD-ROM drive in an MPC 2 system. For starters, it must sustain the 300Kbps transfer rate without relying too heavily on the computer's processor to do so. MPC 2 recommends that no more than 60 percent of the main processor's *bandwidth* (processing power) be used to sustain the higher rate, but it requires only that no more than 40 percent of the bandwidth be used at a 150Kbps transfer rate. Both the required and recommended processor utilization rates apply to read block sizes no less than 16K and a lead time of no more than what is needed to load the CD-ROM buffer with one read block.

What does the computer's processor have to do with throughput? The processor sends and arbitrates all the commands that retrieve data from a CD-ROM. While it is doing that, it can't process other functions such as drawing the screen or generating sound. The faster the processor, therefore, the faster the commands to retrieve information are executed, and the more time the processor has to perform other tasks.

MPC 2 also specifies how fast, on average, a CD-ROM drive must be able to find data. This is called *seek time*, and a drive must locate the desired information within 400 milliseconds.

> **WARNING** Not all CD-ROM drive vendors measure seek time in the same way. The accepted method is to perform the search over at least a third of the disc, called the one-third stroke method. Some vendors give seek times for searching from track to track. This method, of course, results in a better time because the distance the laser read mechanism has to cover is much less. Vendors that use track-to-track seek times in their drive specifications are, to put it bluntly, cheating.

Multisession capability, as defined by the CD-ROM XA standard, is new in MPC 2. This means that your MPC 2-compatible PC can read partially recorded discs such as those produced by Kodak's Photo CD.

CD-ROM drives must be rated for 10,000 hours MBTF (mean time between failure) to ensure that they are robust enough to meet the MPC 2 specification. Finally, MPC 2 recommends that a CD-ROM drive have a 64K buffer with read-ahead capability. *Buffering* allows the CD-ROM to temporarily store requested data in faster-access memory before the system is ready to display or play it. This, in effect, speeds the throughput of data from CD-ROM to the system.

Audio, MPC 2 Style

MPC 2 audio starts with standard audio CD (Red Book) capability. From there, the specification adds 16-bit sound; an MPC 2 drive must have a 16-bit digital-to-analog converter (DAC). The DAC takes the digital signals from the CD-ROM and converts them to analog for playback over the speakers.

The DAC must support linear PCM sampling, and it must be able to sample at the 44.1KHz (audio CD), 22.05KHz, and 11.025KHz rates. Stereo support is, of course, mandatory. MPC 2 requires that the DAC consumes no more than 10 percent of the CPU bandwidth when sampling at 22.05 or 11.025KHz, and it recommends that it uses no more than 15 percent of the bandwidth when sampling at 44.1KHz.

An MPC 2 audio card also has a 16-bit analog-to-digital converter (ADC). This is to convert analog input from, say, a microphone into digital signals. The ADC must sample at the same rates as the DAC, and it must have a buffered transfer capability to ensure a constant flow of data.

To support music playback, MPC 2 requires that an audio card have internal synthesizer capabilities with multi-voice, multi-timbral capacity. That is, an audio card must be able to play six simultaneous melody notes plus two simultaneous percussive notes. This is adequate for playing sound on most CD-ROMs, though you might run into a few that require high-end (extended level) MIDI (Musical Instrument Digital Interface) output. While MPC 2 supports base-level MIDI, you will need special sound hardware to use extended level MIDI. You are not likely to need this level of sound quality unless you are an audio or music professional.

Internal mixing capabilities are also required. They must be able to combine input from three—four are recommended—sources and send the signals back as stereo, line-level audio at the back panel. The four inputs are

▶ CD Red Book

▶ Synthesizer

▶ DAC

▶ Auxiliary input source (recommended)

CD-ROM Standards 73
Chapter 3

Each of these inputs must have at least a 3-bit volume control with eight steps with a logarithmic taper. MPC 2 strongly recommends, however, that a 4-bit or greater volume control be used. Highly recommended are individual source and master digital volume control registers and extra line-level audio sources. Also recommended are CD-ROM XA audio capability and ADPCM support.

You can't tell that a computer soundboard has these capabilities by looking at it. If in doubt, ask to see the soundboard's specification sheet.

Keyboard and Mouse

Any standard or compatible 101-key IBM-style keyboard with a standard DIN connector meets the MPC 2 specification. A two-button mouse with bus or serial connector is required, but you must have at least one other communication port free once the mouse is attached.

Video Specs

You will be viewing multimedia applications from a distance of about three feet. At that distance, low resolution won't cut it. The images will lose definition and become grainy. Your computer's video must be up to snuff if you want to use multimedia software.

An MPC 2 system must be able to produce a display at a resolution of 640 by 480 pixels and with 65,536 (64K) colors. This is barely adequate for demanding multimedia applications such as video sequences, however. For better video performance, MPC 2 recommends that VGA adapters can *bitblt* (bit block transfer; pronounced "bit blit"—it essentially means to copy) 1-, 4-, and 8-bit-per-pixel device-independent bitmaps at 1.2 million pixels per second using no more than 40 percent of the CPU's bandwidth. A *device-independent bitmap (DIB)* is an image format that can be output to any type of device: printer or monitor, for example.

Setting a Standard for Video Movies

MPC 2 does not specify a standard for playback and compressing/decompressing video sequences, or movies. Consequently, you have several competing schemes emerging. These include Microsoft's Video for Windows, Intel's Indeo, and Apple's QuickTime for Windows. (QuickTime has already been described.)

Video requires a lot of storage capacity and bandwidth, which refers to the amount of information that can be transmitted from one part of the computer to another. To minimize the requirements for both, video data is put through a mathematical algorithm so that it requires less space. This makes it easier to store and to transmit.

At 640-by-480-pixel resolution and 24 bits per pixel, you need a bandwidth of over 27MB per second to handle real-time, uncompressed video. Double-speed CD-ROM players deliver 300Kbps. Obviously, full-motion video would be practically impossible on CD-ROM without the ability to compress.

Ideally, you would want video to play at full-screen size at a rate of 30 fps; this is full-motion video. (Your TV displays images at 30 fps.) This is possible using expensive video hardware, but the best you can expect for your average multimedia PC is a quarter-screen at 15 to 30 fps.

Microsoft Video for Windows Microsoft's Video for Windows (VfW) is video playback software. It does not come standard with Windows. Most CD-ROM discs that use VfW load a run-time version—the basic core of the software—on your computer so you can run the videos. You need to purchase it only if you intend to create your own videos. VfW complies with MPC 2.

VfW works on a range of Windows versions, including Modular Windows found in Tandy's VIS system. It uses OLE (object linking and embedding), a Windows feature that allows one OLE-compliant application to share elements—such as video—with another.

Although it comes with its own compression/decompression scheme, VfW provides an interface that allows other hardware and software compression/decompression schemes to be used. In fact, it comes standard with three algorithms, including Media Vision's MotiVE and Intel's Indeo. VfW further extends the Windows architecture by creating a common file format for video information called Audio Visual Interleaved (AVI), and by providing a standard interface for controlling video capture hardware.

A set of tools for playing back, capturing, and editing video come with VfW, along with a CD-ROM containing sample video clips. You also get a file-conversion utility that converts Apple QuickTime video clips for playback using Windows.

VfW provides basic video playback capability. It achieves a rate of 15 fps for video sequences played in a 160-by-120-pixel window—about 1/10th of the screen. What makes VfW a viable standard is its extensibility using other modules, such as Intel's Indeo.

VfW, with Intel's Indeo compression scheme, is destined to be a significant factor for any Windows-based multimedia CD-ROM. Microsoft and Intel wield tremendous clout among developers, whom you can bet will support VfW.

MPEG: THE LEADING VIDEO COMPRESSION STANDARD

If you want full-screen, full-motion video, chances are you will do that using hardware-based MPEG compression. Derived from the JPEG (Joint Photographic Experts Group) standard used to compress and decompress still images, MPEG is the most popular way to compress video sequences.

This video compression standard comes in two flavors: MPEG 1 handles SIF (source input format) resolution signals (360 by 240 pixels) while MPEG 2 handles broadcast quality 720-by-480-pixel video signals.

MPEG compresses consecutive video frames by making the first frame a reference frame. It then finds the difference between this and the rest of the frames, and compresses this difference. MPEG computes the difference by breaking the frame into 8-by-8-pixel blocks and searching for the best match for these pixels in the reference frame. It compresses the difference using a technique called the discrete cosine transform (DCT) that is very similar to the one used in JPEG. This produces a set of coefficients, which are then put through another algorithm to produce the final signal that is often 1/10th to 1/20th the size of the original.

MPEG includes several important functions that are difficult to implement on a general purpose CPU. When each 8-by-8 block of pixels is compared to the reference frame, the best match may not be in the corresponding location because objects often move across the screen. To get high compression ratios, MPEG needs to take advantage of this redundant data even though it has moved relative to the reference frame. It uses a computationally intensive search procedure to find such redundancies.

This computation, therefore, is usually handled by a dedicated video compression processor, such as those made by C-Cube. These video processors are very powerful and free the computer's main processor for other tasks.

Intel Indeo   Intel's Indeo 3.0 can play a quarter-screen video (320 by 240 pixels) at 15 to 24 fps using a 50MHz 486 or better CPU. It achieves this rate without specialized video hardware. It is a lossy technology that can compress video at variable rates, depending on how much data is tossed out. ("Lossy" refers to the fact that the compression algorithm reduces the file size by discarding data.) A ratio of up to 100:1 is possible, though image quality will likely be poor at this level.

Spawned from the Digital Video Interactive (DVI) initiative, Indeo started life in 1983 as an attempt to make RCA's LaserVision videodisc interactive. RCA bailed out of the laser videodisc business a few years later and sold the DVI technology to General Electric. GE briefly toiled with DVI, actually demonstrating it in 1987. Eventually, the company threw in the towel on the project and sold it to Intel, which has finally made it a commercial reality. Intel and other vendors sell professional-quality video hardware based on DVI technology today.

Indeo's compression/decompression software algorithm is *scalable*, which means that it adjusts the rate depending on the performance of the system's CPU. The faster your computer, the better it will play video using Indeo.

To you, Indeo is largely invisible. You might notice the Indeo run time—the core software that lets you use Indeo-based video—load when you install a disc. Otherwise it stays out of your way. CD-ROM publishers, on the other hand, must build Indeo into their titles.

Apple, Microsoft, and IBM all license Indeo for use with their video playback software. This makes Indeo a de facto standard for PC-based video compression/decompression. Each of these "Big Three" might support other schemes as well, but no other method is as heavily supported by all of them.

OS/2 2.1 MULTIMEDIA PRESENTATION MANAGER/2

IBM is aiming its OS/2 operating system straight at people who use multimedia. OS/2 is an ideal multimedia platform because it provides true *multitasking* support. This means that you can run more than one task, or program, at a time. Other operating systems merely give the illusion of multitasking by rapidly switching from one task to another. The centerpiece of this effort is the Multimedia Presentation Manager/2 (MMPM/2) found in OS/2 2.1.

MMPM/2 includes a video player and two video compression schemes: Ultimotion is for high-end, professional publishing, and Photomotion is better suited for presentations. MMPM/2 supports other compression schemes as well, including Intel's Indeo. It also includes a video capture utility.

MMPM/2 Hardware Requirements

MMPM/2 does require some specialized hardware beyond a double-speed, multisession CD-ROM drive. You also need an 8- or 16-bit sound card that supports either Creative Labs' Sound Blaster or IBM's M-Audio. Unfortunately, the OS/2 Sound Blaster drivers support only cards made by Creative Labs. This might change, but for now check with the sound board maker to see if they offer their own OS/2 drivers.

M-Audio supports the DSP (digital signal processor)-based MWave technology developed by IBM, Texas Instruments, and Intermetrics. MWave uses a DSP to compress and decompress audio or video files. The DSP takes this task off the shoulders of the computer's main processor; it can play two audio files at the same time.

CD-ROM drives on an OS/2 system use the SCSI bus interface. Not every drive has an OS/2 driver yet, so confirm OS/2 compatibility with the vendor before making a purchase.

PROPRIETARY FORMATS

Although the preceding CD-ROM and platform standards, with the exception of CD-I and the Mac, are available to any hardware vendor wishing to use them, some still strike out on their own. The perceived payoff is to either add some functionality that existing standards don't yet provide, to maintain control over software development, or both.

The following products use their own formats:

- 3DO
- Atari Jaguar
- Commodore CD32
- SegaCD
- Sony MMCD
- Tandy VIS

Most build on one or more existing standards. These include 3DO, Sony, Atari, and Commodore CD32. Nevertheless, complete compatibility is still lost. While these drives might be able to play discs in those base formats, the reverse will not always be true. For example, while a Commodore CD32 system can read and display Photo CD discs, other Photo CD-capable players will be able to display and execute CD32 discs. See Chapter 4 for more information on these formats and players.

CHAPTER 4

CD-ROM Hardware

If you placed all the different types of CD-ROM players side-by-side on a table, you would find it hard to believe that they all use the same basic hardware. You would see everything from CD-ROM *jukeboxes*—multi-disc players designed to attach to networks—to set-top boxes for your TV, to hand-held devices for portable use. Although the drive hardware found in all CD-ROM players is basically the same, variations occur in the support electronics and software that allow them to read different CD-ROM formats. You will see subtle variations among drives within a given class, too. These differences are the result of manufacturers adding features and improving performance to compete in an increasingly crowded market.

CD-ROM players are broken down into the following classes:

- ▶ Computer-based CD-ROM drives
- ▶ CD-Interactive (CD-I) players
- ▶ CD-Recordable (CD-R) drives
- ▶ Stand-alone, portable players
- ▶ Proprietary TV-based players
- ▶ Related-format players (Sony Minidisc, 3.5-inch CD-ROM)

What separates each class of player are the requirements of the applications, which often dictate which CD-ROM format is used, and the operating environment of the platform. Most of these players use the file system specified by ISO 9660, described in Chapter 3. From there, each diverges.

Computer-based CD-ROM is very dependent on the operating system of a given computer and the way in which it interfaces with other system components. CD-I players have their own operating system and interface built in for playback over a TV. Similarly, proprietary TV-based players have their own, unique operating environments. Stand-alone players and CD-ROM-derivative players are also self-contained, though some are compatible with and capable of attaching to a computer or TV.

CD-R drives have their own special requirements because of their ability to write and, sometimes, read data. They are computer-based, but often require special software, additional magnetic storage, and dedicated processing equipment to ensure a fast, reliable flow of data to disc.

Players can differ within each class, too. Computer-based drives vary by speed, how they implement the support electronics, and by the type of computer interface they use. Some recordable drives can both read and write to discs; some are write-only.

Each class has its specialty application. TV-based players, targeted toward home users, tend to be entertainment and education oriented. Reference and other business-type applications dominate titles available for computer-based drives. If you do not yet own a player, consider the types of applications you want to run before making a purchase. Chapter 6 breaks down the types of applications available for each class of player.

Again, the basic mechanism for reading a CD-ROM is the same for all classes of drives. You will find a detailed, technical description of how a generic drive works at the end of this chapter, in the section, "The Soul of a CD-ROM Drive."

COMPUTER-BASED PLAYERS

Most CD-ROM players today are attached to desktop computers—nearly 6 million at last count. This trend is likely to continue for the foreseeable future. CD-ROM drives are almost standard equipment now for most computers targeted for home use, and they are starting to appear in force in many business systems.

CD-ROM Hardware

Chapter 4

At first, the applications for computer-based CD-ROM were almost entirely reference material: abstracts, specialized databases, collections of documents, and so on. Today, the applications are much more varied, and many make use of multimedia. What's more, recording your own CD-ROMs has become very affordable. This has had a significant impact on CD-ROM hardware. Drives that served reasonably well for a number of years ran out of gas trying to keep up with the demands of the different data types. Consequently, the evolutionary pace of CD-ROM drives has picked up considerably over the last three years. The standard for the transfer rate has doubled, and vendors are constantly tweaking the support electronics to improve throughput. Users and their applications still demand more.

Though there are many subcategories of PC-based drives, you can categorize them according to five general areas:

▶ XA versus standard Yellow Book

▶ Performance

▶ Physical size

▶ Computer interface

▶ Target platform

WHY YOU WANT XA-COMPATIBLE DRIVES

XA drives give you two important things: improved multimedia performance and support for some of the formats produced by CD-R devices. XA drives are designed for concurrent playback of video and audio; garden variety Yellow Book drives were intended mainly for text. Since nearly every category of CD-ROM software is incorporating audio and video to some degree, you want an XA drive.

XA drives generally provide multisession capability, which, remember, is a drive's ability to read discs that have been recorded on a CD-R drive in multiple sessions. The main example of multisession recording is Photo CD, Kodak's technology that allows 35 mm photos to be placed on a CD-ROM. A single-session drive, which most Yellow Book drives are, can only read discs that have been recorded in one session.

CD-R is also becoming increasingly popular in business as a means of distributing and archiving data. Much of this work is done in multiple recording sessions; without multisession capability, that data is unreadable.

Chapter 4

THE FASTER THE BETTER

CD-ROM drives are now available in four speeds: 150Kbps (single speed), 300Kbps (double speed), 450Kbps (triple speed), and 600Kbps (quad speed). They are also referred to as 1X, 2X, 3X, and 4X drives, respectively. The standard base CD-ROM drive for all the major computer platforms is a 300Kbps, multisession unit. The slower 150Kbps drives are obsolete, though still available. Triple-speed drives have only recently become available (from NEC). Few suppliers currently exist for quad-speed drives, but Pioneer, NEC, and Plextor are the leaders in developing this type. Table 4-1 compares the performance of different CD-ROM drives. Notice that access time varies widely within each category.

TIP Some drives are not strictly double-speed, single-speed, and so on. The makers of these drives have boosted the spin rate slightly to get higher performance. Therefore, you might see double-speed drives rated for 330Kbps or quad-speed drives rated at 660Kbps.

Triple-speed drives are likely to be the next base model. The fastest double-speed drives have about a 260 ms access time. NEC claims an access time of about 195 ms for its fastest triple-speed drive. With good buffering and other improvements, the gain in throughput is significant. A triple-speed drive costs about $200 more than a double-speed model, versus $600 to $800 more for a quad-speed drive.

Another factor is that, until recently, quad-speed drives were available only as large external units. The faster spin rate of these drives requires larger

Drive Type	Transfer Rate	Access Time
1X	150 Kbps	400-600 milliseconds
2X	300 Kbps	200-360 milliseconds
3X	450 Kbps	195-250 milliseconds
4X	600 Kbps	140-200 milliseconds

TABLE 4-1
CD-ROM Drive Performance Ranges

mechanisms to rotate the disc and to move the laser. Getting them to the point where you can install them internally has taken time, but it is now an option. A faster spin rate also reduces the tolerances of the laser read mechanism. Poorly recorded discs, therefore, present a challenge to quad-speed drives. To compensate, these drives slow down the spin rate until they can successfully read the disc. Unfortunately, some of them stay at that rate until you put in a new disc. A few of the latest models, such as Plextor's quad-speed drives, will adjust the spin rate according to the readability of a given section of the disc. If you are buying a quad-speed drive, this feature will give you the best performance.

Remember that transfer rates are not the best measure of a CD-ROM drive's performance. What really matters is throughput, which is controlled primarily by three factors: the transfer rate, the load placed on the computer's main processor, and the access time. The transfer rate is pretty well set by the drive's spin rate. Processor utilization is dependent on the interface. The processor is responsible for ferrying requests for data and other commands to and from the SCSI or other kind of controller; each time it handles a command it delays whatever else it is doing—generating an image on the screen, for example. Therefore, the fewer commands you need to handle, the faster the throughput. Manufacturers can reduce the number of commands required by intelligently using the drive's buffer, and this is described in detail in the technical section at the end of the chapter.

The buffer can also be used to improve access time. The larger the buffer, the better; buffer size ranges from 64K to 256K. More important, though, is how the buffer's *firmware*—code placed on an EPROM (electrically programmable read-only memory)—controls the data flow through it. (This is also explained in more detail in the last section.)

ONE SIZE DOESN'T FIT ALL

Without a doubt, computer-based CD-ROM drives represent the most varied type of player when it comes to the physical format, or *form factor*. This is true mainly for external units, but you will find differences in form factor among internal units, too.

In general, internal drives come in two sizes: full-height (roughly 6 inches wide, 8.5 inches deep, and 3.5 inches tall) and half-height (1.7 inches tall). A full-height drive takes up an entire drive bay in a desktop computer. Of course, you can fit two half-height drives in one bay. Virtually all internal drives produced today are the half-height variety. The smaller size does not sacrifice performance or cost any more to produce, so why waste the space?

Different form factors for external drives serve different needs:

- ▶ Portability
- ▶ Performance
- ▶ Use in a work group
- ▶ Use on a network

Even within each of these categories, you will see differences among the available form factors. These differences are described in the following sections, along with an explanation of the circumstances under which you would use each one. You should be able to identify the scenario that most closely matches your needs to determine the form factor appropriate for you.

CD-ROMs to Go

Portable CD-ROM drives come in two basic varieties: stand-alone players with their own display and user interface, and lightweight, enclosed versions of internal drives. The former are actually computers in themselves with built-in connectivity to popular computer platforms. Sony's MMCD (Multimedia Compact Disc) player and others of this type are described in detail in the section "Portable Players," as they represent a distinct class of player.

The lightweight, enclosed drives are becoming increasingly popular for certain types of applications. Lawyers use them to access case abstracts in court, salesmen use them to give presentations, and people who work in finance use them to access regulatory and other data. Unlike portable computers, portable CD-ROM drives are usually used at a destination point, not during transit. Some "portable" drives don't travel at all. Many households have found portable CD-ROM drives a quick and easy way to upgrade the family PC, for instance.

To a degree, all external drives are portable. However, not all external drives are designed explicitly for portable use. A truly portable external drive is smaller in size and lighter in weight—about four pounds. Some are designed to run on batteries if necessary, though CD-ROM drives are comparatively power hungry and can quickly run down batteries.

Although hard disk drives are usually rated for shock resistance, CD-ROM drives generally are not. This is a problem for anyone shopping for a portable drive. You want a drive that will take more abuse than a stationary internal or external model. Your best course of action, therefore, is to query the manufacturer or salesman about a particular drive's "ruggedization" features. You might be met with a blank stare, but vendors need to start thinking about this issue.

Other key features you want to look for in a portable external CD-ROM drive are

- Double-speed performance
- Multisession capability
- EPP (enhanced parallel port) awareness

Until recently, few portable drives met these criteria, particularly the EPP awareness. EPP is a higher speed, bidirectional parallel port, described in Chapter 5.

You can attach portable drives to any computer with a standard parallel or SCSI port. This is not a problem for most portable computers, except in the case of hand-held systems. Some have parallel ports; many don't. Some use standard, popular operating systems for which CD-ROM drivers exist; many don't. Nearly all lack the video capability to run anything but text-based applications.

For these reasons, hand-held systems are a poor match for a CD-ROM drive. If you must have the smallest possible computer/CD-ROM drive combination, you should consider a device such as the Sony MMCD player or one of the notebook-class systems with built-in CD-ROM drives. The problem with the MMCD player is a lack of software. It requires its own CD-ROM format, and relatively few titles exist for it today.

At 8 to 10 pounds, the notebook/CD-ROM combinations aren't exactly hand-held systems, but are currently your best option for a small-sized integrated solution. Several are described in Chapter 5. In general, they offer better power management, guaranteed compatibility, and better integration of options such as sound or networking connections. Integrated notebook/CD-ROMs are used a lot in field service organizations, military training, and the medical profession.

THE RIGHT CONNECTIONS

Chapter 5 describes the bus interfaces used to connect CD-ROM drives to computers. To recap, you have three choices: SCSI, IDE, or parallel port. If at all possible, you should use a SCSI connection. It provides the best performance. Few DOS-based PCs come standard with a SCSI bus, although many multimedia upgrade kits include a SCSI bus interface. All Apple Macintosh computers have SCSI buses, as do most Unix workstations.

Some drives use the 8-bit SCSI-1 connection, and others use the 16-bit SCSI-2 connection. A few drives allow you to use either, giving you added flexibility.

IDE is found only on DOS-based PCs, and its main advantage is low cost. The bus already exists on most PCs, and many non-multimedia systems sold with CD-ROM drives use the IDE bus to keep the price down. IDE does not have enough bandwidth for multimedia applications, however.

The parallel port is a popular means to attach external CD-ROM drives. You pay a performance penalty for using the parallel port, but this might not be true much longer. Faster standards for the parallel interface now exist, and vendors are expected to begin implementing them soon. You also have the option of using a parallel-to-SCSI converter, though this adds some cost. The main advantage to the parallel port is convenience. You don't have to open up the computer to attach the drive. Consequently, the parallel port connection makes it easy to share one CD-ROM drive with several computers (though not at the same time).

THE RIGHT SYSTEM FOR THE JOB

Computers are a varied lot. They come in all sizes with different capabilities and a choice of user interfaces. Regardless of which operating system or CPU a computer uses, you have the following options when it comes to size, or form factor:

- ▶ Hand-held
- ▶ Subnotebook/notebook
- ▶ Laptop/portable
- ▶ Desktop/workstation
- ▶ Network server

You can use a CD-ROM drive with any of these form factors. You want to be careful, however, that you use a CD-ROM drive with good performance. The CD-ROM drives you can use with each form factor are limited.

Hand-held Computers

Though technically possible, you've either got to have a taste for self-punishment or a unique need to want to use a CD-ROM drive with a hand-held computer. The small, roughly one-pound systems present many hurdles to

CD-ROM Hardware

Chapter 4

overcome: slow processors, tiny video displays, nonstandard bus interfaces, lack of software drivers, proprietary operating systems, and so on.

If you still want to attempt the connection, your best bet is to stick with the MS-DOS-compatible systems such as the Hewlett-Packard 100LX (shown in Figure 4-1) or the Fujitsu Poqet PC. With these machines, you have a familiar CD-ROM-supported operating system and a parallel port. You're on your own when it comes to software drivers, though. The batteries in these computers will not be able to run the drive; it will need its own power source. And forget anything but text applications—the displays just won't handle VGA graphics or multimedia.

Subnotebook and Notebook PCs

Going up a size class brings you into more familiar territory: standard operating systems, parallel ports, and driver support. The area where you will most likely run into problems is with the video, especially with subnotebooks. These smaller systems sometimes "squash" the VGA display, taking out horizontal rows of pixels to meet size goals. You will still be able to run most

FIGURE 4-1
The Hewlett-Packard 100LX

applications in this lower resolution, though they won't look as good as on a full VGA display.

All notebook-class systems use LCDs (liquid crystal displays). One problem with most LCDs is that their *refresh rates*—the speed at which they update the image on the screen—are slower than the CRT (cathode ray tube) display on your desktop system. This causes *ghosting*, an example of which would be the trail left by a moving cursor. Ghosting is just a nuisance on most applications, but it creates havoc with video sequences, lowering the quality to unacceptable levels.

The two most popular types of LCD displays are passive matrix and active matrix. The best active matrix displays—both black-and-white and color—do achieve performance levels adequate for displaying video. Of course, you should expect to pay a premium of at least a few hundred dollars for an active matrix display. Most Apple PowerBook notebooks use active matrix displays, as do nearly all premium color notebook PCs.

The types of applications you are likely to run on a small portable, however, are apt to be data-intensive. Lawyer, salesman, CPA, and field engineer are just some of the occupations that require travel and rely on large amounts of information. For them, the video idiosyncrasies of LCD displays won't matter.

It would be extremely difficult to retrofit a notebook or subnotebook system with an internal CD-ROM drive. You would have to remove either a floppy or a hard disk drive to make room, and then you'll probably find that even a half-height drive won't fit. There is no guarantee that the smaller 3.5-inch CD-ROM drives will fit, either. And if a CD-ROM drive did fit in your notebook PC, the connector would likely be of a smaller, nonstandard type. Unless you enjoy this kind of challenge, the effort simply isn't worth it.

Toshiba recently introduced a thinner CD-ROM drive designed for tight spaces such as in a notebook PC (see Figure 4-2). It is called the XM-4101B, and it is only 2.5 centimeters (less than an inch) thick. This double-speed drive is sold only to manufacturers, however, and even if you could buy one, installing it yourself in your small computer is not recommended for the reasons cited above. Scenario is using the XM-4101B in its line of notebook PCs with integrated CD-ROM drive.

Docking Stations to the Rescue   If you need CD-ROM access for your portable computer, but don't need to take it on the road, then you should consider purchasing a docking station. A *docking station* is a box or platform that a portable computer plugs in to, and it provides greater expandability and connectivity (see Figure 4-3). For example, docking stations often have full-

CD-ROM Hardware   89
Chapter 4

FIGURE 4-2
The Toshiba XM-4101B CD-ROM drive

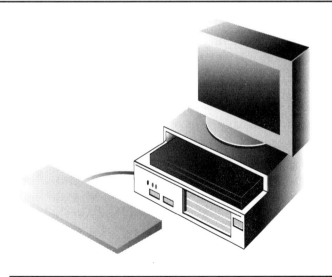

FIGURE 4-3
A docking station

and half-size drive bays, internal expansion slots for add-in cards, and additional external ports.

It is a relatively easy task to install a CD-ROM drive in a docking station; the procedure is virtually the same as for a desktop PC. Docking stations are not available for all portable computers, however. Check with your computer's maker for availability.

Laptops and Portables

The most important differences, besides size and weight, between notebook-class and larger portables are processing power and expandability. Notebook-class systems are usually a generation or two behind in the processors that they use because of power usage and heat dissipation concerns. It takes time for a CPU maker to optimize a given processor for use in small battery-powered systems.

Larger portables (see Figure 4-4) rely less or not at all on battery power and have more space inside to implement cooling schemes—a fan, for instance. Likewise, the extra internal space means there might be room for standard-sized storage components such as a CD-ROM drive. You would, however, have to sacrifice either your hard disk or floppy disk drive.

The easiest and recommended method for attaching a CD-ROM drive to even the larger portables is to go the external route. Laptop systems look like larger versions of the notebooks. In fact, many will present the same problems to anyone wanting to install a CD-ROM drive as notebook-class systems do. Even though they might have the space inside, they just were not designed for CD-ROM.

The so-called lunch-box portables, as shown in Figure 4-5, are bigger yet and provide the best opportunity for you to install a CD-ROM drive. They sometimes have room for a half-height device and a SCSI host adapter.

Desktop PCs and Workstations

Of all the platforms, desktop PCs and workstations place the fewest limitations on what types of CD-ROM drives you can use. (To clear up the semantics here, a *desktop PC* is generally an MS-DOS/Windows or Macintosh system devoted to standard business or consumer applications. A *workstation* is a high-performance system, usually Unix-based, dedicated to applications such as computer-aided design, data analysis, or engineering.)

Assuming that your system has the necessary open slots and drive bays, you can use virtually any type of CD-ROM drive. The limitations you might run into are described in depth in Chapter 5. In a nutshell, you need to make

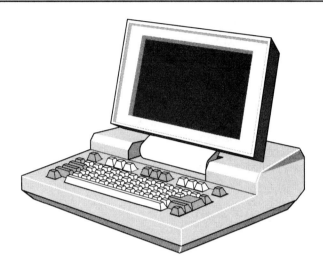

FIGURE 4-4
Full-size laptop computer

FIGURE 4-5
"Lunch-box" luggable PC

sure that your system's components are capable of delivering acceptable performance running the types of applications you wish to use. You can put the fastest CD-ROM drive in the world in your desktop system or workstation, but you'll squander that speed if you have a slow processor or video subsystem, for example.

> **WARNING** If you want to install a CD-ROM drive vertically rather than horizontally in your computer, make sure that the drive you want to use was designed for vertical operation. Not all are, and some could malfunction if mounted vertically.

Networks

More than anywhere else, speed matters when it comes to placing a CD-ROM drive on a network. Quad-speed drives are commonly used in network environments. Why is speed important? You have many people accessing the CD-ROM on a network, and the less time the CD-ROM drive is busy, the faster it can handle multiple requests for data.

For this reason, too, a single CD-ROM drive is not adequate for many network applications. You can probably get away with a single drive with, say, a 10-user network. With 100 users, however, you'll want to go with multiple drives. CD-ROM jukeboxes and servers provide this function. A jukebox is an external enclosure that contains multiple CD-ROM drives (see Figure 4-6). It attaches to the network's main server, or off one of the nodes of a *peer-based* (serverless) network. The jukebox has a controller and software that keeps track of the discs in each drive and the multiple requests for data.

A CD-ROM server has its own processor and can work either with a network's primary server or as a stand-alone server. The CD-ROM server can take much of the processing load generated by requests to the CD-ROM drives off the main server. This not only speeds up response to those requests, but it lessens the performance hit those requests place on other network activity. Some companies or organizations (a library or school, for instance) might want to set up a network solely to access CD-ROM-based information. In this case, they would use a CD-ROM server.

If an organization makes heavy use of CD-ROM on a network, it might have more discs to access than available drives. A minichanger, shown in Figure 4-7, is designed to solve this problem. A *minichanger* (or multichanger) is a drive with a multiple-disc caddy. The controlling hardware and software keep track of which discs are in which caddy, so it can quickly pop the appropriate one into the drive to retrieve requested information. You can find

CD-ROM Hardware 93
Chapter 4

FIGURE 4-6
A CD-ROM jukebox

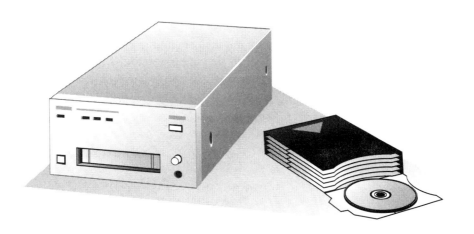

FIGURE 4-7
A CD-ROM minichanger

minichangers used singly or in a jukebox or server. Chapter 8 covers the use of CD-ROM on a network in more depth.

SMALL TOUCHES MAKE A DIFFERENCE

Major differences aside, drive manufacturers find many small ways to add value to their products. These range from the purely cosmetic, such as offering them in different colors, to adding functionality, such as the ability to work as a stand-alone audio CD player.

One area that is receiving attention from many vendors is dust control. After scratches on the disc, dust is perhaps the most common cause of read errors. Three features that combat this problem are dust doors, disc wiping, and self-cleaning lens mechanisms. Dust doors close behind the disc after you've inserted it into the drive and form a seal against dust. If a drive has any of these features, they should be listed on its specification sheet.

Many drives come bundled with an assortment of software. This could include general applications such as a game or reference disc to get you started using the CD-ROM drive. More valuable are the utilities and tutorials that come with some drives. The utilities might help you with installation or allow you to play audio CDs. Tutorials might show you how to use popular software.

CADDY OR TRAY?

Some CD-ROM drives have a built-in tray into which you place a disc for play. The tray closes either manually or automatically to begin play. Other drives require that you first place the disc in a separate caddy, as shown in the following illustration, before inserting it into the drive. Some of these drives then automatically feed in the caddy; others require that you manually push it in.

What's the difference? In terms of playback quality and reliability, virtually none. Manual-feed drives tend to be less expensive, but the automatic insertion and rejection of discs is a great convenience. You are always certain

Chapter 4

that the disc is properly seated, and you never break any fingernails trying to open a tray.

Caddies have the edge when it comes to protecting the discs. This is especially true if you invest in several to permanently house your most frequently used discs.

PHILIPS' CD-I: THE "I" IS FOR "INTERACTIVE"

Compact discs were originally envisioned primarily as a consumer-oriented entertainment medium. The advent of the personal computer forced the CD industry to do some rethinking, but it has never abandoned its goal of creating a mass market for CD technology in the home.

Compact Disc-Interactive (CD-I) is the technology Philips hopes to ride into that market. CD-I differs from computer-based CD-ROM in some obvious and not-so-obvious ways. The players are set-top boxes that attach to your TV, much like a VCR. They don't need a computer because they come with their own processor and operating system. With the player comes what Philips calls a "thumbstick," a point-and-click control device, shown with the player in Figure 4-8. The infrared thumbstick is what you use to interact with the CD-I software. Optional control devices include a mouse, a trackball, and the Roller Controller—a large trackball designed for use by children.

The obvious analogy here is to the Nintendo-class game machines. Actually, CD-I is to Nintendo what IBM mainframes are to desktop PCs. You can do a lot more than just play arcade-style games on the CD-I player, though several Nintendo games have been converted to CD-I format.

The more subtle differences are in the way CD-I records and reads data. CD-I is optimized for real-time, multimedia playback. This means that the different data types—video, audio, text—are encoded in an interleaved format that allows for better synchronization than available with the Yellow Book CD-ROM format. Chapter 3 describes CD-I's Green Book format standard in detail.

The CD-I laser read mechanism is the same basic unit found in CD-ROM drives. It is a single-speed, multisession device with a 64K buffer.

Chapter 4

FIGURE 4-8
The Philips CD-I player and its remote-control "thumbstick" device

PHOTO CD PLAYER

Although Kodak sells four varieties of Photo CD players, many other types of players can read and display Photo CD discs. They include CD-I, CD-ROM XA, Commodore CDTV, and Sony MMCD. The difference is that Kodak has optimized its players to view and manipulate Photo CD images.

The four players are the PCD 270, the PCD 870, the PCD 5870 (shown in Figure 4-9), and the PCD 970. All provide an infrared remote control and come with a single-speed, multisession CD-ROM drive. The player's intelligence is provided by an ASIC (application-specific integrated circuit) custom-designed for Kodak. The PCD 270 is a low-cost player with audio capability and minimal picture manipulation features. It can delete pictures from a sequence, remember the changes, and automatically display the sequence.

The PCD 870 adds the ability to zoom in on pictures, and it provides additional memory to recall individual edited pictures and viewing order selections. The PCD 5870 is the same as the 870, but with a five-disc carousel and an image-indexing feature.

Finally, the PCD 970 is a portable player that can run on four AA batteries. It is about the size of a VHS cassette, and it comes with headphones. The PCD 970 is the only Kodak Photo CD player to offer continuous sound for Photo CD discs that can display a sequence of images over an audio track.

CD-ROM Hardware 97

Chapter 4

FIGURE 4-9
The Kodak PCD 5870 Photo CD player

PORTABLE PLAYERS

Portable players differ from the external portable drives described earlier in that they have their own on-board processors. These processors give them the capability to display and execute software on their own.

The only two examples currently available are Apple's PowerCD and Sony's MMCD player. Apple is expected to announce its SweatPea player in 1994. SweatPea, which might also be produced by Toshiba under a different name, is based on Apple's Newton technology. Newton is the basic architecture for Apple's personal digital assistants (PDAs). PDAs are hand-held devices that act as personal organizers and communicators. SweatPea will, essentially, be a CD-ROM-based PDA, if Apple does indeed release it.

Other reported features of SweatPea include an LCD display, a PCMCIA expansion slot, and a detachable keyboard. Apple also has plans for a wireless mouse and infrared connectivity.

IBM is also rumored to be working on a CD-ROM-based PDA, though few details are available at this writing. In any event, you can expect to see more announcements of hand-held CD-ROM devices.

Chapter 4

APPLE POWERCD

The Apple PowerCD is a three-in-one player that runs Photo CD, CD-ROM, and audio CDs on a TV or a Macintosh. It supports both ISO 9660 and Red Book formats. The SCSI port allows it to be used as a CD drive for a desktop Macintosh or PowerBook portable. It can read both single- and multisession Photo CDs.

This portable player, shown in Figure 4-10, comes with a remote control that allows you to zoom, rotate, crop, and view Photo CDs in the order desired. On a Macintosh with Quicktime, you can cut, copy, and paste Photo CD images into documents and edit them with any image editing software.

You can connect stereo speakers or headphones to the PowerCD. It weighs three pounds and can run on batteries. Its 550 ms access time is slow compared to many other devices, and this is because the PowerCD uses a single-speed drive. A faster-spinning drive would require more power and reduce battery life. Its maximum transfer rate is 175.2Kbps, which is good for a single-speed drive, and probably due to its 256K buffer.

FIGURE 4-10
Apple's PowerCD portable CD-ROM player

SONY'S MULTIMEDIA COMPACT DISC (MMCD)

Sony has pioneered the small, stand-alone CD-ROM player. Its PIX-100 MMCD device is actually a small computer dedicated to playing CD-ROM XA software. It has a NEC V20HL main processor, which is the functional equivalent of an Intel 8088—the processor on which the original IBM PC was based. Its keyboard uses the familiar QWERTY style found on computers.

Sony also provides built-in sound via a stereo headphone jack. You cannot upgrade to 16-bit or MIDI audio, however. Other hardware features include 1MB of system memory plus 512K of ROM containing the operating system. A serial port is also standard.

The PIX-100's five-inch LCD video is relatively low resolution at 320 by 200 pixels (25 lines by 40 characters). Some CD-ROM XA titles, therefore, will not be compatible with the PIX-100's video. Also, its LCD display is not well suited for video sequences, though you do have the option of attaching it to a color monitor or TV set.

Still, the MMCD player's high degree of portability (less than two pounds and approximately 7 by 6 by 2 inches) makes it an excellent tool for mobile access of CD-ROM-based information (see Figure 4-11). It can run on battery or from AC power. Sony has encouraged software development for the

FIGURE 4-11
Sony's PIX-100 MMCD player

MMCD player, though the selection is still somewhat limited, with fewer than 100 available titles.

CD-ROM MAVERICKS: PROPRIETARY TV-BASED PLAYERS

All the vendors of TV-based CD-ROM players share the same vision: to bring interactive entertainment into the home. They don't, however, all share the same vision when it comes to compatibility. Although each uses a fairly standard double-speed CD-ROM drive, and most record according to one or more of the Color Book standards, differences among the players' operating systems and electronics prevent them from playing each others' titles.

In a way, this is good because some of the players provide performance and functionality that would be impossible if compatibility with the lowest common denominator had been required. But as Chapter 3 explained, the downside to proprietary systems is limited software support. Software developers don't like to create separate versions of a title for every different brand of player.

The TV-based player market is also in a state of profound transition. The early players such as Commodore CDTV and Tandy VIS are doing poorly, while a new generation of flashier, more powerful players has just burst onto the scene. These newer players are designed to play full-screen, full-motion video with high-quality audio. Sega recently introduced a CD-ROM-based console system, but as you'd expect, it is targeted at the millions of people who already own cartridge-based game machines.

Some vendors have an eye toward the future, when the so-called Data Highway is built. These systems, such as the one designed by 3DO, can be upgraded to access interactive services off a network, bypassing the need for a CD-ROM.

Interactive home entertainment has not yet caught the fancy of the average consumer. Perhaps it's because the existing players are too expensive, don't offer enough performance, or don't have adequate software support. It is likely due to all of the above. The new generation of players, however, should establish whether or not the public wants an interactive home entertainment system.

3DO: THE VCR OF THE NINETIES?

3DO aims to take interactive consumer-based software to a level above CD-I. Its Interactive Multiplayer offers unparalleled graphics performance in a CD-ROM device for about $700. The list of backers of the 3DO Interactive Multiplayer format includes such heavyweights as AT&T, Matsushita Electric Industrial Co. (Panasonic's parent company), Time-Warner, MCA, and Electronic Arts. With this kind of support, 3DO gained instant credibility before the first player and software titles appeared in late 1993. At last count, over 300 software vendors had announced their intentions to develop 3DO titles.

Powerful investors are not the only thing 3DO has going for it. Its technology is highly innovative. The company developed custom graphics chips to display full-screen animation and full-motion video at 30 frames per second (fps) on your TV. (3DO claims its graphics are 50 times faster than that of a typical PC or game machine, but this has not been independently tested at this writing.) An optional cartridge developed by C-Cube Microsystems will allow hardware-based digital video using MPEG compression. 3DO claims that this upgrade will provide VHS-quality digital video playback.

The player itself is a set-top box somewhat smaller than a VCR (see Figure 4-12). A two-handed controller comes with the player. The box is

FIGURE 4-12

The Panasonic FZ-1 REAL 3DO Interactive Multiplayer

actually a powerful, self-contained computer. Its main processor is a 32-bit RISC CPU made by ARM (it's the same processor found in Apple's Newton MessagePad), though the bulk of the graphics processing is done by 3DO's own graphics processor. A custom DSP (digital signal processor) provides CD-quality digital sound. The player also employs a proprietary technique called 3D Audio Imaging. With headphones, it makes the sounds seem to come from all directions—left and right, up and down. Maximum screen resolution is 640 by 480 pixels with up to 16 million colors. The CD-ROM drive is a double-speed model, and it can play Photo CDs, audio CDs, and video CDs.

The Multiplayer has two expansion ports. The system control port is for devices such as joysticks, keyboards, trackballs, or modems. This port supports up to eight daisy-chained control devices. The second port allows more sophisticated add-ons such as a memory card or sound and video enhancements.

3DO Company, which developed the Interactive Multiplayer technology, does not make or sell players. That is currently being done by Panasonic with its FZ-1 REAL 3DO Interactive Multiplayer, which is aimed at the consumer market. Later in 1994, AT&T is expected to produce its own version designed for use on a telephone network.

This application is broadly known as *interactive TV* (*ITV*). It presents intriguing possibilities for accessing a wide range of interactive services from a remote location and bypassing the CD-ROM altogether. Most telephone and cable TV companies, and some computer companies such as Hewlett-Packard and Silicon Graphics, are actively looking for ways to exploit ITV. It will be years before ITV is a reality for most people, and the topic is explored more deeply in Chapter 9.

3DO has ambitious plans for its technology, and not all of it is CD-ROM-based. Possible future products include

▶ An intelligent cable TV box

▶ Networked Interactive Multiplayers for education

▶ Video production systems

▶ Add-in cards for personal computers

▶ Portable Interactive Multiplayers

The company has stated that these are possible directions for the 3DO technology; no formal product announcements have been made.

Both the industry and general press have devoted a lot of ink to debating whether 3DO will succeed. Serious questions, in fact, have yet to be answered: Is the public ready for, or does it even want, a $700 interactive multimedia player? Will the applications live up to the early hype? How big of a technology lead does 3DO really have over its competitors?

Previous interactive TV players have not set the world on fire. Philips' CD-I is the oldest and most successful, but that's only because Philips has invested millions with little or no return yet. Tandy's VIS is struggling, and Commodore's CDTV has been an outright failure. The Sega CD has enjoyed healthy sales due mainly to the availability of popular game titles and loyal Sega customers upgrading to the newer system.

Software developers report that creating 3DO titles is no picnic, despite the availability of advanced development tools (described in the following section). At the time the player came out, only a third of the number of titles promised were actually available. What has appeared, however, looks impressive.

Sega will soon announce a 32-bit TV console system with a CD-ROM drive. It is too early to know if this will have any effect on 3DO's long-term success. Early reports on Panasonic's Multiplayer, FZ-1, say that sales are strong.

The best advice to prospective 3DO customers is to check it out carefully before you buy. Confirm that the types of titles you want are available now; remember that "real soon now" could just as easily mean "next year" as it could mean "tomorrow." All of 3DO's major investors have deep pockets and a vested interest in its success, so it is likely that the Multiplayer will be around for the foreseeable future.

The 3DO Animation Engine

The Interactive Multiplayer's animation engine is actually two chips. Together, they can display or move up to 64 million pixels per second; most desktop computers and workstations are capable of moving between 1 and 3 million pixels per second.

The animation engine achieves this impressive performance level by organizing the graphics into *animation cels*—high-resolution, full-color images that the engine can animate, scale, rotate, and change in other ways. Animation cels are similar to *sprites*, which are small graphics pictures or a series of pictures that can be moved independently around the screen to create the effect of animation.

Where sprites are limited by size, shape, color, or the number available at a given time, animation cels use layer upon layer of independent art to give a realistic visual depth. The technique is similar to that used in film animation.

A programmer can create and manipulate each cel independently of one another and the background, or in unison. An animation cel might represent an image of a person, a cloud, or any other moving object. The net effect of this is that the animation is limited to only the portion of the image that's moving. There is no need to redraw an entire screen for each frame.

Because animation cels are unique, 3DO developed a set of development tools for programmers. These tools allow a programmer to apply specific effects to a specific animation cel. These tools are just as significant as 3DO's hardware advances, as they save enormous amounts of development time. The available effects are warping, transparency, lighting, anti-aliasing, and texture mapping.

Warping This allows programmers to bend, twist, skew, shrink, and stretch images using a few routines. All the programmer needs to do is define the parameters and the necessary equations—for example, for the path of a bouncing ball.

Transparency A programmer might want to make a solid object see-through to reveal the background. This effect is useful in creating the impression of fog, fire, smoke, water, and so on.

Lighting Programmers can specify a light source as either on the screen or coming from off the screen. The player then illuminates the object according to the light's specified brightness, color, and location. Shadow creation is also possible with this technique.

Anti-aliasing This technique is a common one used to smooth the rough edges, or *jaggies*, often found on bitmapped graphics.

Texture Mapping Texture mapping is the act of wrapping an image onto other three-dimensional objects. For example, a programmer might want to use the image of wood grain to cover a building.

PIONEER'S LASERACTIVE SYSTEM

The laser videodisc is still alive and well in the world of interactive home entertainment. Pioneer recently introduced its LaserActive interactive family entertainment system. This is actually a series of add-on boxes for Pioneer's laserdisc player. The boxes let the laserdisc player run Sega Genesis and NEC

TurboGrafx game cartridges as well as custom laserdisc-based titles. Pricing is competitive with that of CD-I and 3DO players, but availability of software titles is expected to be limited.

TANDY'S VISUAL INFORMATION SYSTEM (VIS)

Tandy is banking on the popularity of Microsoft's Windows operating system to carry over into the world of interactive TV-based CD-ROM players. Based on Modular Windows—a stripped-down version of Windows with a simplified interface—Tandy's VIS has yet to sell in significant numbers.

The key features of VIS are low cost (under $400) and ease of use. For Windows developers, Tandy's use of Modular Windows makes it easier to develop VIS titles; many of the development tools are similar. It is also enticing to Macintosh developers in the process of converting their software to Windows. This has not translated into a slew of VIS titles, though. Tandy claims only 70 so far.

Compared to players from Panasonic, Commodore, and others, VIS is slow. It is based on the older Intel 286 CPU and uses a single-speed, rather than double-speed, drive. This virtually rules out running full-motion, full-screen video on the current incarnation of VIS. VIS supports three sound levels: FM synthesis, MIDI, and audio CD. Only TV video is supported.

The VIS unit itself looks much like a VCR (see Figure 4-13). It comes with a wireless remote control that has six buttons to select options and a directional controller to control onscreen action. One nice feature is the use of Save-It cartridges. These are RAM-based cards that let you save settings for specific CDs, such as which tracks to play, how you want them shuffled, and so on.

The VIS player is sold only in Radio Shack stores as the Memorex MD2500. The vast majority of titles are children-oriented, though a few general home references—cookbooks, dictionary, and so on—are also offered. In a way, the Visual Information System is an entry-level home computer—cheaper and less intimidating than, say, a multimedia PC, which Tandy also sells under the Sensation name.

COMMODORE DYNAMIC TOTAL VISION (CDTV) AND CD32

No sense in beating around the bush: Commodore's CDTV has been a complete failure. Sales have been in the low five-figure range, and it is no

Chapter 4

FIGURE 4-13
The Tandy VIS player

longer in production. But give Commodore credit. It was one of the first companies to produce a CD-ROM-based home entertainment system.

CDTV connects to your TV and stereo. This microprocessor-based system can convert to a multimedia PC with optional keyboard and floppy disk drive. CDTV discs meet Yellow Book specifications, but they work only on a CDTV player. This is because the discs are recorded in ISO 9660 interchange level 2 format, which allows up to 30-character file names. Commodore chose this format to accommodate AmigaDOS files, the operating system for the Commodore Amiga, which can be made to play CDTV discs.

Commodore is giving itself a second chance with the Amiga CD32, a 32-bit CD-ROM-based system designed to compete with the 3DO and Sega systems. The Amiga CD32 uses a Motorola MC68020 processor and the Amiga's Advanced Graphic Architecture (AGA) chip set. This chip set can display up to 256,000 colors on a screen at a time, using a palette of 16.8 million colors.

The Amiga CD32 uses a double-speed CD-ROM drive, and the price is about $400 with 2MB of memory. The unit is capable of playing audio CD, video CD, and games. It will play some, but not all CDTV titles; Commodore is in the process of certifying which ones are compatible. Overall, the company expects 50 to 75 titles to be ready when it appears in stores in early 1994.

MPEG video compression from C-Cube, which provides the same for 3DO, is an option that will allow up to 74 minutes of video playback from one disc. Other options allow the CD32 to become a full-fledged Amiga computer.

There are similarities between the CD32 and 3DO systems, and this is more than just coincidence. Some of the original designers of the Amiga computer are now employed by 3DO. Both systems use specialized chips for graphics and audio to take the processing load off the CPU. The CD32 uses two video chips, called Alice and Lisa, and one audio chip, called Paula, which are found in all Amiga computers. Commodore does not match 3DO's performance, however; the CD32 can render 7 million pixels per second versus 3DO's 64 million. That performance is still significantly faster than most desktop computers.

The CD32 has one advantage in the Amiga's operating system. It is a 32-bit, real-time, multitasking environment ideally suited for playing multimedia. In fact, many people consider the Amiga computer to be the best platform for multimedia development today.

ATARI JAGUAR

Atari once dominated the electronic home entertainment market, and now it hopes to get some of it back with a 64-bit video game system called Jaguar. Jaguar, shown in Figure 4-14, will use both game cartridges and

FIGURE 4-14
The Atari Jaguar

CD-ROM. The Jaguar costs about $400 with the optional CD-ROM drive, making it one of the least expensive of the TV-based players. Atari announced that only 5 titles will be available at launch. A company newsletter, however, describes 10 game titles under development. Atari has been very successful lining up hardware manufacturers to implement Jaguar systems.

At the heart of Jaguar are two chip sets that Atari engineers call Tom and Jerry. Tom is a high-speed RISC-based graphics processor quite capable of generating animation and video. Jerry is designed for networked multiconsole games, and it provides a high-speed connection for modems, cable TV, or other types of networks. The main processor is a Motorola MC68000, the same class of CPU found in Apple Macintoshes. A custom DSP provides a wide range of sound synthesis capability. The CD-ROM drive boasts a transfer rate of 350Kbps.

Despite its low price and advanced technology, Atari will have a tough time finding success with the Jaguar. Having only five titles available at launch is a telling fact. With so many platforms to choose from, software developers are very selective about where they put their resources.

SEGA CD

Sega introduced a CD option for its Genesis game machine in late 1991, but sales have only recently started to take off. This is probably due to the strength of the available software titles—all games—rather than the hardware. Compared to the latest crop of interactive TV-based players, Sega CD looks a little lame. It is inexpensive, however, priced at a little over $200 including the Genesis unit.

The Genesis unit, shown in Figure 4-15, is based on both a Motorola 68000 and a Zilog Z80 (which the Radio Shack TRS-80 computer line used). It has only 64K of main memory, plus another 64K of memory for video. The video is capable of displaying 16 colors on the TV screen simultaneously, out of a palette of 512. The Sega CD option adds another 68000 processor and 768K more of memory, which is needed to load and display the software from the disc.

As you would expect, the Sega CD is unsuited for full-motion video. The game animations for which it was designed work fine, though. Sega offers no option to use Sega CD with any device other than your TV. However, options expected to appear in 1994 make Sega CD a more interesting product. These include a virtual-reality helmet and a modem. *Virtual reality* is a three-dimensional simulation technique that gives you the illusion that you are actually "in" the onscreen environments. The modem can be used to connect Sega Genesis systems remotely using the telephone for multiplayer games.

CD-ROM Hardware   109

Chapter 4

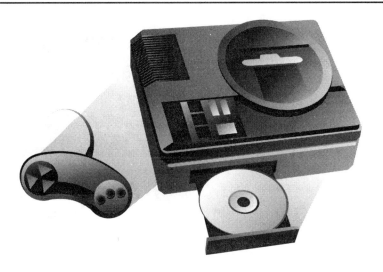

FIGURE 4-15
The Sega Genesis player with Sega CD option

Sega's future products promise to be more exciting. The company has announced it is designing a new multimedia game device with Hitachi, which will provide a new powerful processor for the unit. Hitachi will also provide the software tools to develop the game software. This game machine will use a CD-ROM drive. Don't expect to see this device until 1995, however. Sega is also reportedly working with JVC on another CD-ROM game machine, and with Yamaha to create a music-related device.

TURBO TECHNOLOGIES' TURBO DUO

The Turbo Duo began life as the NEC TurboGrafx CD. NEC still manufactures the product, but the company sold the marketing rights to Turbo Technologies. Unlike Sega CD, the Turbo Duo has a built-in CD-ROM drive (see Figure 4-16). It also has a 16-bit cartridge slot next to the drive. The brains of the unit is a Motorola 6502 processor, the same chip that the old Apple II line used. It has 256K of memory, plus another 384K of special-purpose RAM. This extra RAM is used by a line of SuperCD titles. It can display 241 colors simultaneously on the TV screen from a palette of 512.

A five-player option is available. Other options include the Intelligent Link interface that allows you to use the Turbo Duo as an external CD-ROM

110 BYTE Guide to CD-ROM

Chapter 4

FIGURE 4-16
The Turbo Technologies Turbo Duo player

drive for a Mac or PC, and a 128K memory cartridge allows you to save games once you've filled the standard memory.

Although performance is satisfactory for the few titles currently available (all relatively brainless Nintendo-type fare), the Turbo Duo cannot compete with the likes of 3DO or Jaguar when it comes to graphics and video. Turbo Technologies is working on a new model that reportedly includes video capability, however.

SONY COMPUTER ENTERTAINMENT

Sony has announced plans to introduce a CD-ROM-based game machine in Japan during 1994, and elsewhere in 1995. As yet unnamed, this system will be made by a new company within Sony called Sony Computer Entertainment, which will also develop titles.

The hardware is expected to be based on a speedy 32-bit RISC (reduced instruction set computing) processor. Sony claims that this chip will operate at an astonishing 500 MIPS (millions of instructions per second). This would make it several times more powerful than the fastest computer workstations currently available. If Sony succeeds with launching such a machine, it should provide unparalleled graphics performance.

CD-RECORDABLE: FOR THE PUBLISHER IN YOU

CD-R drives differ dramatically from CD-ROM drives in both the configuration of the drive itself and how it is implemented in a computer. The laser, of course, must be able to burn the pits that represent data into the disc. It is therefore more powerful than and designed differently from a CD-ROM drive, as Figure 2-5 in Chapter 2 illustrates.

You cannot connect a CD-R drive to your computer in the same way that you do a CD-ROM drive. Most CD-R devices are used in CD-ROM publishing applications, where the entire disc is likely to be written at once. They are actually subsystems, like the one shown in Figure 4-17, with their own controlling software and other hardware components. These systems are necessary to create a reliable environment in which to transfer and record data on a CD-R disc. You can, however, buy internal CD-R drives that do not require a lot of supporting hardware and software for use as archiving devices; there are trade-offs, however, as described in the next section.

To properly record, CD-R drives require a constant, uninterrupted flow of data at a rate comparable to the transfer rate of the drive. For example, a double-speed CD-R drive would need to receive data at a rate no lower than 300Kbps. The way most CD-R systems used for CD-ROM publishing handle this is to provide a dedicated high-capacity, high-speed hard disk drive to transfer the data to the drive. The hard disk drive and CD-R drive are connected via a high-speed SCSI interface.

For publishing applications, transferring data from your computer's main hard drive is a bad idea for a number of reasons. Even if your computer has a high-speed, high-capacity hard disk drive, several factors can interfere with a constant data flow. For example, your hard disk might be very *fragmented*; this means that the files are recorded in many different locations on the disk rather than in a single block. To retrieve the entire file, the hard disk drive's read mechanism constantly jumps around the disk, and this slows down access times and transfer rates. With a dedicated drive, you can keep only those files you want to record on the drive, ensuring that they are stored in one contiguous block.

Even with a dedicated hard disk drive, interruptions are possible. For example, many hard disk drives periodically perform a *thermal recalibration*. High-capacity drives have a lot of platters spinning at a rapid rate. This builds up heat, which expands the disk enough to affect the read mechanism. To compensate, a drive will take about a second to recalibrate itself for these changes.

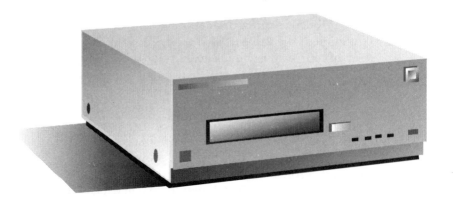

FIGURE 4-17
A typical CD-R device

To keep that one-second delay from ruining a recording session, most CD-R systems use a buffer. Some systems use buffers as small as 64K, which might not be enough for a one-second interruption. Other vendors use more; Sony uses 3MB, for example.

The software that comes with CD-R systems, generally referred to as *formatting software*, has two main components. A set of drivers allows you to write data to the disc, and the other part lets you choose which format—ISO 9660, Apple HFS, and so on—to record the data. Some formatting software also comes with data compression and encryption utilities.

CD-R AS AN ARCHIVING TOOL

Archiving applications allow for a little more flexibility in terms of data transfer. Since data archiving is multisession in nature—usually done incrementally at regular intervals—you are likely to record only a small portion of the disc at any one time. You still need to ensure that you have a fast, constant data flow during each recording session. But this is easier to accomplish for smaller amounts of data.

CD-R drives used for archival purposes, such as the RCD 200 CD-R drive from Pinnacle Micro and the Personal Archiver from JVC, are stripped-down versions of their bigger siblings. They do not come with hard disk drives or large buffers. The Personal Archiver comes in both internal and external versions. The software that comes with them is optimized for archival applications.

Sending data directly from a network to a CD-R drive is very unreliable. Too many other tasks being performed on the network can interfere with the transfer rate. Even if you wait until after hours, someone working late might place enough of a demand on the network to interrupt the data flow. You still need a dedicated intermediary, most likely a hard disk drive. What the archival software does is first copy the data to the dedicated hard disk drive and then transfer that data to the CD-R disc. Otherwise, it works much like any other archiving software, allowing you to choose which data to back up and when to do it.

THE SOUL OF A CD-ROM DRIVE

The remainder of this chapter is a somewhat technical discussion of the manner in which a CD drive reads data. If you do not have an interest in this material, it can be skipped.

A CD-ROM drive is a surprisingly complex device. It contains not one but four motors, or *servomechanisms* (*servos*), the laser read head, a controller chip, signal decoding and processing electronics, and a read-ahead buffer. In a way, a CD-ROM drive has its own simple computer on board. Figure 4-18 shows a relatively complete picture of the internal CD-ROM drive; the rest of this chapter will explain the various components.

Why does it need all this paraphernalia? The drive is complex because it must perform a very difficult task with little margin for error. It must precisely focus a laser on a disc spinning rapidly at varying rates. The reflected light from that laser must be picked up by photodetectors and converted to digital signals. Those signals must then be analyzed, corrected for errors, processed, and then sent to the computer. Microscopic variances in the location of the laser could mean the difference between getting the data you expect or nothing at all.

Here's how it all works: When you insert a disc into a CD-ROM drive, it detects the presence of the disc, and the turntable controller signals the turntable servo (or spindle motor) to spin the disc. From there, the first thing the drive does is to ensure that it is in focus.

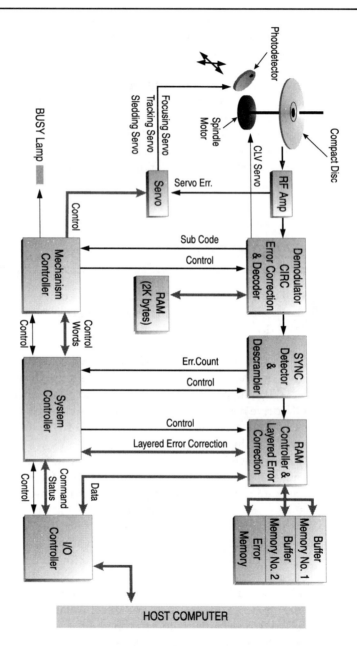

FIGURE 4-18
Components of a typical CD-ROM drive (courtesy of Sony Corp.)

FOCUS, FOCUS, FOCUS

The optical head, or laser mechanism, is on a swing arm and has its own focus servo. It focuses the beam to approximately the size of the pits on the disc, guided by the focus control circuitry. CD-ROMs use semiconductor lasers—also called laser diodes. Their advantage is that they allow for a small mechanism and low-voltage operation.

A photodetector picks up the light reflected from the disc and converts the light into an encoded digital signal. If the laser is out of focus, the photodetector can sense it and signal the focus control to make the appropriate adjustments. To make those adjustments, the focus servo uses two types of lenses—normal and cylindrical—to produce a unique pattern on the detector when the laser is in focus. A normal lens is curved on both its horizontal and vertical axes and causes a parallel light passing through to focus at a point. A cylindrical lens is curved on only the horizontal axis.

Light first goes through the normal lens, focusing it toward the center, and then through the cylindrical lens, which increases the deflection toward the center in only one axis. The two lenses provide two focal points. The combined deflection of the normal and cylindrical lenses brings the light to a focus in front of the detector. The light deflected only by the normal lens is out of focus when it hits the cylindrical lens. Once it passes through the cylindrical lens, a vertical line is produced in front of the photodetector.

The light deflected by the normal lens ultimately converges to a point behind the photodetector. Here, the light that was deflected by both the normal and cylindrical lenses has spread apart and is no longer focused. This results in a horizontal line behind the photodetector. The vertical line will spread to a vertical ellipse as it moves toward the photodetector; the horizontal line will spread to a horizontal ellipse as it moves toward the photodetector. Consequently, when the beam is in focus on the disc surface, the signal at the photodetector is a circle, halfway between the horizontal and vertical lines. This circular pattern on the detector is used to determine correct focus.

The photodetector is divided into four parts to monitor the shape of the light spot on the detector and to correct when it is out of focus. (Figure 4-19 shows it in focus.) The circular spot is the result of equal outputs from all four detector parts: A, B, C, and D. The outputs of the detector are combined into two pairs (A + C, B + D). These output pairs are compared in a "comparator."

Since all outputs are equal, the output from the comparator should be 0 volts DC, indicating that the beam is in focus. This output is applied to a drive amp; if the value is 0, no correction is applied to the objective lens. The *objective lens* is the last lens through which the laser light goes before striking the surface of the disc. It moves on two axes (up and down and side-to-side) to focus the laser beam.

When the disk is too close to the objective lens, the laser beam is out of focus on the disc surface and produces a reflected beam that diverges as it leaves the objective lens. The circular pattern is shifted down, producing an ellipse along the A and C axes of the detector. This causes more light to strike the A and C detectors, producing a higher output than the B and D detectors. This difference in the output of the detector pairs causes the drive amp to amplify the positive output and move the objective lens away from the disc, focusing the light beam and generating the correct pattern. The opposite process occurs when the disc is too far away.

The objective lens position is controlled by applying current to the focus servo from the drive amp via the focus coil wrapped around the objective lens. As current passes through the focus coil, the focusing magnets on the frame of the two-axis device cause the lens to move up or down, depending on the direction of the current—similar to a speaker coil.

THE SIGNAL-TO-NOISE RATIO

Once the beam is focused, the drive still has to deal with interference—or noise—with the light signal. Noise can come from the light source itself, imperfections on the disc, or the optical detector and preamp.

With a laser and photodetector, interference is minimal. Most interference is from the disc itself. Some light is lost during the focusing and deflection, and the photodiode is not 100 percent efficient. To compensate for light loss and these inherent inefficiencies, laser power needs to be 2 to 3 mW. You can minimize noise by taking care when handling discs.

READING THE DATA

Once the laser beam is squared away, the optical head, or pickup system, transfers data from the surface of the disc to the electronics in the player. It has two main parts: the semiconductor laser and the optics that focus the beam on the disc's surface, described in the preceding section; and the detector and the optics that direct the reflection from the disc surface to the detector.

The two systems must be tightly controlled. The semiconductor lasers produce a light beam. Most of the light goes through a semitransparent mirror (some is lost in the process) to the disc surface. Just before reaching the disc, the objective lens focuses the beam on the surface. This servo-controlled lens compensates for mechanical tolerances, temperature changes, or irregularities or warping in the disc.

CD-ROM Hardware 117
Chapter 4

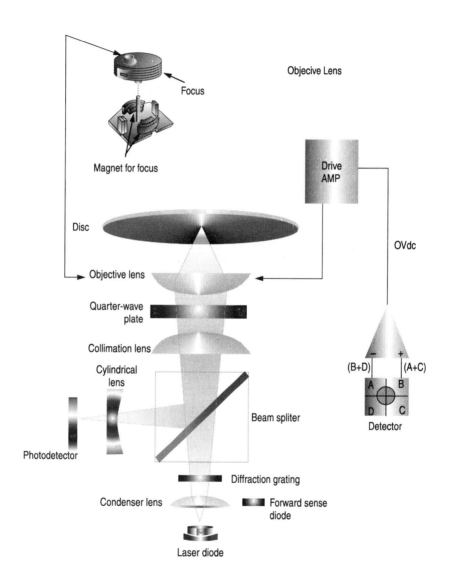

FIGURE 4-19
Correctly focused CD-ROM drive (figure courtesy of Sony Corp.)

The beam striking the surface is reflected back, being *modulated*—meaning its angle is being varied—with the pits and lands. The modulated beam travels over the same path as the light coming from the laser. It passes through the servo-focusing lens, producing a parallel beam traveling in the opposite direction.

The beam is deflected to the semitransparent mirror where part of the beam continues toward the semiconductor laser and is lost. Most of the return beam is focused down toward the detector, producing the output signal.

The mirrors can vary according to the preferences of the drive vendor. Sony uses a semitransparent mirror; some use a polarized mirror, which eliminates light loss and provides higher optics efficiency. Polarized systems have a disadvantage in that they might have trouble reading discs with high *birefringeance* (the refraction of light in two slightly different directions, creating two rays), which affects polarized light.

MAKING DRIVES WORK SMARTER

If you have ever studied the results of a performance test on a large number of CD-ROM drives, it might seem like transfer rates or buffer size have little to do with throughput. This isn't really true; what those results show is how intelligently a manufacturer makes use of a drive's inherent capabilities. This intelligence (or lack of it) resides in the drive's firmware.

The firmware is a chip that contains code to control the flow of data in and out of the disc's buffer and to the drive's controller. It also holds the error detection and correction code. Most of the performance differences among different brands of drives are the result of how each manufacturer uses the buffer. The standard buffer size is 64K, but some drives use 128K or even 256K buffers.

A buffer's function is to hold data for which the computer isn't yet ready. For example, only so much data can be displayed on the screen at one time, so it is not possible to process and display all of a large file all at once. Since the buffer consists of solid-state memory, it provides extremely fast—almost instantaneous—access. As long as the data is in the buffer to be retrieved, it creates virtually no delay.

The standard way to implement a buffer is to read the data off the disc and into the buffer in 2K chunks if the disc uses the ISO 9660 file standard, or 512-byte chunks if it uses the Apple HFS standards. For every chunk of data requested, a command must be issued to the drive's controller. Each command causes an interrupt, which stops the computer's main processor from whatever else it was doing to issue that command. A 20K file, therefore, would generate 10 interrupts, degrading performance.

There is a better way, and it's called a *circular buffer read-ahead*. This method reads data continuously, so that only one command would need to be issued for that 20K file. This speeds throughput by giving the main processor more time to work on compute-intensive tasks such as generating graphics or video. It also does a better job of keeping the buffer full, which in turn gets the data to the display faster. Some drives make even better use of the buffer. With a larger buffer, for example, it is possible to place a disc's table of contents or root directory information in the buffer. The drive can then retrieve this frequently accessed data much more quickly.

Although checksums are placed on a disc in a standard format, drive manufacturers are free to analyze them with whatever error detection and correction code they want. Efficient EDC/ECC code can result in modest performance gains, and it can also improve the data reliability. For practical purposes, however, the differences in reliability are relatively meaningless for most applications.

CHAPTER 5

Do-It-Yourself CD-ROM

Sooner or later, you will want to install a CD-ROM drive in your computer, or upgrade the CD-ROM drive you now have. Installing or replacing a CD-ROM drive is a surprisingly easy task, provided you understand a little about how the drive communicates with your computer.

Even if you prefer to leave the installation to a trained technician, it pays to know what goes on between your CD-ROM drive and system. For instance, you might need to troubleshoot your drive should it stop working. Or, at the very least, you will be better able to explain a problem to a repair person.

You have three basic areas to consider when attaching or replacing a CD-ROM drive:

▶ The physical connection between drive and computer
▶ Software device drivers
▶ Installation of ancillary hardware

The physical connection includes hooking up the drive to a power source, attaching the system interface (or *bus*), and mounting the drive to the computer. A CD-ROM drive usually does not come with a bus interface, since you have several choices (described later in this chapter). Additional hardware might include an interface card or a sound or video board if you want multimedia capability.

Software *device drivers* tell the computer's operating system how to handle the drive. After you've installed the drive, you load the device drivers from a floppy disk that comes with the drive. Some computer operating systems such as Windows NT, OS/2 2.1, and Apple's System 7 have native CD-ROM support for many popular brands of drives; you might not need drivers for the CD-ROM drive you want to use with these environments. Check the list of supported drives in the operating system's manual. If you don't see your drive listed, check with the manufacturer to see if drivers are available.

Installation differs depending on the type of computer you have and the type of CD-ROM drive you want to use. A portable computer, for instance, usually requires that you use an external CD-ROM drive. External drives come in their own enclosures and attach to one of the computer's external ports. The fastest drives available—quad-speed drives—usually come as external units because their mechanics require a larger enclosure.

The type of applications you intend to use from a CD-ROM also affects installation. You might find that you need to upgrade parts of your computer, too. In most cases, however, CD-ROM drive installation is not much more difficult than inserting an add-in board in one of your computer's slots. The trick is getting what you need up front and understanding a few simple concepts.

BEFORE YOU BEGIN

Before you buy a CD-ROM drive, you need to assess how you will use it. Will you be using it mainly for text-based reference CD-ROMs? For entertainment or education? For training? Will you need video playback and high-quality audio capability? The answers to these questions will tell you what kind of performance you need.

You will make different decisions based on the type of computer you have. Installing a CD-ROM drive on a Mac, for instance, is different than installing one on a PC. The discussion that follows deals with the requirements of and procedures for installing a CD-ROM drive on a PC running either MS-DOS or Windows. Macintosh owners will be happy to know that CD-ROM installation is much easier for them. There are some issues to consider, however, and they are covered later, in the section, "The Mac Makes It Easy."

Chapter 5

Today's state-of-the-art entry level for any computer is a double-speed (300Kbps), multisession drive; moving up to quad-speed drives for the most demanding multimedia applications. Single-session 150Kbps drives are obsolete, though you can probably still find them on sale. These slower drives are dirt cheap and will work fine for text and data applications, but for an extra $50 or $100 you can get much better performance—a worthwhile investment. Keep in mind, too, that performance can vary greatly among drives within the same class, as the previous chapter explained.

The first step is to take inventory of your computer's capabilities. You need to know the following:

▶ Is there an open drive bay in the case for a CD-ROM drive?

▶ How many unused expansion slots are there on the motherboard? What type are they?

▶ What type of interface, or bus, does it have?

▶ Does it have the sound capability you want?

▶ Will your video support the applications you want to run?

▶ Does it have sufficient memory and hard disk storage?

▶ Does it have the latest version of the operating system with up-to-date CD-ROM support?

▶ Is the power supply large enough to provide adequate juice to the drive?

▶ Is its CPU powerful enough to run the software you want to use?

This sounds like a lot to think about, but you can determine the answers to most of these questions very quickly by checking your user manual and taking a peek "under the hood." You will easily see whether you have open bays or slots. There should be a label on the power supply giving its specifications. And the CPU should be visible, telling you its type and speed. Look for a CPU upgrade slot near the CPU, too. Many late-model 386 and 486 PCs have them. Figure 5-1 shows a typical layout of a PC motherboard with a CD-ROM installed.

You can get other information by running your system diagnostics or system setup program, which most PCs have. Check your manual for directions on how to access and use them. Third-party diagnostics programs such as Dariana Software's WinSleuth Gold Plus are more "user friendly" and just as good, if not better, at telling you what's in your computer. Better yet, they

Chapter 5

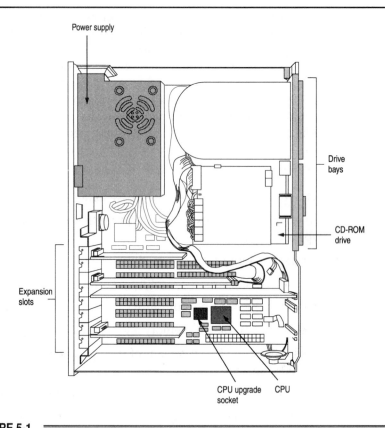

FIGURE 5-1
Typical motherboard for a desktop PC

can be real life-savers if you have to resolve memory or interrupt conflicts caused by installing a CD-ROM drive—more on this in the following sections.

The tough decisions come after you have the answers. Perhaps you won't be able to use the internal model you wanted, or maybe you'll need to upgrade one or more components of your computer.

INTERNAL OR EXTERNAL DRIVE?

The most basic decision is whether to use an internal or external drive. External drives tend to cost more—by about $50 to $300—because they come with their own enclosures and, depending on the type of interface used, require more electronics. There is no performance difference between internal and external versions of a given drive, however. Figure 5-2 shows typical internal and external CD-ROM drives.

If you have a portable computer or a desktop model with no open drive bay, then you must use an external CD-ROM drive. Also keep in mind that you require an open bay that allows external access so you can insert and remove the discs. External drives attach by cable to one of two types of external ports on your computer: parallel or SCSI (Small Computer System Interface—pronounced "scuzzy"). Virtually all computers—portable and desktop—have parallel ports. *Parallel ports* are commonly used to connect printers. *SCSI ports*

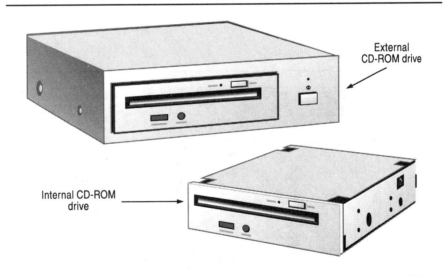

FIGURE 5-2
Internal and external CD-ROM drives

Chapter 5

are usually add-on affairs for PCs, and they are described in detail, along with other computer interfaces, in "Making the Connection," later in this chapter.

Other factors can prevent you from using an internal drive. You might not have enough expansion slots on the computer's motherboard to add a SCSI controller (controllers are also called host-adapter cards), like the one shown in Figure 5-3. For most applications, SCSI requires only an 8-bit ISA (Industry Standard Architecture) bus slot. (ISA refers to the type of expansion slots in your PC and is a standard for connecting devices directly to the motherboard.) Other higher performance bus slots are necessary only for the most demanding applications such as those where you need to constantly pump video data through the system or are running a CD-ROM drive off a network. These include

▶ EISA (Extended Industry Standard Architecture)

▶ Micro Channel (IBM's bus standard)

▶ VL-Bus (a local bus standard that connects directly to the system CPU)

▶ PCI bus (Peripheral Component Interconnect; another local bus standard)

▶ 16-bit ISA

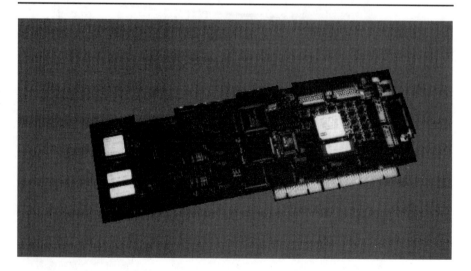

FIGURE 5-3
SCSI host adapter

You can, however, put 8-bit ISA boards into 16-bit ISA, VL-Bus, and EISA slots.

If you have no slots open, you do have some other options, none of which is ideal. First, you could free a slot by removing a board that is already installed. But what do you give up—your modem? Certainly not your graphics card. It would be unlikely that you have a slot filled with something that you can afford to do without.

You might be able to consolidate the functions of two or more cards by buying a *multifunction card*. These cards might combine extra serial or parallel ports with, say, extra system memory functions. Similarly, the sound boards found in most multimedia upgrade kits include a SCSI or other proprietary interface that the CD-ROM drive attaches directly to. Digicom has recently introduced a 16-bit sound card that incorporates a fax/data modem and a SCSI interface. This saves you a slot only if you already had a sound board or modem in your computer.

Another option is to run the CD-ROM drive off the computer's built-in IDE (Integrated Drive Electronics) interface. You will not get the performance that a SCSI interface provides, and this will seriously hamper your ability to run multimedia applications. It will work, though, assuming that your computer has an IDE interface (it probably does if it was made in the last three years), and assuming that it isn't already being used to its maximum capacity (IDE can handle only two devices).

BRINGING THE OLD PC UP TO SNUFF

You want to create the optimum environment for your CD-ROM drive. This means making sure that inadequacies of your PC won't hamper performance, especially for demanding multimedia applications. The most likely parts of your PC that you need to worry about are the main processor, memory, hard disk capacity, video, operating system, and power supply.

The MPC 2 standard described in Chapter 3 says that minimal specifications for a multimedia PC are a 25MHz 486SX-class CPU, 4MB of RAM, a 160MB hard disk drive, 16-bit sound capability, and VGA video. This specification is for manufacturers, however, and does not mean that a lesser machine cannot run multimedia. If you have to, you can get by with less in almost every area.

The Processor

A 286-class, or even an 8088/8086-class, CPU is powerful enough for most text- and data-based applications. For multimedia applications, however, the minimum processor you want is a 25MHz 386; a 486-class CPU is highly recommended.

If you need a faster processor, you can buy CPU upgrade boards or chips for many 286 and higher systems, though you want to be careful about investing too much money in an old, worn out system. You can find a list of companies selling CPU upgrades in Appendix B. Before you buy any upgrade, verify with the upgrade vendor that your particular brand and model of PC is supported. Expect to pay at least a few hundred dollars for the upgrade.

MULTIMEDIA UPGRADE KITS

Multimedia upgrade kits are one option for PC users to upgrade to a CD-ROM drive. They provide an MPC-compatible CD-ROM drive, 16-bit sound capability, and a SCSI interface—the components you are least likely to have in your system. Furthermore, you get extras such as speakers and a microphone. If you are finicky about sound quality, however, you should know that the speakers and microphones in most upgrade kits are of relatively low quality, to keep the price low. If you want the best possible sound input and output, you'll have to invest in higher quality speakers and a microphone.

Many upgrade kits are manufactured by companies noted for their sound boards—Creative Labs, Media Vision, and Aztech. Prices range from $600 to $1200. The best kits provide features such as speakers, a microphone, and plenty of bundled software. A list of multimedia upgrade kit vendors appears in Appendix B.

Memory and Storage: Never Enough

Even though the application and data are on a CD-ROM, they will still use your computer's memory and storage to operate. Again, multimedia applications use the most system resources. Many of these applications require a minimum of 4MB, but realistically you should have at least 8MB, and preferably more. The extra memory allows more of the application to execute from memory, rather than from the slower CD-ROM. Your PC owner's manual should tell you what type of memory your computer uses and how to install it.

Most CD-ROMs load various files onto your hard disk drive. These files could be the *executable data*—the code portion of the application that tells the computer how to access the information on disc—or other data that benefits from being on the faster hard disk. Some CD-ROM applications could place 5MB or more of files on your hard disk. This adds up as you install more and more CD-ROMs. You can get away with an 80MB or even a 60MB hard disk drive if you are dealing only with text-based applications. You want at least 160MB for multimedia applications.

 Before you upgrade your hard disk drive, remember to back it up to tape or floppies. Check your PC owner's manual on how to remove your old hard disk drive and install the new one.

Keeping Up with Updates

The most subtle potential problem in upgrading lurks in your operating system. Even though you might be using the latest version of MS-DOS or Windows, you don't necessarily have the latest version of the Windows CD-ROM extensions, MSCDEX. MSCDEX occupies 35K of memory and comes in MS-DOS 6.2 and Windows 3.1.

MSCDEX must be loaded on boot-up from your AUTOEXEC.BAT file. The setup software that you run when you install a CD-ROM drive often adds the appropriate line to this file. Once loaded, you can tell which version of MSCDEX you have by watching for the "MSCDEX version 2.xx" notice on boot-up.

Using the wrong version could create conflicts with other software or cause your drive not to work at all. Microsoft periodically updates these extensions, so check with the CD-ROM drive vendor to see which version you require. The correct version is often supplied with the SCSI adapter or CD-ROM drive. Earlier versions of MS-DOS don't include MSCDEX at all. Updating MSCDEX is simply a matter of copying the new version into the appropriate MS-DOS directory. See "Troubleshooting Your CD-ROM Drive" at the end of this chapter.

"Scotty, I Need More Power!"

Your power supply regulates the power coming from the AC outlet to the various components of your computer. If those components require more power than the power supply can generate, then you will experience malfunctioning or complete failure of the power supply.

There is no easy way to determine if your computer's power supply can handle the extra load that a CD-ROM drive will place on it. The more add-in boards installed in your computer, the greater the stress on the power supply. As a rule of thumb, you should have at least a 100-watt power supply.

A good power supply costs under $100; check the mail-order ads in popular computer magazines for suppliers. Before ordering, make sure that the power supply is appropriate for your system—that it will fit in your case properly and doesn't require rewiring the line voltage. Power supplies are usually accessible once you have your computer's case off. They are held in place by a few screws, and you have only a couple of cables to deal with. Figure 5-1 shows a typical power supply mounted on the motherboard. Check your computer's manual for specifics.

The Stereo PC

Most CD-ROM drives feature built-in audio circuitry and include headphone jacks and line-output jacks so they can play audio CDs. However, you will not hear the music and sound effects programmed into CD-ROM software simply by plugging a set of headphones into the drive's headphone jack. The sound data programmed into CD-ROM software is different from that on an audio CD and must be played through a sound board.

Multimedia applications require high-quality sound capability. If you expect to run them, you'll need not only a good sound card, but headphones or a good set of speakers, too. The jacks on most sound cards accept headphones commonly used with portable stereos, and will accommodate larger plugs with a converter.

PC speakers generally come with a built-in amplifier to boost the volume (the higher the wattage, the louder the sound possible). Also pay attention to the frequency range—a wider range produces more accurate highs and lows. Some speakers add a *subwoofer*, a separate speaker dedicated to bass, which delivers a deeper bass and richer sound. Don't even think of getting by with the internal speaker that your PC came with.

MPC 2 specifies 16-bit sound capability, but you can get by with an 8-bit sound board. It should be able to produce waveform audio. *Waveform audio*, known simply as *wave*, is digital sound sampled at 11KHz to 44KHz. Faster sampling rates capture more of the original sound, but the resulting data files are much larger than those for sound sampled at a slower rate. Professional-quality is considered to be 16-bit 44KHz sound, which an 8-bit board is incapable of. Low-quality speakers, too, will not adequately match up to 16-bit sound. A minute of sound sampled at that rate can require nearly 10MB of storage space. Therefore, wave is usually used to record voice or sound effects like bangs, pops, or zips. These can be sampled at 11KHz, resulting in much smaller files that sound just fine when played back. Many boards are capable of compressing the waveform data to save disk space.

A multimedia-ready sound board should offer a MIDI interface. MIDI has been used by musicians for years and is a command language, not a recorded sound. It tells the hardware what sound to produce. MIDI files are a stream of commands instructing the MIDI board to produce the desired sounds for the desired length of time at the desired pitch.

Most boards are also capable of FM synthesis, which was developed by Yamaha (whose sound chips are in the vast majority of sound boards). *FM synthesis* generates sound by emulating the target instrument, resulting in a sound that is usually adequate, but not perfectly accurate.

The best sound boards can sample waveform sound at 44KHz and play and record in 16-bit stereo and mono. A 16-bit board lets you sample a larger sequence of data simultaneously, producing much higher fidelity than 8-bit boards.

A good sound card should record sound as well as play it back. This is especially useful if you want to add sound effects or background music to a presentation. Programs such as Microsoft Word let you record your voice to annotate documents. When someone opens the document file later, they can also hear your recorded comments.

Creative Labs' Sound Blaster is considered the dominant industry standard. Most applications that use sound are Sound Blaster compatible, as are many sound boards from other vendors. Other significant standards include Ad Lib, Thunder Board, Media Vision's Pro Audio, and Windows. The more of these standards a sound board supports, the more software it is able to play.

Many boards include a CD-ROM interface, which is especially convenient if you're short on expansion slots because you won't have to also buy a separate host adapter. Only some of these interfaces are SCSI, however. Some are proprietary and only support CD-ROM drives sold by the sound board manufacturer. Many boards also include a joystick port for use with games.

If your board has a SCSI interface, chances are it's an 8-bit variety that supports the older SCSI-1 standard. However, that should be perfectly capable of running a double-speed CD-ROM drive. Be aware, though, that sound and full-motion video together put great demands on your computer's processing power. If, for example, you're trying to run both on a 16MHz 386SX machine, you'll find the sound or the video motion slowing down to an unacceptable pace. For this reason, some of the latest sound boards are providing the faster SCSI-2 interface.

Fortunately, installing a sound board isn't as complicated now as it used to be. Plug the card into a free expansion slot and run the setup program. It should walk you through the installation procedure. See Appendix B for a listing of sound board vendors.

PORTABLE SOUND

Laptop owners are more limited when it comes to adding sound capability to their machines, because few of these miniature PCs can accept standard add-on cards. You can buy devices that plug into a laptop's parallel port and provide many of the features (but not all) of full-blown sound boards. Some, for example, can record at the 44KHz sampling rate and create 16-bit files; some can't. Some provide MIDI and FM synthesis capabilities; some don't.

On the other hand, a few of these devices offer better performance than standard sound boards in areas such as the ability to play sounds in the background while the computer is running animated video or heavy computations. Various manufacturers include different capabilities in their sound devices, so make sure you ask for the features you need when you go shopping.

If you're adding a sound device to support your CD-ROM drive, which probably also plugs into your parallel port, you might have problems trying to run both devices off of a single parallel port. Some vendors offer solutions to this conflict; the best advice is to confirm that you can use the two devices concurrently before you buy.

If your portable PC has a PCMCIA (Personal Computer Memory Card International Association) slot, then you have other options. Several vendors sell sound cards that plug into the PCMCIA slot, and they are listed in Appendix B.

Video You Can Live With

Text-based applications look just fine using even the most basic monochrome video. Once you move into the world of Windows, graphics, and video, however, you must raise your standards. Choose a slow video board or a cheap, fuzzy monitor, and you will likely regret it later.

The best video cards accelerate graphics performance by taking much of the video processing tasks off the shoulders of the computer's main processor. They have their own video processor and video memory. Some computers provide what's called a local bus slot for these video accelerators. The local bus is a direct connection to the computer's main processor.

This speeds communication between the two components, allowing faster graphics generation.

For multimedia applications, you want an accelerator card that can generate a resolution of 640 by 480 pixels and 256 colors—the basic MPC 2 requirement. Fortunately, no self-respecting video card would show itself on the market without this capability. The best resolution any mainstream CD-ROM application will support is 1024 by 1280 and 256 colors. Most video accelerators support that mode, too.

Performance among the different brands of video cards can vary widely. The video accelerator market is extremely volatile. The leading models—in terms of providing the most bang for the buck—change frequently. Your best bet is to check current reviews in popular computer magazines to see which models are recommended.

If you expect to play full-motion video from a CD-ROM, then you want to consider a video playback board. For occasional recreational use of video, the small quarter-screen size that Windows supports through software is adequate. For training applications, presentations, or hard-core use of entertainment software, however, the tiny video windows quickly lead to disappointment. The best video playback boards support the Video CD format, allowing full-screen, full-motion video at 30 frames per second. These boards provide their own video processor to perform MPEG decompression. Audio CD capability is usually a standard feature, as well. Appendix B lists some popular vendors of video playback boards.

If you've been using Windows or another GUI (graphical user interface) for any length of time, you know that 14-inch displays can appear to be very small indeed. The same will be true if you run multimedia applications. For your eyes' sake, you should have a 17-inch monitor with a scan rate of at least 70Hz and a dot pitch of about 0.30. *Scan rate* refers to the speed at which the monitor refreshes the image, and *dot pitch* refers to the proximity of pixels to one another. Using a smaller monitor will not prevent you from running any applications or impair performance. The larger, better monitors will, however, reduce fatigue and help you avoid bloodshot eyes.

Decisions, Decisions

As you've probably guessed, getting your computer ready for CD-ROM can be an expensive proposition. In fact, if you have to upgrade more than one or two components, you might be better off buying a new computer. You should consider the amount of use your computer has had, too. Do you want to invest several hundred dollars in a system that has seen heavy use over a period of years? Probably not. Hard disk drives, keyboards, and monitors wear out, and power supplies weaken over time.

If you absolutely must have a CD-ROM drive now, but can't afford to upgrade your system, then you have to make the best of what you have knowing that some applications will be handicapped on your computer. You can always transfer the CD-ROM drive from your old system to a new one later, or upgrade components as you are able.

MAKING THE CONNECTION

If you've ever gotten on the wrong bus or train, you know the sinking feeling you get when you realize, too late, your mistake. Choose the wrong interface for your CD-ROM drive and you will eventually experience that same feeling.

The interface between a computer and a CD-ROM provides a pathway to exchange data between the two. A CD-ROM drive uses the same types of interfaces as hard disk or floppy disk drives. This interface and the accompanying software also tell the computer what kind of device is attached and establish a protocol for communication.

You can attach a CD-ROM drive using a number of types of interfaces: SCSI, IDE, or parallel port. Each has trade-offs, but once you know your needs and the limits of your system, choosing the interface that fits your situation is easy.

IDE

Many CD-ROM drives use the IDE interface mainly because it's already on most PC motherboards and, therefore, cheaper. IDE is adequate for text and graphics-based applications. If you want to run the latest multimedia applications, however, IDE simply won't cut it. The applications will run, but you won't have the tight synchronization of different data types or as consistent a flow of data as multimedia requires.

IDE is based on the AT Attachment (ATA) specification development by the Computer Association of Manufacturers (CAM). IDE capability is built onto the motherboard of most ISA bus PCs, but the controller logic is built into the drive itself. It is a 16-bit parallel interface that supports up to two hard disk drives (or a hard disk drive and a CD-ROM drive), via the system BIOS, without the aid of additional software drivers. (*BIOS*—Basic Input/Output System—is code that tells the computer how to handle different devices.) IDE is the standard way of attaching hard disk drives with capacities of up to 300MB (or up to 500MB in some cases) to a PC.

IDE can't support multitasking operations. Simply put, what this all means is that IDE can do only one thing at a time. It can't begin one task until it has finished another. For this reason, multimedia applications suffer under IDE.

IDE's maximum data transfer rate is 3MBps (megabytes per second). Table 5-1 compares the transfer rates of the different interfaces used for CD-ROM.

Is IDE's Star Rising? A new IDE standard is on the table and, if approved and accepted, could mean significantly better performance for IDE-based CD-ROM drives. One purpose of this initiative, which might be approved by ANSI by the time you read this, is to provide a fast, inexpensive interface to attach CD-ROM drives to PCs. The backers of this proposal include Western Digital (which makes IDE hard disk drives), IBM, Apple, Compaq, Dell, and NEC. Some reports suggest that one or more of these companies will roll out products using the faster IDE bus, which theoretically offers a transfer rate of 9 to 13 megabytes per second. At this speed, IDE is competitive with SCSI-1.

The new specification, called ATAPI (AT Attachment Peripheral Interface), offers more than just speed. With it, you can attach up to four devices per controller. That way, you can run, say, a hard disk drive, a tape backup device, and your CD-ROM drive off the same IDE controller and still have an open

Interface	Maximum Transfer Rate
IDE	3MBps
SCSI-1	5MBps
SCSI-2	10MBps, 20MBps, 40MBps*
Parallel	200Kbps

*For the three variations of SCSI-2: Fast SCSI, Wide SCSI, and Fast-Wide SCSI, respectively.

TABLE 5-1

Speed Comparison: CD-ROM Bus Interfaces

Chapter 5

node for another IDE device. If system vendors integrate this newer version of IDE on their PCs, you can avoid the expense of buying a separate SCSI controller. CD-ROM installation should also become a much simpler process.

SCSI

As PCs become more powerful, and software and data storage requirements more demanding, an IDE-controlled 300MB hard drive—or sometimes even two—is often too limited to handle large programs, graphics files, and multimedia applications. Therefore, SCSI has become the de facto standard for hard disk drives of 500MB and above, and for a variety of other peripheral devices such as CD-ROM drives, scanners, and streaming tape drives. It comes in two basic flavors: SCSI-1 and SCSI-2, the latter having several variations (as shown in Table 5-1).

SCSI is a fast, intelligent, multitasking I/O channel that can connect many different types of peripherals to one or more host computers. Because it is faster and able to multitask, SCSI is better at synchronizing the display and execution of different types of data—audio, video, text, and graphics. This means that multimedia applications will appear to run much smoother using SCSI.

BUS SPEED VERSUS DRIVE SPEED

If a double-speed CD-ROM drive can transfer data at only 300Kbps, why do you need the 5MBps that SCSI pumps through? The answer has to do with buffering data.

Transfer rates deal only with the speed at which the CD-ROM drive can pull data off a disc. A better measure of overall performance is throughput. *Throughput* is the amount of data that your entire system can process in a given period of time—from getting the data off the medium to displaying it on your monitor.

Your CD-ROM drive does not constantly read data while running an application. Sometimes it must wait for your computer to process and display an image. If it knows what's coming next, it places that data in a buffer, staying ahead of the computer when possible.

All CD-ROM drives have at least a 64K buffer, which is essentially memory coupled with some controlling electronics. The electronics provide the intelligence that controls the flow of data to and from that memory. The benefit of having this data in memory rather than just waiting to pull it off the disc is that it can be accessed at very high speed.

Buffering would be of little help if that data went from the 300Kbps CD-ROM drive to the high-speed memory and then to, say, a 300Kbps bus interface to the computer. With the 5MBps rate of SCSI, however, you can gain a performance advantage from the buffering.

However, buffering can go only so far. Although some drives have as much as 256K, this is tiny compared to the multi-megabyte files often found on CD-ROM. And the CD-ROM drive can strain to keep it full while running read-intensive applications such as video sequences. For this reason, you are not likely to see a significant improvement in throughput by going to a faster version of SCSI until drives become much faster.

SCSI is a combination of hardware and software that lets you connect up to seven SCSI devices to a single card. The hardware always includes the SCSI host adapter card and at least one SCSI peripheral device. The software includes device drivers and utilities that let the computer and operating system communicate with the peripheral.

SCSI permits a wide variety of devices to coexist on a SCSI bus, typically linked to the host computer via a single SCSI adapter. Adding multiple devices to a single adapter is called *daisy-chaining*, and this ability is very important for anyone who wants to use several CD-ROM drives on a network, as Chapter 8 will explain.

Each SCSI device has its own internal controller that communicates with the SCSI host adapter. This allows SCSI to work across a wide range of devices. A CD-ROM drive, for instance, can interpret the SCSI commands from the host adapter and execute them in a manner appropriate for the medium.

Every device attached to a SCSI host adapter gets its own ID number, and they are connected by a ribbon cable. The last device on the chain must have a *terminator*, which is an electrical resistor. The terminator reduces signal noise at the end of the line. You can have more than one host adapter in a PC, each of which can have the maximum seven SCSI devices attached. The total length of your ribbon cable should be no more than 10 feet—beyond that you get electrical interference that can affect reliability.

The external connectors used for SCSI-1 devices usually have 25 pins, while the internal SCSI-1 and basic SCSI-2 connectors have 50. The Apple Mac SCSI uses 25 pins. In the so-called "wide" configurations, SCSI-2 connectors have 68 pins. Unfortunately, some devices use proprietary connectors, so you can't count on the connectors shown in Figure 5-4 to necessarily look like the ones on your CD-ROM drive. Generally, though, you find proprietary connectors on packages that combine both the SCSI interface and the CD-ROM drive. A generic SCSI adapter will have a standard connector. If you plan to add other SCSI devices, such as a scanner or hard disk drive to your system, avoid buying anything with a proprietary connector.

The latest version of SCSI, SCSI-2, allows a data transfer rate of up to 40MBps using a 32-bit EISA, Micro Channel, or local bus slot. However, this is the theoretical limit and assumes that the data is coming from a device a lot faster than a CD-ROM drive. The SCSI-2 specification covers three variations based on the width of the SCSI cable: Fast, Wide, and Fast-Wide. Fast SCSI provides a transfer rate of up to 10MBps using an 8- or 16-bit slot. Wide SCSI allows up to 20MBps using a 16- or 32-bit slot. Fast-Wide SCSI allows up to the maximum 40MBps. Again, these are theoretical limits that are impossible to achieve using a CD-ROM drive.

SCSI-2 also addresses the compatibility issue. It will accept more types of devices, and it restricts the command language used for communication between the host adapter and SCSI devices. This makes it harder for vendors to use a proprietary approach.

Most CD-ROM drives still use SCSI-1 because most of them are not fast enough to take advantage of SCSI-2's throughput. You can expect SCSI-2 to play a key role as a CD-ROM interface in the future, however, as vendors come to grips with compatibility and performance issues.

The SCSI interface is well established in the Apple and Unix workstation markets, but it has been ignored in the mainstream PC market, primarily because, until now, most PC users haven't needed SCSI's capabilities. However, with the current generation of high-performance, 486-based PCs managing large programs and data files, SCSI's high data-transfer and multitasking I/O abilities are

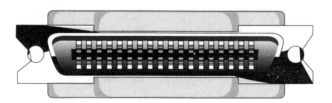

FIGURE 5-4
A 50-pin SCSI connector

much more important. PC users are beginning to use many of the SCSI devices, such as scanners, hard disks, tape drives, and optical drives; but the emergence of important software on CD-ROM has made the CD-ROM drive by far the most popular SCSI device in the PC market.

If you are simply adding a CD-ROM drive to your system, you will likely have to buy a SCSI host adapter separately. Multimedia upgrade kits often provide the SCSI interface on the sound card. In either case, the SCSI interface usually comes preconfigured for a typical PC and the drive. Installation is then simply a matter of plugging the controller into the expansion slot, the drive into the controller, and loading the drivers and utilities on your computer. Utilities might include programs to test or set up the drive; you will most likely encounter these programs if you've installed a multimedia upgrade kit.

The SCSI installation will not affect an IDE interface that your hard disk or floppy drive is using; it will control only those devices that have been assigned to it. Assuming you have the proper device driver, you can use the same SCSI host adapter to run your hard disk drive. However, unless your drive is larger than 300MB, there is little advantage in doing so.

IF YOU ARE MISSING THE DRIVERS

A friend just gave you a used CD-ROM drive for your PC. Unfortunately, he did not have a device driver to give you as well. You have several options to get one.

First, call the drive's manufacturer. Even if the drive is no longer made, it is likely that the vendor will be able to provide the correct driver for a small fee or, if you're lucky, free.

Second, do you have a lot of friends with CD-ROM drives? See if one of them has the same drive as yours. You can then simply copy the drivers onto a floppy to install on your computer. Universal SCSI adapters such as Corel-SCSI (described under "Universal SCSI Adapters") provide drivers to support a wide range of drives, too.

If all else fails, you can put out a call for help on an online service such as CompuServe, America OnLine, or Delphi. These services have conferences dedicated to helping CD-ROM users. You will find a few people professionally involved in the CD-ROM industry there, but most participants are just regular folks like yourself. Someone is bound to have an answer to your missing driver problem, or most other problems for that matter.

Chapter 5

In some cases, other devices or software might compete with the SCSI controller for specific areas of the computer's memory or system interrupts. An *interrupt* is a specific instruction that tells the computer to stop what it's doing and run a particular routine. How you resolve these problems depends on the way your computer is set up. The instructions that come with the interface and CD-ROM drive usually tell you how to get around common types of conflicts. Your MS-DOS and Windows manuals will tell you how to set up your CONFIG.SYS file to move drivers out of the way of one another.

This is where good diagnostics software comes in handy. It can identify and resolve many of the conflicts between drivers in a fraction of the time it would take you. Also, the software is very helpful in optimizing your CONFIG.SYS settings to improve performance and to achieve the most possible free memory.

One reason you might experience a system conflict is that while SCSI is an established standard in principle, each vendor tends to implement it differently. Why? Neither your operating system—MS-DOS or Windows—nor your computer's BIOS supports SCSI directly. Each vendor, therefore, is free to write the SCSI drivers as it sees fit. So, even if your computer already has a SCSI adapter board and drivers, they probably won't work with your CD-ROM drive without some tinkering. Most likely, you will have to use a driver specific to your drive.

Since developers haven't adhered to a strict standard for SCSI device drivers and peripherals, no single driver can adequately support all possible SCSI peripherals. Compounding the problem is the fact that there is no standard host adapter interface for PCs. Each installed SCSI device must have its own driver, and each must be able to share the system's host adapter, though the devices and the adapter may come from different manufacturers.

Fortunately, SCSI is getting easier to deal with, as vendors improve on ease of use and operating systems offer more support. In fact, Microsoft's latest version of Windows, Windows NT, provides native SCSI support. Though NT is considered a high end operating system for networks and workstations, it gives hope that mainstream versions of Windows might soon follow the lead of the Macintosh with full support of SCSI.

UNIVERSAL SCSI ADAPTERS

Are you confused or annoyed by SCSI device drivers? Several off-the-shelf products are available that help ease the pain of installing a SCSI-based CD-ROM drive.

One popular universal SCSI interface is CorelSCSI from Corel Corporation. CorelSCSI is a bundle of drivers and utilities written to control all of the most popular SCSI devices on the market. The CorelSCSI software provides device drivers for most SCSI peripherals, including CD-ROM drives, so you can connect SCSI devices from various manufacturers to a single adapter board. CorelSCSI ensures compatibility between most SCSI devices and most host adapter cards. It also includes managers for those peripherals. CorelSCSI drivers can be loaded into high memory.

CorelSCSI also comes with a CD-ROM driver, CORELCDX. It works much like Microsoft's MSCDEX, except CORELCDX can cache up to eight CD-ROM sectors (MSCDEX only lets you cache two). *Caching* takes data from the CD-ROM drive before you need it and places it in faster-access memory—in effect boosting the throughput of the CD-ROM drive. Unlike MSCDEX, CORELCDX cannot share CD-ROM drives across machines running Windows for Workgroups. Otherwise, Corel claims that there is no performance difference between the two drivers.

Another company, Future Domain Corporation, created its PowerSCSI software as a universal interface between SCSI devices and the DOS and Windows environments. You get it free with Future Domain host adapters. Basically, PowerSCSI lets you use software drivers written to any SCSI interface as is. Any software driver that comes with your SCSI peripheral will work with PowerSCSI. However, it is hardware specific and will only work with Future Domain controller cards, which follow the CAM standard.

PowerSCSI lets multitasking systems, such as Windows, run several SCSI applications simultaneously, and it supports CD-ROM interfaces. To conserve memory, the installation utility allows you to load only those interfaces you need, and you can load PowerSCSI into high memory. PowerSCSI also includes a Windows 3.1 FastDisk emulator, WINDISK, that supports up to seven SCSI hard disk drives, instead of the two IDE drives that FastDisk supports. FastDisk is an option that allows direct, 32-bit communication between Windows and the SCSI controller.

Portable SCSI You can install internal SCSI adapters in portable PCs provided they have PCMCIA slots. Products such as New Media's Visual Media SCSI Adapter and Bus Toaster SCSI Adapter cards are credit-card-sized, 3.3 mm-thick cards that slide into a PCMCIA slot on the laptop, as shown here:

These cards let you attach up to seven SCSI devices to your PC and can sustain data rates of 300Kbps (New Media) and 500Kbps (Bus Toaster). Prices for the cards start at $199.

Parallel Ports

Most external drives are SCSI devices that plug into an external port on a SCSI adapter card or other proprietary card from the drive manufacturer. Once connected, these drives function just as their internal counterparts. However, not all systems have the means for an external SCSI connection—laptops, for instance. To sidestep this inconvenience, many external drive manufacturers offer the option of connecting the drive to the PC's standard parallel port (see the following illustration). This makes it easier to install (because you don't have to open your computer case) and easier to move between machines.

NOTE Connecting an external CD-ROM drive using your computer's parallel port is advisable only when you have no other choice. It is relatively slow and limits the use of the port for other functions.

The external drives connect to the parallel (printer) port in one of two ways. Some use a parallel-port-to-SCSI-port converter, such as the one sold by Trantor Systems. Or they include a driver that puts the parallel port into a non-printer mode so it can transmit SCSI protocol whenever the application that's running needs to access the CD-ROM drive.

Although the installation procedure varies from brand to brand, it is usually fairly simple (see the following illustration). You plug the cable from the drive into the parallel port on your computer, or into the parallel-to-SCSI converter and then into the parallel port. Then you plug in the drive's power cable (if it has one), run an install or setup program to load the necessary drivers, and you're on your way.

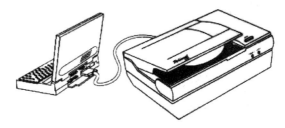

Of course, these drives need to receive SCSI protocol through the parallel port; but since you won't want to sacrifice your system's printer interface, most also include a pass-through printer port (either on the drive or on the cable) to which you can connect a printer. You can switch the parallel port in and out of print mode as necessary. The pass-through port uses the same connector as the parallel port. Note, however, that the pass-through port only supports printer mode and, therefore, will drive a printer but not other non-printing parallel devices. For example, the pass-through port can't drive speakers to hear CD-ROM sound, because the speakers and the CD-ROM drive will both be using the bus (in non-printing mode) at the same time. It is possible, however, to daisy-chain multiple drives or other SCSI devices with an external CD-ROM drive connected to the parallel port, because the port in non-print mode carries the SCSI protocol.

Since these drives can connect to any computer with a parallel port, you can hook them to almost any PC or laptop, including those with the 8088 processor. However, the slower processors—and older parallel port hardware—will give slower disk performance. In fact, the parallel port hardware imposes serious limitations on drives connected to it. For example, a good double-speed CD-ROM drive attached to a SCSI host adapter will have a data transfer rate of 300Kbps, but it won't get that speed when connected to a parallel port that can't handle such fast data transfer. Parallel port transfer rates can vary from 70 to 200Kbps—hardly incentive for investing in a faster drive.

New parallel port standards, such as the Enhanced Parallel Port (EPP) and Extended Capabilities Port (ECP) are on the way. EPP was developed by Xircom and Intel, and it is available now on a number of portable computers. EPP provides a transfer rate of up to 2MBps. At these speeds, you should be able to get most of the benefit of a double-speed CD-ROM drive. ECP was developed by Microsoft and Hewlett-Packard and is a bidirectional standard—the port can send as well as receive signals. Its top transfer rate is about 5MBps—on a par with SCSI-1. The IEEE has combined elements of both ECP and EPP into a proposal for a single, fast parallel port standard. The standard is called IEEE 1284, and it is building support among chip and BIOS vendors.

INSTALLING AN INTERNAL CD-ROM DRIVE

Adding a CD-ROM drive to your PC means plugging a SCSI host adapter (or sound card with its own adapter) into an empty expansion slot in your computer, slipping the CD-ROM drive into a drive bay, plugging the drive cable into the new SCSI port, and loading the device drivers. Figure 5-1 shows an installed internal CD-ROM drive connected to the CD (host) adapter by means of a SCSI ribbon cable. The drivers usually come with the host adapter (unless you buy a product such as CorelSCSI) and are written to support specific drives.

Although the installation procedure for their equipment is similar to hardware that adheres to accepted industry standards, several manufacturers sell their own proprietary adapter cards and drives (which means that the cards and drives will only work with each other and can't connect to hardware from other manufacturers). A standard SCSI connector has 25 or 50 pins, so look first for this visual clue when in doubt. If you don't see 25 or 50 pins, you'll know right away that the hardware is proprietary. This is not necessarily a problem. You should not be handicapped in terms of performance using proprietary adapter cards. You do, however, lose the advantages that SCSI offers; mainly, the ability to add more devices and compatibility. If you don't see any use for SCSI beyond connecting your CD-ROM drive, there is no reason you shouldn't use a proprietary connector.

UPGRADING FROM AN OLDER DRIVE

Owners of machines with older CD-ROM drives who want to upgrade to newer ones to meet current MPC standards, or display full-motion video that's beyond the transfer speed of an older drive, will most likely need to get new driver software also. Driver software is frequently updated to account for new system and CD-ROM drive features. You might also have to replace the adapter card if it doesn't support the drive you want to use. As always, it's a good idea to check with the drive manufacturer to make sure the upgrade is compatible with your system.

INSTALLING EXTERNAL DRIVES

Most external CD-ROM drives are small enough to be easily carried from one location to another, and that can be a valuable feature. For instance, you might want to use one CD-ROM drive for several computers. With external drives, you simply unplug it from one PC and then attach it to another. External drives connect via cable to either a parallel or SCSI port. However, just because a drive is external doesn't mean it's a good choice for portable use. If portability is truly an issue, there are drives available whose size, weight, power supplies, and connectors have been specifically designed to meet that need. Some can be battery powered for use on the road or (literally) in the field.

You might consider an external drive because:

▶ You don't have an empty drive bay in your computer

▶ You don't want to open up your computer

▶ You need a drive that you can move from one computer to another

▶ You need a drive that you can pack along with your laptop

▶ You found a good deal on one

There are differences among external drives, so if you decide to go that route, it's important to know which of the available features best suit your needs, especially if you intend to swap the unit among computers. When shopping in this market, pay special attention to how the drive connects to your computer, and—especially if you need something portable—to the unit's power supply and battery life (if applicable). The drive's performance specifications (its storage capacity, average seek time, and transfer rate) are also important, but if you're connecting it to your computer's parallel port, its performance is more likely to be limited by your particular machine's hardware than by the drive's specifications.

CD-ROMS IN LAPTOPS

If you're serious about traveling with your CD-ROM drive and laptop, several vendors now sell portable systems with built-in CD-ROM drives and multimedia capability. Along with powerful CPUs, these machines offer color displays and sound cards.

Scenario is the pioneer of portable CD-ROM systems. Its DynaVision line of 10-pound notebook computers offers such options as a high-capacity hard disk, up to 20MB of RAM, up to a 50MHz 486DX2 processor, an active or passive matrix color VGA, and a high-speed fax/data modem. You can choose to have either a sound card or network connection built in.

Key features that Scenario offers include a direct SCSI connection to the computer's motherboard, which ensures maximum performance. As a bonus, you also get an external SCSI port. To compensate for the extra draw that the CD-ROM drive places on the battery, Scenario has doubled the size of the battery and developed a power-sharing technology to ensure that both the computer and drive get the power they need.

At 17 pounds, Toshiba's T6600C is heftier than the DynaVision, but includes some powerful features, such as a 66MHz 486DX2 processor, as much as 40MB of RAM, an active matrix super VGA color screen, and a 510MB hard drive. The unit also offers two full-length 16-bit ISA expansion slots, a 16 mm PCMCIA 2.01-compliant slot, a 5 1/2-inch half-height drive bay, and a SCSI port. It has the Microsoft Sound System on the motherboard and comes with two built-in speakers and a microphone.

OCP International offers the Imagepro CD, a lightweight, economically priced way to take high-quality sound and graphics on the road. It has a 33MHz 486DX processor, a double-speed CD-ROM drive, 120MB hard drive, and a 16-bit sound card. You also get a built-in trackball, speakers, and microphone. Displays for this seven-pound unit are sold separately. You have several to choose from, up to a 13-inch active matrix color VGA screen.

THE MAC MAKES IT EASY

Anyone who owns a Macintosh II or later system will have a much easier time of installing a CD-ROM drive. In fact, many current Mac models come standard with CD-ROM drives, making the issue moot. Due to a lack of expandability, it is not advisable to install CD-ROM drives in earlier Macs unless the system has an external SCSI connector.

Mac IIs and later models are already adequately equipped in terms of the SCSI interface, the power supply, and software drivers. Version 6.08 and higher of the Macintosh operating system provide the basic functionality needed for CD-ROM.

Since Apple is the sole manufacturer of Macs, it has been able to control the evolution of the system. You generally do not see the level of competing standards and proprietary approaches to add-on devices such as CD-ROM drives that you see on the PC. As a result, the Mac is a much more integrated and less complicated system.

The main areas of concern when installing a CD-ROM drive in a Mac are

- ▶ Open drive bays
- ▶ Memory and storage
- ▶ Processing power
- ▶ Sound capability
- ▶ Video capability

INSIDE OR OUTSIDE?

On average, Macs provide fewer drive bays than PCs. On some models, such as the SE/30, space for drives of any kind is severely limited. You are therefore more likely to need an external CD-ROM drive with your Mac. Whether you use an internal or external drive, most Macs are already equipped with SCSI interfaces. And since the Mac is a highly integrated environment, the operating system is already on speaking terms with SCSI. Connecting the drive, therefore, is much more of a plug-and-play affair than on the PC.

Apple Macintosh PowerBook owners might consider buying APS Technologies' SCSI DOC, an adapter with a male HDI 30 pin to a female DB 25 connector that lets the PowerBook connect to a variety of SCSI cable types.

SCSI DOC includes a switch that turns the adapter, coupled with a 25- to 50-pin cable, into a docking cable. This allows those PowerBooks that support docking mode to connect as a SCSI device to another Mac.

MAC APPLICATIONS ARE MULTIMEDIA ORIENTED

You should expect to need more RAM and hard disk capacity on a Macintosh than on a PC. The Mac is ahead of the curve when it comes to multimedia applications. A much higher percentage of Mac-based CD-ROM applications are multimedia than on the PC. Consequently, you should prepare your Mac for a CD-ROM drive assuming that you will be running multimedia software. The downside to this is that these applications are very resource hungry. It is not unusual for a Mac to have 16MB of memory or a 300MB hard disk drive. For the average user, you should be able to get by with 8MB of memory and a 160 to 180MB hard disk drive. You can, of course, still run many applications on less, but you will pay a performance penalty.

The minimum recommended processor is a 68030, though a fast 68020 will do in many cases. A number of CPU upgrade options are available from vendors, several of which are listed in Appendix B.

MAC SOUND AND VIDEO

Although the Mac is much more CD-ROM and multimedia ready than the PC, it cannot store audio files to disk or handle 16-bit, 44KHz stereo sound, nor is it MIDI capable. All Quadra models can play 16-bit sound, but not to professional standards.

To meet this need, several vendors, including Media Vision, SuperMac, and Radius, provide sound boards for the Mac. These boards plug into a Mac's LC or NuBus slot and provide MIDI capability and professional-quality 16-bit, 44KHz stereo sound. Speakers, headphones, or microphones are usually extra-cost items. The monitors that come with the Quadra AV models (660AV and 840AV) have speakers and a microphone built in, and you can use these monitors with most Macs being made today.

On the video side, all Macintoshes sold today are capable of at least 16-bit color, even the color PowerBook models. They can display 256 colors simultaneously. Since the Macintosh is a very popular computer for use in the graphic arts, a wide range of professional-quality video boards is available for it. Appendix B lists some of the vendors.

Chapter 5

SOUPED-UP CD-ROM

While you can do little or nothing to increase the speed of a CD-ROM drive itself, you can improve the overall throughput of your system. Your computer imposes a few bottlenecks, and you have a few options available that will help alleviate them.

The simplest action you can take is to use a caching utility. These utilities allow you to use part of the computer's memory as a cache for the CD-ROM drive. Assuming you have the RAM to spare, you can see as much as an 80 percent boost in performance, depending on the type of data being accessed. The average speed increase will be considerably less, however. Examples of caching utilities include Norton Speedcache, Super PC-Kwik, and Lucid's Lightning CD. Caching utilities for the Mac include Anubis CD-ROM All-Cache from ClarisMac Engineering, CD-ROM Toolkit from FWB, and Spot On from MacPeak Research.

The drawback of a caching utility is that it is a TSR (terminate and stay resident) program. On an MS-DOS or Windows PC, it loads into the high area of main memory and remains dormant until needed. The problem is that it competes with drivers for your CD-ROM drive, video card, or audio card for that area. You might find yourself in a situation where you have to give up something to resolve a conflict.

For applications where you absolutely must have the highest throughput you can get, a caching controller with a lot of memory can do wonders. These controllers are SCSI host adapters with RAM and an on-board processor that intelligently manages the caching process. Under normal circumstances, your computer's main processor arbitrates the flow of SCSI commands between the host adapter and the drive. Some caching controllers take most of that responsibility away from the processor, which then only has to tell the controller to issue a command and to be informed when that command's task is finished. Controllers with this capability are referred to as *bus mastering*.

Taking this load off the main processor frees it for other tasks such as drawing images on the screen or generating audio. Therefore, a caching controller—any type of caching, for that matter—boosts throughput by both increasing the flow of data from the drive to the computer, and by giving the main processor more time to produce the output.

As explained earlier in this chapter, you can always boost performance by adding memory or upgrading the computer's processor. Installing a high-performance video board will not only increase your throughput rate, but provide higher resolution, full-screen playback of video movies.

TROUBLESHOOTING YOUR CD-ROM DRIVE

If all goes well with the installation, your CD-ROM drive should be ready to play discs immediately. To make sure, simply place a disc in the CD-ROM drive, type **D:** (or whatever your drive's letter designation is) and press the ENTER key. Then type **DIR** and press the ENTER key. You should see the directory listing for the disc. If you don't, check for the obvious first: loose or improperly attached cables. If that isn't the problem, you will likely see a number of error messages on the screen. These messages are cryptic in nature, giving only the barest clues as to what you should do. Each operating system uses different error messages, too.

What follows is a list of the possible error messages and other problems you might encounter broken down by operating system. More important, suggested actions to take are also listed. The text lists the error or message as it appears on your screen, explains the problem, and then provides a likely solution.

MS-DOS AND WINDOWS ERROR MESSAGES

"Invalid Drive Specification" This indicates that the MSCDEX driver is incorrectly installed. You need to test that it is loading properly. To do so, type **CD BIN** at the C:> prompt and press the ENTER key. (Note that the MSCDEX driver might be located in a directory by a different name, such as CDROM.) Then type **MSCDEX** and press the ENTER key. If MSCDEX is working, you'll see its version number displayed. If not, you'll see the error message "USAGE...".

To solve the problem, make sure that the MSCDEX command line in your AUTOEXEC.BAT file is placed before any menu program command. Sometimes it must be placed before other TSR commands as well.

"Incorrect DOS Version"   Each version of MS-DOS requires specific versions of MSCDEX. MS-DOS 6.x requires MSCDEX version 2.22 and can run with versions 2.10, 2.20, and 2.21. MS-DOS 5.0 requires MSCDEX version 2.21 and can run with versions 2.10 and 2.20. You need to copy the appropriate version of MSCDEX from your MS-DOS disk to the appropriate directory on your hard disk drive. Then you must update the CONFIG.SYS with the line:

DEVICE=C:\DOS\SETVER.EXE

If the error continues, at the C:\DOS> prompt type:

SETVER MSCDEX.EXE 4.01

Press ENTER after entering the command. To verify that this has taken effect, type **SETVER** at the C:\DOS> prompt. You will see a listing of files; look for MSCDEX.EXE. If 4.01 follows it, the change has taken place.

"No host adapter found," "No drives needing support," or "Reset SCSI bus"
These messages could be caused by one of several situations. Your host adapter card might be improperly seated, and you will need to reseat it. You might have a memory address conflict. If so, you need to set the adapter card for a memory address not in use. Don't forget to modify the device line parameters /P: or /B:, if they are used, in your CONFIG.SYS file if you change the memory address.

These error messages might indicate an IRQ (interrupt request) or DMA (direct memory access) conflict. To correct this, you must set the adapter card for an IRQ or DMA address not in use or disabled. If used, modify the device line parameters /Q:, for the IRQ, and /T:, for DMA, accordingly.

You might simply have an incorrect device driver, in which case you need to consult the documentation for the correct driver and install it. Finally, either the slot in which the adapter card sits or its cable have failed. Move the card to another slot or replace the cable.

"CDR 101: Read Fail"   Several problems can produce this error message. You might have an incorrect device driver; check the documentation to find the right one and install it. You might have the incorrect drive identification number; make sure that you have a unique identification number for each CD-ROM drive connected. You also might have a memory address, IRQ, or

DMA interrupt conflict. Set the adapter card for addresses not in use. If used, modify the device line parameters /P:, /B:, /Q:, and /T: accordingly.

"CDR 103: Disc in drive is not High Sierra" Check first to see if the cable is defective or detached. Replace the cable if necessary. Otherwise, you might have installed an ISO 9660 disc using MSCDEX 1.01. Check for which version of MSCDEX you are using with the procedure described previously, under "Incorrect DOS Version." Upgrade to the correct version of MSCDEX if necessary.

Drive Does Not Seem To Be Reading Disk Look for the obvious: a dirty, scratched, or otherwise damaged disc; or a dusty lens reader on the drive. You can do nothing about a damaged disc, but you can clean a disc using the method described at the end of this chapter. You can also clean the laser lens reader by blowing away dust.

You should also check that the adapter card is seated properly and that the cable has not failed. The only way to test this is to replace each, assuming you have spares handy, and see if the problem goes away.

Finally, the power supply on the drive's laser lens reader might be failing. If so, you will have to send the drive out for repair or replace it.

CD-ROM Drive Is Slow to Initialize, or the Starting Screen Refreshes Slowly
One cause of this would be a high number of buffers in MSCDEX. The cure is to set the buffers to four or five for each CD-ROM drive you have connected. Modify the MSCDEX command line parameter /M: accordingly.

Another cause might be multiple CD-ROM device lines in your CONFIG.SYS file. You must eliminate the second device line in CONFIG.SYS, and you must also eliminate the second device name in the MSCDEX command line in the AUTOEXEC.BAT file.

MACINTOSH ERROR MESSAGES

"This is not a Macintosh disc: Do you want to initialize it?" On a Macintosh, ISO 9660 requires the installation of four files on the system: the CD-ROM device driver, the Foreign File Access, ISO 9660 File Access, and High Sierra File Access. Check for their presence and that they have been installed in the correct folder. For System 7, they belong in either the Systems or Extensions folder. You should find them on the installation floppy that came with the CD-ROM drive.

"?" (Appears Within a Floppy Disk Icon) This could be one of two problems. The SCSI ID set might be conflicting with another SCSI device. In this case, you need to set the SCSI ID to the next available number. Second, the terminator might be on or off when it should be off or on. You need to remove or connect a terminator at the SCSI connector of the CD-ROM drive.

The CD-ROM Icon Does Not Appear on the Desktop or Clicking on the Icon Does Not Initialize the Disc Several problems can cause this situation. You might not have the CD-ROM device driver in the Control Panel; you will need to drag it into the Control Panel. The disc might be dirty or damaged, or the laser lens reader might be dusty. Clean the disc or lens reader; replace the damaged disc.

Make sure that the SCSI cable is good and that the host adapter is properly seated. Try using another cable, or put the host adapter in another Macintosh to see if it works.

Finally, the power supply for the laser lens reader might be failing, and the drive will need to be sent out for repair.

The Disc Does Not Eject at Shut Down or When You Press the Eject Button on the CD-ROM Drive Check the SCSI cable and all connections first. If the adapter is properly seated and both it and the cable are good, then your drive could be failing. You will need to replace or repair it.

CARE AND FEEDING OF DISCS AND DRIVES

Taking care of your CD-ROM drive means taking care of your discs. The biggest enemies of your drive are dust and other foreign objects carried into it by the discs. Follow these "Seven Commandments of CD-ROM Care," and both your discs and drive will last longer.

1. Do not put labels on discs.
   Even though the laser reads from the bottom of the disc, a label on the top can throw the disc out of balance when it spins, making it behave as if it is warped or otherwise out of shape in the drive. Also, adhesive can seep through the protection layer and damage the disc surface.

2. Do not write on the disc surface with a felt-tip marker.

The disc's protective lacquer coating is only 30 microns thick. Ink can seep through it and damage the disc.

3. Be careful not to scratch the disc.

   A CD-ROM player can tolerate a few scratches, but severe scratching will interfere with the laser read process and cause data loss, mis-tracking, or total failure to play. Always put the disc back in its protective case when you are finished using it.

4. Keep discs clean.

   Dirt or dust on the surface will interfere with the player reading (via laser light) the data. While some dust and dirt will not affect performance, very dirty discs will not play. Accumulated dust and dirt in the drive itself can cause damage to the drive.

5. Store discs out of direct sunlight.

   Although the plastic substrate will resist sun damage, extended exposure will accelerate the deterioration of the reflective layer that holds the data. CD-ROMs will warp, too, if they become too hot—don't leave them on the dashboard of your car on a sunny day.

6. Never place a warped or misshapen disc into a drive.

   It is unlikely that the drive can read it, and you risk damage to your hardware.

7. Don't touch the bottom of the disc, where the laser must read.

   Even clean hands can leave fingerprints, which can interfere with the laser.

When shopping for a CD-ROM drive, look for a model with a door designed to keep dust out of the drive. The best ones have doors that close snugly and a design that allows air flow to carry dust away from the read mechanism. A few provide a disc-cleaning feature that wipes dust off a disc upon removal from the drive.

TIP Cleaning a dusty or dirty CD-ROM is easy. You can just wipe it down with a damp, clean cloth, preferably cotton. Do not rub or scour or do anything else that might scratch the surface. Never use any kind of solvent, as it could eat into the disc. Make sure the disc is completely dry before inserting it into a drive. If this method does not remove all the dirt from a disc, you can buy cleaning kits at your local computer supply store.

CHAPTER 6

MAKING THE MOST OF CD-ROM SOFTWARE

The number, variety, and quality of CD-ROM software are expanding at a rapid rate. Historically, the lion's share of titles has been oriented toward text-based reference material and custom-made applications for businesses, schools, and other organizations. That is still true, but the picture is changing. CD-ROM now offers something for nearly everyone no matter what your needs or interests are.

Where only a relative handful of consumer titles existed just a couple of years ago, over 1000 are available today. CD-ROM is now an important tool for education at all levels. And professionals of all types can use CD-ROM-based tools and training aimed at their specialties. Many popular computer software titles are also available on CD-ROM, including Quicken, 1-2-3, CorelDraw, and Microsoft Word for Windows.

This diversification of CD-ROM publishing is similar to what you see in the traditional print publishing industry. Titles are categorized roughly along the same lines: home, business, reference, education, and so on. In this chapter, CD-ROM titles are organized in the following categories:

▶ **Art and music:** On-disc studies with images and sound

▶ **Business:** Software, such as presentation programs, spreadsheets, or word processors, distributed on CD-ROM

Chapter 6

- ▶ **Children's:** Storybooks and educational titles for home use
- ▶ **Media clip art:** Collections of image, video, audio, music, and other files used for presentations, multimedia development, or recreational purposes
- ▶ **Database:** Specialized references, abstracts, or listings
- ▶ **Education:** Titles for school use
- ▶ **Electronic books:** Literature adapted to or created for CD-ROM
- ▶ **Entertainment:** Primarily games
- ▶ **Hobbies:** Discs on collecting, sports, and other pastimes
- ▶ **Home:** Family-oriented references such as encyclopedias, cookbooks, atlases, travel guides, and so on
- ▶ **Periodicals:** "Magazines" on disc sold on a subscription basis
- ▶ **Shareware:** Grab-bag collections of software of all types
- ▶ **Training:** Titles that teach a specific task

This chapter looks at each category, citing recommended examples. It also explains the important issues involved with each class of titles. For instance, no real standard exists for search and retrieval methods among the reference titles. This makes life difficult for anyone who has to deal with a lot of reference CD-ROMs—librarians, researchers, educators, and others.

Categorizing some titles is difficult. Many children's titles, for instance, could just as well be used in the classroom. An encyclopedia or atlas could be classified as home-oriented or as a reference. The examples cited in this chapter (and in the listing in Appendix B) are categorized mainly by the audiences that their manufacturers are targeting. Note that these categorizations are somewhat arbitrary; no official classification system for CD-ROM titles exists.

You can skip directly to the types of titles that interest you, but keep an open mind and check out all the categories. Given the rich offerings, you might make an unexpected find that could prove valuable. All of the products listed in this chapter represent the best of what you can expect in each category. Not all are perfect, but each one offers a unique value.

Making the Most of CD-ROM Software   157

Chapter 6

A FEW WORDS ABOUT JEWEL CASES

One of the most frustrating experiences you can have in dealing with CD-ROMs is getting those infernal plastic cases, called *jewel cases*, to open without breaking. The tendency is to squeeze the sides of the case where it opens and pull, but often this only makes matters worse. The easiest way to get them open is to hold the case in both hands. With one hand, hold both sides where the case opens, use your index finger of that hand to hold the top-middle of the lid in place, and pull up with your thumb and other finger on the sides of the case, as shown here:

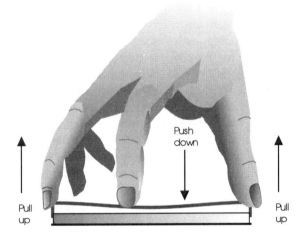

Once you have the case open, you have to get the disc off the hub. Never remove a disc by pulling up on the sides. It is held in by tension at the hub, and if you force it out in this way, you can damage it. Instead, grip the edges of the disc and pull up as you push down on the case's hub with your finger.

Not all CD-ROMs come in the plastic jewel cases, of course. Some use a cardboard and plastic box with a flip-lid; others use a simple cardboard sleeve. Both methods provide marginally less protection than the plastic jewel cases, but they make it up in less aggravation.

Chapter 6

THINGS YOU SHOULD KNOW

There are a few points you should know about all CD-ROM-based titles. First, expect each title to consume some of your hard disk drive space. You can run some titles completely from the CD-ROM, but performance will suffer because the CD-ROM drive is so much slower than a hard disk drive. Most CD-ROMs place about half of a megabyte of executable and other performance-sensitive files on the hard drive. Discs that place 10MB or more on the hard disk are not uncommon. Be aware of the available space on your hard disk.

Some MS-DOS/Windows-based multimedia titles require a significant amount of memory to run—575K or more. This can be a problem if you've used your main memory area for things such as sound or video card drivers. It is not a problem on the Macintosh because the Mac allocates memory dynamically. A diagnostics utility such as Dariana's WinSleuth Gold can help you free some memory, but it might not be enough. Using MS-DOS 6.2 with its MemMaker utility will help free more memory, as will other memory management programs. Unfortunately, the documentation of the CD-ROM title probably won't be much help; it will either ignore the problem altogether or refer you to the DOS or Windows manual. If you are not comfortable moving drivers and other code around in system memory, you should call the technical support department of the CD-ROM software vendor.

Speaking of documentation, expect it to vary dramatically in terms of quality and quantity depending on the class of software. Consumer-oriented titles in particular—games, storybooks, children's software, and so on—are notoriously skimpy. In most cases, the titles are straightforward enough that this isn't a problem. If you have a problem with installation or execution, however, you will likely be forced to call the technical support department. Titles aimed at business tend to provide the best documentation.

TIP During installation, some MS-DOS/Windows titles will modify your AUTOEXEC.BAT and CONFIG.SYS files. Maybe they will tell you about it; maybe they won't. Usually, this isn't a problem. As a safeguard, however, it is always a good idea to have a backup copy of both of those files on hand. If your system crashes after installing a title, you can then copy the original AUTO-EXEC.BAT and CONFIG.SYS files back onto your system and see if the problem goes away. If it does, you know that the software tinkered with one or both and caused a conflict.

ART AND MUSIC: APPRECIATE AND LEARN

An audio CD is a one-dimensional product; you hear the music, and that's it. MTV is not much better, adding just video. But with the multimedia capabilities of CD-ROM, you get an interactive environment that combines audio CD quality with video, text, and animation. The end result is a product that is both entertaining and educational.

Liner notes, for example, take on a whole new meaning in the world of CD-ROM. You can follow the onscreen text describing, say, Beethoven's *Fifth Symphony,* click on the part describing a particular movement, and hear the movement. You might also see the bars appear on the screen with the notes highlighted as they play. For further reference, a music CD-ROM might also include videos of the performer or a critic talking about the work. If you are in a less intellectual mood, you can simply listen to the music as you would an audio CD.

Art discs work much the same way, providing historical background and commentary. While you might buy a music CD-ROM mainly for the music, you probably would not buy an art CD-ROM for the art. All visual art loses something in the translation from its original medium to the video screen; therefore, art discs are mostly educational in nature.

Not all music and art CD-ROMs follow the formats described here. The following examples include some of the exceptions, as well as representative mainstream discs.

COMPOSER QUEST, DR. T'S MUSIC SOFTWARE

Composer Quest is an unlikely mix of jazz and classical music. Using a gamelike format, the disc is primarily education-oriented; it provides no means of simply playing the music other than one song at a time. The object of the game is to listen to a piece of music, hop into your trusty time machine, go to the proper era, identify the composer, and record the piece for posterity. A learn mode helps familiarize you with the composers included on the disc and their work.

All but one of the works on the disc are classical. The only jazz tune is Scott Joplin's *The Entertainer.* Other jazz musicians covered on the disc, without music, include Duke Ellington, Louis Armstrong, and Jelly Roll Morton. Classical composers include Verdi, Beethoven, Brahms, Stravinksy, Vivaldi, and Strauss. The era covered is from 1600 to 1940. Though some composers' music is not on the disc, each one's history and accomplishments are provided.

One fun feature of Composer Quest is that it links each composer to the important news of his era. You can call up a headline for every year from 1600 to 1940 or see the works of significant artists outside of music. You do this by simply clicking on the appropriate icon, as shown in Figure 6-1.

Composer Quest is far from being an in-depth authority on classical and jazz music, but it serves well as an introduction to those genres. The program requires an MPC-compatible computer.

THE GREAT KAT: DIGITAL BEETHOVEN ON SPEED, BUREAU OF ELECTRONIC PUBLISHING

What can you say about a heavy metal guitarist who claims to be both the "number one genius in the universe" and the reincarnation of Ludwig von Beethoven? More than you'd think. The Great Kat, a.k.a. Katherine Thomas, is a graduate of the Juilliard School of Music, where she studied violin. If you can get past the self-promotion worthy of a professional wrestler and lyrics written for maximum shock value, you'll hear a fine musician.

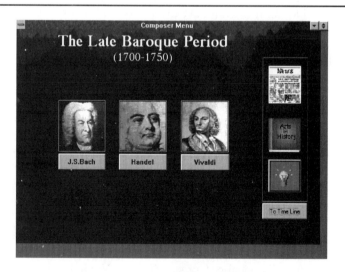

FIGURE 6-1
Composer Quest from Dr. T's Music Software

Making the Most of CD-ROM Software   161

Chapter 6

The MPC-based CD-ROM is not as slick as some of the other music discs, but it's a real delight to play. It includes MTV-like videos, still photos, a biography, and the songs (see Figure 6-2). The interface is menu based and easy to use. Digital Beethoven on Speed is pure entertainment. It is an audio CD, MTV, and fanzine all rolled into one. The Great Kat puts on a great act.

BUSINESS SOFTWARE ON CD-ROM

The Microsofts, Lotuses, and WordPerfects of the world want you to buy your software on CD-ROM. And why not? Distributing business applications such as word processors, spreadsheets, database managers, or even operating systems on CD-ROM has advantages for both vendors and users. Distributing software on CD-ROM saves the vendors money in two ways. First, it is cheaper to produce one CD-ROM than the five, six, seven, or more floppy disks on which most applications are placed today. It costs a vendor 70 to 90

FIGURE 6-2
Main menu of Digital Beethoven on Speed, produced by Bureau of Electronic Publishing

cents to produce 1MB of software on a floppy disk, but only 1/2 of a cent to produce that same 1MB on CD-ROM. Second, installing software from one CD-ROM is faster and simpler than from multiple floppies, and installation problems represent a large portion of the customer support calls a software company receives. Reducing the number of support calls lowers the vendor's costs.

Software distributed on CD-ROM makes life easier for the user for the same reasons: fewer floppies to swap and a better installation procedure. Since most computers are still sold without a CD-ROM drive, however, very few business applications are sold in CD-ROM form exclusively. Those that are distributed primarily on CD-ROM are high-end packages such as operating systems (Windows NT, for example) or complex applications such as CAD (computer-aided design) software. Without CD-ROM, these packages could consume 20 or more floppies. Unix system software and applications in particular have become so immense that CD-ROM is becoming the standard method of software distribution for that platform. Many versions of the Unix operating system are sold on CD-ROM. Digital Equipment Corporation recently announced that it would ship all applications and updates for its Alpha AXP systems on CD-ROM.

Even with the largest applications, a CD-ROM still has capacity to spare. Some vendors have decided to take advantage of that capacity by adding features that enhance their software's marketability. One increasingly popular feature to add is an online tutorial. This tutorial supplements or replaces the printed documentation. It can include any combination of hyperlinked text files, video instruction, sample files and screens, and audio narration. For large corporate users, a good on-disc tutorial can significantly reduce training costs, which sometimes are as much as the purchase price of the software. For all users, the interactive nature of tutorials can reduce the frustration often associated with using printed manuals.

Other packages might include associated reference material. For example, Intuit's Quicken for Windows CD-ROM Deluxe Edition personal finance manager comes with The Wall Street Journal Personal Finance Library. Graphics-based programs take advantage of the CD-ROM by adding image files; Corel's CorelDraw on CD-ROM comes with over 10,000 clip art files.

TRY BEFORE YOU BUY

CD-ROMs have inspired a new twist on the old "try before you buy" marketing ploy. Although shareware vendors have used this tactic to sell software for years, larger software vendors have shied away from it. This was partly because of the fear that many people would use the software and never pay for it—the honor system doesn't cut it for Microsoft, Computer Associates, and other big companies. Also, these companies were concerned about maintaining the perceived value of their products. Distributing software for free, even if payment is eventually expected, puts a second-rate taint on the product.

The larger software vendors can avoid both those drawbacks by distributing test versions of their products on CD-ROM. It works like this: A third party or the vendor itself places a collection of commercial products on a CD-ROM and encrypts or locks them so that they cannot be copied to the hard disk drive. This hamstrings the product so that you cannot use it for real work, but you can sample its features. If you decide you want to buy one of the products on the disc, you call an 800 number, place the order with your credit card, and receive a code that allows you to unlock the product and copy it to your hard disk drive. Usually, the complete package with documentation is also sent to you through the mail.

Using CD-ROM as a distribution medium lowers the cost to the manufacturer, and usually those cost savings are passed on to consumers. As a result, you often pay less for a product purchased off a CD-ROM.

You get these demo discs by purchasing them individually for a low price, or by subscribing to a service that sends them to you at regular intervals. TestDrive Corporation, for example, produces a demo disc with about 40 programs that is sold in retail outlets. Products from Borland International, WordPerfect, Symantec, Lotus, and Broderbund are included on the TestDrive disc. Two of the largest software distributors—Merisel and Ingram Micro—are also heavily promoting demo CD-ROMs. Merisel is packaging demo discs for bundling with computers. Now, when you buy your computer, you might also get a CD-ROM with dozens of demo programs.

Apple Computer is setting up a business unit to sell its own and third-party software on CD-ROM. The program is called the Software Access Initiative. The company expects to bundle the discs with its CD-ROM drives and to sell them through retail stores and via mail order. Apple will produce these discs by categories: games, education, business, and so on.

IBM is also in on the act. IBM's Software Manufacturing Company, which sells software production services, takes the encryption scheme a step further. In addition to the simple lock and key method, IBM offers a means to meter usage. For example, the software vendor might want to bill a customer according to how many people use the product, how long the product is used, or the number of times a product is used. Encryption that controls or meters usage is most important for expensive, specialized software.

Chapter 6

Apple has also extended this concept to traditional mail-order merchandising. The company is distributing a catalog disc with items from mail-order houses such as Hanna Anderson, L. L. Bean, Land's End, and biobottoms. Other companies are using CD-ROM as a promotional medium in other ways: for product demos or as giveaways. The term that has been coined for this is *adware*, and the concept is described in Chapter 9.

MICROSOFT WORD FOR WINDOWS AND BOOKSHELF, MICROSOFT CORPORATION

If you write, chances are you have a dictionary, thesaurus, and other references nearby. Microsoft has placed them all a mouse click or two away. Word for Windows and Bookshelf combines a popular Windows word processor with eight references:

The Concise Columbia Encyclopedia
The American Heritage Dictionary
Roget's II Electronic Thesaurus
The World Almanac and Book of Facts
Bartlett's Familiar Quotations
The Concise Columbia Dictionary of Quotations
The Hammond Atlas
Microsoft Word for Windows User's Guide

This product is actually a combination of two stand-alone packages: Word for Windows and Bookshelf. It makes great sense to combine these popular references with the application for which you are most likely to need them. The Bookshelf references are not merely electronic text versions of the printed books; rather they are multimedia based. The dictionary and encyclopedia, for instance, provide over 65,000 audio word pronunciations. The package has no video, but it does have over 1000 images and graphics as well as a number of animations.

The integration between the word processor and the references is tight (see Figure 6-3). It is easy to switch between them and to keep track of the "path" you've taken during your research. You can have all eight references working at once if you wish. The Word/Bookshelf combination requires an MPC-compatible system. It also requires 13.5MB of your hard disk drive for optimum performance. A minimum hard disk installation requires 4MB.

Making the Most of CD-ROM Software   **165**

Chapter 6

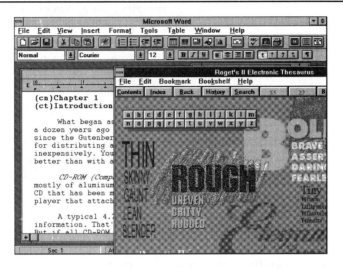

FIGURE 6-3
Word for Windows with Roget's Electronic Thesaurus from Microsoft's Bookshelf

CD-ROMS FOR YOUNG FOLK

Titles for children are one of CD-ROM's strong suits. If you are looking for an educationally redeeming activity to pull your kids away from excessive TV viewing, CD-ROM is one answer. Given the choice, kids will take the interactive nature of the CD-ROM over the passive experience of the TV.

The best children's titles use clever animation, narration, and the element of surprise to keep their attention. One common feature, for example, is to make a lot of elements on the screen "active." Click on an object—say, a mouse (the real kind)—and it skitters across the floor. Click on a cow and it moos.

Another key attribute to look for in a children's title is a consistent, simple interface. Kids are sometimes better than adults at learning the fine points of using a computer, but an interface should offer a minimal amount of choices. Multi-option menus can be confusing; icons are good if used in a clear and limited manner. For example, only those icons appropriate for the screen being viewed should be shown, not every icon used in the program.

Some otherwise good children's titles are marred by long pauses between segments. This is particularly true with storybooks. A storybook is just what its name implies: a story told through pictures, animation, and sound. It can be purely entertaining or have educational content as well. Pauses between images or "pages" are inevitable given the relatively slow transfer rate of a CD-ROM drive. Some storybooks, however, take an excessively long time to switch scenes—long enough for younger children to become impatient. This problem can be minimized by using a CD-ROM drive with a good cache, or by using a software-based caching utility.

Other types of children's software include games, early learning (simple math, alphabet, reading, and so on), and science. You can also find unique titles aimed at children, such as 7th Level's Tuneland. Tuneland is an interactive title somewhere between a storybook and a game. It is pure entertainment, most of which comes from clicking on objects to see what happens.

TUNELAND, 7TH LEVEL

Comedian Howie Mandel provides the voice of the main character in Tuneland, and his wacky style of humor sets the tone for the title. It's hard to categorize Tuneland. It looks like a storybook, but there is no story to tell—at least not in the traditional sense. It is a game only in the sense that you are supposed to find where little Howie is hiding in each scene (see Figure 6-4). This goal is easily forgotten, however, as you move the cursor around, clicking

FIGURE 6-4
7th Level's Tuneland

on objects to see what happens. Click on the cattails and they go off like bottle rockets. Click on the rope hanging in the barn and a mouse makes a Tarzan-like swing into a window. Click on the pig and he breaks out the fiddle and strikes up a tune. Almost everything is active, so a child can spend hours just roaming the scenes clicking on objects.

Tuneland is one of the more delightful children's titles available. It's not terribly original, however, since Broderbund has been using similar effects with its Living Book series for some time (also described in this section). The company, 7th Level, is heavily influenced by the film and music industries, with investors such as Don Johnson, Quincy Jones, and Melanie Griffith. The company sees itself as a natural extension of the traditional entertainment business. Tuneland requires an MPC-compatible system.

DINOSOURCE, WESTWIND MEDIA

Dinosaurs are popular on CD-ROM. At least 10 titles exist, and several of them are very good. DinoSource is one of the better titles. Suited for older children (ages 8 and up), it is both a "catalog" of known species and an educational tool. DinoSource won't win awards for the quality of the graphic images, but it is a well-designed package. You can use the disc in a number of different ways. You can simply scroll through the images of the different kinds of dinosaurs while a narrator reads the accompanying text. The Dinosaur Dig game shown in Figure 6-5 simulates an actual dig; you pick your tools and chisel bones from the side of a cliff. Once you've exposed the bones, you have to identify the dinosaur. A Jeopardy-type game quizzes you about the habits, diet, and other aspects of various dinosaurs.

This disc is bound to be a hit with any kid bitten by the dinosaur bug. DinoSource requires a Macintosh or Windows system.

THE BIG BUG ALPHABET BOOK, MILLIKEN PUBLISHING COMPANY

This early-learning disc teaches the basics of the alphabet, and it is appropriate for either home or classroom. Children have the option of simply listening to the content storybook-style or playing it interactively. In narration mode, each word is highlighted as it is spoken, and simple animation effects help reinforce the lesson.

The theme of The Big Bug Alphabet Book is a circus of bugs that do tricks involving the alphabet (see Figure 6-6). In interactive mode, clicking on objects results in some humorous action or comment, or it reinforces the lesson. Clicking on the letter "G," for instance, might cause the word "goat" to appear as a voice spells it out.

Chapter 6

FIGURE 6-5
Dinosaur Dig game in Westwind Media's DinoSource

FIGURE 6-6
The Big Bug Alphabet Book from Milliken Publishing Company

At certain points, the child can also go to games, which serve to reinforce the lesson. One game asks the child to associate objects with the letter with which they begin. Another asks the child to pick out letters hidden in an object. The last one asks the child to match uppercase letters to lowercase letters.

The Big Bug Alphabet Book is entertaining enough to maintain a young child's interest. It requires a Macintosh system.

SHELLEY DUVALL'S IT'S A BIRD'S LIFE, SANCTUARY WOODS

Actress Shelley Duvall does more than just narrate this story for Sanctuary Woods; she is also one of the company's directors. Hollywood has taken an interest in interactive media, and Ms. Duvall is an early participant in this trend.

It's a Bird's Life is a wonderfully narrated and illustrated storybook. It's about a group of tropical birds kept as pets that flee a fire at their Los Angeles home and go to the Amazon (see Figure 6-7). Unfortunately, the Amazon is being razed by bulldozers, so to escape this destruction, the birds fly back to Los Angeles with many newfound friends from the Amazon. (OK, so that part is a little far-fetched.) The story also features several original songs. Other

FIGURE 6-7

It's a Bird's Life from Sanctuary Woods, narrated by Shelley Duvall

features include hypertext links to word definitions and interactive games. It's a Bird's Life requires a Macintosh system.

THE LIVING BOOK SERIES, BRODERBUND SOFTWARE

The idea behind the Living Book series is to create interactive learning tools from popular print books for children. The first two books that Broderbund has converted are Mercer Mayer's *Just Grandma and Me* and Marc Brown's *Arthur's Teacher Trouble*. Both were charming stories in print, but as interactive CD-ROMs their lessons for children are greatly strengthened.

Just Grandma and Me is aimed at children just beginning to read. The story has Mayer's "Little Critter" character spending the day at the beach with his grandmother. The disc gives the child the option of simply hearing the book read, as the spoken words are highlighted, or to "play" the book. Playing the book means that most of the objects on the screen are active, and the child can click on them with a mouse and get a reaction. Click on the mailbox and a frog jumps out. Click on the ocean and a whale appears. Each of the dozen screens has numerous active items (see Figure 6-8). The child also hears the story read

FIGURE 6-8

Just Grandma and Me, part of Broderbund's Living Book series

in this mode, and has the option of clicking on the individual words to hear them spoken again.

Arthur's Teacher Trouble is a story about a third-grader intimidated by a strict teacher and an upcoming spelling bee. This disc, too, has many active objects (see Figure 6-9), but the actions caused by clicking on objects appeal to an older child's sense of humor. For instance, clicking on the teacher's pants puts him in a Scotsman's kilt. *Arthur's Teacher Trouble* is also more academic, offering a spelling lesson halfway through the story.

Both discs run on the Macintosh and come with print copies of the respective books. Either title could easily be used in a classroom, but each is packaged for the consumer market (parents).

CLIPS, CLIPS, AND MORE CLIPS

The media clip art category is one of the largest categories of CD-ROM software. A media clip art disc is generally a collection of images, sounds,

FIGURE 6-9
Arthur's Teacher Troubles, part of Broderbund's Living Book series

video, animation, or any combination thereof. These discs are exclusive to computer-based CD-ROM, because it provides the necessary editing capability to use the clips. Ostensibly designed for business and professional use in presentations and multimedia production, many media clip art discs are bought by people who just want to play with the clip art.

Unfortunately, this is also one area where the buyer needs to be cautious. Many vendors seem to fill discs with whatever is handy and cheap—which means items that are in the public domain. Too few discs contain original, well produced material. To make matters worse, these discs often have poor user interfaces and almost never tell you anything about what you are looking at or listening to. If you want to know who produced the clip or how they did it, you're out of luck.

The value of some media clip art discs is questionable for other reasons. Is it cost-effective to pay $50 for a disc with 100 images if you only use 1 or 2? A media clip art disc can provide good value in one of two ways: by cramming as much stuff as possible on the disc for the lowest price, or by providing a highly specialized, high-quality collection.

Another hallmark of a good media clip art disc is the user interface. The simplest discs present you with just a directory of files. You access the clips using the built-in media playback capabilities of Windows or the Mac. Other discs might also rely on your computer's playback features, but they provide an easy-to-use interface. For example, a well-designed collection of Photo CD images might present a window of thumbnail images organized by category. You simply browse the images until you find one you want to examine more closely, click on the image, and call up a larger, higher resolution version. This method works well with a relatively few clips.

Some collections, sound clips for example, can number in the thousands. For these discs, you want a quick, efficient search engine and interface. This is often done using pick lists. A *pick list* is a menu of available items. Say you want to find the sound of a girl laughing. You might start with a general pick list that includes categories such as people, animals, nature, and sound effects. You select "people" and see another pick list that includes female adult, female child, male adult, and male child. Clicking on "female child" brings up a list containing talking, crying, laughing, and sneezing. Clicking on "laughing" brings you to the selection of audio clips you desire.

Another common search method uses *Boolean logic*, which allows you to pose queries using key words. For example, typing **girl AND laughing** at the appropriate prompt would find all clips that involved girls and laughing. Typing **girl NOT laughing** would call up all clips of girls not laughing. Boolean logic is described further in "Digging for Data," later in this chapter.

Keep in mind that not all media clip art discs are royalty free. That is, you might not be able to use the files to resell, even if you've incorporated them in a different type of product. In some cases, there is a restriction on the amount of the files on a disc you can use royalty free for commercial purposes. Many media clip art discs prohibit you from using the files in other media clip art products. Not all discs are clearly labeled in regard to the copyrights. If you are buying a disc for personal use only, you have nothing to worry about. But if you are buying media clip art for commercial purposes, make sure you know what the royalty situation is.

KEEPING TRACK OF CLIPS

The popularity of media clips has inspired a number of products designed to help you keep track of them. These packages tend to focus on image files, such as Photo CD, but can handle any standard format media clip that you have copied to your hard disk drive.

Kodak's Shoebox is perhaps the best known package. It runs on either Windows or the Mac and features a very efficient and thorough indexing scheme shown in Figure 6-10. You assign various attributes to a file when you add it to your catalog. For example, for a Photo CD image of a house in a field,

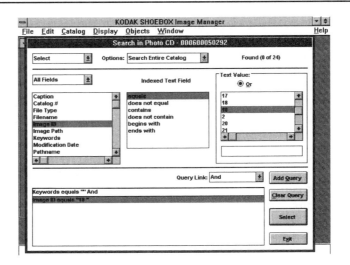

FIGURE 6-10
Search screen from Kodak's Shoebox

you might index it by "house" and "field." Taking it a step further, you might also index it by the dominant color of the image—"green"— or by the season, weather, or time of day. You can even index by the image's format. The more levels of definition you use to index a file, the greater the likelihood that you can pull exactly what you want out of a large database.

Shoebox is intended primarily for image files, but it can handle audio and video files, too. You can group selected images to create custom databases or to display in sequence for presentation purposes. You can even perform some basic editing functions on them. Of course, you can also export the files to other programs such as image editors or presentation software.

Another product is Imspace Systems' Kudo. Kudo is an image browser with many features similar to Shoebox. Its indexing and search mechanism, however, does not quite have Shoebox's depth. It, too, handles most graphics, video, and audio files. Kudo is a very capable browsing and cataloging tool; in fact, several vendors of CD-ROM software use Kudo as part of other packages. Adobe Systems, for instance, uses it as the browsing tool for the clip art collection included with the Deluxe CD-ROM Edition of Adobe Illustrator 5.0 for the Macintosh.

STAR TREK, STAR TREK THE NEXT GENERATION, AND LAWNMOWER MAN, SOUND SOURCE UNLIMITED AND THE MULTIMEDIA PUBLISHING STUDIO

Sound Source Unlimited has secured the rights to publish video and audio clips from the TV shows and movies on which these discs are based. What gives the discs a twist is a utility that the company provides that lets you easily tag any of the clips to a given computer event. For example, you can set it up so that you hear the sound of the Enterprise's transporter to indicate a copy done on the Mac. On a Windows system, you might have Captain Kirk ask, "What have you done with Spock's brain?" when a general protection error occurs.

Lawnmower Man also comes with brief video clips. The movie, *Lawnmower Man*, is about a dim-witted handy man who becomes super intelligent through the use of virtual reality. Much of the movie and all of the clips on the disc consist of computer-generated scenes and excellent special effects (see Figure 6-11).

The clips on these discs cannot be used for commercial purposes; they are intended only to dress up your desktop. These discs were produced by Sound Source Unlimited and are marketed by the Multimedia Publishing Studio, a recent IBM spin-off. This company has an impressive lineup of products

Chapter 6

FIGURE 6-11
Still shot from Lawnmower Man, developed by Sound Source Unlimited

besides those from Sound Source, some of which were developed in-house. Several of them are described elsewhere in this chapter.

JURASSIC (AND OTHER) DINOSAURS, CINEMA EXPEDITIONS, INCORPORATED

Although crudely produced, the 100 Photo CD images on this disc are worthwhile if you're interested in dinosaurs. You get no documentation to speak of—just a terse list of what the images represent. Each image is numbered, and you scroll through them until you find the one you want. The images on the disc are intended for noncommercial use, though a phone number is provided for anyone wanting to resell the images.

1000 OF THE WORLD'S GREATEST SOUND EFFECTS, INTERACTIVE PUBLISHING CORPORATION

They might not all be the world's greatest, but the sound effects on this disc could well be all you will ever need. This is especially true if you use the disc for personal use—presentations, experimenting with multimedia, and so on. The files are all royalty free, so professional publishers will find this disc very useful.

Chapter 6

The sound clips on the MPC-based disc come in both 8- and 16-bit formats. If you don't like what you hear, the disc also includes a Professional Wave Editor to customize the sounds to your liking, or to create new ones.

The indexing system is easy to use and fast. You select the general category you want from a pick list and then browse the selection list to find what you want. A "notes" box provides a somewhat better description of the sound file, and an "info" box gives vital statistics such as the actual file name, length, sample rate, and resolution. An Attach utility lets you link a sound to a system event.

Sounds range from the mundane, such as a car starting, to the obscure, such as an M551 tank firing a shell. You also hear snippets of famous speeches, music bites, and numerous human-generated sounds. With 1000 files, you'd expect a little bit of everything, and that's what this disc delivers.

MPC WIZARD 2.0 AND MEDIACLIPS, ARIS ENTERTAINMENT

Though the MPC Wizard disc is sold primarily as a diagnostics tool for MPC systems, it also includes over 120 images, videos, and sounds. These are from Aris's MediaClips collection. MPC Wizard is a valuable tool that tells you how well your system complies with the MPC 2 standard, and it offers advice for better performance and troubleshooting, as shown in Figure 6-12.

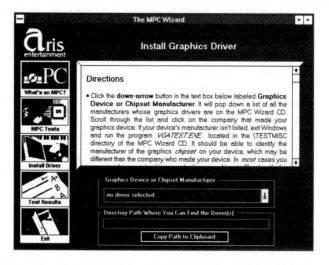

FIGURE 6-12

Advice from Aris Entertainment's MPC Wizard

Making the Most of CD-ROM Software   **177**

Chapter 6

The troubleshooting information is particularly helpful, with good explanations of problems and solutions. MPC Wizard also includes numerous sound and video drivers, and it coaches you on how to install them.

The full MediaClips is a separate product that contains a variety of video, image, and sound files. Although the material is organized into categories, there is no overall theme that ties the files together. The quality of the files and the slick interface, however, make up for the disc's lack of focus. The categories include jets, space, nature, business, and others (see Figure 6-13). Aris allows you to use up to 20 percent of the files for commercial use, but prohibits you from using them in other media clip art discs.

VISUAL VOCABULARY, VOLUME 1, ENERGY PRODUCTIONS

Visual Vocabulary is a collection of over 220 video clips for use with Video for Windows (VfW). VfW (or any other multimedia product capable of running VfW's AVI files) provides the user interface. The main strength of this disc is the quality and selection of the videos (see Figure 6-14). You get aerial shots, sports, buildings, cities, clouds, and much more. The documentation makes no mention of the copyright status and provides only terse descriptions of the files.

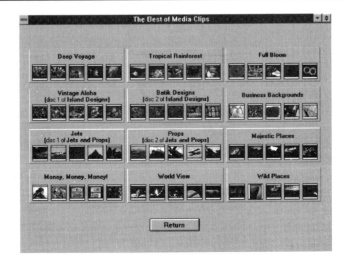

FIGURE 6-13

Sample images from Aris Entertainment's MediaClips disc

Chapter 6

FIGURE 6-14

A sample image from Visual Vocabulary, produced by Energy Productions

COREL PROFESSIONAL PHOTOS, COREL CORPORATION

Corel is most famous for its CorelDraw illustration package. The company has also been a CD-ROM pioneer, having bundled CorelDraw with a CD-ROM containing thousands of clip art images several years ago. You can even purchase the product with a CD-ROM drive. Now Corel is branching out into media clip art discs of Photo CD images for Windows and Mac systems.

Each disc in the Professional Photos series contains over 100 Photo CD images (see Figure 6-15). You also get several utilities that let you use the

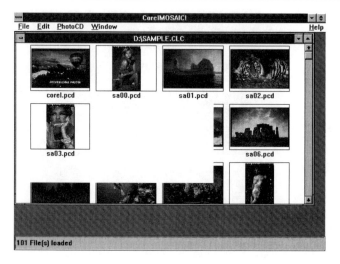

FIGURE 6-15

Sample Photo CD images from Corel's Professional Photos series

images in different ways. You can, for example, convert and edit any of the images for use as a screen saver or as wallpaper. The disc also provides a means of playing audio CDs.

Each of the dozens of discs in the series covers a specific topic. Examples include fireworks, Egypt, executives, auto racing, deserts, and castles. Chances are Corel can sell you a disc with a great selection in exactly the category you want. Unfortunately, Corel restricts the use of the images for resale; if you use the images for commercial purposes, you must purchase the rights to do so.

OSWEGO ILLUSTRATED ARCHIVES, OSWEGO COMPANY

The Illustrated Archives is a CD-ROM version of the classic clip art collection used in advertising and newspaper production. You get over 350 black-and-white images of common items—everything from computers to rocking chairs to musical instruments (see Figure 6-16). All are stored in EPS format, so you can easily use them with any desktop publishing or presentation package.

The illustrations are high quality, and the disc is readable on both Mac and Windows systems. The Kudo image browser, described earlier in this chapter,

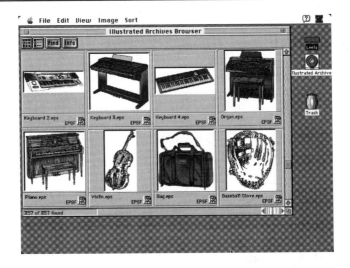

FIGURE 6-16

Clip art images from Oswego's Illustrated Archives

serves as the user interface. Each image is well indexed with information on when it was created, its category, and file size. Graphics designers or anyone who does a lot of presentations will find this disc useful.

DIGGING FOR DATA

The first CD-ROM applications were virtually all text databases. Computer graphics in the mid-1980s were crude by today's standards; video and CD-quality audio were unheard of. Placing large amounts of specialized data was at that time the best, most practical way to take advantage of CD-ROM. Even today, text-oriented references make up the vast majority of CD-ROM titles. Most of these titles, however, cater to niche markets. Few people, for example, require a database of statistics on Norwegian companies. So while these databases are rich in variety, almost none of them generate the sales volume expected of consumer titles.

To make up for the low volume, these databases on disc are usually very expensive; the general rule of thumb is that the more specialized the database, the higher the price. Some of these discs sell only a few dozen copies, but can cost $10,000 or more. Consumer titles need to sell at least 10,000 copies before they are considered successes. Even at those comparatively sky-high prices, CD-ROM-based databases can be extremely powerful competitive weapons. Used properly, they give you the information you need and more of it faster.

Databases on discs compete with online data services such as Dialog, Lexis, CompuServe, and Dow Jones News and Retrieval. Each medium has its own advantages. CD-ROM databases are well suited to serving the need for a lot of information on a narrow topic in a cost-effective manner. You might be able to locate the same information online, but after a point, the connect-time charges and access fees become prohibitive. Searching online is the way to go if you need just a little information on a topic. You might spend as much as $100 or more to get that information, but you could easily spend a lot more for a CD-ROM that you might only use once.

The best advice is to carefully assess your specific information needs. Many professionals and businesses use a combination of CD-ROM databases related to their core needs and online retrieval of infrequently needed information. In fact, several online services such as Dialog and Dow Jones have recognized this trend and now offer CD-ROMs that package some of the data they offer online.

How do you assess your CD-ROM needs? Start with the obvious. If you are an accountant, you can get the federal and state tax codes on CD-ROM. If you are a lawyer, look for abstracts in the area of your specialization. If you export products, look for CD-ROM databases on the economies of the countries you are targeting. If you currently get large collections of spec sheets, catalogs, price lists, or other print data from customers or suppliers, ask if the same information is available on CD-ROM.

Get only those discs you know are going to be immediately useful, and then monitor how you use external information sources. If you find you are spending a significant amount of money in any one area, it probably makes sense to start looking for a CD-ROM database that contains the same information.

One more point on CD-ROM databases: they work best when everyone who needs access has access. This presents a few problems.

▶ Does everyone have access to a CD-ROM drive? It makes sense when purchasing new computers to equip them with CD-ROM drives. The price of doing so is no longer a big barrier; you could pay as little as $200 more. Or you might simply set up one computer with a CD-ROM drive in a central location.

▶ What does the licensing agreement on the disc say about multiple users? By sharing a disc, you could technically violate the licensing agreement. Some discs are priced according to how many people will be using it. In some cases, you can buy a site license, which gives you unlimited use within a specific location.

▶ Is the CD-ROM accessible through your network? This is closely related to the access issue. Network access has the added advantage of disc security. You don't have to worry about anyone walking off with or losing a disc if it is permanently mounted at a central server. If you use multiple CD-ROM drives on the server or a minichanger, you can have instant access over the network to several discs at once—a tremendous convenience.

▶ Is everyone trained in how to use the CD-ROM? Don't underestimate the importance of this issue. People won't use a resource if they don't understand it or they are intimidated by it. It is wise to assume that everyone needs some level of training for each disc, especially since there is little consistency among the various user interfaces.

NOTE The products in this category of CD-ROM are presented in a slightly different format from the others. Since most of these products are highly specialized, and since there are so many of them, only brief descriptions are provided. This way, more products can be listed to better provide a sense of what is available.

Chapter 6

WANTED: SEARCH AND RETRIEVAL STANDARDS

Every one of the 2000-plus database titles has one thing in common: each must provide a means of locating and fetching the desired information. The tool that performs this task is generally referred to as a *search engine*. Most database products use commercially available search engines such as those from Dataware Technologies, Fulcrum Technologies, Folio Corporation, or Silverplatter Information. Some create their own.

The trouble is that no real standard exists for the search engines and, more importantly, their user interfaces. The closest thing to a standard search engine is Dataware's CD Answer, which the company claims is used in 500 applications. Many of those applications, however, are custom databases not intended for resale, and the remainder represent only a tiny portion of the commercial market.

Efforts are under way to standardize the way in which a search engine retrieves data. These methods include SFQL (Structured Full-Text Query Language) and Z39.50, which is useful for unstructured information.

For the end user, however, these standardization efforts will be largely invisible. None actually deals with creating a common user interface for finding and retrieving data. Although most of the search engines use similar schemes, such as key word indexes and Boolean logic, to locate data, each implements them in its own way. On the Macintosh, for example, you can generally expect to use a common command set to access the basic functions associated with using an application: install, copy, move, resize, print, and so on. The application has its own set of commands, too, but it is highly specific to the task it performs. With search engines, very little is consistent from one to another, as you can see from Figure 6-17.

For example, you might simply get a prompt to enter a key word or a Boolean query on one disc. On another, you might select the search criteria from pick lists. *Wildcard searches,* where you can search for partial words, are sometimes implemented differently among database titles. On product A, for instance, you might look for all potential spellings of Smith using SM*TH. Product B might expect the query SM?TH. These differences might seem small, but they can be very confusing to people who must deal with a lot of different database discs.

Chapter 6

Making the Most of CD-ROM Software   183

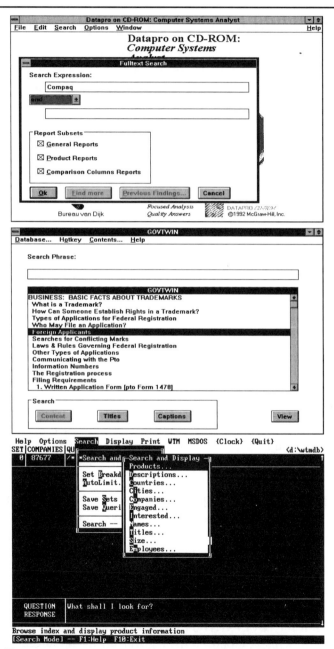

FIGURE 6-17

These three reference discs all contain text-based information, but use very different interfaces for the search function.

Chapter 6

BOOLEAN LOGIC: A COMMON THREAD

The nineteenth century mathematician George Boole created a system to symbolically represent relationships. This system uses the English operators AND, OR, and NOT. Most search engines used in data retrieval today implement Boolean logic in some way, though it is often supplemented or extended with other search mechanisms.

The AND operator is used to find multiple references with the same records or files. For example, the query **dog AND cat** will find all files with references to both dogs and cats. The query **dog OR cat,** however, will locate all files that reference both dogs and cats or that reference dogs or cats alone. NOT is used to focus a search. The query **dog NOT cat** will retrieve all files that reference only dogs.

You can use different Boolean operators within the same query. The query **dog AND cat OR mouse,** for example, will locate all files that reference both dogs and cats plus all files that reference mice. The query **dog AND cat NOT mouse** locates only those files that reference both dogs and cats with no mention of mice. If your Boolean search seems to be moving slowly, try rearranging the order of the operators. Sometimes this speeds performance.

GEOBASE, CD PUBCO

Geobase is a database of oil well production statistics and survey information in Canada. This is a multidisc set. One disc, for example, holds data on 180,000 wells in Alberta alone. It is intended for use on MS-DOS systems.

PHONEDISC USA BUSINESS, DIGITAL DIRECTORY ASSISTANCE

This disc, updated quarterly, provides a phone listing of all businesses—or at least 9.5 million of them—in the United States. Other information provided on this MS-DOS-based disc includes the businesses' standard industrial classification code and address. Digital Directory Assistance also sells a two-disc set containing all the residential phone numbers in the United States.

GOVERNMENT GIVEAWAYS FOR ENTREPRENEURS, INFOBUSINESS

This compendium of government resources for the entrepreneur is "hosted" by Matthew Lesko, a well-known author and expert on information resources. The MPC disc includes over two hours of audio and video explaining how to access the nearly 12,000 resources covered. Government Giveaways is also noteworthy as being one of the few multimedia database titles.

THE MICRO HOUSE TECHNICAL LIBRARY SERIES, MICRO HOUSE INTERNATIONAL

If you work a lot with computers—setting them up, fixing them, or giving advice on them—this series of discs is a treasure trove of specifications for major components. Individual discs include The Encyclopedia of Main Boards, The Encyclopedia of Hard Drives, and the Network Interface Technical Guide. The Hard Drives disc contains specs on over 2100 drives; 1000 of those drives plus 350 controller cards are diagrammed. One drawback: it is difficult to keep up with new products coming on the market, so each disc is always somewhat out of date. This is why Micro House sells the product on a subscription basis.

THE FEDERAL REGISTER ON CD-ROM, COUNTERPOINT PUBLISHING

For the unfortunate souls who must keep tabs on existing and proposed federal regulations, this disc subscription can be a lifesaver. It will cost you nearly $2000 for a subscription that sends a new disc each week, but the time saved doing searches electronically makes it worthwhile.

STREET ATLAS USA, DELORME MAPPING

Delorme claims to have put every street in the United States on a Windows-based CD-ROM, and that appears to be true. Call up any town using a key word search, and you get a full-color map of the streets plus significant landmarks, railroad tracks, bodies of water, and other items you would expect to find on a map. Delorme also sells MapExpert, which lets you produce and print out customized (or canned) maps.

COMPUTER SELECT, ZIFF DESKTOP INFORMATION

Sold on a monthly subscription basis, Computer Select is a collection of material on computers previously published in magazines, newspapers, and newsletters. Much of it is the full text, but some of the articles are merely abstracted. You don't get graphics or fancy formatting, but for researching computer-related topics, nothing else matches up. Computer Select is available for MS-DOS and Macintosh systems.

Chapter 6

THE HEALTH AND MEDICAL INDUSTRY DIRECTORY, AMERICAN BUSINESS INFORMATION

This directory lists over 1 million health and medical related businesses in the United States—dentists, doctors, nursing homes, health clubs, and so on. The disc includes phone numbers, addresses, and the type of business.

DUN'S BUSINESS LOCATOR AND DUN'S MILLION DOLLAR CD-ROM COLLECTION, DUN & BRADSTREET INFORMATION SERVICES

Dun's Business Locator is an MS-DOS-based disc that takes up where other business directories leave off by cross-referencing listings with parent and affiliated companies. This is valuable for anyone performing corporate research or investigating conflicts of interest.

Dun's Million Dollar CD-ROM Collection is a three-disc set that provides comprehensive data on over 200,000 small- to large-sized companies. You can find information such as annual sales, number of employees, line of business, and executive profiles. This is a valuable tool for prospecting potential customers.

PATENT INFORMATION ON CD-ROM, MICROPATENT

This is a database on all U.S. patents issued since 1975—1.7 million of them. Patent Information runs under MS-DOS and includes information on the inventor, issue date, international patent class data, and the primary examiner. You can also trace a patent's subsequent effects on other patents and technology.

NAFTA ON CD-ROM, YOUNG MINDS

Wonder how the North American Free Trade Agreement will affect you? You can get all the important data on the agreement on one CD-ROM. Published in full-text form, this disc is available for MS-DOS, Mac, and Unix systems.

EDUCATION: SLIMMER PICKINGS SO FAR

Relatively few classroom-only discs are available today. This is due to a simple reason: not many schools are yet equipped with CD-ROM, so the market has not fully developed. Consequently, most of the titles that can be used in the classroom are also targeted at the home, where the sales potential is much greater. You can find descriptions of these titles in the part of this

Making the Most of CD-ROM Software   187

Chapter 6

chapter on titles for children and for home use. The titles designed specifically for schools tend to be for the higher levels.

Several publishers and universities have announced interesting CD-ROM projects. Prentice-Hall and Houghton Mifflin, for example, are teaming up to produce interactive courseware. This will include conversion of existing textbooks to multimedia CD-ROM and new projects such as an interactive reading program for Kindergarten through 12th grade. Yale University Press has developed a CD-ROM called Perseus that is used to teach Greek and ancient civilizations.

WHO BUILT AMERICA?, THE VOYAGER COMPANY

Who Built America? is a Mac-based interactive textbook covering the period in American history from 1876 to 1914. In fact, it is based on a two-volume textbook entitled *Who Built America? Working People and the Nation's Economy, Politics, Culture, and Society* (Pantheon 1992). The disc was produced as part of the American Social History Project under the supervision of three historians. You can simply read the text as you would a book, but the real value in Who Built America? is in exploring the different levels of linked information.

Click on an underlined reference to a location, and a map with a marker showing where it is pops up (see Figure 6-18). Key events or concepts are

FIGURE 6-18

Who Built America? from The Voyager Company

placed in bold type at the bottom of some pages; clicking on them provides more graphics and text on the subjects. For example, if you click on "Worshippers of Mammon," you call up text about unionized labor. You can go one level deeper and call up an 1877 editorial from a labor newspaper criticizing the self-made man.

The disc includes sound clips of historical figures, popular music of the time, a few early videos, and the text of historical documents. A time line gives a quick view of the significant events of a given year.

The text portion is substantial, too. It is tough reading a lot of text even on the best monitors, but Who Built America? encourages you to explore the different levels of information on the disc. Reading its text in linear fashion is not what the Voyager Company had in mind.

Who Built America? is appropriate for use at the high school or college level.

20TH CENTURY VIDEO ALMANAC, THE SOFTWARE TOOLWORKS

Although the 20th Century Video Almanac is sold as a consumer product, it is distributed to schools by CEL Educational Resources. This five-disc set for MS-DOS systems covers the highlights of this century: people, sports, science and technology, war, politics, and more. The content is short on text but long on video, images, and audio clips.

Unlike Who Built America?, the 20th Century Video Almanac is not suitable as a stand-alone textbook, but could supplement other coursework. What this almanac offers in breadth, it lacks in depth. Its value is in its ability to encourage and hold a student's interest in twentieth century history.

The discs' user interface is graphically oriented. You can go directly to a topic index, a video index, or category index. You can also select topics from a time line, by a specific date, or geographically. The interface provides a quick and easy way to get a taste of this century's significant events. From this starting point, a student knows the topics that require more in-depth research.

THE PRESIDENTS, NATIONAL GEOGRAPHIC SOCIETY

Everyone is getting into the CD-ROM act, even the National Geographic Society, with a little help from IBM Educational Systems. The Presidents is a multimedia study of all U.S. presidents. It runs under MS-DOS and includes videos, election maps, audio clips, and over 1200 photos and images.

The National Geographic Society is pitching The Presidents as a tool to teach the electoral process. Besides the electoral maps, the disc's content also discusses political parties, the electoral process, and the limits of presidential power.

DISCOVERING FRENCH INTERACTIVE, DC HEATH AND COMPANY

Using multimedia to teach languages makes a lot of sense. You can not only read the vocabulary and text, but also see and hear it spoken. Bringing a CD-ROM home from French class, therefore, is a little like bringing home the instructor as well.

Discovering French Interactive is one of a number of language discs available in CD-ROM format. It allows you to listen to native speakers, record your own pronunciations, and then compare the two. A student can also manipulate the native characters to create different dialogs. Designed for first-year French students, each disc provides three units and a teacher's guide. The program requires a Macintosh computer.

TWAIN'S WORLD, BUREAU DEVELOPMENT

There are a lot of CD-ROMs that contain the lifeworks of well-known authors. Few of them are done well, and Twain's World is a gem. Where other discs might simply compile the text and tack on a simple search engine, Bureau Development has added a graphical interface and provided additional text and multimedia material that adds depth of understanding to the works of Mark Twain and the author himself (see Figure 6-19).

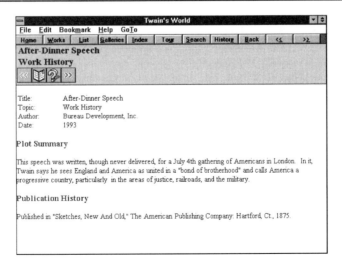

FIGURE 6-19

Twain's World from Bureau Development

You get biographical information on Twain, including "never before released" film footage of the man. In addition to his works, you get his speeches, personal letters, and essays. Some of the more famous scenes from his books are depicted in animation, but these are generally brief and rather silly.

What Twain's World offers that other "lifework" discs don't is perspective. You learn about the author's background as well as the influences of his time. Best yet, the disc is surprisingly inexpensive at $40. It is available for MPC-compatible systems only.

BEST SELLERS ON DISC

"Best sellers" stretches reality a bit. In truth, *electronic books* (also known as e-books), which are both fiction and nonfiction works published on CD-ROM, are hardly best sellers. This is due to a number of factors. First, the potential readership of any given e-book title is limited to people who own CD-ROM drives. Second, traditional book distribution channels have shown little interest in selling CD-ROMs. Finally, reading a book off a monitor or LCD is harsh on the eyes and often inconvenient.

Yet publishing books on CD-ROM has its advantages. You can do hypertext links from one section of the book to another; this is handy for revealing relationships and other threads. You can call up definitions of unusual words or concepts with a mouse click. You can type in your own notes in virtual windows. You can immediately turn to a specific passage with a simple key word search. And the publisher can enhance the text with multimedia features such as video or audio clips. Who Built America?, described earlier, is a prime example of an electronic book. Hyperbole Studios has created what it claims is the first interactive multimedia novel, The Madness of Roland. It is a story about the days of King Charlemagne and his knight Roland.

E-BOOKS AS AN ADAPTIVE TECHNOLOGY

Electronic books are extremely important for one segment of the population: the visually impaired. Once text is converted to digital form, it is relatively easy to then convert the electronic text to speech. Given the capacity of a CD-ROM, it is no problem to provide both text and speech versions of a book (or any other textual information) on one disc.

Chapter 6

ALL WORK AND NO PLAY...

Producing entertainment on disc involves both art and science. You need the creative talent to push the right emotional buttons with your audience, and you need the technical know-how to put all the pieces together into one seamless whole. It is no surprise, therefore, that professionals from the traditional entertainment industry are working side-by-side with programmers to create what are some of the hottest selling discs today. It is not unusual to hear original music scores or see professionally directed and acted skits on video. The onscreen images are often created by artists. Some discs even present movielike credits at the end, listing titles such as "executive producer" or even "casting director."

It really isn't appropriate to use the "game" label to cover everything in the entertainment category. Some discs are pure games, and they include everything from chess to the shoot-the-aliens arcade genre. However, CD-ROM has more to offer in terms of interactive entertainment. Take, for instance, Warner New Media's Funny. Funny is a collection of videos featuring 84 people—some who are famous, such as Dick Cavett—telling their favorite funny stories. Broderbund's Myst could be called a game, but it is more appropriately called an interactive science-fiction mystery.

Think of the variety of ways in which TV entertains you, and then imagine having the ability to manipulate the shows in different ways. You might want to view segments in a different order from which they are presented. You might want to participate in the action. You might want to combine different elements or eliminate others altogether. CD-ROM brings this kind of interactivity to your computer or TV screen.

Entertainment titles stand to benefit a great deal from a number of emerging trends. Most significantly, full-motion, full-screen video is becoming affordable for both TV-based players and computers. Philips recently introduced its Full-Motion Video cartridge for the CD-I player, and add-on video boards for PCs recently broke the $500 barrier. Some are now as low as $400. Expect to see new titles in 1994 that take advantage of full-motion video. Faster drives, players, and computers, too, will give a boost to multimedia-intensive CD-ROM entertainment.

Chapter 6

PLAYTIME CAVEATS

Few other types of titles are as complex and demanding on the hardware as entertainment. Entertainment titles often use an intense mix of audio, video, and high-resolution graphics, which all demand a lot of resources. To make matters worse, these titles often require frequent switching from one multimedia segment to another. On an underpowered system, these demands can result in sluggish performance, "jerky" video, audio that breaks up, or long pauses during play. In some cases, the titles won't run at all.

On TV-based players, this rarely presents a problem because each platform is relatively static. Developers have a stable environment and create the software to work within it. Computers, on the other hand, are not so static. No two are configured the same; memory size, processor speed, storage capacity, and video capability can all vary depending on the manufacturer and user upgrades.

Windows-based systems present the biggest challenge. A common problem here is insufficient main memory. All software requires a certain amount of free memory to run. The most demanding CD-ROM titles can require over 600K, and few list this requirement on the package. This is more than many Windows-based systems have available. Figure savers, drivers, and other software also compete for main memory.

Your best protection against this problem is to use a good memory management utility to free as much main memory as possible. MS-DOS 6.2 comes with MemMaker. Others include Quarterdeck's QEMM386 and Helix Software's Headroom. In some cases, though, you might have to sacrifice a driver or other software to get the needed memory.

Some problems show up on both Macs and Windows systems. A slow processor will cause video and audio to break up, as will a slow CD-ROM drive. Some titles require video capabilities that are not standard on some computer models. Others need a lot of space on your hard disk drive in order to run. Remember, too, that minimum memory requirements are rarely the optimal amount. If you have any doubts about your computer being able to run a title, ask the retailer or vendor before you buy.

Making the Most of CD-ROM Software   193

Chapter 6

MYST, BRODERBUND SOFTWARE

If you like a good mystery, you'll enjoy Myst. Placed abruptly in a strange island world, you are left to discover its secrets. The documentation gives you little guidance, except that you should try everything and look everywhere. As you wander about, you pick up clues about this fantastic world. Without giving away too much of the story, the island Myst is a base for entering and exploring other worlds. The means by which you do so involve a bit of science fiction and, it seems, magic. It is easy to get hooked on Myst, and once you do, expect to spend many hours exploring and solving its puzzles.

Two years in the making, Myst features stunning, highly detailed graphics—art might be a better term (see Figure 6-20). An original soundtrack plays unobtrusively in the background and sets the mood. At certain points, video clips are seamlessly integrated into the artwork. From a technical standpoint, the production of Myst defines the state of the art. Available for both Macintosh and MPC systems, Myst delivers your money's worth.

VIDEO CUBE, ARIS ENTERTAINMENT

Video Cube could become the Tetris of CD-ROM. This deceptively simple game has the same addictive qualities; you can never really win, but you keep trying, hoping to get just a little farther along. The object is to flip cubes within

FIGURE 6-20

The scenery in Broderbund's Myst is highly detailed

a grid so that they form a picture (see Figure 6-21). Once an image is formed, it turns into a video. All the images have a space theme. Each grid can form six separate images, and you must form them all within a time limit. Finish one grid, and you go to another level where there are more cubes within the grid. Video Cube runs on MPC systems.

SPACESHIP WARLOCK, REACTOR

The graphics are good, the story line is interesting, and the dialog with characters is fun. All this comes at the expense of the game play in Spaceship Warlock. This is an action-adventure game set, obviously, in space. The human race has been defeated in a war with robotlike critters, who have rudely swiped Earth and hidden it somewhere in the universe. While traveling in space, the ship on which you are riding is attacked by the pirate Spaceship Warlock, captained by a tough human determined to find and free Earth. After doing some of the captain's dirty work, the two of you accomplish that goal in what seems like record time.

Spaceship Warlock is a fascinating Macintosh title, but the emphasis was put on the graphics and production (see Figure 6-22). This is fairly common with CD-ROM titles. The developer has this wonderful medium to do things

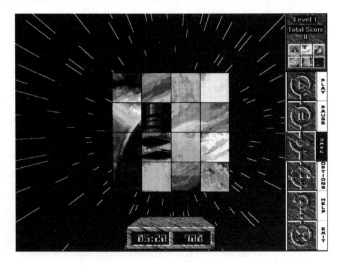

FIGURE 6-21
Video Cube from Aris Entertainment

Making the Most of CD-ROM Software   195

Chapter 6

FIGURE 6-22
Spaceship Warlock from Reactor

that are not practical on floppies, so he or she throws in a lot of bells and whistles to embellish the game. Sometimes, though, the game takes a back seat to those bells and whistles. Spaceship Warlock is a worthwhile product, but it could be better.

KARAOKE SHAKESPEARE, ANIMATED PIXELS AND THE MULTIMEDIA PUBLISHING STUDIO

It was only a matter of time before someone combined karaoke and Shakespeare. This title is based on Macbeth and allows up to 10 people to play parts. Or you can just sit back, watch, and listen as the play unfolds on the monitor of your MS-DOS system. As a bonus, the full text of Macbeth is also available on the disc.

THE CHESSMASTER 3000, THE SOFTWARE TOOLWORKS

The Chessmaster chess program has been around for years in floppy form, but The Software Toolworks recently produced it on CD-ROM. Doing so enabled many intriguing features. You can access a library of 1700 games that have been played between Karpov and Kasparov (see Figure 6-23). On some

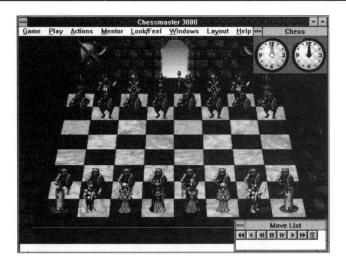

FIGURE 6-23
The Chessmaster 3000 from The Software Toolworks

of them, Karpov annotates the critical moves, explaining his strategy and how he reacted to his opponent.

If you don't know how to play chess—no problem. Animated tutorials get you started. Audio help is always available for the asking. The Chessmaster 3000 requires an MPC system.

SPORTS SPECIALS AND HOBBY HELPERS

Sports and hobbies are an emerging category. The first sports discs were mainly text compilations of sports statistics, but these did not take advantage of the CD-ROM's capabilities. Current titles are becoming more sophisticated. The Sports Illustrated CD-ROM Sports Almanac, for instance, includes statistics on all the most popular sports. However, it also contains articles from *Sports Illustrated* along with sound-captioned photographs. Golfing games have graduated into golfing simulators that claim to help you improve your game.

Philips offers a diverse lineup of CD-I titles for hobbyists. Topics include gardening, cooking, bird-watching, photography, and sailing. Coin and stamp

Chapter 6

collectors can browse through and learn from two titles from Philips' Smithsonian Presents series: Stamps, Windows on the World, and The Riches of Coins.

As the installed base of CD-ROMs grows, the demand for niche sports and hobby titles will grow. The few titles now available are of good quality.

HOME IS WHERE THE CD-ROM IS

The most powerful force behind the sharp recent growth in CD-ROM sales is the consumer, or home user. With TV-based players and multimedia PCs entering households in record numbers, consumers are hungry for new titles. They're here, and more are on the way. Home-based titles can be broken down into three categories:

- ▶ Parental guilt (home reference)
- ▶ Coffee-table discs
- ▶ Self-improvement

Although named with tongue in cheek, the parental guilt category is perhaps the most important. It includes encyclopedias, dictionaries, almanacs, atlases, and other titles that parents buy to help the kids in school and to justify the purchase of a computer or CD-ROM player. The rationale is a good one, though, because these references really shine as multimedia CD-ROM titles.

Reference works are by nature nonlinear; when you need to know something, you want to go directly to the information. Once there, you want to be able to quickly track down data on related items. This isn't easy when the information is printed in books. A research session with the old 20-some-odd-volume encyclopedia could end with a dozen of those volumes scattered about your desk opened to various pages. Not very efficient or neat.

Using CD-ROM and multimedia, you can take a direct path through the research process. You can record your steps, easily explore other avenues, capture the information you want, and compile it into the form you require, and never turn a page or get a paper cut. What's more, your understanding of that information is enhanced because you've seen video clips of actual events, heard an expert describe a concept, and watched a sound-captioned animation explain how something worked.

Chapter 6

Children (and adults) should not rely on these multimedia enhanced references as their only research tools. They will, however, draw curious minds into a topic and provide a better point from which to begin a project.

Coffee-table discs are like the slickly produced coffee-table books that people buy because they are interesting and look impressive when left where others can see them. The best example of a coffee-table disc is From Alice to Ocean made by Against All Odds Productions and sold by Addison-Wesley. In fact, you can buy a coffee-table book version of the disc.

From Alice to Ocean is a compelling story about a woman who trekked across the Australian Outback with four camels and a dog. She kept a journal, and a photographer met her at various points to record the journey on film. She tells the story of that journey through narration of her journal and the photos (see Figure 6-24). Think of it as a PBS special on disc. The disc requires a Macintosh, and is very well produced.

The self-improvement category has a great deal of potential. Existing titles teach you how to play musical instruments, how to improve your photography techniques, or how to draw. What makes CD-ROM such a good vehicle for these how-to discs is its ability to present the material in an interactive multimedia environment. You can learn a subject at your own pace and in the

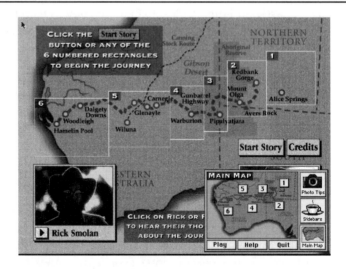

FIGURE 6-24

From Alice to Ocean by Against All Odds Productions

order that suits you. You can repeat different parts at will. Diagrams and text might not get the point across, but a video will.

According to distributors and developers, there should be many new self-improvement titles in 1994. Self-improvement is important in the corporate world, too. Business refers to it as training, and CD-ROM plays a role there as well. There are differences between home and corporate self-improvement applications, however. Training, therefore, is a separate category described later in this chapter.

MICROSOFT ENCARTA, 1994 EDITION, MICROSOFT CORPORATION

Microsoft has a lot of resources to throw at any given project, and it held none of them back on Encarta. Based on the *Funk & Wagnalls New Encyclopedia*, Encarta features over 14,000 media elements including maps, illustrations, video clips, and photos (see Figure 6-25). It also has over 100 animations and seven hours of 16-bit sound clips, including music samples from around the world, nature sounds, jazz and classical music, and recordings of historical events.

You get a lot of information in different forms on this MPC-based title, but what makes it all click is how Microsoft put it together. The interface provides multiple means of locating the information and then of blazing a trail through

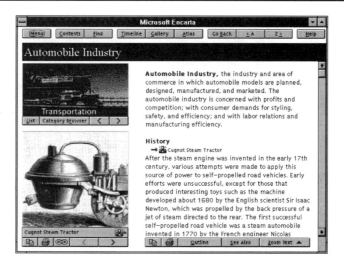

FIGURE 6-25
Microsoft Encarta 1994 Edition

Chapter 6

related references. The sequence of your actions is recorded so that you can return to any point you require. You can also print out or copy any of the information as needed.

Encarta sets the standard for CD-ROM-based encyclopedias. This is not to belittle other such references on CD-ROM. Compton's Interactive Encyclopedia and the New Grolier Multimedia Encyclopedia are excellent products as well. Microsoft has done the better job, however, of integrating all the pieces behind an easy-to-use interface.

REDSHIFT, MARIS MULTIMEDIA LIMITED

Redshift is a superb reference for amateur astronomers both young and old. This Macintosh title combines the *Penguin Dictionary of Astronomy* with over 700 photographs of objects in space (see Figure 6-26). You can also run animations that show, for instance, the orbits of the planets in the solar system and the earth's rotation. You can create your own animations using a Movie Recorder feature.

The user interface will be a challenge for young users; it is a combination of pull-down menus and icons. But the quality of both the information on the disc and the images makes Redshift the premiere astronomy CD-ROM.

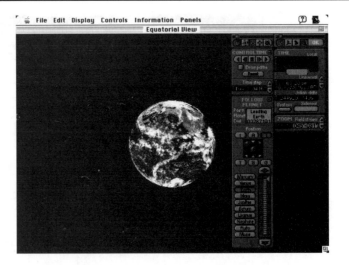

FIGURE 6-26

Redshift from Maris Multimedia

U.S. ATLAS AND WORLD ATLAS, THE SOFTWARE TOOLWORKS

Either of these references is a valuable source of geographic information, but they are also just plain fun to explore. Kids especially have a natural curiosity about places and people. The Software Toolworks seems to have taken that into account. You can find the information you'd expect to see in an atlas: population numbers, birth rates, maps, economic statistics, and so on.

To make it more interesting, both products also include numerous video clips, high-resolution photos, national and state anthems, and pronunciation guides. You can create your own maps and use them with either product, or you can print out maps in multipage form so they take up an entire wall. Both U.S. Atlas and World Atlas require an MPC system.

THE 1993 GUINNESS MULTIMEDIA DISC OF RECORDS, GROLIER ELECTRONIC PUBLISHING

This disc is mostly for fun, but it is useful for some research and settling bets. You can view entries randomly or select them by category through a series of menus and pick lists. You can also search by key words. Many of the entries have accompanying photos, but only a few dozen videos are available. This MPC-based disc does improve on the printed *Guinness Book of Records*.

MAYO CLINIC FAMILY HEALTH DISC AND MAYO CLINIC: THE TOTAL HEART, IVI PUBLISHING

These Windows-based discs pick up where other home medical references leave off. You can more easily find references to specific ailments, then find related references, and follow up on them immediately. Numerous graphics, photos, and animations aid you (see Figure 6-27). The search mechanism is key word and menu based, but the categories are well defined and organized.

Neither title replaces the family doctor. You can, however, get quick answers to less urgent ailments, and sometimes the most important question these references can answer is whether you should see your doctor.

PERIODICALS ON DISC

Folk wisdom has long said that electronically published newspapers and magazines won't replace the printed page until you can take them into the

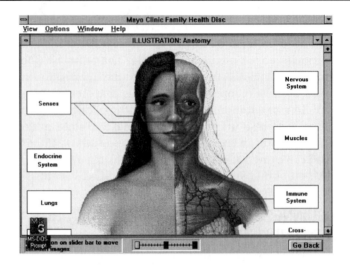

FIGURE 6-27
The Mayo Clinic Family Health Disc from IVI Publishing

bathroom with you. There is truth in that statement; people prefer the printed page over a video display, and for good reason. Not only is the printed page in a higher resolution than a video display, it provides better contrast. More significantly, you see a printed page by reflected light. A video display emits light to create an image. This is harder on your eyes.

Other factors make it unwise to simply convert magazines and newspapers in their existing format to an electronic medium. The Darwinian forces affecting print publications for the last few hundred years have made them highly specialized for the paper medium. It makes absolutely no sense to assume that the printed page format will survive in a video environment. Just as fish had to grow legs and develop lungs to live on land, print publications must evolve for the new electronic medium.

Fortunately, several new and established publishers are taking this evolutionary leap. Some are more daring than others, but all realize that the new CD-ROM medium has its own unique qualities. Established magazines such as *Newsweek, Business Week,* and *Money Magazine* have combined existing material from the print version with new information. Then they've added an array of multimedia elements and hypertext searching capability. These magazines are good choices for CD-ROM versions because they are so data intensive. Their readers use the print publications to make both personal and

Making the Most of CD-ROM Software 203

Chapter 6

business decisions; on CD-ROM in a multimedia environment, they can manipulate that information in ways that make it even more useful.

Several new publications have emerged to specifically play to the strengths of CD-ROM. *Verbum* is focused on the arts. Each issue has graphics, animation, and music. *Nautilus*, from Metatec, is the most interesting of the CD-ROM "magazines." It is part shareware disc, part art disc, part how-to guide, and part club. A sample table of contents is shown in Figure 6-28. In other words, *Nautilus* has captured the same eclectic taste and sense of community that were hallmarks of the early computer magazines. You never knew what you would find in a given issue of *BYTE, Kilobaud Microcomputing,* or *80 Microcomputing* 12 or 15 years ago. You knew, however, that it would be interesting and that it would teach you a little more about your personal computer.

Each issue of *Nautilus* teaches you a little more about topics such as multimedia production. You also get a new collection of software to try out each month. Like the early magazines, *Nautilus* has a few rough edges in terms of production quality, but these are easily overlooked. The computing world needs more publications like *Nautilus*, which is available for both Windows and Mac systems.

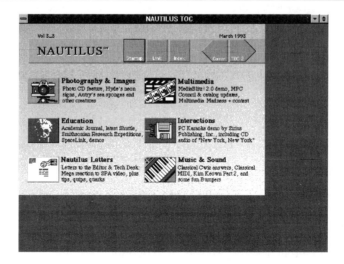

FIGURE 6-28

"Nautilus" CD-ROM magazine, published by Metatec

Chapter 6

DISCS FOR SOFTWARE JUNKIES

If you like trying out new software on your computer, or you just like hunting for software bargains, shareware is the way to go. *Shareware* is software of any type that is sold more or less on the honor system. The way shareware works on CD-ROM is that you pay for the disc, which contains a collection of software. You are then expected to send money to the developers of those programs that you decide to use. Shareware collections on CD-ROM are generally priced in the $20 to $50 range. The individual programs on them request fees as low as $10 but usually no higher than $50.

You can fit a lot of software on one disc, and this is both a blessing and a curse. You get a lot to choose from, but separating the wheat from the chaff can be a tedious chore. This is especially true of discs that include software from all categories.

You need to be aware of two things when buying shareware discs. Look for discs that specialize in areas that interest you; this way you are more likely to find something useful to you. Second, try to determine how the seller of the shareware disc has selected the software. Some vendors simply pull software from online sources without paying much attention to its age or quality. Not only does this mean that you get a lot of very crude material, you also run a higher risk of getting a program that contains a virus. No reputable shareware vendor will place a program on disc without first checking for viruses, but the less care taken in the selection process, the higher the risk.

Several established shareware providers are worth noting. PC-SIG has been in the shareware business since before CD-ROM, and it has a reputation for careful program selection. Walnut Creek offers a wide variety of shareware discs. On a more esoteric note, Network Cybernetics Corporation specializes in artificial intelligence shareware.

IN TRAINING

The training category covers products designed to teach professional skills in a work environment. Most often, these are custom-produced discs aimed at specific tasks: how to operate a specific piece of equipment, how to process a set of forms, or how to interview job applicants. Holiday Inn, for example, has produced a multimedia training course in hotel management on CD-ROM. At least one company, Xebec Multimedia Solutions, produces courses on business and professional skills on CD-ROM.

The most popular commercial training applications are designed to teach people how to use popular computer software. QuickStart Technologies, for instance, has a series of discs that teach various Microsoft applications and operating systems. Topics include Windows NT, Microsoft Access, Microsoft Mail, and Windows for Workgroups.

Many businesses spend a great deal of money on training: purchasing materials, hiring instructors, paying for travel to courses. Indirect costs are incurred for lost productivity while employees are being trained. Interactive multimedia training is a proven means of reducing those costs.

As with education and self-improvement titles, training CD-ROMs allow you to go through a lesson at your own pace. Not only that, you can repeat all or part of it at will, which is useful when you need a refresher for a task that you have not done in a long time. If you don't understand a concept, chances are the disc contains ancillary references to help you out. Best of all, CD-ROM training is comparatively inexpensive. A commercial training disc on CD-ROM costs several hundred dollars. It could cost $15,000 or $20,000 to have a custom training disc produced, and sending employees to a class or hiring an in-house instructor can cost even more.

CONVERT THOSE VCR TAPES

Many companies already have a library of training videos on VCR tape. The trouble with tape is that it is a linear medium, in that it isn't easy to change the order of the presentation or replay a given segment. Doing a hypertext link is impossible. The good news is that you can convert those tapes to CD-ROM format.

Consultants are available who convert VCR tapes to CD-ROM on a professional basis, but VIS Development Corporation provides software that allows you to do it. You can add text and link it to specific video and gain all the advantages of an interactive environment. VIS Development will do the conversion for you if you do not have the resources yourself.

Chapter 6

SPECIAL PROJECTS

CD-Recordable technology has opened up a world of custom CD-ROM possibilities. Just a few of the potential applications are

- ▶ **Presentations:** Impress your clients and boss with slick, interactive presentations on disc. Several portable devices exist that are self-contained or attach to a TV or computer for use on the road (see Chapter 4).

- ▶ **Archiving:** CD-R hardware and software are quickly making CD-ROM a cost-effective and stable environment for long-term storage of important data.

- ▶ **Training:** As this chapter has already stated, interactive multimedia courses on CD-ROM can dramatically improve a company's training program.

- ▶ **Custom publishing:** You can buy your own CD-ROM "press"—hardware and software—for about $8000. Publishing on disc provides unprecedented control over the entire publishing process.

- ▶ **Data distribution:** CD-R technology allows you to get a lot of information out to a sales force or a client base very quickly. That information is also more useful, because you can analyze it and manipulate it in ways that are impossible with print data.

- ▶ **Kiosk:** CD-ROM is becoming an important component of stand-alone, unattended information booths, or kiosks (such as the one shown here). These are popping up in shopping malls, airports, and other public places. You use them to get directions to a location, buy tickets, receive coupons, rent a car, and perform many other transactional and informational applications.

Making the Most of CD-ROM Software 207

Chapter 6

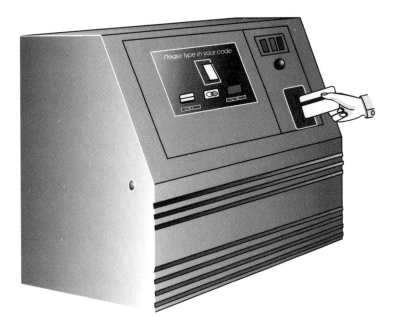

Producing these CD-ROM applications does require some skill in working with electronic media. However, anyone with patience and basic computer skills can produce information on disc. The next chapter covers the tools you need and issues to consider in custom publishing.

CHAPTER 7

CD-ROM PUBLISHING: GETTING STARTED

You can buy many great CD-ROM titles off the shelf. But perhaps the most exciting aspect of CD-ROM is that you can create your own discs relatively inexpensively and more easily than ever. That is not to say that the process is cheap and that everyone can do it. More specifically, it means that anyone with about $25,000 and a basic understanding of computers and publishing has a great opportunity to produce CD-ROM titles for resale.

Similarly, many businesses will find CD-Recordable technology useful for disseminating information to employees and customers. In either case, however, it is easy to get carried away by the notion of do-it-yourself CD-ROM publishing. Although more accessible than ever before, CD-ROM publishing presents many challenges that you must be aware of before beginning.

This chapter outlines those challenges. It is not meant to be a thorough how-to guide to CD-ROM publishing, but the following information will put the task into perspective and show you where to begin. Many who have wandered into the CD-ROM publishing mine field have lost limbs. And while those who pioneered this dynamic industry have smoothed some of its rough edges, there are still many hidden Claymores littering the paths.

Chapter 7

Why venture into this minefield? The rewards can outweigh the risks. This chapter will explain

- What makes a good CD-ROM publishing subject
- How to create a CD-ROM
- Service bureaus versus doing it yourself
- Costs
- How to market and distribute a CD-ROM

Each section will point out the pitfalls and the promise. Preparing for the unexpected is the watchword.

WHY PUBLISH ON CD-ROM?

Consider the following CD-ROM publication examples:

- A government agency regularly updates several hundred manuals on CD-ROM.
- A Fortune 500 company puts its massive, multivolume catalog, complete with photos and video narratives, in the hands of its sales staff and customers.
- An author creates an interactive animated children's story, too massive for floppies or hard drives.
- An international airport installs several informational kiosks offering interactive, multimedia, multilingual tours of the city.
- A software distributor wants to let customers try out, and, if satisfied, buy several programs.
- A major corporation needs to train dozens of employees in scattered locations at varying times.

All of the preceding examples meet the criteria for CD-ROM publications: they contain massive amounts of data, their usage is simplified by a database manager, and multimedia enhances their value. It is cheaper to produce them on disc than on a bunch of floppy disks.

CD-ROM Publishing: Getting Started 211
Chapter 7

The key question you should ask is, will porting content to CD-ROM increase its value? As other chapters have indicated, CD-ROM can enhance value in a number of ways. Packaging a large amount of in-house information so that it is easily accessible could, for example, improve employee productivity, increase sales, or enhance customer relations. Interactivity, though not exclusive to CD-ROM, is a feature more easily implemented on disc. In short, you've got to be able to clearly define the advantages of CD-ROM for any given project. This is true whether you intend to sell the end result or use it within your company.

HOW TO CREATE A CD-ROM

Publishing a CD-ROM *can* be simple, but it rarely is. The most straightforward project would be a text-only, single-platform, in-house application. You are dealing with only one type of data, one type of hardware environment, and your support issues are minimal. Any other type of project is likely to cause more than a few headaches.

The CD-ROM publishing business is at a stage similar to the early days of desktop publishing, when many people called themselves "desktop publishers," but few could do it well. Back then it was "Have Pagemaker will publish;" now it's "Have CD-R, will publish."

Your project may be as simple as an indexed database or as complex as an interactive, multimedia experience. You may want to do it yourself, farm it out to a service bureau, or use some combination of the two. The preparation of the content is similar in all instances. The next several sections explain the 10 steps you need to take to create a CD-ROM; the service bureau versus self-publishing issue will be clarified in its own section later in the chapter.

Creating a CD-ROM title is a multistep process:

1. Identify users and the task.
2. Determine which platforms will run this content and port it to a computer.
3. Acquire and port the content.
4. Formulate the design, the flow of information, and/or the search and retrieval process.
5. Produce an interface.

6. Devise the look and feel of the product.
7. Put the content in a usable format—the "authoring" task.
8. Test with real users.
9. Create a "one-off" or "gold" disc.
10. Mass produce your CD-ROM.

Each of these steps hides its own potential land mines. Each, too, has its own unique learning curves, costs, and options.

IDENTIFY USERS AND THE TASK

Don't assume that you know everything about your target audience. Talk to them, survey them. Find out how they are or are not currently fulfilling the needs you see your CD-ROM delivering. Bounce ideas off them and gauge the reactions. The better you get to know these people, the better you will be able to create a successful CD-ROM. This initial research is essential whether you are working on a commercial product or an in-house project.

Start with your own vision of what you want to accomplish. A little research, however, will go a long way toward focusing that vision. Once you've got that sharper picture, keep it in mind throughout the lengthy and often frustrating production process. This way you stand a better chance of creating a compelling product.

PLATFORMS

Will this CD-ROM run in-house on one computer system? Will it be a stand-alone kiosk? Having just one hardware platform to worry about makes your publishing task fairly straightforward. Add one more, though, and the complexity of your task increases exponentially. Producing for more than two platforms means you are taking on a monumental task. The so-called cross-platform issue is the CD-ROM industry bugaboo. To reach the widest possible audience requires creating a product that will run on several systems. Each target system generally requires its own production process.

The single-platform PC realm presents its own challenges. You have hundreds of processor, motherboard, sound card, and CD-ROM configurations. Most developers just shoot for a lowest common denominator configuration based on who the target user is and the minimum hardware requirements of the project.

There is no VHS-like standard for all CD-ROMs. Accommodating this diversity creates huge headaches for developers. The simple but unsatisfactory answer to this problem is to test your product on as many platforms and configurations as possible. The "Authoring" section later in this chapter will cover this in more detail.

ACQUIRE AND PORT THE CONTENT

Content is key. Those who own content will lead the electronic publishing industry. This can be the most important and costly part of your project. If you already own the content, be it a financial database, collection of photos, or a game, you are well positioned. Most publishers, however, will have to acquire or create content. A critical issue is copyright, which is covered in the section, "Beware of Copyrights," later in this chapter. In the case of a CD-ROM, content can be

- Text
- Structured data
- Page layouts
- Graphics
- Animations
- Audio
- Video

Getting each type of data first into electronic form and then into the appropriate format for publication on CD-ROM is the challenge.

Text Is the Easiest

Text is simple. You can scan it in, port it from existing data files, or type it in using a word processor. Text can be stored in many formats, however, and this can create problems. For instance, Macs and PCs expect different imbedded characters for carriage returns. Different word processors use a wide variety of control characters for the same functions. These formatting issues are critically important on a cross-platform CD. Your safest bet is to start with plain-vanilla ASCII text, which is universally readable, and then format accordingly for the target platforms.

Other text-related considerations include indexing and hypertext links. Both are intended to help the user find data faster. Designing your text for ease in navigation is critical. Text retrieval products can simplify this process. Several are discussed in the "Product Design" section.

Structured Data Is Common

Structured data is the most common data type found on CD-ROMs. Telephone directories, catalogs, databases, and numeric figures are all structured data. Essentially they are organized pieces of information, retrievable in a variety of methods: key word searches, Boolean queries, indexes, and so on. If this is the focus of your CD-ROM project, life is simple. You do not need to do much more than organize the data using a database manager and port this information to CD-ROM. Voilà—instant CD-ROM publishing.

Page Layouts Useful to Print Publishers

Page layouts, or document images, are an easy source of CD-ROM material. Print publishers can put their material directly onto a CD-ROM simply by scanning the pages as bitmapped images, similar to microfiche or microfilm, or by saving them as PostScript or other page-description language files. Companies can keep images of important papers stored on CD-ROM.

Problems arise if you want text search and retrieval; scanned or PostScript files are stored as graphics, not text. You can manually create an index with key words, as in readers' guides to periodicals, but until recently there was no way to search bitmapped images for specific words.

Several tools allow cross-platform viewing of electronic document files. These include Adobe Systems' Acrobat and No Hands Software's Common Ground. Both allow for searches based on indexed images, and both allow hypertext linking of pages. An upcoming version of Acrobat, however, reportedly will allow full-text searches.

Graphics Can Be Demanding

Graphics run the gamut from photos and illustrations to charts and page backgrounds. Problems arise here in the number of colors. Do you use 16, 256, 65,000, or 16 million colors? Each higher level decreases the number of computers capable of displaying the graphics that are on your CD-ROM and slows down performance. There are ways around this. For instance you can offer users a choice based on their video card and processor speed or store some images on the user's hard drive for faster retrieval.

Other problems arise with color palettes. As your CD-ROM changes from one graphics page to the next, you may have distinctly different color schemes. A common example is displaying photographs under a limited number of colors, such as 256 or 16. As you shift from outdoor scenery to interiors or under water to above, you will want to use different color palettes. You use more blues and greens for under water, reds and yellows above. Some systems can handle palette changes easily, others freeze. This becomes a bigger problem when running on more than one platform.

Porting your graphics and photo images into your computer is also critical. In the recent past you had only one option to digitize photos: scan them using expensive and time-consuming equipment. Now there is a simpler and inexpensive option that will work for many projects: Kodak Photo CD. Using 35 mm slides or negatives as your source material, Kodak service bureaus can easily put your pictures or graphics on CD-ROMs for less than a dollar an image, sometimes a little more. Each image is stored in five different resolutions, most of which are of sufficient quality to look good on a PC monitor. Chapter 3 describes the Photo CD format in more detail.

Animations Must Be High Quality

Animations can be as simple as a moving symbol or as complex as a cartoon. You can create animations with a variety of graphic programs, or you can create them like cartoons by using film cels. Animations are useful to draw attention to an item, perhaps by moving a pointer to a particular field. They spice up educational software by giving life to characters. Since animations are frequently used in game and educational software running off hard drives, users have come to expect highly detailed renderings and a fast pace. Re-creating that high-speed quality on a CD-ROM-based program is extremely difficult. If you plan to use animations, keep them simple, small, and limited in movement.

Chapter 7

FROM AN ARTIST'S IDEA TO CD-ROM

The Ugly Duckling on CD-ROM was a bicoastal, collaborative production effort. The author, Shannon Gilligan, wrote the script and oversaw the music and narration of this multimedia version of the children's classic from her home in Vermont. Ed Dua of Morgan Interactive in San Francisco provided funding and marketing. Portland, Oregon-based New Media Magic created the product, and Electronic Arts, of San Mateo, California, is the distributor.

As with most large-scale commercial CD-ROM productions, The Ugly Duckling had its share of difficulties. Virtually everything took twice as long and cost twice as much as budgeted. The developers optimistically planned to use detailed animated characters, but slow CD-ROM playback put an end to that. And they created at least eight masters—or one-off versions—enough to decorate a Christmas tree.

"We learned hundreds of ways to slow up a computer," New Media Magic's producer Jim Swenson said. "We constantly fought that."

They created the 16 background scenes in watercolor, then scanned them in 256 colors. The "click" animations are standard cartoon cel style, with one difference. To keep the color palette simple, they used line drawings and let the computer fill them with solid colors. They authored the project in Macromedia Director to exploit that program's excellent animation and interaction capabilities.

Porting to MPC using Director's Windows player was tedious but finally successful, largely because Swenson and his crew spent so much time on electronic bulletin board systems swapping Director tips.

Audio quality was one cross-platform casualty. The Mac supports 22KHz audio, but the base PC/Sound Blaster standard was, at the time, a lower quality 11KHz. They opted for the lowest common denominator.

Swenson is still licking his wounds but plans to pursue more products of this genre. "We're at the beginning of an industry that hasn't matured yet," he said. "As a tiny group of creative artists we feel like we're dancing with elephants, and it's scary."

Many Options for Audio

Audio includes narration, music, and sound effects. You have a lot of options for recording audio to CD-ROM. You can choose the kilohertz rate, analog versus digital, CD quality versus MIDI, and Red Book versus Yellow Book. Again, each increasing level of quality decreases the number of computers that can play your product and slows performance. Not all computer sound boards, for example, can play MIDI.

To port audio to your computer you typically use digital audio tape (DAT). A sound card translates DAT to sound files that are compatible with your system, such as AIFF (Audio Interchange File Format) for the Mac and WAV for PCs. MIDI files are simply data that, when played through a synthesizer, create instruments and music. Few CD-ROMs use both MIDI and digital audio, but those that do, such as Trilobyte's The 7th Guest, can be mesmerizing. (See the section at the end of this chapter entitled "Escaping the Minefield with $5 Million" for a description of The 7th Guest.)

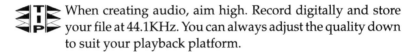 When creating audio, aim high. Record digitally and store your file at 44.1KHz. You can always adjust the quality down to suit your playback platform.

Video Is the Biggest Challenge

Full-motion video is the messiest part of CD-ROM publishing. Video can bring a CD-ROM to a screeching halt. The playback capabilities run from respectable on 3DO and CD-I machines to miserable on most PCs and Macs. Judicious use of video can spice up a multimedia product or cause it to crash and burn. Tread very carefully here.

From the original videotaping to capturing video on your computer, there are many ways to botch a project. Here are a few tips to keep the glitches to a minimum:

▶ Videotape at a minimum format of Hi8 up through 3/4-inch and Beta SP. Do not use S-VHS, VHS, consumer Beta, or 8 mm. Those formats have significant quality degradation with each subsequent edited generation.

▶ Shoot carefully. Avoid pans, zooms, full-screen action, and complex, high-contrast settings.

- Store your video on DAT. Expect to use about 1MB per minute.
- When digitizing, use an S-Video input. Composite video is poorer quality.
- When digitizing, carefully adjust levels, particularly black levels. This cuts down on "noise."
- Capture at a larger size than you need and scale down later.
- Select a frame rate that fits your project. Twelve frames per second is a good compromise. A higher frame rate will likely require a special video card; a slower rate will look choppy.
- Select a data rate that fits the playback platform. Single-speed CD-ROM drives can play movies at 100Kbps, double-speed at about 170Kbps.
- Capture sound at no less than 22KHz.

There are more considerations, but these are enough to give you an idea of the complexity of video and CD-ROMs. It is the most dynamic segment of the CD-ROM publishing industry and requires a lengthy learning curve to get up to speed.

All your decisions regarding video affect the playback platforms. If you have control over your platform and the budget to match, aim high. Use MPEG video cards (described in Chapter 3) that can play full-screen, full-motion video with 32,000 colors. Sigma Designs' ReelMagic MPEG card lists for less than $500.

BEWARE OF COPYRIGHTS

Copyright conflicts can kill a project. This is becoming a quagmire for the entire CD-ROM publishing industry. Recently, a group of writers sued several major publishers, including the *New York Times* and Time-Warner, for publishing their work electronically. These publishers had contracted with the writers for articles to be published in print media. The authors claim that they never sold the electronic media rights to those articles.

Know who owns your content. You may think you have the right to use a photograph; you might even have paid a fee and have a contract to that effect. The person writing that contract may even own the rights to reproduce that photo, but he or she might not own the electronic rights. Those rights probably reside with the photographer. Run that photo in your product and you risk a lawsuit. When in doubt about rights, check with all the involved parties: the original publisher and the creator of the work.

Many so-called royalty-free products are not royalty free if you plan to use them in a product for sale. Or you cannot resell them as images for others to use.

Music is another headache. Sure, Beethoven's Fifth Symphony is in the public domain, but the New York Philharmonic's version of it is not. A MIDI file, even if it's "Old McDonald," can be copyrighted. And here's a kicker: "Happy Birthday to You" is copyrighted!

Obtaining licenses to use content is a very murky issue when it comes to CD-ROMs. Normal licensing rules do not apply. In book publishing or music recording, licensing agencies use a standard formula to determine royalties. Typically it includes the percentage of the product their content takes up and the product's list price. That simple formula does not work with CD-ROMs. There is no set number of pages on a CD-ROM, and due to the interactive nature of most CD-ROM products, it's possible that some people will never view a particular piece of content on a given disc they own.

Take care of your CD-ROM content licensing in the creative stage. Use friendly negotiation. A copyright attorney might be a good idea. Content is critical. Content drives your product. CD-ROMs will not be here forever, but your content can be.

PRODUCT DESIGN

If you haven't yet assembled a production team for your project, and you've gathered your content, now is the time. How users will navigate through your product is a key element in its performance and success. Failure to include your programmer, graphic designer, and interface designer in the overall planning can result in bottlenecks later and, ultimately, a product that does not perform its task. You risk losing that vision "thing" that you worked so hard to develop at the beginning.

An interface designer, by the way, has different skills than a graphic designer. The former deals with human factor issues, i.e., how people use a product. The latter deals primarily with artistic issues.

You're using a CD-ROM because of the massive amount of data it can hold. Organizing that data to create ease of use is your goal. While this book cannot begin to teach design skills, here are some basic tips:

- **Brainstorm:** Place your vision before your team and talk about it. What is your goal? What value will your product add to your data? What do you want the user to get out of your CD-ROM?
- **Flow chart:** There's nothing wrong with using a large blackboard or spreading some butcher's paper on a table and drafting your navigation plan.
- **Keep it simple:** If you're like other potential CD-ROM publishers, you begin with an elaborate, earthshaking vision. Now is the time to tone it down.
- **Narrow the focus while keeping your overall goal in mind:** When the flow chart looks like a Jackson Pollock painting, you're in trouble.
- **Index your data:** Whether your product is a game or an auto parts manual, give the user some additional control through an index or some other simplified system to go directly to a subject area. Design how that will work early in the process. As for index systems, there is no need to reinvent the wheel. Several off-the-shelf tools are available. Multi-Ad Search, from Multi-Ad Service, indexes image files. On Location, from On Technology, performs full-text searches. HyperKRS, from KnowledgeSet, conducts Boolean searches of Hypertext stacks.

PRODUCE AN INTERFACE

Simply stated, the interface is the device connecting the user to the CD-ROM. It usually combines a screen with several navigation buttons, the mouse, and keyboard. It also may tie in to your hard disk drive, printer, or modem for storage, output, or online access, respectively.

Navigating through your CD-ROM should be intuitive. The user shouldn't have to page through a huge manual just to learn how to page through your product. And the faster the user can arrive at a satisfactory destination, the better. Offer as many choices with each option as possible. Your CD-ROM should mimic real-life decision-making processes when it can.

Controlling the navigation process should be simple. Two common methods are mouse clicks, which are intuitive for most people, and typing search words, which is straightforward. If you have hidden "hot spots" on your screen (areas on which you have to click to produce an action), cause your mouse icon to change color or shape as it passes over them.

Make connections to the printer, modem, or hard disk drive transparent to the user. For example, your CD-ROM should automatically take care of configuration conflicts such as drivers competing for the same memory area during setup.

The screen interface should let the user know where he or she is in the program. One idea is to offer a pull-down listing of pages previously called up with the option to return directly to individual pages.

Let the user know what's going on. If the CD-ROM is loading a page (possibly a several-second process), make note of that on the screen display. When a task is completed, make sure the user knows it. Make it easy for the user to quit, start over, and get help.

LOOK AND FEEL

Screen displays make or break a product. Visual appeal, intuitive ease of use, and simplicity can mean the difference between a disc that users love or use as a coaster. Your graphic design is your product's face. Without it, it has no personality.

The look and feel may be nothing more than using the GUIs of the Mac or Windows. Or it may be as complex as creating new graphic backgrounds for each screen page. Many authoring programs have built-in options for a look and feel, and they are covered in the next section. If your product will run in-house and marketability is not a factor, these prepackaged options might be adequate. Otherwise the selection of your graphic artist is critical. Unless you know a good computer graphic artist or have one on staff, a service bureau can be a big help. This chapter will discuss service bureaus in more detail later.

AUTHORING

You have all this wonderful content, your graphics look hot, the interface is simplicity itself, and your design is a knockout. Now you need to put it all together. The least complex method is to use an off-the-shelf authoring tool. Creating your own proprietary authoring system or authoring a CD-ROM from scratch is a monumental task reserved for the Sierra On-Lines and LucasArts of the world.

Authoring software brings all the pieces of your product into one cohesive unit. Good authoring software can use a variety of file formats, including graphics, audio, and video. It allows users to create products heavy in interactivity and branching, permits access to a database, and tracks user responses. Software that can accomplish all that is, by definition, powerful. And taking full advantage of powerful software requires a lengthy learning curve.

If incorporating video into a CD-ROM is the most dynamic part of CD-ROM publishing, authoring is a close second. Keeping up with the latest authoring software is not for the fainthearted. Unless you intend to author several CD-ROMs, you might be better off leaving the authoring chore to a service bureau.

The principal factor that will narrow your authoring tool selection is the playback platform. Despite several authoring tools claiming to port across multiple platforms, at the moment there is no authoring language that is truly cross-platform transparent. At best they require some tweaking when the product is ported to a new platform. At worst, cross-platform porting is problematic. There are several pretenders to this throne and a couple more in the wings.

The number of potential platforms for which you can produce a disc is daunting: MS-DOS, MPC, Mac, CD-I, Sega, 3DO, and so on. No CD-ROM or authoring product runs on all these systems. Most have common format standards such as ISO 9660 or CD-ROM XA, but this is useful only for raw data files, not for the software required to access that data. Still, a common file format is important.

All authoring software can handle ISO 9660. Significant authoring software for CD-ROM XA includes Mammoth Micro Production's Studio XA. Studio XA allows for simultaneous development on Windows/MPC, OS/2, and Sony MMCD systems. Kaleida, an Apple and IBM partnership, is also working on an authoring language called ScriptX. It is intended to be the cross-platform solution, a truly device-independent, multimedia description language. Kaleida says it will have authoring software for Mac, Windows, and OS/2.

For the moment then, if you plan to go cross platform, that will likely be Mac to Windows, and some tools are geared to that. Multimedia artists and developers have traditionally favored Macs for their ease in graphics production. Therefore, most multimedia authoring tools have been Mac based, but parity between Mac and Windows has almost been reached. However, artists are reluctant to shift to the more popular PC platform. Projects on other platforms will probably require separate authoring for each playback system.

The platform, complexity of your product, and your budget dictate which authoring package will be right for your project. The following are descriptions of several popular authoring titles for the Mac and MS-

DOS/Windows PCs—the most popular CD-ROM authoring environments and playback platforms.

HyperCard

HyperCard, from Claris Corporation, is the grandfather of authoring tools. This Mac-based product is easy to use; allows integration of text, graphics, video, and audio; has a huge developer base; and has no run-time charges (i.e., Claris charges no royalties for its use in commercial products). Its retail price is about $200. Custom installation on the end user's part is one drawback, as is its lack of depth compared to more fully featured products.

Supercard

A step up from HyperCard is Supercard from Aldus. The added depth of this product brings with it an incremental increase in the user learning curve. Improvements over HyperCard include better animation and color support plus multiple window applications. It too has no run-time charges, and it retails for about $300.

Director

Director, from Macromedia, seems expensive at $1200, but it is the workhorse of Mac authoring tools. Its strong suit is its animation capabilities. The number of popular CD-ROM-based games authored on Director—Iron Helix, Journeyman Project, Spaceship Warlock, and C.H.A.O.S. Continuum, to name a few—bears this out. Director is interactively oriented and expects minimal text input from users. Macromedia describes it as lightning fast, yet most Director-authored games are very slow. Version 4 might correct that. It has good cross-platform porting to Windows and no run-time charges.

Producer Pro

At the higher end, Producer Pro, from Passport, uses a time line, much like an offline video editor, as its authoring system. Its forte is multimedia presentation using a variety of sources with frame-accurate playback. It allows for easy interactivity and graphic production, and incorporates dozens of built-in scene transitions and special effects. It has no run-time charges and has cross-platform support for Windows. Producer Pro sells for about $1500.

Authorware Pro

The first four authoring tools use scripting as the basis for development. Macromedia's Authorware Pro is an object-oriented, icon-based tool that allows for rapid design without scripting. Its quality and development speed live up to its $5000 price tag. The learning curve is minimal, as the tools are intuitive and powerful. The Mac version ports easily to Windows but the reverse is not the case. Its price puts it out of reach for most developers, but educational institutions can buy it for $1000. At that price it is a clear winner over Macromedia's other authoring tool, Director.

Multimedia Toolbook

Multimedia Toolbook, from Asymetrix, is the equivalent of an enhanced HyperCard for Windows. It is the authoring system of choice for many Windows-based developers. A series of linked pages with "hot" text buttons, media control objects, and text capturing capability, this authoring tool stands out in interactive multimedia products. Its drawbacks are its inadequate animation support, lack of depth, and single platform playback. However, it is a bargain at $400, and there are no run-time fees.

Multimedia Grasp

Multimedia GRASP (GRaphic Animation System for Professionals), from Paul Mace Software, is a high-end, script-based authoring system. This $1200 product is multimedia oriented, with a rich command set and video mode support. It has a lengthy learning curve but is a favorite among animation and special effects artists. GRASP is MS-DOS-based, but an add-on product, WinGrasp, allows demos to run in Windows. Interactivity is not its strong suit.

Icon Author

AimTech Corporation's Icon Author is at the top end of Windows-based authoring titles. It is an icon, flow chart system. Its ease of use, flexibility, and power make it a standout. Icon Author is one of those elegant programs that you can use right out of the box. But a four-day training program is included in the steep $5000 price. Its drawbacks are the price, plus heavy run-time fees for more than six users, and the basic limitations of visual-based authoring. Sometimes all those icons can clutter the screen.

THE NEXT GENERATION PRODUCTION TOOL?

MultiDoc from Foundation Solutions is a high-end production tool aimed at major reference-work publishers, who incorporate massive amounts of text, graphics, video, and sound into their CD-ROMs. It incorporates a very powerful search engine and text-capture and formatting capabilities. MultiDoc has built-in features to speed up CD-ROM performance, allowing complete text searches in as few as two CD-ROM seeks. It has already been used to create the Macintosh versions of Microsoft's Encarta '94 Multimedia Encyclopedia and Cinemania. This $7500 product works only on System 7 Macs.

TESTING

Testing should be an ongoing process. The purpose at this point in your production is not necessarily to see how your project will run on CD-ROM. Ask friends, co-workers, family members, and computer illiterates to try out your product before making your first trial CD-ROM pressing. What you want to learn here is

- ▶ **Interface:** Does it work? Where do users have problems?
- ▶ **Look and feel:** Is it effective? Too glitzy or cluttered? Understated or empty?
- ▶ **Vision:** Do users walk away having gained, learned, experienced what you intended way back when you first dreamed up this project?
- ▶ **Multimedia elements:** How does it sound? Is the video acceptable? Are there color shifts from one scene to another?

CREATE A ONE-OFF OR GOLD DISC

Once you're satisfied with your program, it's time to test its operation on a CD-ROM. Gird yourself for some unpleasant surprises. True, you can avoid some of these surprises by using software intended to simulate CD-ROM access speeds, but with bargain basement prices for single recordable CDs, you might as well check the real thing. What you'll need is a one-off.

A *one-off* or gold disc is a one-time creation of one or a very small number of CD-ROMs. These CD-ROM one-offs are produced on a CD-Recordable machine, which is described in Chapter 4. You want to use the gold disc to see how well your project really works on disc. This is the acid test. Don't be too disappointed if you find that it doesn't work as well as you'd like. Videos and graphics that quickly popped on screen from your hard disk drive will take a couple of seconds to load from your CD-ROM. Music that flowed smoothly from one screen shot to the next may cut off unexpectedly.

Does your one-off run on every platform and configuration? Testing on the Mac is straightforward; there just aren't many configuration options. PC configurations, on the other hand, are nearly infinite. Aim for standards such as MPC and Sound Blaster and still expect to run into setup conflicts. Some glitches go with the territory. Others you can repair with careful sequential placement of files on the CD-ROM. You can also load some material from your CD-ROM to the user's hard disk drive to create smoother transitions. Some CD-ROM-based entertainment titles put as much as 30MB on the hard drive. That is extreme, but a couple of megabytes is reasonable.

TIP CD-ROMs read files faster off the inner tracks, so place speed-critical files first.

Maybe you'll get it right the first time; more likely it will take several one-offs. The goal is to use the one-offs as the critical, final testing before mass production.

The next question is, how much of the one-off production process do you want to do? It's a two-step process: premaster the data and then copy it to the gold disc. Premastering basically converts your data into CD-ROM-readable files by adding error detection and error correction codes. Premastering software adds 144 bytes of coding to each kilobyte.

To premaster you need some expensive software, which you usually acquire when purchasing a CD-R machine. But you can buy it separately, premaster your data, and take it to a service bureau for a straight one-off copy. Blank gold discs run as low as $20 each, and service bureau one-off charges begin at $130. Expect to pay $6000 to $10,000 for a hardware/software CD-R bundle.

MASS PRODUCE YOUR CD-ROM

Congratulations! If you've reached this point with your original product vision intact, you have completed 99 percent of your task. You can mass produce your CD-ROM straight from your one-off. And you can do it in large quantities (10,000 or more) for as little as $1.50 per disc, printed with a two-color label, placed in a jewel case with artwork inserted. Smaller quantities (100 or so) can run up to $10 per disc. You can go to a number of production houses for your project, many of which are listed in Appendix B.

There are pitfalls here to be sure. Comparison shopping is encouraged, and close contact throughout the process is essential. But, if you use a one-off for your data master, very little can go wrong. Problems arise for those who insist on using some other portable form of data transfer such as DAT, U-Matic, or SyQuest Magneto Optical storage. There's nothing wrong with these formats, but glitches can occur with additional premastering and data transfer. Stick with one-offs.

DO-IT-YOURSELF VERSUS SERVICE BUREAUS

Multimedia production service bureaus save time. Also, for first-timers considering publishing in-house, service bureaus can ease that transition. Here are some of the advantages of using a service bureau:

- ▶ **Speed:** You hire an experienced staff accustomed to working in multimedia authoring and designing. No learning curve for you; no need to hunt for free-lance contractors to handle each development segment.

- ▶ **Depth:** Most service bureaus have multiple authoring tools, platforms, graphical, and interface production styles.

- ▶ **One-stop shopping:** You can have all the design, authoring, data handling, artwork and photo scanning, and video and audio digitizing done at one place.

- ▶ **No electronic paperweights:** If you bought a CD-R machine in 1990, you would have a $50,000, washing machine-sized dust collector sitting in some dark corner today.

Service bureaus present some disadvantages, too:

- ▶ **Higher costs:** You pay for the bureau's overhead.
- ▶ **Loss of control:** Inherent in any extra layer of product management is some loss of control.

A SERVICE BUREAU STORY

This example is indicative of the fragmented yet collaborative nature of low-level commercial CD-ROM publishing. The School Company in Vancouver, Washington, specializes in products intended to help young people make early career choices. They have an extensive video library and wanted to use some video clips in an interactive CD-ROM focusing on the Occupational Outlook Handbook, but they did not have the expertise or the time to acquire that expertise. So they hired a Portland, Oregon, video production company to oversee the project. This company subcontracted with Planet Productions, a Portland multimedia service bureau, to do the authoring, interface, graphics, and content capturing. Planet further subcontracted some HyperCard authoring to a company specializing in Mac-based systems.

The finished product was to be a CD-ROM, playable on Mac and MPC systems. Since this was an interactive product with a large database and substantial use of video, Planet Productions opted to author it in Multimedia Toolbook. Planet digitized the edited video and audio clips, enhanced some existing graphics, fine-tuned the extensive database, and created a straightforward button interface. In addition, they altered the client's proposed flow chart to improve the product's presentation on CD-ROM.

Planet put the MPC and Mac versions on separate SyQuest removable media and used a Seattle service bureau for the one-off. That bureau created a hybrid disc, hard partitioned with the MPC and Mac versions in different locations on the disc. The first one-off had a few bugs, which Planet corrected in the second.

Sony did the final production run using the second one-off as a master and charged $1000 for the first 100 discs with jewel case, label art, and insertion of client-provided manuals.

Chapter 7

Publishing in-house requires dedicated hardware and probably additional personnel. Personnel costs are too variable for an estimate here, but the following table gives you an idea of equipment and software costs. You will need a reasonably powerful computer with at least twice as much hard disk storage as your project plus authoring software, a CD-R drive, and some other data handling items:

486 PC or Mac system with 1.3Gb hard disk drive	$5,000
Authoring software, both high and low end	6,000
Color scanner, video input card, DAT drive	3,000
CD-R machine with premastering software	10,000
Total	$24,000

This does not have to be an all-or-nothing proposition. There is middle ground. Your decision about publishing in-house depends on the number and frequency of CD-ROMs published, the existing expertise, and budgets.

Try a combination approach at first. Contact some multimedia service bureaus. All major metropolitan areas should have several. You can begin your search by calling an established video production company, which may have a service bureau subsidiary or will know where to turn. Present your proposal and evaluate the responses.

Select a bureau with the understanding that you want to do as much of the preliminary work as possible—for instance: data acquisition, product flow charting, and video editing. Then turn interface, graphic and final product design, authoring, and data porting over to the bureau. Get your feet wet by looking over the shoulders of the artists and programmers. You will learn that, like laws and sausage, multimedia is something painful to watch in the making.

One other benefit from this process is the knowledge you will gain of your region's multimedia community. It is likely to be a close-knit group of people. For future projects you might want to farm out some of your work to the better free-lance contractors who you will meet or learn about.

Chapter 7

MARKETING AND DISTRIBUTING YOUR CD-ROM

Most CD-ROM publishers create titles for sale. InfoTech, a Vermont-based CD-ROM research firm, estimates two out of every three CD-ROM titles are produced for the commercial market. At last count about 5000 commercial titles were vying for the public's dollars. Not many are successful. Merisel, a software distribution company, estimates that only 1 out of 10 CD-ROM titles it carries sells well enough to warrant keeping in its catalog.

The CD-ROM market is immature, unsophisticated, and experiencing serious growing pains. CD-ROMs do not fall into a convenient sales niche. They are not simply software. They are encyclopedias, photo libraries, medical reference material, and even X-rated movies. Traditional retail outlets are reluctant to stock CD-ROMs, since they can't pigeonhole them (though this is changing, as Chapter 9 points out). In addition, the distribution network is just starting to take form. This is a growing industry that has yet to clearly define where it fits in the marketplace.

As a commercial CD-ROM title developer you have a mind-numbing plethora of marketing and distribution possibilities. The basis for your decision will be your willingness to spend time and money. Ask yourself this: Do you want to make dozens of sales deals with retail chains, wholesalers, individual retail customers, mail-order outfits, and CD-ROM manufacturers and distributors? How about marketing? Do you want to design and place advertisements, attend trade shows, and stuff envelopes? And then there's technical support. Do you have the patience, time, and personnel to answer technical calls from up to half of those who buy your CD-ROM? Your answers will determine what kind of marketing and distribution scheme is best for you. Here are a few options:

▶ **Self-publish:** This is for those who answered "yes" to all of the preceding questions. Your risks and work load will be overwhelming. You also stand the best chance of reaping the highest rewards.

▶ **Affiliate:** In this case you take your product to the final packaged stage. Then you work out a deal with one of several affiliate labels to have them distribute and possibly do the marketing and provide technical support. You usually receive approximately 30 percent of the list price. Claris Corporation and Electronic Arts, for example, both have affiliate programs.

▶ **Develop only:** In much the same way as a book author, you finish your product and pass the gold disc (the manuscript) to a publisher. If that publisher likes your work, it does the packaging, marketing, technical support, and pays you a royalty. Unlike the book publishing industry, where a 15 percent royalty is common, CD-ROM publishers typically pay only about 10 percent. Some well-known publishers are Broderbund, Software ToolWorks, Compton's NewMedia, Electronic Arts, and Time-Warner Interactive Group.

The truth is, you may be better off using all three approaches to varying degrees, along with several other sales tools. You might work out an affiliate arrangement and still approach major distributors such as Baker & Taylor Software, Ingram-Micro, and Merisel. You can call on retail chains such as CompUSA, Egghead, and Software Etc. And you can sell direct through mail order.

Your goal may be to eventually self-publish. This will work especially well if you plan a series of similar, niche-oriented products. Using registration cards in your product, even if it is sold through an affiliate or publisher, you can create a database of loyal customers who might buy directly from you if you later turn to self-publishing.

You can bundle your CD-ROM. Most CD-ROM drive upgrades come with several CD-ROM titles. This is bundling. The CD-ROM drive distributor typically pays a royalty to the developer or publisher and presses its own copies of the title. This is usually a very low-profit margin process, but it provides excellent exposure.

CD-ROMs lend themselves to rental and "try before you buy" schemes. This is one market that rankles software executives who believe, justifiably, that many who rent software copy it to their hard drives and continue to use it long after returning it to the rental store. CD-ROMs change that. Compton's NewMedia is leading this charge. It is practically impossible to copy its Interactive Encyclopedia and most other CD-ROM-based titles to a hard disk drive, so Compton's has worked out a rental arrangement with Blockbuster Video and other rental chains. If it is as successful as similar "try before you buy" programs for video games, this will be an excellent CD-ROM sales tool.

CD-ROMs also exploit one other new sales technique: data-file unlocking. CD-ROM distributors can place several programs, font files, or entertainment titles on a CD-ROM and have them run in a demo or limited-access format. The cost to create such CD-ROMs is minimal, as they need only a simple interface. Thus a distributor, publisher, or developer can put their products in the hands of potential purchasers for less than $2 per prospect.

Potential customers can then try out the titles. If they want one or more titles, all that's needed to make a purchase is a phone call and a credit card. The order taker gives customers a set of file-unlocking alphanumeric codes to key into their computer, and they can immediately begin using the titles ordered. Any manuals or other support material will come in the mail. This is a marketing concept that the CD-ROM industry has barely begun exploiting, but it could become a major sales tool.

Finally, don't forget international sales, where a huge market exists. If you have a product with universal appeal, CD-ROMs are an excellent delivery platform. It is reasonably easy to add multilingual sound tracks and text, especially with CD-I titles. Distribution, on the other hand, is at least as complicated as it is in the United States. One good contact is the Federation of International Distributors in Boston, Massachusetts. Their telephone number is (617) 742-5599.

COMMERCIAL CD-ROM PRODUCTION CONSIDERATIONS

For those planning to produce a CD-ROM for the commercial market there are a few other points to ponder:

- ▶ **Advertising:** Recent data from PC Data show, 9 out of 10 of the top-selling CD-ROM titles advertise. Out of those ranked 21 through 30, only 1 advertised. One action does not necessarily lead to the other, but there is a pattern here.

- ▶ **More advertising:** Do not underestimate the value of bulletin boards. Word of mouth can drive sales, as can properly placed news releases and review copies.

- ▶ **Platform:** The same survey in PC Data showed that 90 of the top 100 titles were PC based. Six were dual format (PC and Mac) and only four were Macintosh only.

- ▶ **CD-ROM-drive installed base:** Half are only single-speed drives.

- ▶ **CD-ROM drive users:** Nearly all are male, and most are adults between 30 and 45 years old.

- ▶ **Packaging:** Why do CDs need such large boxes? Exciting packaging pumps up retail sales. Grab customers' attention and show them your product with screen shots.

BOTTOM LINE TIME

The question now is, can you make any money at this? The answer is yes, but it won't be easy. Consider the following: A typical consumer CD-ROM title might cost $50,000 to develop. That covers content, design, authoring, gold discs, and artwork for packaging and advertising. This is just a ball-park figure; some game titles cost more than $1 million.

If you work with an affiliate, you provide the CD-ROM and packaging. That amounts to about $2 per disc in quantity. The affiliate pays you 30 percent of list price, which, for the example used here, is $40. You can also bundle your title and receive a royalty of only $2 to $5 per disc. There is no additional cost to you since the bundler presses and packages the disc.

You also may sell directly through the mail—high gross profit margin but a headache to administer. Plus you can work deals with mail-order distributors by buying pages in catalogs or providing your CD-ROM at a greatly reduced cost. This is another way to get exposure but at a minimal profit.

A title is considered reasonably popular if it sells 5000 copies. Table 7-1 presents one basic scenario.

Type of Sales	Units	Cost per Unit	Total Cost	Revenue per Unit	Total Revenue
Affiliate sales	2,500	$2 ea.	$ 5,000	30% of $40	$30,000
Bundled sales	2,000	$0	$ 0	$3 royalty	$ 6,000
Mail order	500	$2 ea.	$ 1,000	$38 gross	$19,000
Administration, tech support (approximate cost)			$20,000		
Development cost			$50,000		
TOTALS	5,000		$76,000		$55,000

TABLE 7-1

Sample Cost/Revenue Breakdown

As mentioned before, the development cost was $50,000. Add another $20,000 for administrative and technical support costs. The total costs, therefore, are $76,000. The revenues are $55,000. So in this example you lose $21,000. The break-even sales figure for this simplified scenario is slightly more than 7000 units. This is a rough-and-tumble industry. The public has just begun to see the value of CD-ROM drives. As of this writing, no developer has created a killer CD-ROM application to drive hardware sales.

ESCAPING THE MINEFIELD WITH $5 MILLION

Sales of The 7th Guest will likely hit 1 million by the time this book is printed. No other CD-ROM has had that level of success. This interactive horror drama has ratcheted CD-ROM entertainment technology and gaming several notches forward. Its developers are gurus of this evolving industry.

Those developers are Guest's programmer, Graeme Devine, and its graphic designer, Rob Landeros. Both worked for Virgin Games' U.S. division in 1990. "Back then," Devine says, "CD-ROMs had a home penetration of zero." They concluded that this emerging platform would demand a new genre of computer game, one with more dramatic content, better plots, real people with real voices, more interactivity, and greater ease of play.

Devine and Landeros had an idea for a Clue-type game with *Twin Peaks* overtones that evolved into an interactive drama in a haunted house. Virgin Games put up $400,000 against future royalties. "Virgin believed we would create a profitable floppy disk product," Devine says. "They were certain a CD-ROM version would lose money hand over fist." Nintendo kicked in $300,000 more, and Devine and Landeros formed their own company, Trilobyte. "An ugly little fossil but an instant logo and instant history," Devine says.

Bringing full-screen, 256-color graphics and video, plus CD and MIDI audio to a PC required creating an authoring system and video compression technology from scratch. This consumed more than two years of Devine's time. Meantime Landeros created a 22-room, fully 3-D rendered haunted mansion using Autodesk's 3D Studio.

Virgin Games previewed The 7th Guest at the January 1992 Consumer Electronics Show to overflow crowds and rave reviews. "People started calling it the most anticipated product ever. It just blew us away," says Devine. "We looked at each other and said 'We bloody well better finish this.'"

They did not know it then, but they would need 15 more months to complete Guest, nearly three years in all. They ran out of money and steam several months before completion. "The final three months were the deepest, darkest, most abysmal I've ever lived," Devine recalls. "They were horrible, very depressing times."

They released Guest in April 1993. It has generated $5 million in royalties. Its sequel, XIth Hour: The 7th Guest Part II, will come out in the Spring of 1994. Devine and Landeros have several other titles in production, and at last word, 10 Hollywood entertainment companies were trying to buy a piece of Trilobyte.

CD-ROMs offer infinite possibilities. Never before has one product combined audio, video, and interactivity in such depth. Soon the technology will be transparent, simply another tool in an increasing spectrum of creative possibilities. Those who exploit this dynamic technology's assets will lead the creative revolution.

CHAPTER 8

Using CD-ROM on a Network

In an ideal work situation, all employees with a need to access CD-ROM-based data would have a CD-ROM drive attached to their computer and, within arm's reach, a copy of every title that they might need. But for most companies, economics dictate otherwise. Accessing CD-ROM-based data often means borrowing someone else's computer or sharing a dedicated workstation. The most popular discs are sometimes hard to track down, as people tend to use them for a project and not return them to their proper location.

Buying drives and discs for everyone is rarely practical. For a rough comparison, the average bare-bones double-speed CD-ROM drive today costs about $200. This does not include installation and setup charges. It is not unusual to find businesses with 100, 200, or even thousands of employees with a need for data on CD-ROM.

It may not even be a question of buying stand-alone versus networked CD-ROM drives and titles. Some databases sold on CD-ROM are also available via online services. Over time, the access and connect-time fees for online information can become prohibitively expensive and inefficient. What often happens is that several people within a company access the same information at different times. It makes no sense for a company to pay for that same information more than once.

Chapter 8

There has to be a better way to share and access both commercial and in-house databases, and there is: place both the hardware and the software on the company's network.

There are a number of good options that provide network access to information on CD-ROMs. These range from simply attaching a single drive on the server to building a dedicated CD-ROM-based network. New tools are making the job easier and, once installed, more manageable. Best of all, networked CD-ROM is the most cost efficient and productive way to get data to where it is needed in the company.

There are two main types of local area networks (LANs): server-based and peer-based. On a *server-based LAN*, one or more systems act as servers (also called hosts). The computers attached to the server via the LAN are called *clients* or *nodes*. The client computers access the network's services—printers, stored data (including that on CD-ROM), electronic mail, modems, and so on—by going through the server. Novell Netware and Banyan VINES are two examples of server-based networks. Figure 8-1 shows a typical server-based LAN setup.

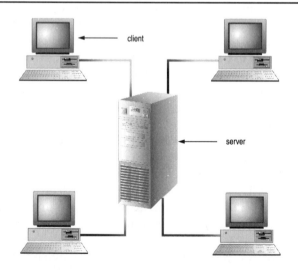

FIGURE 8-1
Typical server-based LAN

Using CD-ROM on a Network   239

Chapter 8

A *peer-based LAN* has no dedicated server. Every computer on the network is more or less equal and "aware" of one another. Everyone on the peer-based LAN has access to the same types of resources, but those resources are more distributed throughout the network. For example, a CD-ROM drive can reside as a dedicated unit attached to the network, or it can be part of someone's desktop system. That person, then, is sharing his or her CD-ROM drive with everyone else on the network. Artisoft's LANtastic is the most popular peer-based LAN. Figure 8-2 shows a typical peer-based LAN setup.

This chapter assumes some familiarity with basic networking concepts. The creation and maintenance of networks is a complex topic and beyond the scope of this book. Many good networking references are available, including Tom Sheldon's *Novell NetWare 4: The Complete Reference* (Osborne/McGraw-Hill, 1993).

SERVER-BASED LANS

CD-ROM drives may be connected to a network simply to provide text-based information in databases to a group of people. Or, depending on your vision of long-term needs, CD-ROM networking may be merely one

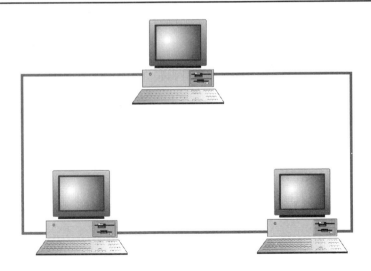

FIGURE 8-2
Typical peer-based LAN

Chapter 8

spoke of a wheel that encompasses distributed multimedia applications in many forms across a multiplatform network. Needless to say, this complicates the process. First, however, let's deal with the task of connecting a drive to a LAN.

If what you need is to network one or more CD-ROM drives to a server-based LAN without connecting additional SCSI devices—for example, a magneto-optical drive—to the same controller, a plethora of solutions awaits. These solutions are split into three major groups: Tower products (also called jukeboxes) comprise the CD-ROM drive/cabinet components you need in order to hook up multiple drives to a dedicated server. Second, the CD-ROM server package incorporates a server PC with the tower cabinet.

Finally, a Netware Loadable Module (NLM) uses the standard cache RAM on the Novell file server to accommodate directly connected drives that do not use a separate server. An NLM is software that adds to or enhances features of a Netware server. Two of the NLM solutions worth considering, Micro Design's SCSI Express and Corel's CorelSCSI, also support other SCSI devices. NLMs will be discussed in the section, "Netware and NLMs," later in this chapter.

TOWER PRODUCTS

Tower products are born of convenience. Rather than stack a bunch of CD-ROM drives, perhaps bought from and manufactured by several vendors, you purchase a sleek, all-in-one case with streamlined connections to a computer you designate as a CD-ROM or multimedia server. Towers typically have one controller driving up to seven CD-ROM or other SCSI drives. Each additional controller can support another seven devices. Depending upon the product, the server may not need to be dedicated exclusively as a CD-ROM or other type of SCSI server. Data traffic over the computer's I/O bus, however, may demand that the server be dedicated. The best of these products will let you add more drives or combine towers like building blocks. As more and more CD-ROM titles become available, after all, you might discover you provided for too little CD-ROM access. Buy a system you may need to supplement, not replace.

One computer-less solution is Online Computer Systems' Optical Storage Units (OSUs). Available in SCSI or non-SCSI versions, OSUs can work with a minimum of two drives. The SCSI version supports up to seven drives off a controller installed in a CD server. (OSUs support several brands besides the one made by Online Computer Systems.)

For a four-drive setup, consider the CD/Quartet from Optical Access International (OAI). Shown in Figure 8-3, this tower case integrates four

Using CD-ROM on a Network **241**

Chapter 8

FIGURE 8-3
CD/Quartet from Optical Access International

SCSI-2, 180 or 240 ms drives (depending on the model). It also includes two isolated 150W power supplies, a cooling fan, and OAI's SuperCache software, which installs on your CD server PC and works in concert with that system's cache to speed throughput. Networks can include Apple's AppleShare, Apple's System 7 with its built-in file-sharing facility, Novell's Netware, and Sitka's TOPS (no longer manufactured). Clients can be Macintosh or MS-DOS/Windows PC systems.

Legacy Storage Systems' M.A.S.S. SL CD-ROM is an eight-drive subsystem that supports MS-DOS, Windows, OS/2, and Netware 3.x or higher. Included with the tower is a utility that lets network administrators test the drives, the interface card, and the cable connection. A locking front door keeps prying hands from the discs kept in the drives.

Near the high end of processor-less tower systems are products like CD/Maxtet, also from OAI. The 7-drive tower, shown in Figure 8-4, places the drives under a single SCSI ID. This placement lets you add up to five more CD/Maxtets for a total of 42 drives. Four isolated 300W power supplies, SuperCache software, and three cooling fans round out the package. The isolated power supplies and fans help ensure system reliability.

If your CD-ROM access needs lie in the 100Gb range, you may want to consider a multidisc changer instead of a tower system. A changer may

Chapter 8

FIGURE 8-4
CD/Maxtet from Optical Access International

include as few as one actual (standard) CD-ROM drive and one read head; typically they have one to four drives. A robotic changing mechanism switches discs in and out, jukebox-style, using control software and a SCSI interface. Minichangers are simply small multidisc changers. One such product, the Kubik CD240 Compact Disc changer from Kubik Technologies, lets you store and retrieve about 160Gb of data (240 discs) through a 7-by-18-by-18-inch unit (see Figure 8-5). The company claims an average 7-second access to any disc. A four-drive unit is also available, and you can stack changers if you need more capacity.

Most vendors of CD-ROM tower products don't leave the choice of computer brand to the end user, believing themselves to be the best judges of how best to optimize the computer-to-CD-ROM subsystem. However, vendors like Online Computer Systems, Meridian Data, and Micro Design do let you purchase the software separately for use with another vendor's computer/tower combination. And once you add on a processor, a few megabytes

Using CD-ROM on a Network   **243**

Chapter 8

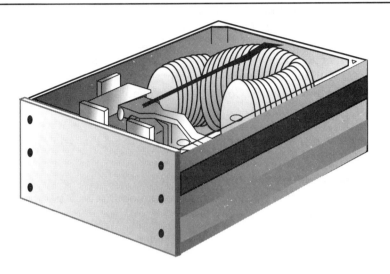

FIGURE 8-5
Kubik CD240 Compact Disc changer

of RAM, and other components, the number of drives supportable in a single tower goes up as well. Here are a few CD-ROM tower systems:

▶ **Meridian Data's CD Net Model 100NC:** This is a 7-, 14-, or 28-drive tower that includes a 386 or 486 processor, a 3.5-inch floppy drive, and 4MB RAM. CD Net software (covered later in "Netware and NLMs") is included, and the server supports NetBIOS or Netware LANs.

▶ **Virtual Microsystems' CDWorks 1000:** The CDWorks 1000 can act as an application server for PCs, Macintoshes, DEC VAX clients, and VT terminals on Ethernet networks. Up to seven processors can combine with up to 49 CD-ROM drives, although systems start with 14 or 21 drives and 8MB RAM.

▶ **CBIS' CD Server 2000:** This actually represents a family of servers that, depending on the model, can put a 14-drive tower subsystem (or a 28-drive, two-unit system) on a dedicated-only server supplied by the vendor. Full systems include a 386 or 486 processor, 4MB RAM, and a floppy drive; conversion towers add 7-drive capability to existing PCs.

Chapter 8

At the high end of SCSI servers is Digital Equipment Corporation's InfoServer 1000 (see Figure 8-6), which is impressive for its scalability. Of course, DEC is not alone in its modular, building-block approach, though other solutions fall short in overall functionality. Where DEC also stands out is with the sheer number of different platforms it supports as clients over an Ethernet network. Components available in the InfoServer 1000 line include:

▶ **InfoServer Local Area CD (LA CD):** This is the InfoServer 1000 base unit—a single tabletop CD-ROM drive that you can combine with other drives.

▶ **InfoServer Librarian:** This is a four- or seven-drive cabinet housed with the base unit; it can accommodate any 5.25-inch SCSI device.

▶ **InfoServer Scribe:** This consists of the base unit and tape backup software for OpenVMS systems. Norton Backup for Windows, from Symantec, lets you extend InfoServer Scribe's functionality to users of Windows and InfoServer Client for DOS.

▶ **InfoServer Publisher:** This lets you write to CD-Recordable (CD-R) discs.

FIGURE 8-6
DEC's Infoserver 1000

Clients that can access InfoServer include MS-DOS (including DEC's Pathworks and Novell Netware), Windows, Macintosh, Ultrix/RISC and /VAX, OpenVMS, and Unix. KI Research separately licenses Unix-variant clients.

BEYOND CD-ROM, BEYOND SCSI

The products discussed in this chapter up to now are mostly CD-ROM-only solutions, typically SCSI-based. For companies that want to integrate not only SCSI devices like CD-ROM but also multimedia devices like analog or digital full-motion video, audio, data services, and graphics, a much broader view is necessary. One such view is expressed in IBM's Ultimedia strategy, which is now coming to fruition.

IBM's Ultimedia has been years in planning and runs the gamut of company divisions and product lines. It can best be described as the transparent delivery of multimedia information, in all forms, across a heterogeneous network. Ideally, this means that any network user, anywhere in a company, could access not only CD-ROM drives but also other multimedia in VHS, laser videodisc, and other forms of storage—not to mention the vast amounts of text, graphics, and data—no matter where the devices are physically located.

IBM is expected to support all popularly accepted standards of compression and transmission. A developer should be able to write an application once for network stations comprising any hardware platform through ScriptX, a cross-platform development tool made by Kalieda in a joint venture with Apple Computer.

Supported Ultimedia clients so far include only MS-DOS, Windows, and OS/2 over Ethernet or Token Ring. IBM expects, however, that network users should be able to access all this through MS-DOS, Microsoft Windows, IBM's OS/2, Apple's System 7, Novell's Netware, IBM's AIX, or any other operating system. Not surprisingly, Big Blue is hinging much of its strategy on the operating system it feels will deliver the most capability: OS/2. As a multimedia environment, OS/2 does have a lot to offer with its multitasking capability and multimedia extensions. At this writing, it was uncertain whether Microsoft would support ScriptX for Windows NT across Intel-based and other hardware platforms.

Network Support Under OS/2

So far, OS/2 provides no specific support for CD-ROM networking. The operating system sees a CD-ROM drive or tower as just another device—subject to security that the network administrator sets up through OS/2 LAN

Server (IBM's network operating system for OS/2). Consequently, OS/2 manages simultaneous multiuser access and maintains complete control of cache RAM for CD-ROM drives and other devices that require caching. It is up to the application running the drive(s) to provide specific functions such as recognizing multiple-disc titles.

Nonetheless, OS/2 LAN Server does address the issues of accessing multimedia across a LAN. LAN Server Ultimedia, announced in November 1993, does much to prioritize the streams of audio and video information that, if mishandled, can result in a choppy, unsynchronized flow of information. Audio and video streams hold a higher priority than ordinary data, which helps deliver audio and video *isochronously*, (at the same time).

As you might expect, the difficult part of this shows up when your data simply cannot wait, or cannot wait for long, behind multimedia streams. If you're the one accessing the multimedia, one challenge is mechanical: keeping the flow when more than one network user is accessing full-motion video with audio—say, a training video clip—from a single disc at the same time. In a network with heavy multimedia traffic, sometimes bumping up the Ethernet from 10Mbps (megabits per second) to 100Mbps will help alleviate the delays. Of course, increasing performance to that level is an expensive proposition.

If you plan to have network users accessing multimedia from other networks using TCP/IP (transmission control protocol/Internet protocol), rest assured that TCP/IP will get the packets there and in the right order. What TCP/IP won't ensure without help is that the gap between one block of video and the next one that follows is within an acceptable amount of time to prevent dropped video frames and choppiness. The smaller audio stream itself can be sent in advance and buffered as necessary.

OS/2's chief competition, Windows NT, supports CD-ROM sharing among clients running MS-DOS, Windows (including Windows for Workgroups), Windows NT, OS/2 1.x and 2.x, and FTP (file-transfer protocol) agents on any machine that can make the physical connection. FTP allows CD-ROM sharing over the Internet, but this is chiefly intended for ordinary data, not multimedia. Macintosh clients can access NT Advanced Server's CD-ROM drives, but NT does not support the Macintosh HFS (Hierarchical File System) format. However, Apple will provide a redirector for ISO 9660 and MSCDEX support on a heterogeneous network.

MS-DOS and Windows clients run Workgroup Connection, a redirector provided by Microsoft for free or, for a site license, a fee for the documentation. Rights are handled through the shared system's File Manager, with metering capability if the company needs to limit the number of copies of a title in use at any one time. Also, a tool called Performance Monitor gives you a variety of statistics on CD-ROM and other device usage.

NETWORK TO NETWORK

Sending data from a CD-ROM from one network to another presents its own problems. A network made up of different LANs in different locations is called a *wide area network (WAN)*. The connections are usually made through devices called routers and bridges. A *router* is a hardware device that routes messages from one LAN to another similar one. A *bridge* is a hardware device that connects two similar LANs.

Until recently, one of the problems with WANs was that network users who needed to access CD-ROM and other data on another network across a router often met resistance. Wide-Area Network Broadcast, the routing mechanism most commonly used, didn't always let clients' requests for data get across a router from one subnetwork to the rest of the network. Bridges present no such problem, since they connect subnetworks into one logical whole.

Through another broadcast mechanism that has actually been available since Netware 2.15, Service Advertising Protocol (SAP), clients accessing one or more CD-ROM drives across a router from a subnetwork can now find their way to the server with the help of Netware's bindery (called Directory Services from version 4.0 onward). Meridian Data is one of many vendors that are employing this more reliable means of internetworking CD-ROM and other services.

PERFORMANCE ISSUES: THE CACHING ADVANTAGE

The typical access speed of today's double-speed CD-ROM drives falls in the range of 200 to 400 ms. When you consider the speeds of average hard disk drives—12 to 14 ms—you quickly see how far behind CD-ROM remains in comparison with other electronic storage media. Put a CD-ROM drive on a network, however, and you see a performance advantage. This is ironic considering that a stand-alone computer can often run an application faster locally than it can over the network. The biggest reason for the CD-ROM's advantage is caching. A stand-alone CD-ROM drive commonly includes a 64K

Chapter 8

to 256K buffer, which acts mostly to maintain an even flow of accessed information. But on a dedicated CD-ROM server, a megabyte of properly implemented cache RAM devoted to each networked CD-ROM drive achieves far speedier access than possible from a stand-alone station.

CD Connection 3.0 from CBIS is one example of CD-ROM networking software that makes the most of caching algorithms. The software can run with your existing hardware, with the vendor's full CD Server PC/drive-chassis packages, or with one of CBIS' drive chassis towers added onto your existing server. Supported networks are Novell Netware, Banyan VINES, CBIS' Network-OS Plus, and all NetBIOS-compatible LANs.

Adding cache memory to your file server can improve performance, providing that the data you are accessing off the CD-ROM is accessed with enough frequency that the cache can play a role. Consider, for instance, a CD-ROM server outfitted with several CD-ROM drives, each of which is running a different CD-ROM title that is accessed about as frequently as the next. If networked users typically access the server, perform a single search, and then move on to other applications that don't involve the CD-ROM, then the cache advantage may seldom come into play. Cache, after all, shows its stuff on subsequent queries. After that first query, subsequent queries to that same application from the same or different users could see performance double or better.

Of course, a properly implemented cache isn't a perfect solution even for multiple networked drives running the same CD-ROM application. A 100 percent *hit rate* (meaning the data is accessed from cache memory and not from the disc) on cache queries won't help you if you typically have too many users accessing the CD-ROM data at the same time. What is the solution? Choose a CD-ROM networking solution that permits as many drives per server as you expect you will ever need. Or go with a product that lets workstations with available extended memory devote some of that RAM to client-side caching of frequently used CD-ROM data. Online Computer Systems' Opti-Net NLM 2.0 for Netware is one such product.

Multitasking improves performance, too. A server with the ability to multitask, through an advanced operating system such as Windows NT, OS/2, or Netware, can receive one or more requests just as it is completing another. Operating systems with symmetric multiprocessing (SMP) capability (OS/2 2.2 or Windows NT, for instance) have another advantage. *Symmetric multiprocessing* is a system architecture that incorporates more than one main processor. Servers with multiple processors can simultaneously handle several requests for data from the CD-ROM, even while non-CD-ROM applications are being run from the same server. Note that both multitasking and multiprocessing capability shows the most benefit amid CD-ROM data requests from many users. The fewer the users, the more the cache alone acts to speed networked access.

NETWARE AND NLMS

Beginning with version 3.12, Novell Netware includes a loadable volume, CDROM.NLM, which lets you load CD-ROM drives as network disk volumes without any need for workstations to load TSRs or MSCDEX. The NLM lets you list available CD-ROM devices (in groups of 10 at a time) by device and drive numbers, mount drives by device number and volume name, change the disc within a mounted drive, and view the contents of the volume's root directory. Novell recommends you devote 1.2MB of cache for each drive you intend to network.

If you expect many (say 10 or more) users to access the Novell-mounted CD-ROM drives simultaneously, you may find the I/O traffic brings your server performance to a virtual standstill or even hangs the server. Your best bet then, is to go with a third-party NLM or another solution that allows the option of putting your drives on a separate, dedicated CD-ROM server. The latter solution includes Meridian Data's CD Net and CBIS' CD Connection. Lotus Development's Lotus CD/Networker (a software solution for NetBIOS, Banyan VINES, or Netware IPX/SPX) will install only on a dedicated CD-ROM server.

If Novell's CDROM.NLM won't work for you, several third-party products available for Netware install as NLMs and enjoy similar status to CDROM.NLM: full integration with Netware security features and ample means of configuring and accessing CD-ROM resources on a network. A few vendors, including Meridian Data, CBIS, and Micro Design, sell hardware/software combinations as well as the software component alone. These companies advise you to use their hardware, too, for optimal performance; but if you've already made a substantial hardware investment and have the know-how, there's no reason why you couldn't realize similar performance levels using other hardware.

CD Net 4.4 for Netware, from Meridian Data, is an NLM for Netware 3.x and 4.x servers that lets you configure up to 28 CD-ROM drives per server as either DOS drives or Netware volumes. Workstations can use any of the networked discs to which the network administrator has permitted access (though they each must run Meridian's driver or MSCDEX), and CD Net's 12K workstation driver is a removable TSR.

Chapter 8

A technique Meridian calls dynamic load balancing (the name differs from product to product) has CD Net distribute CD requests to the least-used duplicate title in the CD Net server (see Figure 8-7). If you're running CD Net from Windows, one feature worth mentioning is the software's ability to transparently map several CD-ROM applications, one at a time, to a single local drive letter and make the change as you go from window to window.

In addition to the NLM version, Meridian's software is available in a NetBIOS version for Netware (not running IPX), 3Com 3+Open, Microsoft LAN Manager, Ungermann-Bass, AT&T StarLAN, and IBM's LAN Server. Network topologies can be Ethernet, Token Ring, or Arcnet; and drives may be run from a separate CD-ROM server, using Meridian's hardware if you desire.

Another solution, SCSI Express 600CDX from Micro Design (see Figure 8-8), is a hardware/software solution that supports MS-DOS, Netware 3.x, OS/2, Sun, AIX, HP/UX, and Unix (SCO Unix and Xenix, Interactive Unix). The Netware 3.x version also provides access to CD-ROM drives (ISO 9660, High Sierra, and Macintosh HFS formats) as Netware volumes. You'll need to add at least 1MB of nondedicated cache RAM to the server for each networked CD-ROM drive. The good news is that, in most cases, you need to load nothing

FIGURE 8-7
Meridian Data's CD Net server

FIGURE 8-8
Micro Design's SCSI Express 600CDX

whatsoever on the client workstations even if the CD-ROM application requires MSCDEX. As the name implies, SCSI Express also supports other SCSI devices such as hard disk drives, digital audio tape (DAT) backup drives, and multifunction drives.

One new feature of SCSI Express, a utility called CDUTIL.NLM, guides the user through the process of making a file set containing the most-often queried data to speed database searches. It lets you assign trustees who have access to a particular file set upon its creation. CDUTIL.NLM also provides work-arounds for deficiencies if the CD-ROM was mastered slightly off the proper file format specification.

Opti-Net NLM 2.0 for Netware from Online Computer Systems is a software-only solution that can support servers in a mixed Netware 3.x and 4.x environment or a Netware or other LAN running NetBIOS. A nice feature of Opti-Net is that although it requires you to load device drivers and MSCDEX onto each client workstation, users can remove them from memory when they are no longer needed without rebooting the system. For the LAN administrator, a monitoring tool allows enforcement of licensed concurrent-user limits.

Because Opti-Net can address CD-ROM drives by Logical Unit Numbers (LUNs), each of seven SCSI devices connected to the board can in turn support seven additional drives. In other words, a server hosting four SCSI adapters under the LUN system could accommodate a maximum of 224 CD-ROM drives per server.

Typically, CD-ROM networking solutions take either a standard Novell Netware NLM approach—with little or nothing taking up workstation RAM—or a MS-DOS redirector approach, where device drivers on workstations running MS-DOS or Windows redirect workstation requests for CD-ROM data to the remote CD-ROM server. CorelSCSI 2 takes both routes: it's an NLM that also uses a redirector and drivers at the workstation. The NLM mounts drives at the server as drives rather than Netware volumes, creating a database of CD-ROM drive information. Like SCSI Express, CorelSCSI has extensive support for SCSI devices other than CD-ROM drives. Operating system support includes MS-DOS, Windows, and OS/2.

CD-ROM NETWORK CONNECTIONS WITHOUT A PC

Much discussion about implementing CD-ROM services into a new or existing network has centered on whether to use a dedicated or nondedicated server. In the past, any existing network limited your options to whatever would peacefully coexist with your current scheme and available resources. From either approach, CD-ROM networking has implied footing the bill for a new PC or devoting (though not necessarily dedicating) some memory or, say, resources of a Netware file server to the task.

At least for Netware 3.11 and 4.0 users, those days are past. With Microtest's Discport, you can access one or more CD-ROM drives as if they were a hard disk drive on a Netware file server. Discport, shown in Figure 8-9, is a 4-by-7 1/2-by-1 1/8-inch device with 10BaseT and Thin Ethernet connections and a SCSI port for linking up to seven CD-ROM drives. For more drives, you can connect multiple Discports to the LAN. All Netware features are available, including caching, drive mapping, and security. The security feature allows departments or workgroups to control access to their particular titles.

Included with Discport is a Windows-based software application called Discview that lets the LAN administrator mount or unmount drives and perform other administrative tasks. Users can drag and drop icons to map network drives to CD-ROM volumes, and Discview will retain information on an individual user's last session. To reuse previous mappings, for instance, the user simply selects the icon from a drop-down list. There's a plus for client workstations, too. Because of Discport's integration with Netware, this solution needs no redirector or TSR loaded on the workstation.

Using CD-ROM on a Network   253

Chapter 8

FIGURE 8-9
Discport from Microtest

THE MAC DIFFERENCE

If you need to share CD-ROM drives among two or more Macintoshes, you have the easiest job of all. File Sharing, a feature of Apple's System 7 that lets you share any volume, teams up with the drivers sold with an Apple CD-ROM drive (or another vendor's that supports the Mac) to provide instant peer-to-peer networking for up to 10 simultaneous users. This networking pertains to Apple's HFS format that governs Macintosh hard disk and floppy disk storage as well as CD-ROM. ISO 9660 and High Sierra formats are no trouble, either. Foreign File System extensions for these formats, included with the CD-ROM drive, need only be copied to the client's system folder. Another extension is available for CD audio discs.

For the network size of 10 or fewer simultaneous users accessing, say, text files archived on CD-ROM or another SCSI device, the built-in networking support is sufficient. Macintosh systems come equipped with at least twisted-pair LocalTalk connections for use with the AppleTalk protocol, and Ethernet or Token Ring is better for heavier traffic. But if CD-ROM activity is great—for example, if users will be accessing QuickTime videos from CD-ROM—Apple recommends that you dedicate the system sharing the CD-ROM drives. Beyond that, if you need to ease the network load, your best option is to run

AppleShare on top of System 7 with a dedicated server for up to about 50 users. AppleShare Pro is intended for greater numbers of users.

There's also good news for heterogeneous networks that include Macintoshes. Netware 4.0's Netware for Macintosh NLM makes Netware look like an AppleShare server to connected Macintoshes, AppleTalk packets and all. Connecting Macintoshes to a Unix Network File System (NFS) server is another option for heterogeneous networks. And, if your workgroup of Macs is small but you still need to hook up with a larger, non-Mac network, gateways and routers from vendors such as Cayman Systems or Shiva Corporation can provide the link between LocalTalk wiring and Ethernet.

PEER-BASED LANS

In a true peer-based LAN such as Artisoft's LANtastic 5.0 and Invisible Software's Invisible LAN 3.4, one PC is outfitted with the CD-ROM drive and the necessary drivers as well as MSCDEX. Through the redirector software, that drive is added to the list of network resources available to whoever the network administrator chooses. For a handful of users and a CD-ROM application that's needed only occasionally, this setup may never pose a problem provided the nondedicated machine has enough high memory to accommodate the SCSI and other drivers. Otherwise, RAM-hungry applications may not have room to run. For light usage, it's by far the easiest approach to set up and maintain.

Where trouble begins, however, is when workstations access the CD-ROM on a regular basis. If the host PC is merely running MS-DOS or Windows, caching on a peer-to-peer LAN may not be sufficient to keep the host PC from slowing to a crawl. And a CD-ROM with a typical 300 ms access speed on a stand-alone machine may deliver data two or three times slower, depending on what the host PC user is running at the time and whether another user is also trying to access the CD-ROM. A server-based system, by contrast, can implement caching routines that actually speed CD-ROM database queries when the same disc is routinely accessed.

SITE LICENSING

In the early days of CD-ROM networking, two obstacles stood in the way of its acceptance in business. First, in-house CD-ROM production was minimal due to the expense (well into the tens of thousands of dollars) of producing a master disc. Second, off-the-shelf CD-ROM titles were sold on a one-license-per-user basis. Even popular products like Ziff Desktop Information's Computer Library did not allow even a slight bending of the single-user license that would have permitted legal, simultaneous users. Eventually, CD-ROM title vendors took a page from the software industry's playbook and adopted the concept of site licensing.

Site licensing had already caught on for computer software. Rather than pay full price for a given product, companies would pay one fee based on the number of anticipated users. This often amounts to a fraction of the retail price per user, but software vendors still come out ahead because they would sell far fewer products otherwise.

Now it's by far the exception to the rule to find a CD-ROM title that does not have a site-licensing option. The usual rule of thumb is that the owner of the software (you only buy a limited license to use the software) expects you to have a reasonable mechanism in place for assuring that the number of simultaneous users at any given time does not exceed the number of licensed users. This is sometimes accomplished by using *metering software,* which automatically keeps track of how each title is used.

WRITABLE SYSTEMS

One of the best reasons for setting up networking CD-ROMs on a new or existing network is that the cost of putting your own company's data on disc has dropped significantly with the debut of under-$5000 CD-R drives. CD-R is intended not so much for high-volume distribution (the exception is inexpensive prototyping prior to conventional pressing), but for small, even single-copy runs. This lends itself handily to networking the data for internal use as well as archiving.

CD-R products intended for network use include Sony's Multimedia Formatter, which lets you link a master rack-mountable CDW-900E to as many as 15 "slaves" for the simultaneous writing of multiple CDs in either ISO 9660 or Sony MMCD Player formats. If what you're writing to disc with a CD-R system will include document images—scanned forms, for example—or multimedia presentations, a viable solution may be the Kodak PCD LAN writer 200, which bundles Meridian Data's Netscribe Access Client Software. Kodak claims that MS-DOS, Windows, and Windows for Workgroups users on any Netware-based Ethernet network can produce standard CD-ROM discs for about four cents per megabyte. Available formats include standard CD-ROM, CD-ROM XA, and CD-I. Recently, the Kodak PCD LAN writer 200 package received a software upgrade, available to new and existing users, that permits it to record Photo CD Portfolio discs.

Lotus has embraced CD-R in its Notes workgroup software. Lotus Notes: Document Imaging Release 2, a follow-up to Imagery Software's Notes Companion Product, uses Microsoft's Object Linking and Embedding (OLE) technology to let Notes users view and manipulate images from within Notes. This includes support for Photo CD images.

CHAPTER 9

The Future of CD-ROM

Just two or three years ago, few people would have believed that CD-ROM would become the versatile and important medium that it is today. Today's titles make the early versions look crude in comparison, and the latest hardware provides performance that is several magnitudes better than the original models. Yet CD-ROM as a publishing medium is just starting to gather steam. Sharp rises in demand for CD-ROM players and titles have started the industry's competitive and creative juices flowing. Larger, established companies are grabbing for market share, and new companies are popping up regularly. All will use innovation and creativity as a means to differentiate themselves from their competition.

This innovation will take place in several ways, and not all of it will be specific to CD-ROMs. Many current and upcoming titles will benefit from better platform hardware and operating systems, which are expected to appear soon. You will see both long- and short-term progress in areas such as:

▶ Software
▶ Platform hardware and operating systems
▶ CD-ROM drives and media
▶ New applications

SOFTWARE CHALLENGES

A lot of the challenge in writing software for CD-ROM lies in the creative rather than technical area. CD-ROM title development uses many of the same tools used to create standard computer applications: compilers, debuggers, illustration software, interface design tools, and so on. The trick is to use those tools to produce software that capitalizes on the unique qualities of CD-ROM.

It's been a long learning curve for developers. The latest titles are exciting, but they only hint at what's possible in the future. Each category of titles follows its own evolutionary path. The following text suggests what you can expect in a few of those areas.

INTERACTIVE CD-ROM: HOLLYWOOD AND SILICON VALLEY DO LUNCH

Interactive CD-ROM titles have a unique set of standards to live up to. They combine elements of other, familiar media: TV, audio CD, computer games, educational software, and so on. At the same time, interactive CD-ROM software is really in a class by itself. More often than not, however, it is compared to and judged by media that people already know. And since interactive CD-ROM has similarities to so many other established media vehicles, it must meet the minimum expectations of them all. This is especially true of entertainment titles.

For example, people generally do not expect much from video games in terms of plot or character development. What counts is fast action and playability. You do, on the other hand, expect a good story and believable characters from the next video you rent. When interactive CD-ROM uses video to combine a story line with a game, it must meet viewers' expectations of both genres. The game must be good, and the story must be believable and well developed.

The entertainment CD-ROM titles themselves encourage this dual comparison, with movielike introductions, trailer clips, and rolling credits. Eventually, entertainment titles will be reviewed much the way movies are now. Critics will evaluate the direction, acting, script, and special effects along with the action of the game itself. "Siskel and Ebert on CD-ROM" is not too farfetched a concept.

It is no surprise, therefore, that software publishers and Hollywood are collaborating more and more frequently on CD-ROM titles. The results of this collaboration are just now appearing, with titles such as 7th Level's Tuneland, Media Vision's Critical Path, Broderbund's Myst, and Activision's Return to

Zork. The first title, Tuneland, was created by a company with strong entertainment industry connections, both financial and creative. The latter three titles all integrate professionally produced and acted video into a game-oriented story line.

These titles represent the best of what's available in interactive entertainment. In many ways, however, they are still works in progress. The level of integration in terms of graphics/video and story/game is still rough. No one has yet produced an interactive title that is both a good, believable story and a challenging, interesting game. One or both aspects suffer. Matching graphics and video has not been seamless (Myst comes very close, however).

From the developer's perspective, the problem is a creative one. The leading publishers recognize this, and that is why you see the movielike credits on many new titles. A lot of those people came from a film or music background. The next generation of interactive entertainment titles that will appear in 1994 will blur the line between film and game even more. You will see feature-length films running full-screen, full-motion video on all the major platforms: MPC, Macintosh, CD-I, 3DO, and so on. You will be able to interact in more realistic ways.

Nerds and Rock Stars

Interaction is becoming a new element with music on CD-ROM. You can make the case that CD-ROM will someday replace the audio CD as a music medium. Where audio CD is more or less a one-dimensional, linear medium, CD-ROM is a multidimensional, interactive medium. It allows you to not only play the music at the same quality level but to manipulate it and combine it with video or graphics.

A number of well-known musicians are starting to experiment with CD-ROM—most notably Peter Gabriel, Todd Rundgren, and David Bowie. What these and other artists are creating are interactive records on CD-ROM. If you've ever wanted to be a music producer, now is your chance. Don't like Bowie's latest hit? Just pop the CD-ROM into your player, remix, record, and voilà! You have your own personal version. In fact, you could choose to play the tune differently every time.

Heavy-metal artist The Great Kat, whose Digital Beethoven on Speed is described in Chapter 6, is working on a software program she calls Riff Checker. Riff Checker takes interactivity a step further; you can change the guitar riffs to your liking on the Kat's next CD-ROM. If you run into trouble, however, Riff Checker can give you technical advice and even help change the mood of the music.

Chapter 9

Interactive records are the result of a collaboration between programmers and musicians, although some of the pioneering artists are also well-known nerds—Todd Rundgren, for example. The CD-ROMs are generally produced by the artist and a multimedia development company and then marketed in partnership with the artist's record label. Other artists and professionals might also collaborate on a multimedia record production—a process that Peter Gabriel refers to as an "interdisciplinary soup." These other collaborators might include film professionals, architects, or artists in nonmusic mediums.

Gabriel recently released a CD-ROM titled Xperience1: Peter Gabriel's Secret World that features many elements you can expect to find in music discs in the future. The disc is in four parts: music videos from the "Us" album, World Music, Behind the Scenes, and a biographical section on Peter Gabriel. The "Us" portion contains all the music videos from the album. You can also see interviews with people involved in making the album, including Gabriel. World Music features music and instruments from around the world. You can call up background information on all the international recording artists included in the section. You can not only hear what they sound like, but "play" them from the disc.

Behind the Scenes gives you a tour of how the "Us" album was put together. At one point, you can actually help mix the songs. A "jam session" puts you in partnership with producer Brian Eno. You have 15 artists to work with to produce music. The biographical section includes older songs, as well as insights to Gabriel's music. Throughout the contents of the disc, you can find passes, which give you virtual backstage access to a concert or even to the Grammies.

Don't expect any two interactive records to use the same format or techniques. CD-ROM is a versatile enough technology that an artist has the range to experiment and produce something that is unique to his or her talents.

The fact that there is not currently a large installed base of interactive CD-ROM players—compared to audio CD players—limits the amount of work being done today on interactive records. Ideally, an interactive record should be conceived of and produced from the start as a multimedia production. What usually happens is that a record is produced primarily as an audio-only product, and video and other elements are added on later. Audio CD, therefore, is in no immediate danger of going the way of the LP record player. As interactive CD-ROM players and multimedia computers become better established, the incentive to move album publishing to that medium will be intense.

Chapter 9

A DATABASE FOR EVERY NEED

Although they number in the thousands, database titles have a long way to go before they truly offer something for everyone. The current offerings are very much oriented toward business and government; consumer reference titles are rare. Most are highly specialized and therefore have a limited audience. Consequently, prices are high—another barrier to more widespread use. Finally, the search and retrieval interfaces are usually arcane and not standardized.

The explosion in the number of consumers with CD-ROM drives and players will inspire new database titles. The first signs of a consumer-oriented class of reference discs are beginning to appear for activities such as cooking and collecting. As the potential number of users increases, publishers can bring down prices to consumer levels.

It is unrealistic to expect that someday all database titles will have the same search and retrieval interface. Each type of database has its own requirements. As a result, you might see some standardization within a given category—say, one type of interface for all legal abstracts and another for all business statistics listings. Vendors of database titles have long assumed—and rightly so—that what they are selling is the information and not the interface. Millions of new CD-ROM users, however, will encourage more competition in this area. Given the choice between two similar databases, people will choose the one that's easier to use. So expect better interfaces for database titles, but keep in mind that these Darwinian forces act slowly.

At the consumer level—the encyclopedias, cookbooks, atlases, and so on—there is hope for a consistent standard. This is partly because most consumer titles are very graphics-oriented and focused on ease of use. This often means adhering more closely to the conventions of the user environment's command structure, be it Windows, the Apple Macintosh, or CD-I.

Microsoft, which created Windows, has also made a splash with its Multimedia Viewer product. Multimedia Viewer is a GUI-oriented (Windows, of course) search and retrieval utility (see Figure 9-1). For a small fee (under $200), a developer can purchase the package and use it for resale in his or her product royalty free. This is a strong incentive, especially for the many small developers of CD-ROM titles. Competition is tough, and the fewer costs developers have to pass on to their customers, the better. Developers can port Multimedia Viewer to the Macintosh, though Microsoft does not yet sell a Mac version.

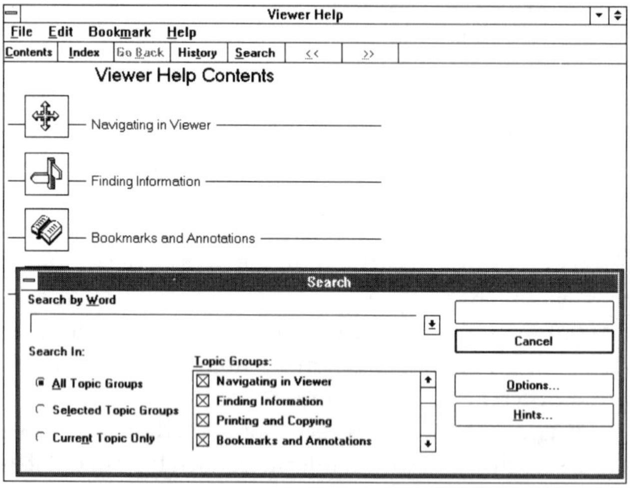

Chapter 9

FIGURE 9-1
Microsoft's Multimedia Viewer

APPLICATIONS ON DISC

CD-ROM is already starting to revolutionize how computer software is distributed. If every computer had a CD-ROM drive today, in fact, virtually every software publisher would abandon floppy disks and offer their wares only on CD-ROM. It's cheaper for them and makes installation easier for the user. You can expect to see many more software vendors offering computer software on CD-ROM either as an option or as the exclusive medium. In addition, expect those same vendors to take advantage of CD-ROM to add value to their product as a means of differentiating it from its competitors.

Take, for example, Microsoft Word for Windows and Bookshelf, described in Chapter 6. You get a complete set of writing reference tools with your word processor. Within a few years, you will expect extras like those that Word for Windows offers to come with many of the computer applications you buy.

It's easy to imagine, say, Lotus, Borland International, and Microsoft competing in the spreadsheet market not only in terms of features, but in terms of how many templates they offer on a CD-ROM; or how good their video tutorial on disc is; or how much reference material on accounting rules they provide. Database vendors might offer 500 of the most commonly used templates. How about a word processor with dictionaries for the 100 most-used languages in the world?

The Future of CD-ROM

Chapter 9

PRINT PUBLISHERS CATCH THE CD-ROM WAVE

Every conscious print publisher right now is scratching his or her head wondering how to translate what he or she does on paper to electronic media. Though many are already posting their content on online services, this adds little value. In fact, some value is lost; since nearly all online services are text-based, graphics, charts, photos, and other visual elements are impossible to reproduce. A number of these publishers, consequently, are turning their attention to CD-ROM.

The first impulse that many publishers have is to use the same model for CD-ROM as they use for print: periodical versions of those print publications sold on a subscription basis. In most cases, this doesn't work. As Chapter 6 explained, people resist reading from a video display. The greatest asset that CD-ROM gives a print publisher, therefore, is the ability to repackage existing data, or create new material, in a reference form. *Business Week,* for example, sells its Business Week 1000 listing on CD-ROM. You can now interact with the same data published in the magazine to find relationships and to group different types of information in ways that are impossible with print.

It is better, then, to think of CD-ROM as an enhancement to the print publication rather than a parallel medium. In the parlance of the publishing trade, this is known as an ancillary product—one that leverages the editorial content to produce a new revenue stream. Don't expect CD-ROM to replace print publications, but don't be surprised if your favorite magazines and newspapers start offering related products on disc.

"This Disc Is Sponsored By..."

Don't look now, but advertising is already working its way into CD-ROM. This advertising can take many different forms, from TV-commercial-like videos, to product demonstrations, to user-selected product descriptions. Disc-based content adapted from print is the most common category to contain advertising. Publishers and advertisers, however, seem to recognize that the interactive nature of CD-ROM places limits on the traditional in-your-face approach used on TV and in print. In those media you can't easily avoid the advertising to read a story or watch a show. With CD-ROM, you choose just what you want to see.

A publisher could attach an ad to a story or video so that you had to read it, but CD-ROM users expect to be able to avoid this. Publishers and advertisers, therefore, are experimenting with subtle yet compelling ways to get you to *want* to look at disc-based advertising. Many of the gimmicks are familiar: humor, intriguing teasers, and so on. The most significant methods, however, blur the line between advertising and what has traditionally been considered editorial.

Consider the hypothetical case of a construction-trade publication on CD-ROM. This particular disc might be a comprehensive reference to windows, listing dimensions, insulating qualities, costs, and so on. All listings provide a basic set of data for each window. Some listings, however, have little icons next to them. These icons indicate that you can click on them to get more information on a particular product. What may or may not be clear, though, is that the company that makes that particular window provided the information and paid the publisher to include it—the information is essentially paid advertising.

No reputable publisher would try to pass off this type of printed information as editorial. Many of them, however, do not yet fully understand the CD-ROM medium and see first the opportunity to create a new source of revenue. What's worse, some custom-development services are using this blurring of editorial and advertising as selling points to publishers—saying, in essence, that by making the advertising seem more like other information on disc, advertisers will be more likely to accept the concept.

The ethics issue has yet to be fully defined or addressed by professional publishing organizations. This is partly due to the fact that all the possible permutations of disc-based advertising have not yet been implemented. Until the publishing industry has established guidelines for these new ways to advertise, it's buyer beware.

CATALOGS AND JUNK MAIL ON DISC

CD-ROM is a natural environment in which to produce a catalog. Catalogs are visual in nature, data intensive, and read randomly. With, for example, the Lands' End catalog on disc, a potential mail-order customer could go directly to the section he or she desires. Once there, the items can be displayed in more complete and interesting ways than in print. Every coat can be displayed in the same size in all the colors, for example. The viewer can zoom in on specific details. For the most popular items, perhaps a video will show them being modeled—your own virtual fashion show.

Apple recently took the lead in this category with its En Passant CD-ROM. This disc contains 21 catalogs from 18 retailers, including L.L. Bean, The

Chapter 9

Nature Company, Williams Sonoma, Pottery Barn, and Apple itself. It is mailed to registered owners of CD-ROM drives. Each catalog's style is in keeping with the print version. Viewers can select and group items of interest from different catalogs, and they can dynamically change the color of a given item. Searching is possible either within a given catalog or across the entire disc.

In addition to catalog entries, En Passant provides interviews and video clips to embellish the merchandising. For example, a consultant might discuss the latest fashions. Some editorial content on topics such as personal finance or travel is also provided. At first, you must call an 800 number to order, just as you do for a print catalog. Once connected, you are transferred to the appropriate mail-order company. Apple anticipates that some type of online ordering could be implemented in the future, however.

Some high-tech-minded marketers are beginning to explore CD-ROM as a means of distributing promotional material. The concept—referred to as adware—is not new; Ford Motor Company, for instance, has been mailing floppy-disk-based "road tests" of certain car models to potential customers for years. CD-ROM, however, vastly expands what is possible with the adware content. It also allays concerns about computer viruses among consumers, who are increasingly wary of placing unrequested floppy disks in their systems.

Marketers count on slick, interactive multimedia presentations and the curiosity of the recipient to get their CD-ROM-based message across. You get an unsolicited disc in the mail, which includes some accompanying print material that serves as a teaser. Your interest piqued, you pop the disc into your computer or player to check it out. If the disc is properly done, you should be able to easily access those portions you find most interesting.

Computer software and hardware vendors have already executed promotions on CD-ROM. For now, computer owners are the only demographic group likely to have the ability to play the discs. Apple, for example, has produced a disc that its salespeople use to sell its education products to schools. WordPerfect mailed out CD-ROMs that demonstrate WordPerfect 6.0 for Windows that also includes 12 original songs. Once you've checked out the software, you still have what amounts to a hype-free audio CD.

Chapter 9

HARDWARE NEEDS TO GET BETTER

No question about it, the quickest way to improve the quality of CD-ROM titles is to build better platform hardware. This is especially true in the areas of graphics and video playback. Improving the main processing capabilities of computers and players is also important.

Today, no computer or player can run the most demanding CD-ROM titles without some trade-offs. Those trade-offs range from a slight pause while switching scenes to severely degraded audio and video. The good news is that development of the hardware platforms is accelerating at a rapid pace. The not-so-good news is that improvements in CD-ROM drive performance will be slower in coming and most likely expensive.

FASTER PROCESSORS, AFFORDABLE VIDEO

The price/performance ratio on desktop computers has been steadily dropping almost since they were invented. The pace of this decline is about to accelerate fantastically with the appearance of systems based on new high-performance processors. These processors include Intel's Pentium processor and the PowerPC processor developed by IBM, Motorola, and Apple. Not that you will pay less for a computer based on these chips; in fact, you might pay a little more. The potential boost in performance, however, far outstrips the premium on the price tag. By the time you read this, you should see Pentium systems and PowerPC systems selling for about the same price. These prices are for a multimedia-capable machine with a CD-ROM drive.

Early tests show that you can expect double the performance in many instances. At these speeds, you'll see smoother video, shorter pauses, and cleaner sound. That's assuming, of course, that you have at least a reasonably fast double-speed CD-ROM drive.

TV-based players will provide an even greater improvement in their price/performance ratio. These systems will emphasize interactivity and video. Consequently, companies such as Sony, Hitachi, Sega, Nintendo, and others are designing new systems built around extremely powerful graphics processors. Most will be targeted at owners of cartridge-based game machines who want to upgrade. Many in the industry expect that disc-based game boxes, in fact, will overtake the cartridge-based systems in volume unit sales sometime after 1995. The target prices for these units average about $500. The vision for these set-top boxes is twofold: provide a disc-oriented platform for in-home entertainment and education titles, and provide a means of connecting to the anticipated "Data Highway," described later in this chapter.

Video movies are fast becoming a vital part of many CD-ROM titles, especially for the entertainment, education, home reference, and how-to/training categories. Unfortunately, few existing desktop computers have the hardware needed to run this video, and fewer still can execute full-screen, full-motion video. The reason is primarily cost. Video hardware until recently was almost exclusively used for professional purposes. Only the most dedicated hobbyist splurged on an expensive video board. A lack of popular consumer software that required video hardware kept demand low. Things have changed. Affordable (under $500) video playback boards for both Mac and MS-DOS/Windows PCs are now common. These boards offer features such as Video CD compatibility, audio CD-quality sound, and high resolution (1024 by 768 pixels).

More important than the advent of low-cost video playback boards is the growing interest among system manufacturers in building video playback capability into desktop computers. Apple, in fact, has already done this with its AV series Macs, as has Silicon Graphics with its Indy workstation. Selling desktop systems is a low-margin proposition, and adding video playback is one way for a manufacturer to differentiate itself from its competitors. This allows some freedom to raise the retail price and, consequently, margins. There is some understandable concern among the vendors about whether the demand for such a feature is large enough to warrant adding the cost to the system. Still, you will likely see some tentative steps toward on-board video playback in desktop PCs during 1994.

SPEEDIER DRIVES IN THE WORKS, BUT AT A PRICE

Right now you can purchase a quad-speed CD-ROM drive for your computer and see a big boost in playback performance of your titles. For most people, however, this option is too expensive. Considering the price-curve history of double-speed drives, it could be two years before quad-speed drives become affordable for consumers. In the labs, however, faster and higher density drives are being built. You can expect these to be expensive at first, just as most new technology commands a premium. Building faster, higher capacity drives is not the main challenge, however. Maintaining backward compatibility with older drives is.

Making a denser drive is relatively simple. You reduce the size of the pits and narrow the distance between tracks (the pitch), which allows more pits to be placed on the same area of disc surface. The laser must then be built so that it is calibrated to the smaller pits and narrower tracks. This means that older drives will not be able to read the denser discs.

In the United Kingdom, Nimbus Technology has demonstrated a CD-ROM with a storage capacity of over 1Gb. This double-density disc looks just like any other audio CD or CD-ROM. It can store 135 minutes of full-motion color video with stereo sound. The company claims that existing players need only minor modification to be able to read these discs.

However, no one will want to throw out their old discs when they buy one of these newer drives. Drive manufacturers know this, so compatibility with the discs you use today is a key goal for companies such as Nimbus and Philips, which are working on the problem. How will they achieve it? Probably by building intelligence into the drive's firmware so that it recognizes what type of disc it is reading. The drive then focuses the laser according to the type of disc.

The faster access rate is also the result of the smaller pits and narrower tracks. The smaller the pits, the more of them can be read within a given amount of time at a given spin rate. As with today's drives, however, faster read rates require greater precision. The need for greater precision and the requirement for backward compatibility with today's discs represent a significant investment in research and development. For this reason, the first higher density drives are likely to be premium-priced items.

There is a need for these denser drives and discs. Most titles don't use the full 680MB capacity of today's discs. However, more and more frequently, titles in a number of categories are being published as multidisc sets. Many business directories and phone number listings, for example, just don't fit on one disc. As multimedia titles become more sophisticated, they too will demand more storage space. Even today, for example, The Software Toolwork's 20th Century Video Almanac requires five discs.

Hybrid discs, which have software code and data for more than one hardware platform, are often crunched for space as well. The separate sets of platform-specific code and data represent storage overhead that single-platform discs don't have. The ability to produce a hybrid disc is important for publishers of consumer titles, who can create just one package that works on the two most significant platforms. It is also important to businesses who want to ensure that valuable information is available across platforms within the organization.

Chapter 9

THE UBIQUITOUS CD-ROM

Today you have to search for a retail store that sells CD-ROMs. Computer stores are almost certain to carry them. Other stores that sell books, video tapes, or music rarely carry them. The same holds true for department stores. This will change shortly. CD-ROM publishers and distributors are all quick to point out that the business model for disc-based content most closely resembles that of the book publishing industry. It makes sense, therefore, that you should expect to buy many of your CD-ROMs in a bookstore. Certainly storybooks, on-disc references, self-help, and education titles are natural categories for bookstores. Games will soon start to appear in department, toy, and video stores.

CD-ROMS TO RENT

Compton's NewMedia, best known for its interactive encyclopedia, now makes its titles available for rental in video stores. Many of Compton's titles, which include children's storybooks, a movie guide, and a multimedia golf guide, are targeted at the home market and appear to be a good fit. Several rental chains are expected to take up Compton's offer.

Rather than steal sales, Compton's is betting that CD-ROM rental will spur demand by letting consumers try out a title before buying. The company claims that it has found that a relatively high number of VCR owners also own CD-ROM drives.

Blockbuster Entertainment also recently announced that it would begin carrying CD-ROM titles from Compton's and others for rent along with its VCR tapes.

THE DATA HIGHWAY: ROUTE 66 WAS NEVER LIKE THIS

It's hard to pick up a newspaper or business publication and not see a story on dramatic changes in the communications and media industries.

Chapter 9

Phone companies are buying cable companies, which are buying movie studios, which are buying publishing houses, which are buying software companies. To what end no one really knows for sure, but it is broadly referred to as the Data Highway (also known as The Information Highway or the Data Superhighway).

The vision that is almost universally painted is this: Someday, probably by the turn of the century, every home and business will have an information pipeline attached to it. This pipeline will probably be a fiber-optic cable or, at worst, high-speed copper cable. The pipeline can attach to your telephone, your TV, or computer, which by the year 2000 might be converged into one. Through this pipeline you will have a seemingly limitless range of services, including:

- Movies on demand
- Online shopping
- Home banking
- Interactive TV
- Reference material of all types
- Virtual libraries
- Online games
- Video communications
- Basic networking connectivity

If this vision is realized, you'll have more reasons than ever to become a couch potato. Theoretically, however, you'll also have enormous resources designed to enrich your life if you so choose.

How does this affect CD-ROM? If fully implemented—that is, available to everyone in the format just described—there will be no need for an intermediary distribution device. You'll simply download everything you'd want on a CD-ROM from some central repository. Full implementation of the Data Highway, however, is a long shot at best.

The dream of the Data Highway is unlikely to be realized in its full glory. The reasons are part economic, part technical, and part political. Briefly, it will cost hundreds of billions of dollars to connect everyone from source to residence. That's a huge investment that will have to be amortized over decades. Although experts agree that fiber-optic cable can provide the bandwidth that the Data Highway requires, no one has yet built the complex servers required at the source or the set-top boxes to receive the information, and no one has written the software to make it all work. Projects are under way at companies such as Silicon Graphics, Sun Microsystems, Oracle, and Gain Technology. Results are hardly around the corner, however.

The politics represent the toughest issue. Every involved party—phone companies, content providers, cable companies, and government—has its own agenda for how the Data Highway should be implemented. Unfortunately, no one has yet seriously sought consumer feedback. A few trials are currently under way in different parts of the United States, but by and large they've been implemented on the "if you build it, they will come" mentality. People have been confused by what those trials provide, so usage rates are low. It will take years of trial and error before information providers understand how consumers will use the Data Highway.

What is likely to happen is this: The Data Highway will be implemented piecemeal over the next 10 to 20 years. Trade-offs will be made in terms of who gets access when, who pays and how much, and who provides what where. To clarify, areas with the greatest population density are likely to be the first to go online. This is pure economics; you build first where you're likely to get the greatest return for the investment.

For similar reasons, individuals and businesses in areas that are difficult to service will possibly pay more to connect to the Data Highway. (Some people in government, however, are working to ensure that this doesn't happen.) Available services will differ, too, depending on which companies provide them in a given area.

This means that CD-ROM's role in society is assured for the foreseeable future. Partial implementation of the Data Highway—in terms of both connecting people and variety of content—won't satisfy the demands of everyone. Since CD-ROM does not require such an immense infrastructure, it can fill the gaps left open by the Data Highway.

As Chapter 1 points out, however, CD-ROM technology is just one means of delivering content digitally. If something better comes along, many publishers will move to that new medium. Besides the Data Highway, potential candidates to replace CD-ROM include solid-state memory chips and rewritable optical.

The Data Highway is the medium that many of the set-top box manufacturers have placed side bets on. Sega, 3DO, Nintendo, and others have plans to add online connectivity to their systems. Sega, in fact, has already launched the Sega Channel on cable. The Sega Channel delivers video games on demand in the few areas where it is available (New York City and Orlando, Florida). This dual strategy will become increasingly important to vendors of both CD-ROM software and hardware.

AN ENDING, A BEGINNING

What's important about CD-ROM is that it is the most exciting medium going for both reference and interactive multimedia software. It is a valuable tool for distributing information within a company. In the home, CD-ROM technology turns your computer or TV into an unparalleled entertainment and education medium.

The titles available today are just the tip of the iceberg compared to what's coming. Although CD-ROM technology is nearly a decade old, it is just now beginning to show its full potential.

A P P E N D I X A

GLOSSARY

Active matrix A type of LCD that is generally expensive, but of high quality.

ADC (analog-to-digital converter) A device that converts analog data to digital form.

ADPCM (adaptive differential pulse code modulation) An audio compression standard. It usually offers a 4:1 compression ratio.

Adware Promotional material distributed using a digital medium such as CD-ROM.

Analog Data that consists of continuously variable physical qualities.

Animation cel High-resolution, full-color images that can be animated, scaled, rotated, and changed in other ways.

Anti-aliasing A technique used to remove jaggies from bit-mapped graphics.

Archival storage The long-term storage of infrequently used data.

ATA (AT Attachment) The specification on which IDE is based.

Appendix A

Audio CD   A compact disc designed to play only audio, though some have limited graphics capability as well. *See also* Red Book, CD+G.

Authoring software   Software that lets you pull different elements together —text, graphics, video, audio—into an integrated application.

Auxiliary data   Checksum data stored in each Mode 1 sector of a CD-ROM that the EDC/ECC use to locate and repair read errors.

Bandwidth   The capacity of a bus or other connection to carry data.

Binary 0   Represents a "no transition" state during a read of a CD-ROM.

Binary 1   Indicates that a transition has occurred during a read of a CD-ROM.

BIOS (basic input/output system)   Code imbedded in every MS-DOS/Windows PC that tells it how to handle various system components.

Birefringeance   The refraction of light in two slightly different directions, creating two rays.

Bit structure   The way in which bits form bytes.

Bitblt (bit block transfer)   A term that refers to the act of copying graphics from one location to another on a video screen.

BLER (block error rate)   The number of disc read errors that occur per second.

Block   *See* Sector.

Boolean logic   A method used to locate and retrieve information from a database. Boolean logic uses the operators AND, NOT, and OR to form relationships among keywords, thereby narrowing the parameters of a search.

Bridge   A hardware device that connects two similar networks.

Bridge disc   A type of CD-ROM disc that works with more than one format standard.

Glossary

Appendix A

Buffer   On a CD-ROM drive, a buffer is 64Kb to 256Kb of memory that acts as a temporary storage area for data read off a disc that the computer is not yet ready for.

Bump height   The depth of the pits that have been burned into a CD-ROM.

Bus   An interface used to connect a computer to other devices such as a CD-ROM drive. SCSI is the primary bus used to connect CD-ROM drives to computers.

Bus mastering   The taking control of a process or task from the computer's main processor through the system bus. Bus mastering controllers, including many caching controllers used with CD-ROM drives, usually have their own processor.

Caching   The use of high-speed memory to hold data read from a storage device until the computer is ready to access it.

Caching controller   A controller used with storage devices that contains its own caching hardware.

Caddy   The removeable case used by some CD-ROM drives to hold a disc while it is being read.

CAV (constant angular velocity)   The method used by hard and floppy disk drives to seek and access data off the medium. The drive maintains a consistent spin rate as it scans the concentrically arranged tracks.

CD+G (compact disc plus graphics)   The part of the Red Book audio CD specification that allows the incorporation of limited graphics.

CD-I (compact disc interactive)   A compact disc format developed by Philips that better enables the playback of multimedia, interactive software. CD-I is defined by the Green Book specification.

CD-I Bridge   Also referred to as the White Book standard, it defines how CD-I data is recorded on CD-ROM XA discs.

Appendix A

CD-I Ready A bridge format between the audio CD (Red Book) and CD-I standards.

CD-R (compact disc recordable) A recordable compact disc. It uses a gold reflective surface rather than aluminum, and adds a dye-based layer to enable the recording of data. Also referred to as CD-WO (compact disc write-once).

CD-ROM (compact disc read-only memory) A 4.72-inch plastic and aluminum disc designed to optically store audio, text, video, and graphics data. *See also* Yellow Book, CD-ROM XA.

CD-ROM XA (extended architecture) An enhanced CD-ROM format standard that allows for multisession playback and better synchronization of multiple data types.

CD-quality audio Sound produced at a sampling rate of 44.1KHz

CD-WO (compact disc write-once) *See* CD-R.

Channel bit The bits formed by the conversion of 8-bit bytes to 14-bit bytes.

Checksum A number generated by a special algorithm that is used to ensure data integrity.

CIRC (cross interleave Reed-Solomon Code) Error correction code developed specifically for CD-ROM.

Circular buffer read-ahead A technique used to read data continuously into a CD-ROM drive's buffer, thereby keeping it full and speeding throughput.

Client On a network, an attached desktop computer.

CLV (constant linear velocity) The data on a compact disc is stored in one long spiral track. A drive must maintain a constant speed (linear velocity) as it scans this track. Therefore, the disc must spin slower to read the inner track and faster to read the outer track.

Comparator The circuitry in a CD-ROM drive that measures the outputs produced by the focusing circuitry.

Appendix A

Condenser lens   A lens that increases the intensity of the laser light in CD-R drives.

Controller   A device, usually an add-in card, that controls a specific device or component of a computer. A SCSI controller is often referred to as a host adapter.

Cross-coding   An error-detection and correction algorithm used to generate checksums.

Cross-platform development   The act of developing one application for more than one platform, or the conversion of an application from one platform to another.

CRT (cathode ray tube)   The standard type of video display used in computer monitors. It employs an electron gun to excite phosphors on a glass screen.

DAC (digital-to-analog converter)   A device that converts digital information into analog data.

Daisy-chain   With SCSI devices, the act of connecting multiple units using one host adapter.

Decibels (dB)   A measure of amplitude or intensity of sound.

Density   In terms of storage media, density refers to the amount of data that can be placed in a given area of the media.

Device driver   Software that tells a computer's operating system how to communicate with a peripheral such as a CD-ROM drive.

Digitize   To convert images, sound, text, and other types of data to a binary numerical form understandable by a computer.

DMA (direct memory access)   A technique for moving data directly between main memory and a peripheral.

Appendix A

Docking station   An expansion unit for portable computers that provides additional storage, I/O ports, and slots for add-in cards.

Dot pitch   The measurement used to indicate the proximity of pixels to one another on a video display.

Double-speed drive   A drive that reads data at 300Kbps, twice the single-speed rate.

Drive   The basic hardware unit that reads and/or writes a CD-ROM, audio CD, CD-I, CD-R, or other type of disc.

DSP (digital signal processor)   A type of processor specialized for one task, such as video or audio. Takes the processing load off the main system CPU.

DVI (digital video interactive)   Intel's video compression scheme. DVI is the basis for Indeo.

Dye-recording layer   A chemical layer found on CD-R discs that reacts with the recording laser to form the pits that represent data.

Ebook (electronic book)   A print book that has been converted to a digital medium such as CD-ROM, or a book that has been created for digital publication.

EDC/ECC (error detection code/error correction code)   The software that resides within a CD-ROM's firmware that identifies and corrects read errors from a disc.

Editor   A software tool that allows you to modify individual elements. There are text editors, audio editors, image editors, and so on.

EFM (Eight-to-Fourteen Modulation)   The process of converting 8-bit bytes to 14-bit bytes.

EISA (extended industry standard architecture)   An enhancement of the ISA standard that allows for faster expansion slots.

Glossary

Appendix A

Encryption The scrambling of data for security reasons. The data is unscrambled using a decoding key.

EPROM (electrically programmable read-only memory) An integrated circuit chip that can be programmed to record and permanently hold data.

Father The metal die created from the glass master during the compact disc manufacturing process.

File attribute A piece of information about a particular file, such as a timestamp of when it was recorded.

Firmware Code that is stored within a chip, usually an EPROM.

FMV (full-motion video) The ability to play video sequences at 30 frames per second.

Focus coil Part of a CD-ROM's focusing mechanism.

Focus servo The motor that adjusts the focus of the laser in a CD-ROM drive.

Format The method or standard by which a CD-ROM is recorded and played back.

Formatting software Software used with CD-R drives to write and format data to a recordable disc.

Forward sense diode A diode found in CD-R drives that measures the intensity of the laser light.

Fragmentation The phenomenon where files become widely dispersed on a hard disk drive because frequent reads and writes have limited the amount of contiguous free space.

Frame A single image within a video sequence.

Appendix A

Frankfurt Group   An industry consortium that has devised a CD-ROM file format standard to replace ISO 9660. It is likely to be formally adopted as ISO 13490.

Frequency response   The range of sound a sound board can generate, usually no lower than 30Hz and no higher than 20KHz.

FTP (file-transfer protocol)   A communications protocol used to transfer files across or between networks.

Ghosting   The effect seen when a moving image on a video leaves a "trail." This trail is the result of the persistence of the phosphors or LCD crystals, which do not immediately turn off but fade.

Gigabyte   One thousand megabytes.

Glass master   A glass disc used in the compact disc manufacturing process to create a die to stamp out copies.

Green Book   The CD-I format standard established by Philips.

GUI (graphical user interface)   A "shell" or abstraction between you and the underlying software that allows you to graphically manipulate applications. Microsoft Windows is a GUI.

Header bytes   The bytes within each sector on a CD-ROM that provide address and mode information.

HFS (hierarchical file system)   The file system used by the Apple Macintosh.

Hierarchical directory tree   A file structure that uses a root directory and subdirectory structure. On a CD-ROM, the directory structure is eight levels deep.

High Sierra   The unofficial CD-ROM file format standard that was eventually modified and accepted as ISO 9660.

Hit rate   The rate at which the computer finds information it requires in cache memory, and not on the storage device.

Glossary

Appendix A

Host adapter   A type of controller.

Hybrid disc   A CD-ROM that uses more than one type of file format.

Hybrid Disc Standard   The format standard on which Photo CD is based.

Hypertext   On-screen data that is linked to other, related data. Most often used with text, but it can also include graphics, video, or audio.

IDE (integrated drive electronics)   A bus standard common on MS-DOS/Windows PCs and sometimes used to connect CD-ROM drives.

Interrupt   A specific instruction that tells the computer to stop what it's doing and run a particular routine.

IRQ   Interrupts used for the COM (communications) ports on an Intel-based PC. COM1 and COM3 usually share IRQ4; COM2 and COM4 usually share IRQ3. You can't have two devices using the same IRQ at the same time.

ISA (industry standard architecture)   The standard architecture for MS-DOS/Windows PCs.

ISO 9660   A file format standard for CD-ROMs established by the International Standards Organization. Most types of CD-ROMs use ISO 9660.

ISO 10149   The official ISO designation for the Yellow Book CD-ROM standard.

ISO 13490   *See* Frankfurt Group.

Isochronous   Two events that happen at the same time.

ITV (interactive television)   Television programming that has been modified using hardware and software to be interactive. This can be done using set-top boxes, which might also contain a CD-ROM drive, or in the future by connecting a modified TV to a special cable service.

Jaggies   The rough edges often found on bit-mapped graphics.

Appendix A

Jewel case   The plastic cases used to store CD-ROMs.

JPEG (Joint Photographic Experts Group)   A common compression scheme for photographic images.

Jukebox   A term sometimes used to describe a multiple-drive CD-ROM server.

Karaoke CD   *See* Video CD.

Kiosk   A booth-like device that uses a computer and often a CD-ROM drive to allow people to perform financial transactions or to gather information without human assistance.

Lacquer coating   The protective coating sprayed onto a disc during the manufacturing process.

LAN (local area network)   A group of computers at a specific location linked together for communications and resource sharing.

Land   The flat area between pits on a compact disc track. The transitions between pits and lands represent data.

Laser diode   *See* Semiconductor laser.

Laser videodisc   A larger (12-inch) ancestor to the compact disc that is used primarily to play back movies.

Latency   The time spent by the disc read mechanism locating requested information.

Lead-in area   The place on a CD-R disc where the final table of contents is written.

Lead-out area   The place on a CD-R disc that tells the drive that there is no more data to be read.

LECC (layered error correction code)   The scheme by which errors that cannot be corrected by CIRC are processed again by the EDC and ECC.

Glossary

Appendix A

Local bus   A system bus type that provides a direct connection to the main processor.

Logical file format   The way in which the directories and files are organized on a CD-ROM or other storage medium.

Logical sector structure   The way in which sectors are organized on a storage medium.

Markup   To insert codes in electronic text to indicate structure.

MBTF (mean time between failure)   The expected amount of time a type of hardware unit will operate before it fails.

MCI (Media Control Interface)   A component of Microsoft Windows that determines which device you play from the Media Player—CD-ROM, sequencers, etc.

MD Data   A proprietary data format used by Sony's 3.5-inch MiniDisc player. MD-ROM is the read-only version of the disc.

Media clipart   Collections of images, videos, sound clips, and other media elements distributed using a digital medium such as CD-ROM.

Metering software   Software that keeps track of software or database usage for billing purposes.

Micro Channel   A system bus standard developed by IBM.

MIDI (musical instrument digital interface)   An interface standard for music synthesis.

Minichanger   A CD-ROM drive with a mechanical assembly that can hold a number of discs and automatically swap among them.

Mixed-mode disc   CD-ROMs that have Red Book audio tracks (Mode 2) recorded on them along with CD-ROM (Mode 1) tracks.

MO (magneto-optical)   A writable and readable optical storage technology.

Appendix A

Mode 1   The CD-ROM encoding scheme that incorporates EDC/ECC.

Mode 2   The data-only CD-ROM encoding scheme (Red Book audio).

Modulate   To vary.

Mother   A metal die created from the father die during the compact disc manufacturing process.

MPC (multimedia PC)   A standard created by the Multimedia Marketing Council that establishes the minimum acceptable requirements for running multimedia applications on Windows-based PCs.

MPEG (Moving Picture Experts Group)   A popular compression scheme for video.

Multifunction card   A computer add-in card that performs more than one function; many sound boards, for example, also provide a SCSI bus.

Multimedia   The use of multiple types of data—audio, video, text, graphics—to convey information.

Multisession   The ability to record a disc in more than one session, or the ability to read a partially recorded disc.

Multitasking   The ability of a computer to perform more than one task simultaneously.

NLM (NetWare loadable module)   Software that adds features to or enhances Novell Netware.

Objective lens   The last lens that the laser light travels through before striking the surface of the disc.

OLE (object linking and embedding)   A component of Microsoft Windows that allows different applications to share data.

Glossary

Appendix A

One-third stroke   The accepted method to measure the performance of CD-ROM and other optical drives. It requires that a search take place over at least one-third of the disc surface, not track to track.

Online data retrieval   The access of remote information using telecommunications.

Optical head   The laser read mechanism in a CD-ROM drive.

Optical media   Storage media that uses laser light to record and read data. CD-ROM is an optical medium.

Orange Book   The format standard for CD-R and MO discs.

O-ROM (optical read-only memory)   A hybrid media that is part CD-ROM format and part magneto-optical (writable) format. Also called P-ROM (partial ROM).

Parallel port   An I/O port found on virtually all computers and most commonly used to connect printers. It can, however, be used to connect external CD-ROM drives as well.

Passive matrix   A type of LCD that features low cost at the expense of some lost image quality.

PCA (program calibration area)   The area on a CD-R disc that the laser reads to calibrate itself to the disc.

PCI (peripheral component interconnect) bus   A high-speed local bus standard.

PCM (pulse code modulation)   A method of digitizing analog sound. PCM matches samples against a predefined set of permitted values. It then codes the selected value as a series of pulses representing "on" or "off" (or the binary 0 or 1).

PCMCIA (Personal Computer Memory Card International Association) Standard   A bus standard for small, credit-card-sized add-in cards often used in portable computers.

Appendix A

PDA (personal digital assistant)   A small, handheld computer designed for personal information management and communications.

Peer-based network   A network that does not use a central server. Instead, resources are distributed throughout the network's nodes.

Pit   A depression in the reflective layer of a compact disc that represents data.

Pitch   The distance between tracks on a compact disc.

Platform   The hardware and operating system on which a CD-ROM is played.

Player   A self-contained unit to play compact discs. It contains a drive and other controlling electronics.

PMA (program memory area)   The part of a CD-R disc that contains the track numbers and their starting and stopping addresses.

Premastering software   Software used to prepare data for the proper format to be recorded on CD-ROM.

P-ROM (partial read-only memory)   *See* O-ROM.

Quad-speed drive   A CD-ROM drive that reads data at 600Kbps, four times the single-speed rate.

Quantization   Measurement of how much data a sound board can accumulate per sample. Most boards sample at 8 bits of data; better CD-quality boards sample at 16 bits. A higher sampling rate provides greater accuracy of the sampled sound.

Quarter wave plate   The part of a CD-R drive that rotates the beam toward the photodetector.

Random access   The ability to go directly to and retrieve a discrete piece of data from a storage medium.

Glossary   Appendix A

Read-ahead   The ability to access data from a CD-ROM or other medium and place it in a buffer before the computer needs it.

Red Book   The digital audio standard, developed by Philips and Sony, for compact discs.

Reflective layer   The middle part of a compact disc that consists of the aluminum layer containing the data.

Refresh rate   The rate at which a video display updates the screen. Also referred to as the scan rate.

RLL (run-length limited)   The distance between transitions during a read of a CD-ROM.

Rock Ridge Extensions   CD-ROM file format extensions to ISO 9660 that accommodate the Unix file structure.

Router   A hardware device that routes messages from one network to another similar one.

Runtime   A core piece of executable code that allows you to access or view data created by the fully featured version of the software.

Sampling rate   The speed at which a sound board generates sound, measured in frequency, typically ranging from 4 to 44KHz.

SAP (Service Advertising Protocol)   A broadcast mechanism found in versions of Novell NetWare that is used to send information over a WAN.

Scan rate   *See* Refresh rate.

Scripting language   A high-level software development language where code is written using natural-language-like scripts.

SCSI (small computer system interface)   A high-speed bus standard that is the preferred method of connecting CD-ROM drives to computers. The latest implementation, SCSI 2, comes in three varieties: Fast, Wide, and Fast Wide.

Appendix A

Sector   On a CD-ROM, a sector is the minimum unit of data that a drive can access. It is 2352 bytes long. Also referred to as a block.

Semiconductor laser   The type of laser used in a CD-ROM drive. Also called a laser diode.

Sequential access   The retrieval of data by scanning sequentially a storage medium until the data is located.

Server-based LAN   A network where control and resources are centered in one computer—the server.

Servo mechanism   A small, precise motor. A typical CD-ROM drive contains four. Also referred to as a "servo."

SGML (Standard Generalized Markup Language)   A coding method used to represent the structure of an electronic document.

Shareware   Commercial software that is distributed collectively on CD-ROM or via other electronic media. You are free to try the software, but expected to pay for it if you find it worthwhile.

Single session   A drive that cannot read a partially recorded disc (one that is recorded in multiple sessions).

Single-speed drive   A CD-ROM drive that reads data at a rate of 150Kbps.

Site license   An agreement between a software provider and a customer where the customer pays one fee to use the product at a particular location or within the entire company. The amount of a site license fee is often determined by the estimated number of users.

SMP (symmetric multiprocessing)   A system architecture that permits the use of more than one main processor.

SNR (signal-to-noise ratio)   Difference in decibels between the lowest and highest sounds a sound board can generate. The higher the SNR, the more realistic the sounds. For CD quality, the SNR should be 100dB.

Glossary

Appendix A

Son A metal die created from the mother die during the compact disc manufacturing process. Also called a daughter.

Sprite Small graphics pictures or a series of pictures that can be moved independently around the screen to create the effect of animation.

Stamper The metal die actually used to press compact discs.

Subcode byte An auxiliary signal read by the CD-ROM drive circuitry that contains the address (same as the header value), track number, and detection signals.

Substrate The plastic portion of the compact disc.

Sync bytes The identifying part of each sector on a CD-ROM.

Synthesizer The part of a sound board that reproduces specific sounds, such as a musical instrument or speech.

TCP/IP (transmission control protocol/Internet protocol) A set of communications protocols that support peer-to-peer connectivity for both local and wide area networks.

Terminator A resistor placed at the end of a chain of SCSI devices that reduces signal noise.

Texture mapping The act of wrapping an image onto other 3-dimensional objects.

THD (total harmonic distortion) The amount of total distortion or background noise a sound board generates, measured in percent. A good THD is in the 0.5% range.

Thermal recalibration A function that a hard disk drive performs to compensate for physical changes in the recording surface caused by temperature variations.

Throughput The amount of data that a system can process in a given amount of time, from input to output.

Appendix A

Track   Both CD-ROMs and rotating magnetic media arrange data in tracks. On a CD-ROM, the tracks are arranged on a spiral and logically separated according to how the files are arranged. On rotating magnetic media, the tracks are concentric and physically discrete.

Track-at-once   The process of recording an entire CD-R disc at once.

Triple-speed drive   A CD-ROM drive that reads data at 450Kbps, three times the single-speed rate.

TSR (terminate and stay resident)   Software that loads into high memory and remains dormant until needed. Most driver software are TSRs.

Turn-table controller   The circuitry in a CD-ROM drive that controls the servo that rotates the disc.

Turn-table servo   The motor that turns the disc in a CD-ROM drive.

Video CD   A format standard that covers the use of video sequences on CD-ROM. It uses the MPEG compression algorithm, and is also called the Karaoke CD standard.

Virtual reality   A 3-D simulation technique that "immerses" the viewer into the image being viewed. Virtual reality applications usually require the use of a special optical helmet.

Virus   Computer code designed to clandestinely "infect" a computer and perform unwanted tasks. Can be either destructive or simply annoying.

VL-Bus   A local bus standard.

Voice   A specific synthesized sound made by a sound board.

Volume   A related set of files on a CD-ROM or other storage medium.

Volume descriptor   Data placed on a disc that contains information about a related set of files.

Glossary

Appendix A

WAN (wide-area networking)   A network that connects LANs that are in separate locations.

Waveform audio   Sound that is played digitally.

Wavelength   A measured distance traveled by a beam of light.

White Book   *See* CD-I Bridge.

Wide Area Network Broadcast   A broadcast mechanism used to send information over a WAN.

WORM (write once, read many)   An optical storage technology used primarily for archival storage.

Yellow Book   The basic format standard for CD-ROM, developed by Philips and Sony.

APPENDIX B

VENDOR RESOURCE GUIDE

The following is a comprehensive, though not complete, listing of companies that sell CD-ROM-related products and services. The companies appear in alphabetical order within each category. Space does not permit listing every product or service a company provides. While this listing might not lead you immediately to the specific product or service you require, it will give you a good starting point to begin your search.

ACCESSORIES

CD Technology
766 San Aleso Ave.
Sunnyvale, CA 94086
(408) 752-8500
(408) 752-8501 fax
Disc caddy

Appendix B

BUSINESS APPLICATIONS ON CD

Corel Corp.
1600 Carling Ave.
Ottawa, Ontario
Canada K1Z 8R7
(613) 728-8200
(613) 728-9790 fax
Illustration software: Windows, OS/2, Unix

DeLorme Publishing Co., Inc.
Lower Main St.
P.O. Box 298
Freeport, ME 04032
(800) 227-1656 or (207) 865-1234
(207) 865-9628 fax
Mapping software: Windows

InfoBusiness
887 S. Orem Blvd.
Orem, UT 84058-5009
(801) 221-1100
(801) 225-0817 fax
Business how-to: MS-DOS

Media Vision
47300 Bayside Pkwy.
Fremont, CA 94538
(510) 770-8600
(510) 770-8648 fax
Daily planner: Windows, MPC, Mac

Microsoft Corp.
One Microsoft Way
Redmond, WA 98052-6399
(800) 323-2577
Integrated software package: Windows

Appendix B

Software Toolworks, The
60 Leveroni Ct.
Novato, CA 94949
(800) 234-3088 or (415) 883-3000
(415) 883-3303 fax
Reference: Windows, MPC

Sony Electronic Publishing Co.
9 W. 57th St.
New York, NY 10019
(212) 418-9439
Travel guide: MMCD, Windows, Mac

CD-ROM-PUBLISHED PERIODICALS

Business Week 1000
McGraw-Hill
1221 Avenue of the Americas
New York, NY 10020
(212) 512-2882
News magazine: Mac, Windows

ComputerWorld
Emerging Technology Applications
111 Speen St.
Framingham, MA 01701-9107
(508) 820-8649
(508) 820-4396 fax
MS-DOS

Nautilus
Metatec Corp.
7001 Discovery Blvd.
Dublin, OH 43017
(800) 637-3472 or (614) 761-2000
(614) 761-1258 fax
MPC, Windows, Mac

Appendix B

New England Journal of Medicine
Creative Multimedia Corp.
514 NW 11th, Ste. 203
Portland, OR 97209
(800) 776-9277 or (503) 241-4351
(503) 241-4370 fax
MS-DOS

Newsweek InterActive
444 Madison Ave.
New York, NY 10022
(212) 350-4000
News magazine: Windows

UMI
300 N. Zeeb Rd.
Ann Arbor, MI 48106
(800) 521-0600
(313) 761-1203 fax
Various magazines and newspapers

Verbum
P.O. Box 189
Cardiff, CA 92007-0189
(619) 944-9977
(619) 944-9995 fax
Music and multimedia: Mac

CONSUMER CD-ROM SOFTWARE

7th Level, Inc.
1771 International Parkway #101
Richardson, TX 75081
(214) 437-4858
(214) 437-2717 fax
Children's software: Windows

Appendix B

Access Software
4910 W. Amelia Earhart Dr.
Salt Lake City, UT 84116
(800) 800-4880 or (801) 359-2900
(801) 359-2968 fax
Game: Windows, MPC

Activision Studios
11440 San Vicente Blvd.
Los Angeles, CA 90049
(310) 207-4500
(310) 820-6131 fax
Game: MPC, Windows, VIS

Aditus, Inc.
5756 Royalmount Ave.
Montreal, Quebec H4P 1K5
Canada
(514) 737-8547
(514) 737-0922 fax
Game: Mac

Advanced Multimedia Solutions, Inc.
300 Fairview Ave. N.
Seattle, WA 98109
(800) 626-4105 or (206) 623-4011
(206) 382-9200 fax
Movie listing: Windows MPC, VIS

Against All Odds Productions
P.O. Box 1189
Sausalito, CA 94966-1189
Storybook: Mac, Photo CD

Allegro New Media
387 Passaic Ave.
Fairfield, NJ 07004
(201) 808-1992
(201) 808-2645 fax
Electronic book

Appendix B

American Laser Games
4801 Lincoln Rd. NE
Albuquerque, NM 87109
(505) 880-1718
(505) 880-1557 fax
Game: Windows, 3DO

Applied Optical Media Corp.
1450 Boot Rd.
Bldg. 400
West Chester, PA 19380
(800) 321-7259 or (215) 429-3701
(215) 429-3810 fax
Wildlife encyclopedia, atlas: Windows, MPC, VIS

Aris Entertainment
310 Washington Blvd.
Ste. 100
Marina Del Rey, CA 90292
(310) 821-0234
Game: Windows

Azeroth, Inc.
3020 Issaquah Pine Lake Rd.
Ste. 341
Issaquah, WA 98027
(206) 392-9941
(206) 392-6899 fax
Game: VIS

Broderbund Software, Inc.
500 Redwood Blvd.
P.O. Box 6121
Novato, CA 94948-6121
(800) 382-4600 or (415) 382-4400
Storybook, educational game: Windows, Mac, VIS

Appendix B

Candlelight Publishing
1136 E. Harmony Ave.
Ste. 204
Mesa, AZ 84204-5844
(800) 274-1048
(801) 224-3888 fax
Bible: VIS

CMC Research, Inc.
7150 SW Hampton
Ste. C-120
Portland, OR 97223
(503) 639-3395
Wildlife

Compact Publishing, Inc.
5141 MacArthur Blvd.
Washington, DC 20016
(800) 964-1518 or (202) 244-4770
(202) 244-6363 fax
Almanac: Windows, MPC, VIS

Compton's NewMedia
2320 Camino Vida Roble
Carlsbad, CA 92009
(800) 862-2206 or (619) 929-2500
(619) 929-2511 fax
Interactive encyclopedia, music, children's: Windows, MPC, VIS

Context Systems, Inc.
The Technology Center
2935 Byberry Rd.
Hatboro, PA 19040
(215) 675-5000
(215) 675-2899 fax
Bible stories, children's software, atlas, dictionary: Windows, MPC, VIS

Appendix B

Creative Multimedia Corp.
514-NW 11th
Ste. 203
Portland, OR 97209
(503) 241-4351
(503) 241-4370 fax
Baseball statistics, astronomy, medical reference, role-playing game, wildlife: MS-DOS, Mac

Cruise Watch
3151 Airway Ave.
Ste. I-1
Costa Mesa, CA 92626
(714) 241-1512
(714) 241-1350 fax
Travel: VIS

Crystal Dynamics, Inc.
2460 Embarcadero Way
Palo Alto, CA 94303
(415) 494-7316
(415) 858-3640 fax
Game: 3DO

Deep River Publishing
P.O. Box 9715-975
#100 Fore St.
Portland, MA 04104
(800) 643-5630 or (207) 871-1684
(207) 871-1683 fax
Home design: Windows, MPC

Discis Knowledge Research, Inc.
P.O. Box 45099
5150 Yonge St.
Toronto, Ontario
Canada M2N 6N2
(800) 567-4321 or (416) 250-6537
Storybook: Mac, VIS

Appendix B

Dr. T's Music Software, Inc.
124 Crescent Rd.
Ste. 3
Needham, MA 02194
(800) 989-6434 or (617) 455-1454
(617) 455-1460 fax
Music, children's software: Windows, MPC

Dynamix, Inc.
1600 Mill Race Dr.
Eugene, OR 97403
(503) 343-0772
(503) 345-1460 fax
Game: 3DO

EBook, Inc.
32970 Alvarado-Niles Rd.
Ste. 704
Union City, CA 94587
(510) 429-1331
(510) 429-1394 fax
Storybook, music: Windows, MPC, VIS

Edmark Corp.
6727 185th Ave. NE
P.O. Box 3218
Redmond, WA 98073-3218
(800) 426-0856 or (206) 861-8200
(206) 861-8998 fax
Early learning: VIS

Eduquest
6269 B Variel Ave.
Woodland Hills, CA 91367
(818) 992-8484
(818) 992-8781 fax
Natural park guide: Windows, MPC

Appendix B

EE Multimedia Productions
1455 S. 2200 W.
Salt Lake City, UT 84119
(801) 973-0081
(801) 973-0184 fax
Tutorials

Electronic Arts
1450 Fashion Island Blvd.
San Mateo, CA 94404-2064
(415) 571-7171
(415) 571-1893 fax
Game: 3DO, VIS

Forward Records
10635 Santa Monica Blvd.
Los Angeles, CA 90025
(800) 827-4466
Interactive music: CD-I

Gale Research
835 Penobscot Bldg.
Detroit, MI 48226
(313) 961-2242
(313) 961-6083 fax
Genealogy software, movie video listing

Grolier Electronic Publishing, Inc.
Sherman Turnpike
Danbury, CT 06816
(800) 356-5590 or (203) 797-3530
(203) 797-3835 fax
Encyclopedia: Windows, MPC

IBM Multimedia Publishing Studio
1374 W. Peachtree
Ste. 200
Atlanta, GA 30309
(800) 995-9999
Astronomy, children's software: Mac, Windows, MPC

ICOM Simulations
648 S. Wheeling Rd.
Wheeling, IL 60090
(708) 520-4440
(708) 459-3418 fax
Interactive game: Mac, VIS

InfoBusiness
887 S. Orem Blvd.
Orem, UT 84058-5009
(801) 221-1100
(801) 225-0817 fax
Movie guide: MS-DOS

Integrated Systems, Inc.
11361 Sunset Hills Rd.
Reston, VA 22090
(703) 471-7453
(703) 471-1126 fax
Early learning: VIS

Intellimedia Sports, Inc.
3565 Piedmont Rd.
Two Piedmont Center Ste. 300
Atlanta, GA 30305
(404) 261-8330
(404) 261-2282 fax
Sports, game: 3DO

Interactive Publishing Corp.
300 Airport Executive Park
Spring Valley, NY 10977
(914) 426-0400
Children's software, music, game: MS-DOS, Mac

Interplay Productions, Inc.
17922 Fitch Ave.
Irvine, CA 92714
(800) 969-4263 or (714) 553-6655
(714) 252-2820 fax
Game: Windows, MPC, 3DO

Appendix B

JLR Group, The
214 Lincoln St.
Ste. 104
Allston, MA 02134
(617) 254-9109
(617) 254-9170 fax
Game: VIS

Kinder Magic Software
1680 Meadowglen Ln.
Encinitas, CA 92024
(619) 632-6693
Early learning: VIS

Legacy Software
9338 Reseda Blvd.
2nd Fl.
Northridge, CA 91324
(818) 885-5773
(818) 885-5779 fax
Home education: VIS

Llerrah, Inc.
2701 W. 15th St.
Ste. 631
Plano, TX 75075
(214) 422-1122
Music: Windows, MPC

LucasFilm Games
P.O. Box 10307
San Rafael, CA 94912
(415) 721-3300
(415) 721-3344 fax
Game: MS-DOS, VIS

Macmillan New Media
124 Mt. Auburn St.
Cambridge, MA 02138
(800) 342-1338
(617) 868-7738 fax
Children's dictionary: Windows, MPC

Maris Multimedia, Ltd.
99 Mansell St.
London E1 8AX
England
44-71-488-1566
44-71-702-0534 fax
Astronomy: Mac, Windows

Maxwell Electronic Publishing
124 Mt. Auburn St.
Cambridge, MA 02138
(800) 342-1338
Children's dictionary: Windows MPC

MCA, Inc.
100 Universal City Plaza
Universal City, CA 91608
(818) 777-1747
(818) 777-7180 fax
Game: 3DO

McGraw-Hill
11 W. 19th St.
New York, NY 10011-4285
(800) 772-4726
Wildlife encyclopedia

MediAlive
766 San Aleso Ave.
Sunnyvale, CA 94086
(408) 752-8500
(408) 752-8501 fax
Travel guide: Windows, MPC, Mac

Media Vision
47300 Bayside Pkwy.
Fremont, CA 94538
(510) 770-8600
(510) 770-8648 fax
Interactive game, children's software,
interactive movie: Windows, MPC, Mac

Appendix B

Medio Multimedia, Inc.
2703 152nd Ave. NE
Redmond, WA 98052
(206) 867-5500
(206) 885-4142 fax
Popular culture, movie listing

MicroProse Software, Inc.
180 Lakefront Dr.
Hunt Valley, MD 21030-2245
(410) 771-0440
(410) 527-0765 fax
Music, game: 3DO

Microsoft Corp.
One Microsoft Way
Redmond, WA 98052-6399
(800) 323-2577
Home reference, encyclopedia, movie listing, music: Windows, MPC

Midisoft Corp.
P.O. 1000
Bellevue, WA 98009
(800) 776-6434 or (206) 881-7176
(206) 883-1368 fax
Music: Windows, MPC, VIS

Multicom Publishing, Inc.
1100 Olive Way
Ste. 1250
Seattle, WA 98101
(206) 622-5530
(206) 622-4380 fax
Children's software: Mac, Windows, MPC, VIS

National Geographic Society
Washington, DC 20036
(800) 368-2728
Wildlife encyclopedia

New Media Schoolhouse
Box 390
69 Westchester Ave.
Pound Ridge, NY 10576
(800) 672-6002 or (914) 764-4104
Storybook

Parallax Publishing
471 Lighthouse Ave.
Pacific Grove, CA 93950
(408) 646-1015
Home education: VIS

Park Place Productions
5421 Avenida Encinas
Carlsbad, CA 92008
(619) 929-2010
(619) 929-2020 fax
Game, sports: 3DO

Philips Interactive Media of America
11111 Santa Monica Blvd.
Ste. 700
Los Angeles, CA 90099-3663
(800) 845-7301 or (310) 444-6600
(310) 479-5937 fax
Music, tutorial, sports, children, games, art, hobby: CD-I

Psygnosis
S. Harrington Buildings
Sefton St.
Liverpool, UK L3 4BQ
44-51-709-5755
44-51-709-6466 fax
Game: 3DO

Appendix B

Quanta Press, Inc.
1313 5th St. SE
Ste. 223A
Minneapolis, MN 55414
(612) 379-3956
(612) 623-4570 fax
Poetry: Mac, MS-DOS

Queue
338 Commerce Dr.
Fairfield, CT 06430
(800) 232-2224 or (203) 335-0906
Storybook

ReadySoft, Inc.
30 Wertheim Ct.
Unit 2
Richmond Hill, Ontario
Canada L4B 1B9
(416) 731-4175
(416) 764 8867 fax
Game: 3DO, MS-DOS

Sanctuary Woods
1124 Fort St.
Victoria, BC
Canada V8V 3K8
(800) 665-2544 or (604) 380-7582
(604) 388-4852 fax
Storybook: 3DO, Mac, Windows, MPC, VIS

ScanRom Publications
P.O. Box 72
Cedarhurst, NY 11516
(516) 295-2237
(516) 295-2240 fax
Movie trivia: MS-DOS

Appendix B

Sierra On-Line, Inc.
P.O. Box 485
Coarsegold, CA 93614
(800) 326-6654 or (209) 683-4468
(209) 683-3633 fax
Game, storybook: Windows, MPC, VIS

Sirius Publishing
7655 E. Gelding Dr.
Ste. B-1
Scottsdale, AZ 85260
(800) 247-0307 or (602) 951-3288
(602) 951-3884 fax
Music, karaoke: Windows, MPC

Softbit, Inc.
One Whitewater
Irvine, CA 92715
(714) 251-8600
Educational and entertainment multimedia software

Software Toolworks, The
60 Leveroni Ct.
Novato, CA 94949
(800) 234-3088 or (415) 883-3000
(415) 883-3303 fax
Wildlife, education, encyclopedia, almanac, atlas, game: Windows, MPC, Mac, MS-DOS, 3DO

Sony Electronic Publishing Co.
711 5th Ave.
New York, NY 10022
(212) 702-6273
Travel guide, game: MMCD, Windows, MPC, Mac

Spectrum Holobyte, Inc.
2490 Mariner Square Loop
Alameda, CA 94501
(510) 522-3584
(510) 522-2587 fax
Game: 3DO

Appendix B

Sumeria, Inc.
329 Bryant St.
Ste. 3D
San Francisco, CA 94107
(415) 904-0800
(415) 904-0888 fax
Wildlife: Windows, Mac

TeleTypesetting
311 Harvard St.
Brookline, MA 02146
(617) 734-9700
(617) 734-3974 fax
Cookbook, Bible, literature: Mac, MS-DOS, Windows

Texas Caviar, Inc.
3933 Spicewood Springs Rd.
Ste. E-100
Austin, TX 78759
(512) 346-7887
(512) 346-1393 fax
Wildlife: Windows, Mac

Trilobyte, Inc.
110 S. 3rd St.
Jacksonville, OR 97530
(503) 899-1113
(503) 899-7114 fax
Game: 3DO

Virgin Games, Inc.
18061 Fitch Ave.
Irvine, CA 92714
(714) 833-8710
(714) 833-8717 fax
Game: 3DO, VIS

Voyager Company, The
1351 Pacific Coast Hwy.
Santa Monica, CA 90401
(310) 451-1383
Storybook, movie, movie listing: Mac

Warner New Media
3500 W. Olive Ave.
Ste. 1050
Burbank, CA 91505
(800) 593-6334 or (818) 955-9999
(818) 955-6499 fax
Sports, humor: Windows, MPC

Westwind Media
Box 5833
Lake Ariel, PA 18436
(800) 937-3200 or (717) 937-3000
(717) 937-3200 fax
Storybook, dinosaurs: Mac, MS-DOS

World Library, Inc.
12914 Haster St.
Garden Grove, CA 92640
(714) 748-7197
(714) 748-7198 fax
Literature

Xiphias
8758 Venice Blvd.
Los Angeles, CA 90034
(310) 841-2790
(310) 841-2559 fax
Electronic book, dictionary, tutorial

DATABASES, DIRECTORIES, AND OTHER REFERENCES

Access Innovations
4314 Mesa Grande SE
Albuquerque, NM 87108
(505) 265-3591
Russia

Appendix B

American Business Information
5711 S. 86th Circle
Omaha, NE 68127
(402) 593-4656
(402) 331-6681 fax
Business directory, phone listing medical directory: MS-DOS, Mac

Bancroft-Whitney
3250 Van Ness Ave.
San Francisco, CA 94120
(800) 848-4000
(415) 673-9776 fax
Legal

Biosis
2100 Arch St.
Philadelphia, PA 19103-1399
(800) 523-4806
(215) 587-4800
(215) 587-2016 fax

Bowker Electronic Publishing
P.O. Box 31
New Providence, NJ 07974
(800) 323-3288
Library

Bureau Development, Inc.
141 New Rd.
Parsippany, NJ 07054
(800) 828-4766 or (201) 808-2700
(201) 808-2676 fax
Geography: MS-DOS, Mac

CAB International
Wallingford
Oxon, UK OX10 8DE
0491-32111
0491-33508 fax
Agriculture, forestry, environment, public health abstracts

Appendix B

Cambridge Scientific Abstracts
7200 Wisconsin Ave.
Bethesda, MD 20814-4823
(800) 843-7751 or (301) 961-6750
Science abstracts

CD PubCo, Inc.
Ste. 2050, 777-8 Ave. S.W.
Calgary, AB
Canada T2P 3R5
(403) 294-0080
(403) 294-0082 fax
Oil industry

Compact Cambridge
7200 Wisconsin Ave.
Bethesda, MD 20814
(800) 843-7751 or (301) 961-6750
(301) 961-6720 fax
Medical abstracts

Context Limited
Tranley House
Tranley Mews
London, UK NW3 2QW
071-267-7055
071-267-2745 fax
Legal

Creative Multimedia Corp.
514-NW 11th
Ste. 203
Portland, OR 97209
(503) 241-4351
(503) 241-4370 fax
Medical: Mac

Appendix B

Delorme Publishing Co., Inc.
Lower Main St.
P.O. Box 298
Freeport, ME 04032
(800) 227-1656 or (207) 865-1234
(207) 865-9628 fax
Maps: MS-DOS, Windows

Dialog Information Services, Inc.
3460 Hillview Ave.
Palo Alto, CA 94304
(800) 2-DIALOG
Online data on disc

Digital Directory Assistance, Inc.
5161 River Rd.
Bldg. 6
Bethesda, MD 20816
(800) 284-8353 or (617) 639-2900
(617) 639-2980 fax
Phone directory: MS-DOS

DISC Information Services Corp.
800 S. Highway 10
St. Cloud, MN 56304
(800) 328-4827
(612) 253-9195 fax
Automotive: MS-DOS

Dun & Bradstreet Information Services
3 Sylvan Way
Parsippany, NJ 07054-3896
(800) 526-0651
Business directory

EBSCO Publishing
P.O. Box 2250
Peabody, MA 01960-7250
(800) 653-2726
(508) 535-8545 fax

Appendix B

Facts on File
460 Park Ave. S.
New York, NY 10016
(800) 322-8755
(800) 678-3633 fax

GeoSystems
227 Granite Run Dr.
Lancaster, PA 17601
(717) 293-7500
(717) 293-7467 fax
Geographic

Horizons Technology, Inc.
3990 Ruffin Rd.
San Diego, CA 92123
(619) 292-8331
Maps: MS-DOS

InfoBusiness
887 S. Orem Blvd.
Orem, UT 84058-5009
(801) 221-1100
(801) 225-0817 fax
Guide to databases: MS-DOS

Information Access Co.
362 Lakeside Dr.
Foster City, CA 94404
(415) 378-5249
Periodical directory

InterOptica Publishing, Ltd.
1213-1218 Shui On Centre
6-8 Harbour Rd.
Hong Kong
852-824-2868
852-824-2508 fax
Travel: MS-DOS, MPC, Windows, Mac

Appendix B

Johnston & Co.
P.O. Box 446
American Fork, UT 84003-0446
(801) 756-1111
(801) 756-0242 fax
U.S. Constitution papers: MS-DOS, Windows

Lightbinders, Inc.
2325 3rd St.
Ste. 320
San Francisco, CA 94107
(415) 621-5746
(415) 621-5898 fax
Charles Darwin's writings

Micro House International
4900 Pearl East Circle #101
Boulder, CO 80301
(800) 926-8299 or (303) 443-3389
(303) 443-3323 fax
Technical database: MS-DOS, Windows, Netware

MicroPatent
25 Science Park
New Haven, CT 06511-9787
(800) 648-6787 or (203) 786-5500
(203) 786-5499 fax
Patent database

Moody's Investor Service
99 Church St.
New York, NY 10007
(800) 955-8080
Investment

NewsBank
58 Pine St.
New Canaan, CT 06840
(800) 223-4739
Newspaper and newswire articles

Appendix B

NTC Publishing Group
4255 W. Touhy Ave.
Lincolnwood, IL 60646-1975
(708) 679-5500
(708) 679-2494 fax
Multilingual dictionary: MS-DOS, Windows, Mac

Online Computer Systems, Inc.
20251 Century Blvd.
Germantown, MD 20874-1196
(800) 922-9204 or (301) 428-3700
(301) 428-2903 fax
Medical

PennComp Software Development
P.O. Box 271529
Houston, TX 77277
(800) 326-6145
(713) 669-1014 fax
Quotations: Windows, MS-DOS, Mac

Quanta Press
1313 Fifth St. SE
Ste. 223A
Minneapolis, MN 55414
(612) 379-3956
(612) 623-4570 fax
Consumer references, geography, movie listing, astronomy: MS-DOS

SilverPlatter Information, Inc.
1750 Bridgeway
Ste. A200
Sausalito, CA 94965
(800) 874-1130
Medical

Slater Hall Information Products
1301 Pennsylvania Ave. NW
Washington, DC 20004
(202) 393-2666
(202) 638-2248 fax
Census data

Appendix B

Sociological Abstracts, Inc.
P.O. Box 22206
San Diego, CA 92192-0206
(619) 695-8803
(619) 695-0416 fax
Sociology and linguistics

Sony Electronic Publishing Co.
711 5th Ave.
New York, NY 10022
(212) 702-6273
Business directory: MMCD, Windows, Mac

U.S. Department of Commerce, Economics, and Statistics Administration
Office of Business Analysis
Room H-4885
Washington, DC 20230
(202) 482-1986
(202) 482-2164 fax
Economics, social statistics, environmental, trade: MS-DOS

Wayzata Technology, Inc.
P.O. Box 807
Grand Rapids, MI 55744
(800) 377-7321 or (218) 326-0597
(218) 326-0598 fax
Geography: MS-DOS, Windows, Mac

Young Minds, Inc.
1910 Orange Tree Ln.
Ste. 300
Redlands, CA 92374
(800) 569-3472
NAFTA database: Mac, MS-DOS, Unix

Ziff Desktop Information
25 First St.
Cambridge, MA 02141
(617) 252-5000
(617) 252-5551 fax
Computer-industry articles and abstracts: MS-DOS, Windows, Mac

DEMO SOFTWARE

Apple Computer, Inc.
20525 Mariani Ave.
Cupertino, CA 95014-1010
(408) 996-1010
(408) 974-5192 fax
Mac

Ingram Micro, Inc.
1600 E. St. Andrew Pl.
Santa Ana, CA 92799
(714) 566-1000

Instant Access International
The Access Centre
Colindeep Ln.
London NW9 6DU
England
Mac

SelectWare Technologies
29200 Vassar
Ste. 200
Livonia, MI 48152
(313) 477-7340
(313) 477-6488 fax
MS-DOS, Windows

TestDrive Corp.
2933 Bunker Hill Ln.
Ste. 101
Santa Clara, CA 95054-1124
(408) 496-0555
(408) 496-6810 fax
MS-DOS, Windows

Appendix B

DEVELOPER PROGRAMS AND ASSOCIATIONS

Apple Multimedia Program (AMP)
(716) 871-6555
Apple-based multimedia developers

Information Technologies (ITC)
1011 E. Main St.
Richmond, VA 23219
(804) 780-2677
Full-service agency for developers and marketers of electronically published media

Interactive Multimedia Association
3 Church Circle
Ste. 800
Annapolis, MD 21401-1933
(410) 626-1380
(410) 263-0590 fax

Multimedia PC Marketing Council
1730 M St. NW
Ste. 707
Washington, DC 20036-4510
(202) 331-0494
MPC standard

Optical Publishing Association
P.O. Box 21268
Columbus, OH 43221
(614) 442-8805
(614) 442-8815 fax

SGML Open
c/o Pres. Larry Bohn
Interleaf
Prospect Place
9 Hillside Ave.
Waltham, MA 02154
(617) 277-7114 ext. 5536
SGML professionals

Software Publishers Association (SPA)
1730 M St. NW
Ste. 700
Washington, DC 20036
(202) 452-1600
(202) 223-8756 fax

DEVELOPMENT TOOL VENDORS

Adobe Systems, Inc.
1585 Charleston Rd.
P.O. Box 7900
Mountain View, CA 94039-7900
(800) 833-6687 or (415) 961-4400
(415) 961-3769 fax
Document interchange software, photo editing software: Mac, Windows, Unix

Aimtech Corp.
20 Trafalgar Sq.
Nashua, NH 03063-1973
(800) 289-2884
(603) 883-0220
(603) 883-5582 fax
Multimedia authoring tool: Windows, VIS

Altura Software, Inc.
510 Lighthouse Ave.
Ste. 5
Pacific Grove, CA 93950
(408) 655-8005
(408) 655-9663 fax
Help system, multimedia viewer: Mac, Windows

Apple Computer, Inc.
20525 Mariani Ave.
Cupertino, CA 95014-1010
(408) 996-1010
(408) 974-5192 fax
QuickTime, authoring tool: Mac, Windows

Appendix B

Asymetrix Corp.
110-110th Ave. NE
Ste. 700
Bellevue, WA 98004
(800) 448-6543
(206) 462-0501
(206) 637-1504 fax
Multimedia toolkit: Windows

Avalanche Development Co.
947 Walnut St.
Boulder, CO 80302
(303) 449-5032
(303) 449-3246 fax
Markup software

Avid Technology, Inc.
One Park West
Tewksbury, MA 01876
(508) 640-6789
(508) 640-1366 fax
Video production software: Mac, Unix, Photo CD

Brodart Co.
500 Arch St.
Williamsport, PA 17705
(717) 326-2461
(717) 999-6799 fax
Cataloging system

CD-ROM Strategies, Inc.
6 Venture
Ste. 208
Irvine, CA 92714
(714) 453-1702
(714) 453-1311 fax
Premastering software: MS-DOS, Unix, Mac

Appendix B

Creative Labs, Inc.
1901 McCarthy Blvd.
Milpitas, CA 95035
(408) 428-6600
(408) 428-2394 fax
Video capture board: Mac, Windows

Dataware Technologies
222 Third St.
Ste. 3300
Cambridge, MA 02142
(617) 621-0820
Authoring software, hypertext software: Unix, MS-DOS, Windows

Eastman Kodak Co.
343 State St.
Rochester, NY 14650
(800) 242-2424
(716) 724-1983
Photo CD software: Mac, Windows

Electronic Book Technologies, Inc.
One Richmond Sq.
Providence, RI 02906
(401) 421-9550
(401) 421-9551 fax
Electronic book authoring software: Windows, Mac, Unix

Enigma Information Retrieval Systems, Ltd.
10 Kishon St.
Bnei Brak
P.O. Box 2080
Israel 51203
972-3-579-7061
972-3-579-7062 fax
Authoring software: Windows

Appendix B

Exoterica Corp.
1545 Carling Ave.
Ste. 404
Ottawa, Ontario
Canada K1Z 8P9
(613) 722-1700
(613) 722-5706 fax
SGML reference, evaluation software,
markup software: MS-DOS, Mac, Unix

Farallon Computing, Inc.
2470 Mariner Square Loop
Alameda, CA 94501
(510) 814-5100
(510) 814-5020 fax
Document interchange software: Windows, Mac

Handmade Software, Inc.
15951 Los Gatos Blvd.
Ste. 17
Los Gatos, CA 95032
(408) 358-1292
(408) 358-2694 fax
Imaging software: MS-DOS, Unix

HSC Software
1661 Lincoln Blvd.
Ste. 101
Santa Monica, CA 90404
(310) 392-8441
(310) 392-6015 fax
Multimedia authoring software: Windows

IBM Ultimedia Tool Series
1055 Joaquin Rd.
Mountain View, CA 94043
(800) 887-7771
Authoring software, multimedia development tools: OS/2

Appendix B

Incat System
One Faneuil Hall Marketplace
Boston, MA 02109
(617) 227-8541
(617) 742-3431 fax
Authoring software: Windows, MPC, MS-DOS, Unix

Kaleida Labs
1945 Charleston Rd.
Mountain View, CA 94043
(415) 966-0400
(415) 966-0496 fax
Scripting language

Knowledge Access International, Inc.
2685 Marine Way
Ste. 1305
Mountain View, CA 94303
(415) 969-0606
(415) 964-2027 fax
Premastering software: MS-DOS, Windows, MPC

Macromedia
600 Townsend
San Francisco, CA 94103-9632
(800) 288-4797 or (415) 252-2000
Multimedia authoring software: Windows, Mac, 3DO

Mammoth Micro Productions
1700 Westlake Ave. N., Ste. 702
Seattle, WA 98109
(206) 281-7500
(206) 281-7734 fax
CD-ROM XA title production toolset

Media Cybernetics, Inc.
8484 Georgia Ave.
Silver Spring, MD 20910
(301) 495-3305
(301) 495-5964 fax
Image processing software: Windows, MS-DOS, Unix

Appendix B

Meridian Data, Inc.
5615 Scotts Valley Dr.
Scotts Valley, CA 95066
(408) 438-3100
(408) 438-6816 fax
Authoring software: MS-DOS

Microsoft Corp.
One Microsoft Way
Redmond, WA 98052-6399
(800) 323-2577
Programming language: MS-DOS, Windows

Moon Valley Software
21608 N. 20th Ave.
Phoenix, AZ 85027
(800) 473-5509 or (602) 375-9502
(602) 993-4950 fax
Icon creation software: Windows

Multicom Info Systems GmbH
Arheilger Weg 17
W-6101 Rossdorf
Germany
49-6154-699-5155
49-6154-699-5159 fax
Multimedia authoring software: Windows

No Hands Software
1301 Shoreway Rd.
Ste. 220
Belmont, CA 94002
(415) 802-5800
(415) 593-6868 fax
Document interchange software: Windows, Mac

Appendix B

Ntergaid, Inc.
2490 Black Rock Tpke.
Ste. 337
Fairfield, CT 06430
(203) 380-1280
(203) 380-1465 fax
Authoring software, hypertext software: MS-DOS, Windows

Optical Media International
180 Knowles Dr.
Los Gatos, CA 95030
(800) 347-2664
(408) 376-3511
(408) 376-3519 fax
Premastering, authoring software: Mac, MS-DOS, Unix, Windows

Pacific Gold Coast Corp.
15 Glen St.
Ste. 201
Glen Cove, NY 11542
(800) 732-3002
(516) 759-3011
(516) 759-3014 fax
Multimedia authoring software: Windows

Passport Designs, Inc.
100 Stone Pine Rd.
Half Moon Bay, CA 94019
(415) 726-0280
(415) 726-2254 fax
Music production software: Windows

Philips Professional Interactive Media Systems
One Philips Dr.
P.O. Box 14810
Knoxville, TN 37914-1810
(800) 835-3506
Authoring software: Mac, MS-DOS

RasterOps Corp.
2500 Walsh Ave.
Santa Clara, CA 95051
(408) 562-4200
(408) 562-4065 fax
Video production hardware: Mac, QuickTime

Sony Electronic Publishing
One Lower Ragsdale Dr.
Monterey, CA 93940
(800) 654-8802
(408) 372-9267 fax
Mastering software

SuperMac Technology, Inc.
215 Moffett Park Dr.
Sunnyvale, CA 94089-1374
(800) 334-3005
(408) 541-5004 fax
Video production card: Mac

TextWare Corp.
P.O. Box 3267
Park City, UT 84060
(801) 645-9600
Authoring software, indexing software

TMS, Inc.
P.O. Box 1358
Stillwater, OK 74076
(405) 377-0880
(405) 377-0452 fax
Imaging software, utilities: MS-DOS, Windows, Unix, Mac

Twelve Tone Systems
44 Pleasant St.
P.O. Box 760
Watertown, MA 02272
(800) 234-1171 or (617) 926-2480
(617) 924-6657 fax
Music production software: Windows, MPC

Video Associates Labs
4926 Spicewood Springs Rd.
Austin, TX 78759
(800) 331-0547
(512) 346-5781
(512) 346-9407 fax
Video and audio capture boards: MS-DOS, Windows

Voyager Co., The
1351 Pacific Coast Hwy.
Santa Monica, CA 90401
(310) 451-1383
Electronic book authoring software: Mac

Voyetra Technologies
333 5th Ave.
Pelham, NY 10803
(800) 233-9377 or (914) 738-4500
(914) 728-6946 fax
Music/audio production software: Windows, MPC

WordPerfect Corp.
1555 N. Technology Way
Orem, UT 84057-2399
(801) 225-5000
(801) 228-5077 fax
Markup software: MS-DOS, Unix

Young Minds, Inc.
1910 Orange Tree Ln.
Ste. 300
Redlands, CA 92374
(909) 335-1350
(909) 798-0488 fax
Authoring software and hardware: Unix, Windows, Mac

Appendix B

DISTRIBUTORS

Baker and Taylor Software
124 E. 36th St.
New York, NY 10016
(212) 689-0777
(212) 689-0930 fax

EduCorp
7434 Trade St.
San Diego, CA 92121
(619) 536-9999
(619) 536-2345 fax

TestDrive Corp.
2933 Bunker Hill Ln.
Ste. 101
Santa Clara, CA 95054-1124
(408) 496-0555
(408) 496-6810 fax
Demo disc

DRIVE VENDORS

3DO Company, The
600 Galveston Dr.
Redwood City, CA 94063
(415) 261-3202
(415) 261-3230 fax
3DO licensing

Acculogic, Inc.
13715 Alton Pkwy.
Irvine, CA 92718
(714) 454-2441
(714) 454-8527 fax
Portable CD-ROM

Appendix B

ACS Computer
Blk. 211 Henderson Industrial Pk., #10-03/04
Singapore 0315
(65)4793888
(415) 875-6729
CD-ROM

Alea Systems, Inc.
5016 Dorsey Hall Dr.
Ste. 102
Ellicot City, MD 21042
CD-R

Apple Computer, Inc.
20525 Mariani Ave.
Cupertino, CA 95014-1010
(408) 996-1010
(408) 974-5192 fax
CD-ROM, PowerCD

APS Technologies
6131 Deramus
P.O. Box 4987
Kansas City, MO 64120-0087
(816) 373-5800
(816) 478-6506 fax
CD-ROM

CD Technology, Inc.
766 San Aleso Ave.
Sunnyvale, CA 94086
(408) 752-8500
(408) 752-8501 fax
Portable CD-ROM, CD-ROM

Chinon America, Inc.
615 Hawaii Avenue
Torrance, CA 90503
(800) 441-0222
CD-ROM

Appendix B

CMS Enhancements, Inc.
2722 Michelson Dr.
Irvine, CA 92715
(714) 222-6000
CD-ROM

Creative Labs, Inc.
1901 McCarthy Blvd.
Milpitas, CA 95035
(408) 428-6600
(408) 428-2394 fax
CD-ROM

DC Technologies
(800) 937-6257
CD-ROM

Eastman Kodak Company
343 State St.
Rochester, NY 14650-0519
(800) 242-2424
(716) 724-1983
Photo CD

Fidelity International Technologies
106 Campus Plaza
Raritan Center
Edison, NJ 08837-3936
(908) 417-2230
(908) 417-5994 fax
Portable CD-ROM

FWB, Inc.
2040 Polk St., Ste 225
San Francisco, CA 94109
(415) 474-8055
(415) 775-2125 fax
CD-ROM

Appendix B

Hitachi Home Electronics, Inc.
401 W. Artesia Blvd.
Compton, CA 90220
(800) 369-0422
(310) 537-8383
(310) 515-6223 fax
CD-ROM

Insight
1912 W. 4th St.
Tempe, AZ 85081
(800) 927-7848
(602) 902-1176
(602) 350-1150 fax
CD-ROM

Interpreter, Inc.
11455 W. I-70
N. Frontage Rd.
Wheat Ridge, CO 80033
(800) 232-4687 or (303) 431-8991
(303) 431-9056 fax
Portable CD-ROM

Introl Corp.
2817 Anthony Lane S.
Minneapolis, MN 55418-3254
(612) 788-9391
(612) 788-9387 fax
CD-ROM

JVC Information Products Company of America
19900 Beach Blvd.
Ste. I
Huntington Beach, CA 92648
(714) 965-2610
(714) 968-9071 fax
CD-R

Appendix B

Knowledge Access International, Inc.
2685 Marine Way
Ste. 1305
Mountain View, CA 94043
(415) 969-0606
(415) 964-2027 fax
CD-R

Liberty Systems
160 Saratoga Ave., Ste. 38
Santa Clara, CA 95051
(408) 983-1127
CD-ROM

MacProducts USA, Inc.
608 W. 22nd St.
Austin, TX 78705-5116
(800) 622-3475
(512) 472-8881
(512) 499-0888 fax
CD-ROM

MASS Microsystems
810 W. Maude Ave.
Sunnyvale, CA 94086
(800) 677-8333
(408) 733-5499
CD-ROM

Micro Design International, Inc.
6985 University Blvd.
Winter Park, FL 32792
(407) 677-8333
(407) 677-8365 fax
CD-ROM

Micronet Technology
80 Technology
Irvine, CA 92718
(714) 837-6033
CD-ROM

Appendix B

Micro Solutions, Inc.
132 W. Lincoln Hwy.
DeKalb, IL 60115
(815) 756-3411
(815) 756-2928 fax
Portable CD-ROM

Mirror Technologies, Inc.
305 Second St. NW
New Brighton, MN 55112
(800) 654-5294
(612) 633-4450
(612) 633-3131 fax
CD-ROM

NEC Technologies, Inc.
1255 Michael Dr.
Wood Dale, IL 60191
(708) 860-9500
CD-ROM, portable CD-ROM

Optical Access International, Inc.
500 W. Cummings Park, Ste. 3250
Woburn, MA 01801
(800) 433-5135
(617) 937-3910
(617) 937-3950 fax
CD-ROM

Optical Media International
180 Knowles Dr.
Los Gatos, CA 95030
(408) 376-3511
(408) 376-3519 fax
CD-R

Peripheral Land, Inc. (PLI)
47421 Bayside Pkwy.
Fremont, CA 94538
(800) 288-8754
(510) 657-2211
(510) 683-9713 fax
CD-ROM

Appendix B

Philips Professional Interactive Media Systems
One Philips Dr.
P.O. Box 14810
Knoxville, TN 37914-1810
(800) 835-3506
CD-I, CD-ROM, CD-R

Pioneer New Media Technologies, Inc.
2265 E. 220th St.
Long Beach, CA 90810
(310) 952-2111
(310) 952-2990 fax
CD-ROM, CD-R, minichanger

Plasmon Data Systems
1654 Centre Pointe Dr.
Milpitas, CA 95035
(408) 956-9400
(408) 956-9444 fax
CD-R

Plextor
4255 Burton Dr.
Santa Clara, CA 95054
(800) 886-3835 or (408) 980-1838
(408) 986-1010 fax
CD-ROM

Procom Technology
2181 Dupont Dr.
Irvine, CA 92715
(714) 852-1000
(714) 852-1221 fax
CD-ROM

Sony Electronics, Inc.
Data Storage Products Div.
3300 Zanker Rd.
San Jose, CA 95134
(800) 352-7669
CD-ROM

Appendix B

SyDOS
6501 Park of Commerce Blvd.
Ste. 110
Boca Raton, FL 33487
(407) 998-5400
(407) 998-5414 fax
Portable CD-ROM

Teac America
Data Storage Products Division
7733 Telegraph Rd.
Montebello, CA 90640
(213) 726-0303
CD-ROM

Todd Enterprises, Inc.
224-49 67th Ave.
Bayside, NY 11364
(718) 343-1040
CD-ROM

Toshiba America Information Systems, Inc.
Disk Products Div.
9740 Irvine Blvd.
Irvine, CA 92718
(714) 457-0777
CD-ROM

Wearnes Technology Corp.
1015 E. Brokaw Rd.
San Jose, CA 95131
(408) 456-8838
CD-ROM

Young Minds, Inc.
1910 Orange Tree Ln.
Ste. 300
Redlands, CA 92374
(909) 335-1350
(909) 798-0488 fax
CD-R

Appendix B

EDUCATIONAL CDS

Applied Optical Media Corp.
1450 Boot Rd.
Bldg. 400
West Chester, PA 19380
(800) 321-7259 or (215) 429-3701
(215) 429-3810 fax
History: Windows, MPC

Broderbund Software, Inc.
500 Redwood Blvd.
Novato, CA 94948-6121
(800) 521-6263 or (415) 382-4600
(415) 382-4419 fax
Early reading, geography: Windows, MPC, Mac

Bureau Development
141 New Rd.
Parsippany, NJ 07054
(800) 828-4766 or (201) 808-2700
(201) 808-2676 fax
Literature, history: MS-DOS, Mac

Compton's NewMedia
2320 Camino Vida Roble
Carlsbad, CA 92009
(800) 862-2206 or (619) 929-2500
(619) 929-2511 fax
Music history, early learning: Windows, MPC

Compu-Teach Educational Software
78 Olive St.
New Haven, CT 06511
(800) 448-3224 or (203) 777-7738
Early learning, math: VIS

Appendix B

DC Heath & Co.
125 Spring St.
Lexington, MA 02173-9911
(800) 235-3565
Language: Mac

Decision Development Corp.
2680 Bishop Dr.
Ste. 122
San Ramon, CA 94583
(800) 835-4332 or (510) 830-8896
(510) 830-0830 fax
History: MS-DOS, Windows

Digital Theater
5857 Peachtree Industrial Blvd.
Ste. 150
Norcross, GA 30092
(404) 446-1332
(404) 446-9164 fax

Dr. T's Music Software, Inc.
124 Crescent Rd.
Ste. 3
Needham, MA 02194
(800) 989-6434 or (617) 455-1454
(617) 455-1460 fax
Music history: Windows, MPC

Ebook, Inc.
32970 Alvarado-Niles Rd.
Ste. 704
Union City, CA 94587
(510) 429-1331
(510) 429-1394 fax
Art history, music history, history, literature: Windows, MPC

Appendix B

EduQuest
6269 B. Variel Ave.
Woodland Hills, CA 91367
(818) 992-8484
(818) 992-8781 fax
Windows, MPC

Follett Software Co., The
809 N. Front St.
McHenry, IL 60050-5589
(800) 323-3397 or (815) 344-8774

HyperGlot Software Company, Inc.
P.O. Box 10746
Knoxville, TN 37939-0746
(800) 726-5087 or (615) 558-8270
(615) 588-6569 fax
Language: Windows, MPC

Ibis Software
140 Second St.
Ste. 603
San Francisco, CA 94105
(415) 546-1917
(415) 546-0361 fax
Musical instrument instruction: Windows, MPC

Knowledge Adventure, Inc.
4502 Dyer St.
La Crescenta, CA 91214
(800) 542-4240
(818) 542-4205 fax
Science, astronomy: MS-DOS, Windows

Maris Multimedia, Ltd.
99 Mansell St.
London E1 8AX
England
44-71-488-1566
44-71-702-0534 fax
Astronomy: Mac, Windows

McGraw-Hill, Inc.
11 W. 19th St.
New York, NY 10011
(800) 722-4726 or (212) 337-5961
(212) 337-4092 fax
Biology: MPC, Windows

Microsoft Corp.
One Microsoft Way
Redmond, WA 98052-6399
(800) 323-2577
Music history

Milliken Publishing Co.
1100 Research Blvd.
P.O. Box 21579
St. Louis, MO 63132-0579
(800) 325-4136
Early learning: MS-DOS, Windows, Mac

National Geographic Society
Washington, D.C. 20036
(800) 368-2728
Natural science and geography

Pacific HiTech, Inc.
4530 Fortuna Way
Salt Lake City, UT 84124
(800) 765-8369 or (801) 278-2042
(801) 278-2666 fax
Early learning: MS-DOS

Quanta Press, Inc.
1313 5th St.
Ste. 223A
Minneapolis, MN 55414
(612) 379-3956
(612) 623-4570 fax
History

Appendix B

Software Toolworks, The
60 Leveroni Ct.
Novato, CA 94949
(800) 234-3088 or (415) 883-3000
(415) 883-3303 fax
Typing: Windows, MPC

Sony Electronic Publishing Co.
9 W. 57th St.
New York, NY 10019
(212) 418-9439
Language: MMCD, Windows, Mac

Sumeria, Inc.
329 Bryant St.
Ste. 3D
San Francisco, CA 94107
(415) 904-0800
(415) 904-0888 fax
Natural science: Mac, Windows

Syracuse Language Systems
719 E. Genesee St.
Syracuse, NY 13210
(800) 688-1937 or (315) 478-6729
(315) 478-6902 fax
Language: Windows, MPC

Texas Caviar, Inc.
3933 Spicewood Springs Rd.
Ste. E-100
Austin, TX 78759
(512) 346-7887
(512) 346-1393 fax
Early learning: Windows, Mac

Voyager Co., The
1351 Pacific Coast Hwy.
Santa Monica, CA 90401
(310) 451-1383
(310) 394-2150 fax
Culture, language: Mac

Appendix B

Warner New Media
3500 W. Olive Ave.
Ste. 1050
Burbank, CA 91505
(800) 593-6334 or (818) 955-9999
(818) 955-6499 fax
History, current events, astronomy, cosmology: Windows, MPC

World Library, Inc.
12914 Haster St.
Garden Grove, CA 92640
(714) 748-7197
(714) 748-7198 fax
Literature

Xiphias
8758 Venice Blvd.
Los Angeles, CA 90034
(310) 841-2790
(310) 841-2559 fax
History, science, business, art, music, literature: MS-DOS, Data Discman, CDTV

MARKET RESEARCH

InfoTech
P.O. Box 150
Woodstock, VT 05091
(802) 457-1037
(802) 457-1038 fax

MEDIA CLIPART

Applied Optical Media Corp.
1450 Boot Rd.
West Chester, PA 19380
(800) 321-7259
(215) 429-3701
(215) 429-3810 fax
Photos, sound: MPC, Windows

Appendix B

Aris Entertainment
310 Washington Blvd.
Ste. 100
Marina Del Rey, CA 90292
(800) 228-2747 or (310) 821-0234
(310) 821-6463 fax
Graphics, video, photos, sound: MPC, Windows

Autologic, Inc.
1050 Rancho Conejo Blvd.
Thousand Oaks, CA 91320
(805) 498-9611
(805) 499-1167 fax
Fonts: Mac

Cinema Expeditions, Inc.
17 Leisure Dr.
Kirksville, MO 63501
Image: Photo CD

Comstock, Inc.
The Comstock Bldg.
30 Irving Pl.
New York, NY 10003
(212) 353-8600
(212) 353-3383 fax
Photo: Mac

Digital Zone, Inc.
P.O. Box 5562
Bellevue, WA 98006
(800) 538-3113 or (206) 623-3456
(206) 454-3922 fax
Image: Photo CD

Educorp
7434 Trade St.
San Diego, CA 92121
(800) 843-9497 or (619) 536-9999
(619) 536-2345 fax
Image: Mac

Appendix B

Hopkins Technology
421 Hazel Ln.
Hopkins, MN 55343-7116
(800) 397-9211
(612) 931-9377 fax
Astronomy images: MS-DOS, Windows

InterActive Publishing Corp.
300 Airport Executive Park
Spring Valley, NY 10977
(914) 426-0400
(914) 426-2606 fax
Sound: Windows, MPC

Killer Tracks
6543 Sunset Blvd.
Hollywood, CA 90028
(800) 877-0078 or (213) 957-4455
(213) 957-4470 fax
Music: Windows, Mac, MS-DOS

Laboratory for Atmospheric and Space Physics
University of Colorado
Campus Box 590
Boulder, CO 80309
(303) 492-7666
(303) 492-6444 fax
Astronomy images: MS-DOS, Mac

Marr Design Associates
977 Oakland Ave.
Cincinnati, OH 45205
(513) 251-7014
(513) 861-2932 fax
Image: Mac

Appendix B

Mediacom, Inc.
P.O. Box 36173
Richmond, VA 23235
(804) 794-0700
(804) 794-0799 fax
Video: Mac

Midisoft Corp.
P.O. 1000
Bellevue, WA 98009
(800) 776-6434
(206) 881-7176
(206) 883-1368 fax
Music: Windows

Mirror Technologies, Inc.
2644 Patton Rd.
Roseville, MN 55113
(800) 447-5393 or (612) 628-6295
(612) 633-3136 fax
Image, photo: Mac

Prosonus
11126 Weddington
N. Hollywood, CA 91601
(818) 766-5221
(818) 766-6098 fax
Sound effects, music: Windows, MPC, Mac

Sound Ideas
105 W. Beaver Creek Rd.
Ste. 4
Richmond Hill, Ontario L4B 1O6
Canada
(800) 387-3030
(416) 886-5000 fax
Sound effects: Windows, MPC

Swifte International, Ltd.
724 Yorklyn Rd.
Hockessin, DE 19707
(800) 237-9383
(302) 234-1716 fax
Font: MS-DOS, Windows

Walnut Creek CD-ROM
1547 Palos Verde Mall
Ste. 260
Walnut Creek, CA 94596
(800) 786-9907 or (510) 674-0783
(510) 947-0821 fax
Image: MS-DOS, Windows, Mac

MEDIA SOURCES

3M Optical Recording
3M Center Bldg.
St. Paul, MN 55144-1000
(612) 733-2142
CD-ROM and CD-R

CD-ROM Service Bureau
Rte. 3 Box 1108
Gainesville, VA 22065
(800) 328-2347 or (703) 347-2111
(703) 347-9085 fax
CD-R

DIC Digital
Glenpointe Centre W.
500 Frank W. Burr Blvd.
Teaneck, NJ 07666
(201) 692-7700
CD-R

Appendix B

Eastman Kodak Co.
343 State St.
Rochester, NY 14650
(800) 242-2424
(716) 724-1983
CD-R

Kao Optical Products Div.
1857 Colonial Village Ln.
Lancaster, PA 17601
(800) 525-6575 or (717) 392-7840
(717) 392-7897 fax
CD-R

Knowledge Access International, Inc.
2685 Marine Way
Ste. 1305
Mountain View, CA 94303
(415) 969-0606
(415) 964-2027 fax
CD-R

MTC America, Inc.
Two Central Tower
140 E. 45th St.
New York, NY 10017
(800) 367-2479 or (212) 867-6330
(212) 867-6315 fax
CD-R

Verbatim Corp.
1200 W.T. Harris Blvd.
Charlotte, NC 28262
(800) 759-3475
(704) 547-6609 fax
CD-ROM and CD-R

Appendix B

MULTIMEDIA UPGRADE KIT VENDORS

ACS Computer PTE Ltd.
260 E. Grand Ave.
San Francisco, CA 94080
(800) 282-5747 or (415) 875-6633
(415) 875-6636 fax
Windows, MPC

Apple Computer, Inc.
20525 Mariani Ave.
Cupertino, CA 95014-1010
(408) 996-1010
(408) 974-5192 fax
Windows, MPC

Aztech Labs, Inc.
46707 Fremont Blvd.
Fremont, CA 94538
(510) 623-8988
(510) 623-8989 fax
Windows, MPC

Cardinal Technologies, Inc.
1827 Freedom Rd.
Lancaster, PA 17601
(717) 293-3000
(717) 293-3055 fax
Windows, MPC

Creative Labs, Inc.
1901 McCarthy Blvd.
Milpitas, CA 95035
(408) 428-0233
(408) 428-6611 fax
Windows, MPC

Appendix B

Insight
1912 W. 4th St.
Tempe, AZ 85081
(800) 927-7848 or (602) 902-1176
(602) 350-1150 fax
Windows, MPC

Media Vision
3185 Laurelview Ct.
Fremont, CA 94538
(800) 348-7116 or (510) 770-8600
(510) 770-8648 fax
Windows, MPC

Micro Express
1801 Carnegie Ave.
Santa Ana, CA 92705
(800) 989-9900
Windows, MPC

Plextor
4255 Burton Dr.
Santa Clara, CA 95054
(800) 886-3935 or (408) 980-1838
(408) 986-1010 fax
Windows, MPC

Saturn Technology, Inc.
3945 Freedom Circle
Ste. 770
Santa Clara, CA 95054
(408) 982-5910
(408) 982-5923 fax
Windows, MPC

Sigma Designs
47900 Bayside Pkwy.
Fremont, CA 94538
(510) 770-2654
(510) 770-2640 fax
Windows, MPC

NETWORKING PRODUCTS

DEC
Digital Dr.
Merrimack, NH 03054
(800) DIGITAL
Server

Flexsys Corp.
24 Graf Rd.
Newburyport, MA 01950
(800) 533-7756 or (508) 465-6060
(508) 465-6633 fax
CD-ROM network

IBM
Old Orchard Rd.
Armonk, NY 10504
(800) 426-3333
(914) 765-1900
Server

Info Line
2391 Zanker Rd.
Ste. 340
San Jose, CA 95131
(408) 428-0268
(408) 428-9174 fax
Server: MS-DOS, Netware

Logicraft
22 Cotton Rd.
Nashua, NH 03063
(603) 880-0300
(603) 880-7229 fax
Server

Appendix B

Lotus Development Corp.
55 Cambridge Pkwy.
Cambridge, MA 01242
(617) 577-8500
LAN software

Meridian Data, Inc.
5615 Scotts Valley Dr.
Scotts Valley, CA 95066
(408) 438-3100
(408) 438-6816 fax
Server, jukebox

Microtest Inc.
4747 N. 22nd St.
Phoenix, AZ 85016-4708
(602) 952-6400
(602) 952-6401 fax
LAN port adapter and software

TAC Systems, Inc.
P.O. Box 650
Meridianville, AL 35759
(205) 828-6920
(205) 828-6922 fax
Server

Todd Enterprises, Inc.
224-49 67th Ave.
Bayside, NY 11364
(718) 343-1040
(718) 343-9180 fax
Server

Virtual Microsystems, Inc.
1825 S. Grant St.
Ste. 700
San Mateo, CA 94402
(415) 573-9596
(415) 572-8406 fax
Server: MS-DOS, Mac, VAX

Appendix B

PHOTO CD PROCESSING

Boston Photo Lab
20 Newbury St.
Boston, MA 02116
(617) 267-4086
(617) 267-8711 fax

Eastman Kodak
343 State St.
Rochester, NY 14650
(800) 242-2424
(716) 724-1983

Fedco Electronics, Inc.
184 W. Second St.
Fond du Lac, WI 54936
(414) 922-6940

Lazerquick Images
2959 SW Cedar Hills Blvd.
Beaverton, OR 97005
(800) 937-9196 or (503) 520-3180
(503) 641-5151 fax
Oregon, Washington, and California only

PORTABLE COMPUTERS WITH CD-ROM DRIVES

Aquiline, Inc.
283 Old Catham Rd.
Latham, NY 12110
(518) 785-6517
(518) 785-0283 fax

Appendix B

Scenario, Inc.
3 Bridge St.
Newton, MA 02158
(800) 468-1119
(617) 965-6460 fax

PRESENTATION SOFTWARE

Ask Me Multimedia Center, Inc.
7100 Northland Circle
Ste. 401
Minneapolis, MN 55428
(612) 531-0603
(612) 531-0645 fax
Windows

Asymetrix Corp.
110-110th Ave. NE
Ste. 700
Bellevue, WA 98004
(800) 448-6543 or (206) 462-0501
(206) 637-1504 fax
Windows

Gold Disk, Inc.
3350 Scott Blvd.
Bldg. 14
Santa Clara, CA 95054-3107
(408) 982-0200
(408) 982-0298 fax
Windows

Lotus Development Corp.
55 Cambridge Pkwy.
Cambridge, MA 01242
(617) 577-8500
Windows, Mac

Q/Media Software Corp.
312 E. 5th Ave.
Vancouver, BC V5T 1H4
Canada
(604) 879-1190
(604) 879-0214 fax
Windows

Zuma Group, Inc.
6733 N. Black Canyon Highway
Phoenix, AZ 85015
(800) 332-3492 or (602) 246-4238
(602) 246-6708 fax
Windows

PROCESSOR UPGRADES

Kelly Micro Systems
25 Musick
Irvine, CA 92718
(800) 854-3900
PC

PUBLISHING SERVICES

3M Corp.
3M Center
St. Paul, MN 55144-1000
(800) 328-1303
(612) 733-1110
Replication, distribution, packaging, and fulfillment

Appendix B

Andromeda Interactive
1050 Marina Village Pkwy.
Ste. 107
Alameda, CA 94501
(510) 769-1616
(510) 769-1919 fax
Image resource bank

CD-ROM Technologies, Inc.
5711 S. 86th Circle
P.O. Box 27347
Omaha, NE 68127-0347
(402) 593-4511
(402) 331-6681 fax
Metering software, production

Disc Manufacturing, Inc.
1409 Foulk Rd., Ste. 102
Wilmington, DE 19803
(302) 479-2500
Replication

Disctronics, Inc.
Plano, TX
(214) 881-8800
(214) 881-8500 fax
Replication, production

Ehrlich Multimedia
One Maynard Dr.
Park Ridge, NJ 07649
(201) 307-8866
(201) 307-8884 fax
Custom publishing services

IBM Software Manufacturing Co.
6300 Diagonal Hwy.
Boulder, CO 80301-9191
(800) 926-0364
(800) 925-7479 fax
Production

Appendix B

Knowledge Access International, Inc.
2685 Marine Way
Ste. 1305
Mountain View, CA 94303
(415) 969-0606
(415) 964-2027 fax
Prototyping, production

Media Presents
3233 Clay St.
Ste. 5
San Francisco, CA 94115
(415) 771-6126
Multimedia production service

Metatec Corp.
7001 Discovery Blvd.
Dublin, OH 43017
(800) 637-3472 or (614) 761-2000
(614) 761-1258 fax
Production services

Nimbus Information Systems
Guildford Farm
Ruckersville, VA 22968
(800) 782-0778 or (804) 985-1100
Replication, production

Northeastern Digital Recording, Inc.
2 Hidden Meadow Lane
Southborough, MA 01772
(508) 481-9322
(508) 624-6437 fax
Premastering

One-Off CD Shop, Inc.
304-8th Ave. SW
Ste. 610
Calgary, AB
CANADA, T2P 1C2
(800) 387-1633 or (403) 263-1370
(403) 228-6480 fax
Franchise CD-ROM service bureau

Appendix B

R.R. Donnelley Database Technology Services
7501 S. Quincy
Willowbrook, IL 60521
(708) 655-8232
Multimedia publishing

Roger East Design
600 Townsend St.
Ste. 415W
San Francisco, CA 94103
(415) 552-2300
(415) 552-2371 fax
Multimedia production

Vanguard Media Corp.
132 W. 22nd St.
5th Fl.
New York, NY
(212) 242-5317
Interactive multimedia service for traditional publishers

VIS Development Corp.
100 Fifth Ave.
Waltham, MA 02154
(617) 466-6678
VCR-to-CD-ROM conversion

Young Minds Publishing Services Group
1910 Orange Tree Ln., Ste. 300
Redlands, CA 92374
(909) 335-1350
(909) 798-0488 fax
Production services

Appendix B

RETRIEVAL SOFTWARE VENDORS

Apple Computer, Inc.
20525 Mariani Ave.
Cupertino, CA 95014-1010
(408) 996-1010
(408) 974-5192 fax

BRS Software Products
8000 Westpark Dr.
McLean, VA 22102
(703) 442-3870
(703) 827-0686 fax

Creative Multimedia Corp.
514-NW 11th
Ste. 203
Portland, OR 97209
(503) 241-4351
(503) 241-4370 fax

DataDisc
Rte. 3, Box 1108
Gainesville, VA 22065
(800) 328-2347 or (703) 347-2111
(703) 347-9085 fax

Dataware Technologies
222 Third St.
Ste. 3300
Cambridge, MA 02142
(617) 621-0820
(617) 621-0307 fax
MS-DOS, Unix, Mac

Appendix B

Eastman Kodak Co.
343 State St.
Rochester, NY 14650
(800) 242-2424
(716) 724-1983
Windows, Mac

Folio Corp.
2155 N. Freedom Blvd.
Ste. 150
Provo, UT 84604
(801) 375-3700
Windows, MS-DOS

Fulcrum Technologies, Inc.
785 Carling Ave.
Ottawa, Ontario K1S 5H4
Canada
(613) 238-1761
(613) 238-7695 fax

H.W. Wilson Company
950 University Ave.
Bronx, NY 10542
(800) 367-6770
(718) 588-1230 fax

Imspace Systems Corp.
4747 Morena Blvd.
Ste. 360
San Diego, CA 92117
(800) 488-5836 or (619) 272-2600
(619) 272-4292 fax

Information Management Research, Inc.
5660 Greenwood Plaza Blvd.
Ste. 210
Englewood, CO 80111
(303) 689-0022
(303) 689-0055 fax

Appendix B

Johnston & Co.
PO Box 446
American Fork, UT 84003-0446
(801) 756-1111
(801) 756-0242 fax
U.S. Constitution papers; DOS, Windows

Knowledge Access International, Inc.
2685 Marine Way
Ste. 1305
Mountain View, CA 94303
(415) 969-0606
(415) 964-2027 fax
MS-DOS, Windows, MPC

MicroRetrieval Corp.
101 Main St.
Cambridge, MA 02142
(617) 577-1574
(617) 577-9517 fax

Personal Library Software
2400 Research Blvd.
Ste. 350
Rockville, MD 20850-3243
(301) 990-1155
(301) 963-9738 fax

SandPoint Corp.
124 Mount Auburn St.
Cambridge, MA 02138
(617) 868-4442
(617) 868-5562 fax

Appendix B

SilverPlatter Information
100 River Ridge Dr.
Norwood, MA 02062-5026
(617) 769-2599
(617) 769-8763 fax
or 1005 N. Glebe Rd.
Ste. 605
Arlington, VA 22201
(800) 521-0574

TextWare Corp.
P.O. Box 3267
Park City, UT 84060
(801) 645-9600

TMS, Inc.
P.O. Box 1358
Stillwater, OK 74076
(405) 377-0880
(405) 377-0452 fax
MS-DOS, Windows, Unix, Mac

SCSI PRODUCTS

APS Technologies
6131 Deramus
P.O. Box 4987
Kansas City, MO 64120-0087
(816) 373-5800
(816) 478-6506 fax
Cable adapter: Mac

Corel Corp.
1600 Carling Ave.
Ottawa, Ontario K1Z 8R7
Canada
(800) 836-7274 or (613) 728-8200
(613) 728-9790 fax
Universal driver

Future Domain
2801 McGaw Ave.
Irvine, CA 92714
(714) 253-0400
(714) 253-0913 fax
Host adapter, universal interface

New Media Corp.
Irvine Spectrum
15375 Barranca, Bldg. B101
Irvine, CA 92718
(800) 453-0550 or (714) 453-0100
(714) 453-0114 fax
PCMCIA adapter

Shuttle Technology Ltd.
Rubra 1
The Mulberry Business Park
Workingham, Berkshire RG11 2QJ
England
44-734-770441
44-734-771709 fax
Parallel-to-SCSI converter

Ultrastor Corp.
15 Hammond
Ste. 310
Irvine, CA 92718
(714) 581-4100
(714) 581-0826 fax
Caching controller: PC

SECURITY SOFTWARE VENDORS

Digital Delivery, Inc.
54 Middlesex Turnpike
Bedford, MA 01730
(617) 863-8807
(617) 861-6752 fax
Encryption software

Appendix B

Glenco Engineering, Inc.
270 Lexington Dr.
Buffalo Grove, IL 60089-6930
(708) 808-0300
(708) 808-0313 fax

InfoSafe Systems, Inc.
67-15J 190th Ln.
Fresh Meadows, NJ 11365
(718) 990-6364

SHAREWARE

CD-ROM Users Group
P.O. Box 2400
Santa Barbara, CA 93120
(805) 965-0265
(805) 965-5415 fax
MS-DOS

Crosley Software
Box 276
Alburg, VT 05440
(514) 739-9328
(514) 345-8303 fax
Windows, OS/2

Max Systems, Inc.
P.O. Box 1087
Winter Garden, FL 34787
(800) 444-6723
(407) 877-3834 fax

Most Significant Bits
15508 Madison Ave.
Lakewood, OH 44107
(800) 755-4619
MS-DOS, Windows

Appendix B

Network Cybernetics Corp.
4201 Wingren Rd.
Ste. 202
Irving, TX 75062-2763
(214) 650-2002
(214) 650-1929 fax
Artificial intelligence software: MS-DOS, Mac, Unix

PC-SIG
1030-D E. Duane Ave.
Sunnyvale, CA 94086
(800) 245-6717 or (408) 730-9291
(408) 730-2107 fax
MS-DOS

PC Software & Supply
2404 Dakota Ave.
Sout Sioux City, NE 68776-0278
(800) 728-5031
(402) 494-8711 fax
MS-DOS, Windows, MPC

Pier Exchange, The
128 Carmel Rd.
Buffalo, NY 14214
(716) 875-4931
Windows, OS/2

Profit Press
2956 N. Campbell Ave.
Tucson, AZ 85719
(800) 843-7990 or (602) 770-0000
(602) 770-0005 fax
MS-DOS, Windows

S&S Enterprises, Inc.
P.O. Box 552
Lemont, IL 60439
(800) 766-3472 or (708) 257-7616
(708) 257-9678 fax
MPC, Windows

Appendix B

Walnut Creek CD-ROM
1547 Palos Verde Mall
Ste. 260
Walnut Creek, CA 94596
(510) 674-0783
Games, business software, religious, home: MS-DOS, Windows, OS/2

SHOWS AND CONFERENCES

CD-ROM Expo
Mitch Hall Associates
260 Milton St.
Dedham, MA 02026
(617) 361-8000
(617) 361-3389 fax

Interactive Media Festival
3945 Freedom Circle
9th Floor
Santa Clara, CA 95054
(408) 982-0400
(408) 982-0403 fax

Intermedia
Reed Exhibitions
999 Summer St.
P.O. Box 3833
Stamford, CT 06905-0833
(203) 352-8254
(203) 352-8445 fax
Electronic publishing

SIGGRAPH Conference Management
401 N. Michigan Ave.
Chicago, IL 60611
(312) 321-6830
(312) 321-6876 fax
Graphics

Appendix B

SOUND PRODUCT VENDORS

Apple Computer, Inc.
20525 Mariani Ave.
Cupertino, CA 95014
(408) 996-1010
Speakers

Aztech Labs, Inc.
46707 Fremont Blvd.
Fremont, CA 94538
(510) 623-8988
(510) 623-8989 fax
Sound board: Windows, MPC

Best Data Products, Inc.
21800 Nordhoff St.
Chatsworth, CA 91311
(818) 773-9600
Sound board

Bose Corp.
The Mountain
Framingham, MA 01701
(508) 879-7330
Speakers

Cardinal Technologies
1827 Freedom Rd.
Lancaster, PA 17601
(717) 293-3000
Sound board: Windows

Creative Labs, Inc.
1901 McCarthy Blvd.
Milpitas, CA 95035
(408) 428-6600
(408) 428-2394 fax
Sound board: Windows

Appendix B

Diamond Computer Systems, Inc.
1130 E. Arques Ave.
Sunnyvale, CA 94086
(408) 736-2000
(408) 730-5750 fax
Sound board: Windows

Labtec Enterprises, Inc.
11010 NE 37th Circle
Unit 110
Vancouver, WA 98682
(206) 896-2000
(206) 896-2020 fax
Speakers

Logitech, Inc.
6505 Kaiser Dr.
Fremont, CA 94555
(510) 795-8500
(510) 792-8901 fax
Sound board: Windows

Kenwood USA Corp.
P.O. Box 22745
2201 E. Dominguez St.
Long Beach, CA 90801-5745
(310) 639-9000
Music software: Windows

Media Vision
3185 Laurelview Ct.
Fremont, CA 94538
(800) 348-7116
(510) 623-5749 fax
Sound board: Windows

Microsoft Corp.
One Microsoft Way
Redmond, WA 98052-6399
(206) 882-8080
(206) 936-7329 fax
Sound software: Windows

Roland Corp.
7200 Dominion Circle
Los Angeles, CA 90040-3696
(213) 685-5141
Sound board: Windows

Sigma Designs
47900 Bayside Pkwy.
Fremont, CA 94538
(510) 770-2654
(510) 770-2640 fax
Sound board: Windows, MPC

Video Associates Labs
4926 Spicewood Springs Rd.
Austin, TX 78759
(800) 331-0547 or (512) 346-0547
(512) 346-5781 fax
Parallel port sound device: MS-DOS, Windows

SYSTEM INTEGRATORS

Virtual Microsystems, Inc.
1825 S. Grant St.
Ste. 700
San Mateo, CA 94402
(415) 573-9596

TRAINING CD-ROMS

Canadian Centre for Occupational Health and Safety
250 Main St. E.
Hamilton, Ontario
Canada L8N 1H6
(416) 572-2981
Chemical industry

Appendix B

Computer Directions
2712 W. Shaw Ave. #234
Fresno, CA 93711
(209) 276-5777
(209) 276-5656 fax
Physical fitness: VIS

National Education Training Group
1751 W. Diehl Rd.
Naperville, IL 60563
(708) 369-3000
Professional skills

QuickStart Technologies, Inc.
5862 Bolsa Ave.
Bldg. 103
Huntington Beach, CA 92649-1169
(714) 894-1448
(714) 894-4814 fax
Software: Windows

TV-BASED PLAYERS

3DO Company, The
600 Galveston Dr.
Redwood City, CA 94063
(415) 261-3202
(415) 261-3230 fax
3DO licensing

Commodore Business Machines
1200 Wilson Dr.
West Chester, PA 19380
(215) 431-9100
CD32, CDTV

Panasonic
1 Panasonic Way
Secaucus, NJ 07044
(201) 348-7000
3DO

Philips Consumer Electronics Co.
1 Philips Dr.
P.O. Box 14810
Knoxville, TN 37914-1810
(615) 521-4316
CD-I

Sega of America
255 Shoreline Dr.
Ste. 200
Redwood City, CA 94065
(415) 508-2800
Sega CD

Tandy Corp.
1800 One Tandy Center
Fort Worth, TX 76102
(817) 390-3011
(817) 390-2774 fax
VIS

Turbo Technologies, Inc.
6701 Center Drive W.
Ste. 500
Los Angeles, CA 90045
(310) 641-4622
Turbo Duo

Appendix B

UTILITIES

Animotion Development Corp.
3720 4th Ave. S.
Ste. 205
Birmingham, AL 35222
(800) 536-4175 or (205) 591-5715
(205) 591-5716 fax
Audio control: Windows

Apriori Software Corp.
63 Washington Ave.
Streamwood, IL 60107
(708) 830-6844
CD-ROM cataloger: Windows

Aris Entertainment
310 Washington Blvd.
Ste. 100
Marina Del Rey, CA 90292
(800) 228-2747
(310) 821-0234
(310) 821-6463 fax
Diagnostic software, audio drivers: Windows

C&D Programming
P.O. Box 581012
Salt Lake City, UT
(800) 847-5676
Caching software: MS-DOS

ClarisMac Engineering, Inc.
66D P&S Ln.
Newcastle, CA 95658
(800) 487-4420 or (916) 885-4402
(916) 885-1410 fax
Caching software: Mac

Appendix B

DiagSoft, Inc.
5615 Scotts Valley Dr.
Ste. 140
Scotts Valley, CA 95066
(408) 438-8247
(408) 438-7113 fax
Diagnostic software: MS-DOS, Windows

FWB, Inc.
2040 Polk St.
Ste. 215
San Francisco, CA 94109
(415) 474-2125
(415) 775-2125 fax
Caching software: Mac

Landmark Research International Corp.
703 Grand Central St.
Clearwater, FL 34616
(800) 683-6696 or (813) 443-1331
(813) 443-6603 fax
SCSI diagnostics: MS-DOS, Windows

Lucid Corp.
101 W. Renner Rd.
Ste. 450
Richardson, TX 75082
(800) 925-8243
Caching software: MS-DOS

MacPeak Research
3701 Bee Cave Rd.
Austin, TX 78746
(210) 327-3211
(210) 327-9553 fax
Caching software: Mac

Appendix B

PC-Kwik Corp.
15100 SW Koll Pkwy.
Beaverton, OR 97006-6026
(503) 644-5644
Caching software: MS-DOS

Symantec Corp.
10201 Torre Ave.
Cupertino, CA 95014-2132
(408) 253-9600
Caching software: MS-DOS, Windows

Touchstone Software Corp.
2130 Main St.
Ste. 250
Huntington Beach, CA 92648
(800) 531-0450
(714) 960-1886 fax
Diagnostics: Windows

VIDEO HARDWARE/SOFTWARE VENDORS

Aztech Labs, Inc.
46707 Fremont Blvd.
Fremont, CA 94538
(510) 623-8988
(510) 623-8989 fax
Video board: Windows, MPC

Media Vision
3185 Laurelview Ct.
Fremont, CA 94538
(800) 348-7116 or (510) 770-8600
(510) 770-8648 fax
Video board: Windows

Appendix B

Microsoft Corp.
One Microsoft Way
Redmond, WA 98052-6399
(206) 936-4974
Video capture software: Windows

New Video Corp.
1526 Cloverfield Blvd.
Santa Monica, CA 90404
(310) 449-7000
Video board: Mac

Radius, Inc.
1710 Fortune Dr.
San Jose, CA 95131
(408) 434-1010
Video board: Mac, Windows

RasterOps Corp.
2500 Walsh Ave.
Santa Clara, CA 95051
(408) 562-4200
(408) 562-4065 fax
Video board: Mac, Windows

Sigma Designs
47900 Bayside Pkwy.
Fremont, CA 94538
(510) 770-0100
(510) 770-2640 fax
Video board: Windows

SuperMac Technology
215 Moffett Park Dr.
Sunnyvale, CA 94089
(408) 541-6100
Video board: Mac

Appendix B

TouchVision Systems, Inc.
1800 W. Winnemac
Chicago, IL 60640-2662
(312) 989-2160
(312) 989-2144 fax
Video board: MS-DOS, Windows

Index

A

Access, CD-ROM, 181
Access speed
    CD-ROM, 247
    hard disk, 247
Access to data
    random, 21
    sequential, 21
Accessories, vendors for, (list, 293)
Acrobat, document searches with, 214
Adaptive Differential Pulse Code Modulation (ADPCM), 56
Ad Lib, 131
Adobe Systems, use of Kudo by, 174
ADPCM (adaptive differential pulse code modulation), 273
    and XA discs audio capacity, 56
    compression of sound by, 56
    decompression capability, 56
Adult titles, on CD-ROM, 7
Advertising
    blurring of editorial and, 264
    commercial CD-ROM production and, 232
    contained on CD-ROM, 263-264
Adware, 164, 265, 273
AIFF (Audio Interchange File Format), 217
AimTech Corporation, Icon Author by, 224-225
Aldus, Supercard by, 223
Algorithms, caching in networking, 248
Almanac, 20th Century Video, 188
Alpha AXP systems, applications for on CD-ROM, 162
Alphabet, teaching basics of, 167-169
Amazon, destruction of in children's CD-ROM, 169
American history, on CD-ROM, 187-188
American Social History Project, 187
Amiga CD32
    capabilities, 106
    competitors of, 106

cost, 106
defined, 106
similarities to 3DO, 107
titles of, 106
Analog, 273
bytes, 27
text, sound and video, 27
Analog sound, recording, 51
Ancillary product, CD-ROM to print publishing, 263
Animation
cels, 103, 104, 273
full-screen with 3DO, 101
for "Ugly Duckling," 216
using quality in CD-ROM creation, 215
Anti-aliasing, 104, 273
Anubis CD-ROM All-cache, 149
Apple Animation Compressor, 68
Apple Computer
demos sold by, 163
mail-merchandising by, 164
Apple Macintosh, 11
platform sets an example, 67-69
Apple Photo Compressor, 68
Apple PowerCD portable CD-ROM player, 98, (illus., 98)
Apple QuickTime, 67-69
Apple Raw Compressor, 68
AppleShare, 241
server, 254
Apple's Newton technology, 97
Apple Sweetpea Player, 97
Applications explosion, 14
Archival applications, features of CD-R drives for, 112-113
Archival data, accessing, 22
Archival disc, placing files on, 22
Archival storage, use of optical media for, 21, 273

Archiving, CD-ROM use for, 206
Aris Entertainment, maker of MPC Wizard, 176
Arthur's Teacher Trouble, children's CD-ROM storybook, 170, 171, (illus., 171)
Arts and music
background and commentary on, 159
as CD-ROM classification, 155
contents of, 159
liner notes on, 159
ASCII text, in CD-ROM publishing, 214
Astronomy, Redshift CD-ROM on, 200, (illus., 200)
Asymetrix, Multimedia Textbook by, 224
ATAPI, 135
Atari Jaguar, 47, 107-108, (illus., 107)
Atlas, on CD-ROM, 201
Audio
MPC2 style, 72-73
quality of in production, 216
recording to CD-ROM, 217
Audiocard, 72
Audio CD, 9, 274. *See also* Standards
applications of, 26
architecture of, 36
bit structure, 46
block, 36
and CD-ROM, 10
CD-ROM as an extension of, 25
cross-interleavened Reed-Solomon Code, 40-41
defined, 3
future of, 260
maximum capacity of, 26
physical block structure, 36
played on CD-ROM drives, 25
read with CD-ROMs, 51

recordable, 26
Red Book for, 50-52
sector, 36-37
spiral, 50
Audio CD player
and data error, 41
and reading discs, 50
speed of reading, 50
Audio code
analog, 50
digital, 50
Audio errors
and Red Book, 51-52
correcting, 51-52
Audio optical standard, Red Book, 27
Audio quality, deciding on creating CD-ROM, 217
Audio tracks, parallel, 58-59
Australian outback, story on CD-ROM, 198
Authoring software
defined, 221, 274
using, 221-223
Authoring systems, 222-225
Authorware Pro, authoring tool, 224
AUTOEXEC.BAT file, CD-ROMs modifying on installation, 158

B

Backup medium, CD-ROM as a, 22
Banyan VINES, server-based network, 238
Best sellers, on disc, 190
Big Bug Alphabet Book, 167, 169, (illus., 168)
Birds, in children's CD-ROM, 169
Bitmapped images
scanned, 214
searching for words in, 214

Bits
counting, 67
maximum, 39
Block error rate (BLER), 70, 274
Books, color, 47-66
Books, electronic, 190
advantages of publishing in, 190
as CD-ROM classification, 156
disadvantages of, 190
Bookshelf, Microsoft
properties of, 164
references on, 164
Boole, George, 184
Boolean logic, 184, 274
in search engines, 184
search method, 172
Borland International, on TestDrive Corp. demo, 163
Bridge, between LANs, 247
Bridge discs, 57, 274
Broderbund
"Just Grandma and Me," by, 14
Living Book Series, 167, 170-171, (illus., 170)
Myst by, 193
on TestDrive Corporation's demon, 163
Brown, Marc, author of children's CD-ROM storybook, 170
Buffer, 275
CD-ROM, 136
function of a, 118
implementing, 118
size, 118
size and access time, 83
Buffering data, 136-137
Bundling, CD-ROM, 231
Bureau Development, CD-ROM by, 189-190

Bureau of Electronic Publishing, 160, 161
Business applications on CD, vendors of, (list, 294-295)
Business directories, on CD-ROM, 186
Business software
    advantages of, 161
    as CD-ROM classification, 155, 161-164
Business Week, on CD-ROM, 202, 263
Bus interfaces, 275
    CD-ROM drive and, 121
    to connect CD-ROM drives, 85-86
Bus mastering, 149
Bus slots, higher performance, 126
Bus speed, contrasted to drive speed, 136-137
Bytes. *See also* Bits
    and maximum bit rule, 39
    and stored data, 39

===== C =====

Cache memory, adding to file server, 248
Caching, CD-ROM in network, 247-249, 275
Caching controller, and memory, 149, 275
Caching utility, 148
    drawback of the, 149
    for the Mac, 149
    to speed storybooks, 166
CAD (computer-aided design), on CD-ROM, 162
Caddy, for discs, 94-95, 275
Capacity, CD-ROM, 28, 162
Cartoons, using in CD-ROM creation, 215
Case, jewel
    tips on removing discs from, 157

Catalogs
    on CD-ROM, 264-265
    as structured data, 214
CBIS, CD network tower by, 243
CD, three layers on a, (illus., 30)
CD Answer search engine, 182
CD Connections, networking software, 248
CD Digital Audio, 25
CD-I, 103, 275
    and color variations, 58
    compared to computer-based CD-ROM, 95
    and corporate activity, 57
    defined, 3
    Green Book for, 57-59
    laser read mechanism, 95
    and Nintendo, 95
    Philips, 95-96
    portable, 57
    TV-based consistent with CD-ROM, 47
    video planes and, 58
CD-I based device, 12
CD-I Bridge, 275
    and Mode 1, 59
    and Mode 2XA, 59
    and Photo CD pictures, 59
    and playing discs, 59
    and reading partially recorded discs, 59
    and recording data, 59
    for White Book, 60
CD-I disc, and real time, 58
CD-Interactive, 11. *See also* CD-I
CD-I operating system, 58
CD-I players, 80
CD-I Ready, 276
    and expansion of gap, 59
    format defined, 59

Index 381

purpose of, 59
CD-I technology, 57
CD-Magneto-optical, Orange Book for, 60-66
CD/Maxtet network tower, 241, (illus., 242)
CD/Quartet for networks, 240-241, (illus., 241)
CD-R (compact disc recordable), 276
    as an archiving tool, 112-113
    for business, 81
    and data transfer, 21-22
    defined, 3
    multisession, 61
    overwriting, 61
    as a publishing tool, 61
CD-R device, typical, (illus., 112)
CD-R discs
    construction of, 31
    dye recording layer of, 31
    layers of, 31
    limitations, 33
    recording data by burning pits, 35
    size of, 28
    three layers of a, (illus., 31)
CD-R drive
    as a backup device, 22
    compared to CD-ROM drives, 111
    cost of, 11, 256
    laser energy of, 32
    laser of CD-ROM drive and, 33
    and recording discs, 61
    requirements, 80
    use of in LANs, 255-256
CD-Recordable, 11, 111-113. *See also* CD-R
    applications of, 26
    cost of drive, 21
    maximum capacity of, 26
    recordable, 26

CD-R laser mechanism, (illus., 32)
CD-R media
    fully recorded, 61
    multisession, 61
    partially recorded, 61
    states of, 61
    unrecorded, 61
CD-ROM. *See also* Disc, Standards
    accessing data randomly with, 37
    adaptation to the, 15
    applications, 26
    block error rate, 42
    capacity, 27, 36
    composition of a, 30-31
    content, 14-15
    defined, 1, 3, 113-119
    duplication process of, 33-34
    effect of dirt on, 19
    encoding music with, 51
    enhancement to the, 149-150
    evolving, 28-29
    fiber optic cable and, 15
    future of, 14-15
    history, 6
    introduction to, 1-15
    layer architecture for the, 52
    layers of, 30
    life of, 18, 31
    material on a, 1-2
    materials used to make a, 31
    maximum capacity of, 26
    multimedia, 2-3
    multiple stampers, 34
    number of megabytes in a, 1
    played on audio CD players, 25
    pressing, 33
    production of, 33
    recordable, 26
    recording in mixed-mode discs, 37
    recording of first track of, 37

reflective layer of the, 30
rentals of, 269
retail sales of, 269
sales, 6
software on, 3
stampers, 33
storage of data on, 37
substrate layer, 31
uses of, 12
Yellow Book for, 52-57
CD-ROM applications, memory for, 129
CD-ROM compatibility, with standard and platforms, 10
CD-ROM data
   amount of, 4
   errors and, 41
CD-ROM delivery system, features of, 17
CD-ROM drive
   average cost of, 237
   with built-in audio circuitry, 130
   components of typical, (illus., 114)
   computer companies and, 6
   connecting or replacing, 121
   correctly focused, (illus., 117)
   costs of, 4
   creating an optimum environment for, 127
   features of, 113
   focus, 115-116
   form factor of, 83-84
   installation, 121
   installing an internal, 144-145
   laser beam, 116
   light, 115-116
   motors, 113
   objective lens, 116
   optical head, 115
   output, 115-116
   performance of, 118-119
   performance ratings, (table, 82)
   photodetector, 115
   portable, 84-85
   and reading on tracks, 23
   server, 92
   slow initialize error message, 152
   speed, 82
   troubleshooting, 150-153
   upgrading, 145
   vertical and horizontal installation, 92
   workings of, 113-116
CD-ROM extensions, windows, 129
CD-ROM hardware, 79-121
CD-ROM icon message, 153
CD-ROM jukeboxes, 92, (illus., 93)
CD-ROM minichanger, (illus., 93)
CD-ROM players
   classes of, 79
   tracks in, 36
CD-ROM production, 33
CD-ROM published periodicals, vendors of, (list, 295-296)
CD-ROM publishing, cost of, 5
CD-ROMs, creating, 211-215
   as multi-step process, 211
CD-ROM sectors, 37
CD-ROMs in Print, 1993, 6
CD-ROM standards, 45-77
   history of, 45-46
CD-ROM titles, number of, 6
CD-ROM Toolkit, 149
CD-ROM XA, 55, 276
   authoring software for, 222
   compressed audio data, 56
   discs and CD-I drives, 57
   extended Yellow Book for, 55-57
   interweaving sectors for, (illus., 56)

standard, 11
CD-RTOS, 58
CDR 101: Read Fail, error message, 151-152
CDR 103 error message, 152
CDTV
    Amiga Dos files, 106
    failure of, 105-106
    features of, 106
CD Write-Once, 11, 276. *See also* CD-WO
    Orange Book for, 60-66
Changer, multidisc for networks, 241-242
Channel bits, 39-40, 276
Checksum, 119, 276
    defined, 41
    diagonal, (illus., 43)
    horizontal and vertical, (illus., 42)
Chess, multimedia, 195-196
    tutorials to learn, 196
Chessmaster 3000, 195-196, (illus., 196)
Children
    CD-ROM titles for, 7, 165-171
Children's books
    on CD-ROM, 14
    as CD-ROM classification, 156
    cost of, 8
Cinema Expeditions, Inc., clip art CD-ROM by, 175-176
CIRC (cross interleave Reed-Solomon Code), 51-52, 276
Claris Corp., HyperCard by, 223
Classical music, on Composer Quest, 159-160
Classification
    arbitrary nature of, 156
    CD-ROM title, 155-156
Clicking, error messages, 153

Clients (computers attached to servers), 238, 276
Clip art, 171-180
    as CD-ROM classification, 156
    files on CD-ROM, 162
    keeping track of, 173-174
    quality of, 172
    royalty fees for, 173
CLV (constant linear velocity), 276
Coffee-table disc, 198
Coins, CD-ROM in collecting, 197
Collections, CD-ROM use in stamp and coin, 197
Color palette, problems with in creating CD-ROMs, 215
Color video, storing full-motion, 268
Commercial CD-ROM production, considerations in, 232
Commodore CD32, 47, 105-107
Commodore Dynamic Total Vision (CDTV), 105-107
Common Ground, document searches with, 214
Compact Disc Real-Time Operating System (CD-RTOS), 58
Component Manager, 68
Composer Quest, 159-160, (illus., 160)
    features, 160
    linking news to music with, 160
Compton's Interactive Encyclopedia, 200
Compton's New Media, rental of, 269
Computer-based players, 80-95
Computer components, database on, 185
Computers
    ability to handle multimedia by, 192
    articles about on CD-ROM, 185
    capabilities of, 123

hand-held, 86-87
Computer Select, CD-ROM database, 185
CONFIG.SYS file, CD-ROMs modifying on installation, 158
Constant linear velocity, 25
Consumer CD-ROM software, vendors of, (list, 296-311)
Content
    acquiring for CD-ROM publishing, 213
    licensing in CD-ROMs, 219
    types of, 213
Controller cards, 277
    diagrams of, 185
Conversion, VCR tape to CD-ROM format, 205
Copyright, 213
    in CD-ROM clip art, 172, 173
    problems in CD-ROM publishing with, 218-219
CorelDraw, available on CD-ROM, 155, 162
Corel Professional Photos, clip art CD-ROM, 178-179, (illus., 178)
CorelSCSI, 141
Corporations
    CD-ROMs for use by, 24-25
    internal use of CD-ROM by, 25
    presentations on CD-ROM by, 25
Costs
    CD-R drive, 11
    CD-ROM, 19
    CD-ROM drive, 4
    CD-ROM title, 4
    CDs cheaper than discs, 163
    children's titles, 8
    databases, 7
    of making CD-ROMs, 161-162
    multimedia PC, 6

online services and CD-ROM, 180
    TV-based player, 4
Courseware, interactive, 187
CPU
    checking the, 123
    8088 class, 127
    486 class, 127
    286 class, 127
Creative Labs, SoundBlaster by, 131
Critical Path, 258
Cross-interleavened Reed-Solomon Code (CIRC), 40-41
Cross-platform issue, in CD-ROM publishing, 212, 277

D

DAC, and MPC2 drive, 72, 277
Daisy-chaining, defined, 137, 277
Dariana, WinSleuth Gold by, 158
DAT, storing video on, 218
Data
    bits of, 38
    breaking, 52
    converted to CD-ROM, 21
    differences in storage of, 36
    distribution on CD-ROM, 206
    encoded for error detection, 41
    increasing density of, 20
    random access of, 52
    read continuously, 119
    reading the, 116-118
    recorded to disc, 61-62
    reliability, 42
    selecting rate, 218
    storage on ISO 9660, 54
Data Highway, 15
    effect of on CD-ROMs, 269-272
    politics of the, 271
Database manager, using to create CD-ROM, 214

Database software, as CD-ROM
   classification, 156
Databases
      cost of, 8, 180
      properties of current on
         CD-ROM, 261
      vendors of, (list, 311-318)
Databases, text
      on CD-ROM, 180
      cost of, 180
DC Heath and Company, interactive
   French by, 189
DeLorme Mapping, Street Atlas USA
   by, 185
Demo discs, ordering, 163
Demo software, vendors of, (list, 319)
Desktop PCs, 90-94
      using CD-ROM drive with, 90
Desktop publishing, clip art for, 179
Detection code (EDC), 37
Developer programs and associations,
   (list, 320-321)
Development tool vendors, (list,
   321-331)
Device-independent bitmap (DIB), 73
Devine, Graeme, 234
Diagnostics, CD-ROM, for MPC2
   standard, 176
Dialog online service, 180
Dictionaries, on CD-ROM, 262
Digicom, 127
Digital audio tape (DAT), 217
Digital Beethoven on Speed, 160,
   (illus., 161)
Digital data, 27
Digital Directory Assistance database,
   184
Digital Equipment Company,
   applications of Alpha AXP systems
   on CD-ROM, 162

Digital-to-analog converter (DAC), 72
Digital Video Interactive (DVI), history
   of, 76, 278
Digitizing, photo, 215
Digitizing, video, 218
Dinosaurs
      in CD-ROM titles, 167
      clip art, 175
Dinosource, 167, (illus., 168)
Director authoring tool, 223
      cost, 223
      games authored on, 223
Direct-overwrite technology, with MD
   DATA, 57
Disc
      compatibility of, 46
      creating a master, 33
      forming, 34
      playing the, 59
      quality checks of the, 34
      spiral tracks, 23
      tips on removing from the case,
         157
      tracks compared to hard disk
         drives, 23
Disc density, problems with, 21
Disc Does Not Eject error message, 153
Discovering French Interactive
   CD-ROM, 189
Discport, accessing CD-ROMs by, 252,
   (illus., 253)
Discrete cosine transform (DCT), 75
Discview, software application for, 252
Disk, structure of a hard, (illus., 24)
Distributing, CD-ROM, 230-232
      affiliate, 230
      methods of, 231
Distributors, (list, 330)
Docking stations, 88-89, 278, (illus., 89)
      installing a CD-ROM drive in a, 90

Document images, saving on CD-ROM, 214
Document storage, on CD-ROM, 214
Documentation, for CD-ROMs, 158
Dot pitch, defined, 133, 278
Double-speed CD-ROM drives, 23, 82, 278
Dow Jones online service, 180
Drive Does Not Seem to be Reading Disc error message, 152
Drivers
    CD-ROM and, 67
    missing, 139-140
    obtaining, 139
    software device, 122
Drives
    defined, 3, 278
    double-speed multisession, 123
    equipping computers with CD-ROM, 181
    future of speedier, 267-268
    hard disk and CD-ROM, (illus., 20)
    internal or external, 125-127
    loading CD-ROM as network disk volumes, 249
    making faster, 23
    manual-feed, 94
    multiple, 92
    problems with faster-speed, 24
    single-session, 123
    taking care of, 153-154
    upgrading from older, 145
    XA-compatible, 81
Drive vendors, (list, 330-337)
Dua, Ed, 216
Dun and Bradstreet Information Services, 186
Dun's Business Locator on CD-ROM, 186
Dun's Million Dollar CD-ROM collection, 186
Dust control, 94
Duvall, Shelley, 169
Dye, properties of the, 33
Dynamic load balancing, in networking CD-ROMs, 250
DynaVision line, of notebook computers, 146

E

Eastman Kodak CD-based media, 11. *See also* Kodak
EDC/ECC (error detection code/error correction code) sections, 55, 278
Education CD-ROMs, 155, 186-190
    titles, 7
Education software, as CD-ROM classification, 156
Educational CDS, vendors of, (list, 338-343)
EISA (extended industry standard architecture), 126, 278
Elections, learning about on CD-ROM, 188
Electronic Arts, 216
Electronic books, 190
11-bit maximum rule, 39
Encarta, Microsoft, 199-200, (illus., 199)
    as standard for encyclopedias on CD-ROM, 200
    created on MultiDoc, 225
Encyclopedia
    on CD-ROM, 14
    Encarta as, 199
    Funk and Wagnall's, 14
    of Main Boards, 185
Encryption, controlling use by, 163, 279
Energy Productions, video clips by, 177
Enhanced Parallel Port, 144

En Passant CD-ROM, catalogs on, 264-265
Entertainment
    on CD-ROM, 6
    features of Sony Computer, 110
    sophistication of interactive, 191
EPP, 85
Erasing and rewriting data, with MD DATA, 29
Error-corrected data, capacity of disc with, 28
Error correcting code (ECC), of CD-ROM, 37
Error correction, 40
    and audio CD, 40
Error detection codes, adding, 226
Error detection scheme, in CD-ROM drives, 41
Error messages
    for the Macintosh, 152-153
    for MS-DOS and windows, 150-152
Error rate, block, 42
Errors
    correcting audio, 51-52
    and CD-ROM data, 41
Ethernet, bumping up to avoid transmission delays in network, 246
Executable data, 128
Expansion slots, 126
Exports, CD-ROM with information on, 181
Extended capabilities port, 144
Extended Yellow Book, for CD-ROM XA, 55-57
External drives, 125
    differences among, 145-146
    form factors for, 84
    installing, 145-146
    for the Mac, 147
    portability of, 84
    reasons for, 145

F

Federal Register, on CD-ROM, 185
Federal regulations, on CD-ROM, 185
Fiber optic cable, 270-271
    and CD-ROM, 15
Fiber optic network, national, 15
File-naming, on ISO 9660, 54
File sharing, with Macs, 253-254
File system
    accommodation on ISO 9660, 55
    CD-ROM, 11
    defined by a logical structure, 37
Film footage, on CD, 60
Firmware, 279
    buffers, 83
Floppy disks, compared to CD-ROM, 161-162
FM synthesis, 131
Foreign languages, learning with CD-ROM, 189
Form factor, 83
    options for, 86
Form 1, and CD-I standard, 56
Form 2, and CD-I standard, 56
Formats
    of CD-ROMs, 19
    proprietary, 77
Format standards, 9-12
    defined, 9, 10
Formatting software, 112, 279
Foundation Solutions, MultiDoc authoring system by, 225
14-bit patterns, 39
Frame differencing, 68
Frame rate, choosing correct, 218
Frankfurt Group, 62-64, 280
    and CD-R, 62

and ISO, 62
and Rock Ridge Extensions, 63
and Unix files, 62
Frankfurt specification, 11
French, learning interactively, 189
From Alice to Ocean coffee-table disc, 198, (illus., 198)
Full Motion Video (FMV), 58, 279
cartridge, 191
Funk and Wagnall's New Encyclopedia, 199
Funny (video collection), 191
Future of CD-ROM, 257-272

=== G ===

Gabriel, Peter, 259
on multimedia records, 260
"Secret World" CD-ROM, 260
Game boxes, disc-based, 266-267
Games
advantages with CD-ROM for, 7
on CD-ROM, 5-8
as CD-ROM classification, 156
Geobase, oil well database CD-ROM, 184
Geographic information, on CD-ROM, 201
Gigabyte, 17, 280
Gilligan, Shannon, 216
Glossary, 273-291
Gold disc (one-off)
creating a, 225-226
use of, 226
Government Giveaways for Entrepreneurs, 184-185
Government resources, database of, 184-185
Graphical User Interfaces (GUI), 12, 280

Graphic artists, using in screen display creation, 221
Graphic designer, function of, 219
Graphic processor, 102
Graphics
demands for, 215
placed on a CD, 51
problems with color, 215
Great Kat, 160-161
heavy metal on CD-ROM, 259
Greek, teaching with CD-ROM, 187
Green Book, 11, 280
for CD-I, 57-59
and Form 1 and 2, 55-56
history of, 57
interweaving sectors, 58
Mode 2, 58
qualities, 58
specifications, 47-48
standards defined, 11
Griffith, Melanie, 167
Grolier Electronic Publishing, 201
GUI. *See* Graphical User Interface
Guinness Book of Records, 201
Guinness Multimedia Disc of Records, 201

=== H ===

Hard disk drives, disadvantages of, 111-112
Hard disk space
CD-ROM use of, 18
consuming, 158
Hard Drives, Encyclopedia of, 185
Hardware, CD-ROM, 79-121
future improvements in, 266-268
pressures on by interactive titles, 192
HDTV (High Definition Television), 65-66

Head crash, 4
Headroom, memory manager, 192
Health and Medical Industry
    Directory, on CD-ROM, 186
Health CD-ROMs, Mayo Clinic, 201
Hewlett-Packard 100LX, (illus., 87)
Hierarchical file system (HFS), 52, 280
High Sierra Standard meeting, 53, 280
History, American, on CD-ROM,
    187-188
Hit rate, of cache query, 248, 280
Hobbies, as CD-ROM classification,
    156
Hobby helpers, CD-ROMs as, 196-197
Hollywood, collaboration with on
    CD-ROM titles, 258
Home references, as CD-ROM
    classification, 156
Houghton Mifflin, interactive
    courseware by, 187
Hybrid CDs, 55, 281
    Kodak Photo CD as, 64-66. *See
        also* Kodak
    producing, 268
Hyperbole Studios, first interactive
    novel by, 190
HyperCard, authoring tool, 223
Hypertext linking, 8, 214

=========== I ===========

IBM, demo meter usage by, 163
IBM Dictionary of Computing, 27
Icon Author authoring system, 224-225
IDE (integrated drive electronics) hard
    disk drives, 86, 281
        attaching hard disk drives, 135
        capability, 134
        data transfer rate, 135
        interface, 127, 134-136
        interface and AT attachment, 134

manufacturers of, 135
maximum data transfer rate, 135
multitasking operations, 135
standard, 135-136
Image Compression Manager, 68
Image files, indexing, 173-174
Incorrect DOS version error message,
    151
Indeo, 68
Index systems, choosing for CD-ROM
    creation, 220
Indexing
    schemes for clip art, 172-174
    on sound effects CD-ROM, 176
    text in CD-ROM creation, 214
Information, distribution and
    production of, 5
Information gap, bridged by
    CD-ROMs, 12-13
Information storage and retrieval, 10
InfoServer 1000, CD network tower,
    244
Ingram Micro, demo CD-ROMs by, 163
Installation
    CD-ROM drive, 121
    modifying AUTOEXEC.BAT and
        CONFIG.SYS files during, 158
Installing
    internal CD-ROM drive, 144-145
    speed of CD-ROM, 162
Intel, Indeo by, 75-76
    compression standard, 65
Interactive CD-ROM, elements in, 258
Interactive novel, the first, 190
Interactive Publishing Corp., sound
    effects CD-ROM by, 175-176
Interactive television, 102
Interactive Ventures, 14
Interface
    AT attachment peripheral, 135

choosing consistent and simple
for children, 165
defined, 134
producing in CD-ROM creation,
220-221
Interface designer, function of, 219
Interfaces
between computer and CD-ROM,
134
IDE, 134-136
parallel ports, 134, 142-144
SCSI, 134-144
Internal CD-ROM drives, (illus., 125)
for the Mac, 147
installing, 144-145
sizes, 83
International sales, of CD-ROMs, 232
International Standards Organization,
52. *See also* ISO
9660 standard, 10
Internetworking, CD-ROM, 247
Interrupt, defined, 140, 281
Invisible LAN, 254
ISA (industry standard architecture),
281
16-bit, 126
ISO, and American National Standards
Institutes, 53
ISO 9660, 53-55, 64, 281
compatibility with, 62
deficiencies, 63
description, 54-55
format standard, 222
purpose of, 11
reading data, 53
record organization, 53
standard, 53
standard file system of, 54
It's a Bird's Life, children's CD-ROM,
169-170, (illus., 169)

J

Jaguar, 108
cost and features of, 108
Jazz, on Composer Quest, 159
Jewel cases, tips on opening, 157
Johnson, Don, 167
Joint Photographic Experts Group
(JPEG), 68
Jones, Quincy, 167
Jukebox, 92, 282
Julliard School of Music, 160
Jurassic Dinosaurs, clip images, 175
"Just Grandma and Me," children's
CD-ROM storybook, 170

K

Kaleide, authoring language by, 222
Karaoke Shakespeare, 195
Karpov, Anatoly, accessing chess
games by, 195, 196
Keyboard and mouse, 73
Key word searches, in structured data,
214
Kiosks, CD-ROM use in information,
206, 282
Kodak PCD 5870 Photo CD player,
(illus., 97)
Kodak PCD LAN writer, 256
Kodak Photo CD, 215
cost of, 215
hybrid disc, 64-66
Kodak players, 96
Kodak's Shoebox, for keeping track of
clips, 173-174, (illus., 173)
Kubik CD240 Compact Disk changer,
242, (illus., 243)
Kudo image browser, 174, 179

L

LAN (Local Area Network), server-based, 238, 239-247, 282, (illus., 238)
    solving transmission delays in, 246
LAN, peer-based, 238, 239, 254, (illus., 239)
Landeros, Rob, 234
Lands, on the disc, 35, 282
LAN Server Ultimedia, 246
LANtastic, peer-based LAN, 239, 254
Laptop computers, 90
    attaching a CD-ROM drive to, 90
    CD-ROMs in, 146
    full-size, (illus., 91)
Laser
    advantages of the, 19-20
    binary, 38
    bump height, 38
    of CD-ROM drive compared to CD-R drive, 33
    condenser lens, 33
    and the dye, 33
    forward sense diode, 33
    light, 38
    mirrors and use with CD-ROMs, 38-40
    pit depth, 38
    quarter-wave plate, 33
    recording data with a, 19
    synchronized with a spinning disc, 38
    use in reading a CD-ROM, 38
    wavelength, 38
Laser beam
    functions of the, 117-118
    mirrors for, 118
    size of, 20-21
Laser energy, of CD-R drives, 32

Laser light, described, 19
Laser mechanism, distance from disk of the, 20
Laser videodisc, 282
    compared to CD-ROM, 26
    history of, 26
    interactive home entertainment, 104
    predecessor to CD-ROM, 46
Lawnmower Man, video clips from, 174, (illus., 175)
Layered ECC (LECC), 41
LCD displays, 88
Legacy Storage Systems, 8-drive system by, 241
Lesko, Matthew, 184-185
Library
    CD-ROM advantages in the, 13
    CD-ROM stations in the, 12-13
    online data retrieval in the, 13
    online data search in the, 13
Licensing, music for CD-ROMs, 219
Lighting, 104
Liner notes, in music CD-ROMs, 159
Linked information, in CD-ROM American history textbook, 187
Living Book series, children's CD-ROM, 167, 170-171, (illus., 170)
Logical file format, defined, 36, 283
Logical file structure, 37
Logical sector structure, 37, 283
Logical Unit Numbers, addressing drives by, 251-252
Lotus, on Test Drive Corporation's demon, 163
Lotus Notes: Document Imaging, 256
Lucid's Lightning CD, 149

M

Macbeth, on multimedia, 195

Macintosh
    caching utilities, 149
    CD-ROM for the, 10
    color, 148
    drive bays, 147
    error messages, 152-153
    graphic art, 148
    installing CD-ROM drive on the, 147-149
    memory area in, 158
    platform, 67
    sound and video, 148
Macintosh applications
    multimedia orientation of, 148
Macintosh HFS (Hierarchical File System), 246
Macintosh PowerBook, SCSF DOC, 147
Macintosh II
    installing CD-ROM drive on, 147
    SCSI interface, 147
Macromedia
    Authorware Pro by, 224
    Director authoring tool by, 223
Macromedia Director, project creation with, 216
Madness of Roland, as first interactive novel, 190
Magazines, on CD-ROM, 202-203
Magnetic fields, effects of, 21
Magnetic optical. *See also* CD-MO
    applications of, 26
    maximum capacity of, 26
    recordable, 26
Mammoth Micro Production, Studio XA by, 222
Mandel, Howie, voice in Tuneland, 166
MapExpert, 185
Maps, Street Atlas USA CD-ROM, 185
Market, for CD-ROMs, 230-232
Market research specialists, (list, 343)

Mass production, CD-ROM, 227
Master, formation of a, (illus., 34)
Mayer, mercer, 14, 170
Mayo Clinic Family Health disc, 201, (illus., 202)
Mayo Clinic: The Total Heart, 201
MD Data, 283
    advantages over floppy disks, 29
    benefits from, 19
    and Personal Digital Assistants, 29
    and portable computers, 29
    storage capacity of, 29
    variations of, 29
MD Data discs, interactive applications and, 29
MD recordable discs, cost of, 29
MD-ROMs, 29
Media Clip Art. *See also* Clip art vendors, (list, 343-347)
MediaClips collection, 176-177, (illus., 177)
Media sources, vendors, (list, 347-348)
Medical information, on CD-ROM, 186
Medical references, on CD-ROM, 201
Megabyte capacity, 17
MemMaker, freeing main memory with, 158, 192
Memory
    freeing with MemMaker utility, 158
    freeing with WinSleuth Gold, 158
    insufficient main, 192
    for multimedia applications, 128-129
    required to run CD-ROM titles, 158
    requirement for free, 192
    and storage needs, 128-129
Memory manager, need for optional running, 192

Meridian Data, CD Net server, 249-250, (illus., 250)
   network tower, 243
Merisel, demo CD-ROMs by, 163
Message, spread by CD-ROM, 4-5
Metatee, publisher of Nautilus, 203
Metering software, for CD-ROM on LANs, 255
Micro channel, 126, 283
Micro House Technical Library Series, CD-ROM database, 185
Microsoft applications, learning with CD-ROM training course, 205
Microsoft Encarta, 199-200
Microsoft Encarta 94, defined, 14
Microsoft Video for Windows, 74
Microsoft Windows, 11
Microsoft Word, recording voice with, 131
Microsoft Word for Windows
   available on CD-ROM, 155
   on CD-ROM, 262
MIDI (musical instrument digital interface), 131, 283
MIDI sound, 217
   files, 217
Milliken Publishing, maker of Big Bug Alphabet Book, 167
Minichanger, 92, 283
Minute: sector scheme, 23
Mixed-mode discs, recording in, 37
MMPM/2 hardware requirements, 76-77
MO (magneto-optical), 283
   optical media, 26
   shared recording format with, 61
   speeds, 60
Mode 0, 37
Mode 1, 37
   CD-ROMs recorded in, 37
   defined, 52
Mode 2, 37, 284
   CD-ROMs recorded in, 37
   defined, 52
   and Green Book, 58
Modes, on a CD-ROM, (illus., 38)
MO drive, and recording data, 60
Money Magazine, on CD-ROM, 202
Mouse clicks, using in navigation, 220
Motherboard, typical PCs, (illus., 124)
Movie Recorder feature, in Redshift, 200
Movies, future reviews of CD-ROM like current reviews of, 258
Moving Picture Exports Group (MPEG), 58
MPC (multimedia PC) system, 9, 10, 284. *See also* Multimedia PC
MPC Wizard CD-ROM, 176-177, (illus., 176)
MPC 2 (Multimedia PC), 71
   audio, 72-73
   buffering, 72
   CD-ROM drive, 71-72
   costs, 70
   mixing inputs, 72-73
   requirements, 69-70
   sets windows standard, 69-76
   sound capability for, 130
   standard for video movies, 73-74
   video specs, 73
MPEG (Moving Picture Experts Group), 284
   leading video compression standard, 60, 75
   video cards, 218
MSCDEX, 254
   driver, 150, 151
   updating, 129
   Windows CD-ROM extension, 129

MS-DOS, freeing memory in, 158
MultiDoc authoring system, 225
Multifunction card, defined, 127, 284
Multilingual sound tracks, adding, 232
Multimedia, 284
    accessing between with TCP/IP, 246
    CD-ROM and, 2-3
    Macintosh, 148
    pixel resolution, 71
    sound requirement for, 130
Multimedia applications
    accelerator card for, 133
    memory for, 128-129
Multimedia capabilities, on CD-ROM XA, 55
Multimedia Compact Disc, features of the, 99-100
Multimedia Formatter, 256
Multimedia Grasp authoring system, 224
Multimedia PC. *See also* MPC
    cost of, 6
    marketing council, 69
    minimal specifications for, 127
    standard, 69
Multimedia Presentation Manager, 76-77
Multimedia-Ready Windows PC, requirements for, 9
Multimedia Toolbook authoring system, 224
Multimedia Upgrade kits, 128
    vendors of, (list, 349-350)
Multimedia Viewer, 261, (illus., 262)
Multiple CDs, simultaneous writing of, 256
Multiple users, on CD-ROM, 181
Multisession, defined, 11, 284

Multisession CD-ROM drive, and single-session, 62, 63, 123
Multisession recording, 62
Multitasking, 76, 284
    improving network performance by server, 248
Music. *See also* Art and Music
    copyrights for, 219
    on future CD-ROM, 259-260
    liner notes on CD-ROMs, 159
    listeners' ability to change on CD-ROM, 259
    playback, 72
Musical Instrument Digital Interface (MIDI), 72
Musical instruments,
    self-improvement in playing from CD-ROMs, 198
Myst (interactive game), 191, 193, 258, 259, (illus., 193)
Myths, CD-ROM, 18-19

N

NAFTA, on CD-ROM, 186
National Geographic Society, CD-ROM by, 188
Nautilus, CD-ROM magazine, 203, (illus., 203)
Navigation process, in CD-ROM creation, 220
NEC triple-speed drive, 23, 82
Netware, 241
Network, CD-ROMs on, 237-256
Network connections, CD-ROM without a PC, 252
Network environments, with quad-speed drives, 92
Network Interface Technical Manual, 185

Network Loadable Module (NLM), 240, 284
Networking products, vendors of, (list, 351-352)
Networks, 92-94
    accessibility of CD-ROM through a, 181
    using Apple for CD-ROM, 253-254
New Grolier Multimedia Encyclopedia, 200
New Media Magic, 216
News magazines, on CD-ROM, 14
Newsweek, on CD-ROM, 202
Nimbus Technology, increased storage capacity of discs by, 268
Nintendo games, conversion to CD-I, 95
NLM (NetWare loadable module), loading CD-ROMs in network by, 249
No drive needing support error message, 151
No host found error message, 151
Noise, signal, 137
Norton Speedcache, 149
Notebook PCs, 87-90
Novell Netware, 238
    loading CD-ROMS with, 249
Novell Netware 4: The Complete Reference, 239

========= O =========

OCP International, Imagepro CD by, 146
Oil well production, Canadian on CD-ROM, 184
OLE (object linking and embedding), 68, 284
One-off (gold disc)
    creating a, 225-226

mass production from the, 227
use of, 226
Online data retrieval, 13, 285
Online data search, 13
Online data services, databases on discs competing with, 180
Online services
    competing and complementary, 13
    cost compared to CD-ROMs, 237
Operators, Boolean, 184
Optical disc, defined, 60
Optical media, 26, 285
    CD-ROM as, 19-30
    other, 26-27
Optical ROM (O-ROM), 28, 285
Optical Storage Units (OSU), in networks, 240
Optical technology, 21
    stability of, 21
Opti-Net NLM for Netware, 248, 251
    features, 251-252
Orange Book, 11-12, 285
    for CD-Magneto-optical, 60-66
    and CD-MO, 60
    for CD-Write Once, 60-66
    standards, 11
OS/2 compatibility, 77
OS/2 Multimedia Presentation Manager, 76-77
OS/2 Multimedia standard, 10
OS/2 operating system
    in Ultimedia, 245
    network support under, 245-247
OS-9 operating system, 58
Oswego Illustrated Archives, clip art CD-ROM, 179-180, (illus., 179)
Overwrite, 4
    and CD-R, 61

P

Packaging, CD-ROM, 232
Panasonic FZ-1 interactive
  multiplayer, 47, (illus., 101)
Parallel port, transfer rates, 144
Parallel port hardware, limitations of,
  143-144
Parallel ports, 86, 142-144, 285
    and external drives, 125
      connecting external CD-ROM
        drive, 142
Parallel port standards, new, 144
Parallel-port-to-SCSI-port converter,
  143
"Parental guilt" (home reference) CD
  titles, 197-199
Partially recorded discs, reading, 59
Partial ROM (P-ROM), 28, 286
    availability of, 29
    disc size, 29
      permanently recorded area of, 29
      recording discs permanently
        with, 29
      rewritable portion of, 29
Patent Information on CD-ROM, 186
Patents, on CD-ROM, 186
Paul Mace Software, Multimedia
  Grasp by, 224
PC, luggable, (illus., 91)
PC-based drives, areas of, 81
PCI (peripheral component
  interconnect) bus, 126, 285
PCMCIA (Personal Computer
  Memory Card International
  Association), 285
    slot and sound cards, 132
Peer-based network, 286. *See also* LAN
Pentium processor, hardware
  improvements resulting from, 266
Periodicals

  on CD-ROM, 201-203
  as CD-ROM classification, 156
Perseus, CD-ROM, 187
Philips
  hobbyist titles by, 196-197
  patent on CDs, 27
  TV-based format, 11
Philips CD-I, 12, 95-96
  player, (illus., 96)
Philips compact disc, 6
Philips Green Book, 47-48
Philips Orange Book, 60
Phonedisc USA Business database
  CD-ROM, 184
Photo CD, 11, 65-66
  and ID numbers, 65
  and image resolution, 65
  master format, 65
  recording on, 65
  35mm film and, 65
Photo CD images
  accessing, 172
  manipulation of, 66
Photo CD Master disc pro, 65
  scanning resolutions of, 65
Photo CD players, 64, 96
Photo CD processing, vendors, (list,
  353)
Photo CD resolutions, 65
Photodetector, light reflected to the,
  (illus., 39)
Photographs, displaying on CD-ROM,
  215
Pick list, in media clip art CD-ROMs,
  172
PICT graphic files, 68
Pioneer Corp., Laseractive system by,
  104-105
Pitch, 36, 286
Pits, described, 35-36, 286

Index 397

Pits and lands
    creation on the disc of, 35-36, (illus., 35)
    transition patterns on a CD, (illus., 40)
Planets, running orbits in Redshift, 200
Platform, 9-12, 286
    Apple Macintosh, 9
    CD-ROM, 232
    defined, 9
    incompatible, 10
    Multimedia PC, 9
    playback as factor in authoring tool selection, 222
Platform formats
    built on existing standards, 77
    use of own standards, 77
Platform requirements, meeting, 66-77
Platforms, hardware
    deciding on before creating CD-ROM, 212-213
Playback, in real time, 18
Player, 286
    computer-based, 80-95
    defined, 3
    portable, 97-100
    proprietary TV-based, 100-110
    standard, (table, 48)
Portability, 4
Portable CD-ROM drives, 84-85
Portable computers
    attaching a CD-ROM drive to, 90
    with CD-ROM drives, (vendors list, 353-354)
    docking station for, 88-89
    and MD DATA, 29
Portable external CD-ROM, features of, 85
Portable Operating System Interface (POSIX), 64
Portable players, 97-100
Portable sound, 132
POSIX files and directories, 64
PowerCD, features of, 98
Power PC processor, hardware improvements resulting from, 266
PowerSCI, defined, 141
Power supply, computer, 129-130
Premastering software, 226, 286
    costs of, 226
Prentice-Hall, interactive courses by, 187
Presentation software, vendors of, (list, 354-355)
Presentations, on CD-ROM, 206
Presidents, CD-ROM multimedia study, 188
Prices, of CD-ROM databases, 8
Printed page, reader preference for the, 202
Printing press, and recordable CD media, 60
Print publications, inevitability of evolution of, 202
Print publishers, moving toward CD-ROM publishing by, 263
Pro Audio, 131
Processor, defined, 127-128
Processor upgrades, vendors of, (list, 355)
Producer Pro authoring tool, 223-224
Product design
    in CD-ROM creation, 219-225
    tips in, 220
Professional Wave Editor, on sound effects CD-ROM, 176
Profits, from CD-ROM publishing, 233-234, (table, 233)
Promotional materials, distribution of by CD-ROM, 265

Pronunciations, on Bookshelf, 164
Proprietary formats, 77
Proprietary software, 45
Proprietary TV-based players, 100-110
Publishers, and in-house production, 11
Publishing
    CD-R as tool in, 61
    CD-ROM, 5, 155, 209-235
    classifications in CD-ROM, 166
    cost of CD-ROM, 209
    custom on CD-ROM, 206
    in-house CD-ROM, 229
    mistakes, 8-9
    reasons for CD-ROM, 210-211
    recordable CD media and, 60
Publishing services, vendors of, (list, 355-358)
Pulse, 50

Q

QEMM 386 memory manager, 192
Quad-speed drive, 82, 286
    and poorly recorded discs, 83
    vendors, 23
Quad-speed players, 23
Quicken, availability of on CD-ROM, 155
Quicken for Windows, reference material for, 162
QuickStart Technologies, 205
QuickTime, 66, 67-69
    movie toolbox, 68
    parts of, 68
QuickTime for Windows, 67, 73

R

Random access to data, 21, 286
RCA LaserVision, 26

Read, teaching children to with CD-ROM, 170-171
Read-ahead circular buffers, 119, 287
Reading data, 116-118
Reading discs, 23
    problems with, 23
Reading information, 4
Recordable CDs, 31-33
    drives, 19
Recordable media and players, 11
Recording
    difficulty of CD-ROM, 21
    laser calibration and, 61
    multisession, 11
Records, Guinness Disc of, 201
Red Book, 10, 287
    for audio CD, 50-52
    and graphics on a CD, 51
    and large data errors, 52
    Layer O structure, 37
    and Level 1 error correction, 51-52
    logical file structure, 50
    specifications, 50
    standard, 10, 25
    two-layer architecture specification, 50
Red Book audio, CD standard, 36
Redshift, astronomy reference, 200
Redirector software, for peer-based LANs, 254
ReelMagic MPEG card, 218
References
    finding multiple, 184
    on Word for Windows, 164, (illus., 165)
    working in combination in Microsoft Word for Windows, 164
    works for CD-ROM home use, 197-199

Rentals, CD-ROM, 231, 269
Research, audience before creating CD-ROM, 212
Research process, speeding with CD-ROM, 197
Reset SCSI bus, error message, 151
Retrieval software vendors, (list, 359-362)
Return to Zork, 258-259
Rewritable portion, of Partial-ROM, 29
Riff Checker, 259
Rock Ridge extensions, 63, 287
Router, defined, 247, 287
Royalty-free products, 219
RRIP, 63, 64
Run length, 38
Rundgren, Todd, 259, 260

=========== S ===========

Sample
    defined, 54
    values, 51
Sampling rate, 50, 51, 287
Sanctuary Woods, 169
Scan rate, defined, 133
Scanning, documents for CD-ROM storage, 214
Schools, equipped with CD-ROMS, 186
Screen displays, importance of clear, simple, easy-to-use, 221
ScriptX authoring language, 222
SCSI (Small Computer System Interface), 136-139, 287
    buffering data and, 137
    controller, 126
    data transfer rate of, 138
    defined, 136, 137
    Fast-Wie, 138
    hardware, 137
    host adapter, (illus., 126)

    latest version, 138
    multitasking I/O channel, 136
    PC markets and, 138
    port, 85, 125-126
    portable, 142
    protocol, 143
    requirements, 126
    software, 137
SCSI adapters
    connector for a generic, 138
    installed in portable PCs, 142
    universal, 141-144
SCSI bus, interface, 85
SCSI cable, width of the, 138
SCSI connector,
    50-pin, (illus., 138)
    standard, 144
    using a, 85
SCSI drivers, 140
    and external port, 142
    vendor writings of, 140
    and Windows NT, 140
SCSI Express, 240, 250-251, (illus., 251)
    features in, 251
SCSI host adapter, (illus., 126)
    communicating with a, 137
SCSI installation, effect on IDE interface, 139
SCSI interface
    and Macintosh II, 147
    and multimedia upgrade kits, 139
SCSI products, vendors of, (list, 362-363)
SCSI-1
    connection, 86
    connectors for, 137
    and speed of CD-ROM drive, 138
    standard, 131
SCSI-2
    connectors for, 137-138

data transfer rate of, 138
latest version of, 138
Search and retrieval methods, lack of standard in, 156
Search and retrieval systems, need for standardized, 261
Search and retrieval utility, Multimedia Viewer, 261
Search engine, 182
    lack of standard for, 182
    schemes for, 182
    using Boolean logic, 184
Search function, different interfaces in, (illus., 183)
Search words, using in navigating, 220
Sectors, 288
    of an audio CD player, 36-37
    of CD-ROMs, 37
    size of uncorrected, 28
Security disc, 181
Security software vendors, (list, 363-364)
Sega, game machine by, 109
    features, 108
Sega CD, 47, 108-109
Sega Channel, 271-272
Sega Genesis player, (illus., 109)
Self-improvement CD-ROMs, 198-199
Sequential access to data, 21, 288
Serial ports, multifunction cards and, 127
Server, 288
    CD-ROM disc on a, 181
    peer-based system, 254
Server, CD network, 249-250, (illus., 250)
    options for, 250
Service Advertising Protocol (SAP), 247, 287

Service bureaus, multimedia production, 227-229
    costs of, 228, 229
    working with, 228-229
"7th Guest", on CD-ROM, 217
    success of, 234-235
7th Level (company), 166, 167
SFQL (Structured Full-Text Query Language), 182
Shareware, 288
    on CD-ROM, 204
    as CD-ROM classification, 156
    defined, 8
    prices of, 204
    vendors, (list, 364-366)
Sheldon, Tom, 239
Shows and conferences, (list, 366)
Signal-to-noise ratio, 116, 288
Site license, purchase of, 181, 288
Site licensing, for CD-ROM on LANs, 255
Sitka's TOPS network, 241
Sizes, CD-ROM, 27-28
Slides, 35 mm
    transferring to CD-ROMs, 215
Slots, high performance bus, 126
Software
    compatible, 11
    future of, 258-264
    monthly available by subscription, 203
    move toward CD-ROM in distribution of, 262
    need for standards for, 45
Software, CD-ROM, 155-207
    availability of consumer titles, 155
    producing quality, 9
Software Access Initiative Apple Computer, 163
Software Manufacturing Co., IBM, 163

Index 401

Software Toolworks, almanac by, 188
Sony, 110
    compact disc, 6
    and Orange Book, 60
    patents on CDs, 27
Sony MiniDisc, 28. *See also* MD DATA
    computer data storage on, 19
    error correction of, 28
    recording of, 28
Sony MMCD (multimedia CD), 47
    defined, 99-100
    PIX-100 player, (illus., 99)
    standalone CD player, 12
Sound
    capture, 218
    Mac video and, 148
    portable, 132
SoundBlaster, 77, 131
    standard, 216
Sound board standards, 131
Sound boards, 127
    with CD-ROM interface, 131
    with FM synthesis, 131
    industry standard, 131
    installing, 131
    manufacturers of, 128
    with MIDI interface, 131
    with SCSI interface, 131
Sound capabilities
    on laptop computers, 132
    parallel ports and, 132
Sound cards, for PCMCIA slot, 132
Sound effects, on CD-ROMs, 175-176
Sound product vendors, (list, 367-369)
Sound qualities, Green Book, 58
Sound requirements
    MPC 2, 130
    for multimedia, 130
Sound Source Unlimited, rights to clips, 174

Spaceship Warlock game, 194-195, (illus., 195)
Speakers, PC, 130
Speech, converting text to, 190
Speed
    and capacity of CD-ROM, 22-24
    CD-ROM, 22-24
    CD-ROM drives, 82
    increased for CD-ROM drive, 149
    increasing with a caching utility, 148
    problems with, 23
Spinning, disc
    with CD-ROM drive, 23
    and read mechanism, 23
Spelling lessons, on children's CD-ROMs, 171
Spiral tracks, advantages of, 23
Sports Almanac, on CD-ROM, 196
Sports Illustrated, on CD-ROM, 196
Spot on, 149
Sprites, 103, 289
Standalone CD players, 12, 84
Standard
    proposed Frankfurt Group, 63
    sampling rate, 51
Standards
    "book", 10-11
    for hard drives, 136
    for hardware, 46
    history of industry, 25
    industry, 10-11
    for recordable media, 11
    related color book, (illus., 49)
    search and retrieval, 182
    for software producers, 46
Standards, CD-ROM, 9-12, 45-77
    absence of a, 213
Starting Screen Refreshes Slowly error message, 152

Star Trek clips, 174
Stereo PC, features, 130-131
Storage, data on CD-ROMs, 36-37
Storage capacity, increases in
 CD-ROM, 267-268
Storage medium, CD-ROM as a, 21-22
Storybooks, CD-ROM, 165-166
Street Atlas USA, CD-ROM, 185
Streets, maps of all U. S., 185
Structured data, as component data
 type in CD-ROM, 214
Studio XA authoring software, 222
Subcode byte, 40, 289
Subnotebook, 87-90
SuperCache software, 241
Supercard authoring tool, 223
Super PC-Kwik, 149
SUSP extension, 63, 64
S-Video input, using in digitizing, 218
Sweatpea player, features of, 97
Swenson, Jim, 216
Symantee, on Test Drive Corp. demo,
 163
Symmetric multiprocessing, defined,
 248-249
Synthesizer, MIDI for, 217, 289
System files, used on disc, 22
System integrators, (list, 369)
System 7, Macintosh, 9, 10

T

Tandy VIS (Visual Information
 System), 47, 105
  player, 12, 103, (illus., 106)
Tax codes, on CD-ROM, 180-181
Telephone directories, as structured
 data, 214
Telephone listings, database of all
 business, 184
Terminator, defined, 137, 289

TestDrive Corporation, demo disc by,
 163
Testing, in CD-ROM creation, 225
Test versions, CD-ROM software,
 162-163
Text, as easiest in CD-ROM
 publishing, 213-214
Text and graphic information,
 standards for, 11
Text-based reference, CD-ROM, 12
Textbooks, converted to multimedia,
 187
Text databases, CD-ROM as, 180
Text searches, speeding up CD-ROM,
 225
Texture mapping, 104, 289
Thesaurus, on MS-Word for Win, 164,
 (illus., 165)
This is not a Macintosh disc... error
 message, 152
Thomas, Katherine ("Great Kat"), 160
Toshiba T6600, 146
Toshiba XM CD-ROM drive, 88, (illus.,
 89)
Tower products
  as CD-ROM server, 240
  properties of, 240
3DO
  Animation Engine, 101-104
  costs, 103
  defined, 101-104
  features, 101-104
  future products of, 102
  graphic processor of, 102
  multiplayer, 102
  players, 12, 47
Throughput, defined, 136, 289
Thunder Board, 131
Track, description of a, 27-28, 290
Track-at-once, 62, 290

Track density, 36
Tracks, music placement on, 50
Training
    CD-ROM on, 206
    for CD-ROM use, 181
Training CD-ROMs, 204-205
    costs of, 205
    vendors of, (list, 369-370)
Training software, as CD-ROM classification, 156
Transfer rate, 23, 83
Transparency, 104
Tray, for discs, 94-95
Trilobyte, CD-ROMs by, 217
Triple speed, cost of, 82
Triple-speed drives, 82, 290
Tuneland, 166-167, 258, 259
Turbo Duo, 109-110
    competitors of, 110
    features, 109
    player (illus., 110)
Turbo Technologies, Turbo Duo by, 109-110
Tutorials, on-line, 162
TV-based CD-I, 47
    and "book" specifications, 47
TV-based CD-ROM player, (illus., 2)
TV-based player, 4, 6
    compatibility with CD-ROMs, 47
    cost of, 4
    vendors of, (list, 370-371)
TV entertainment, and CD-ROM, 6-7
TV hookup, with players, 12
TV player, 12
    interactive, 103
Twain, Mark (Samuel Clemens), works by on CD-ROM, 189-190
Twain's World, CD-ROM, 189-190, (illus., 189)
20th Century Video Almanac, 188

space required for, 268

U

"Ugly Duckling" (CD-ROM production), 216
Ultimedia, IBM
    features of, 245
    supported clients, 245
Unix, 11
Unix file system, 64
Unix files, and Frankfurt group, 62
Unix Network File System, connecting Macintoshes to, 254
Unix software
    immensity of, 162
    versions of on CD-ROM, 162
Updates, keeping up with, 129
Updating a disc incrementally, 22
Upgrading, problems with, 129
Usage, measuring CD-ROM on network, 246-247
US Atlas, CD-ROM, 201
User interface, weakness in some clip art CD-ROMs, 172
Users
    identifying for CD-ROM creation, 212
    profile of CD-ROM, 232
Utilities, vendors of, (list, 372-374)

V

VCR tape, converting into CD-ROM format, 205
Vendor Resource Guide, 293-376
Verbum magazine, 203
VGA display, 87-88
Video, full-motion, 133
    CD-ROM publishing and, 217
    storage of, 60
    with 3DO, 101

Video, full-screen, full-motion, 133
Video boards, cost of, 191
Video cards, MPEG, 218
    costs of, 218
    and graphic performance, 132
    performances among, 133
Video CD, 60, 290
    defined, 60
    format, 133
    player, 60
Video clips, 177
Video Cube game, 193-194, (illus., 194)
Videodisc, optical media, 26
Video display, size of, 133
Video features, 132-133
Video for Windows (VFW), 67, 73, 74
    and file conversion utility, 74
    and OLE, 74
    video clips for, 177
Video frames, reference, 75
Video games, compared to interactive CD-ROM, 258
Video hardware/software vendors, (list, 374-376)
Video movies, as part of CD-ROM titles, 267
Video playback boards, 133, 267
    adding to standard computers, 267
Video specs, 73
Videotape
    pitfalls in using, 217
    tips for using, 217-218
Virgin Games, "7th Guest" investment by, 234
Virtual Microsystems, CD network tower by, 243
Virtual reality, 290
    Sega CD and, 108
Viruses, 4, 290
    on shareware CD-ROM, 204
VIS, 105
    defined, 105
    titles of, 105
VIS Development Corp., conversion software by, 205
Visually impaired, E-books for, 190
Visual Vocabulary video clips, 177, (illus., 178)
VL-Bus, 126, 290
VMS, 52
Voice recording, with Microsoft Word, 131
Voyager Co., interactive textbook by, 187-188

W

Wall Street Journal Personal Finance Library, on CD-ROM, 162
Warping, 104
Washington Post Newsweek Interactive, 14
WAV sound file, 217
Westwind Media, makers of Dinosource, 167
When You Press the Eject Button on the CD-ROM Drive error message, 153
White Book, for CD-I Bridge, 59-60
Who Built America? CD-ROM textbook, 187-188, (illus., 187)
Wide Area Network (WAN), 258, 291
    Broadcast, 247
    problems with, 247
Wildcard searches, in database titles, 182
Windows-based systems
    challenges of, 192
    insufficient main memory in, 192
Windows CD-ROM extensions, 129

Windows NT, CD-ROM sharing supported by, 246
Windows PC, CD-ROM for the, 10
Windows standard, 69-76
    sound board, 131
WinSleuth Gold, freeing memory with, 158
Word for Windows
    references on, 164
    system required for, 164, (illus., 165)
WordPerfect, on TestDrive Corp. demo, 163
Workgroup Connection redirector, 246
Workstation, 90-94
World Atlas, CD-ROM, 201
WORM (Write Once Read Many), 26, 291
    applications of, 26
    maximum capacity, 26
    recordable, 26
Writable systems, 255-256

X-Y-Z

Yale University Press books on multimedia, 187
Yellow Book, 10-11, 52, 291
    extended, 55-57
    for CD-ROM, 52-57
    Layers, 52-53
    and Mode 1 and 2, 52
    and random access, 52
    standard, 37, 46
    standard defined, 10-11
    and supporting formats, 52
Ziff Desktop Information, CD-ROM on computers by, 185
Z39.50 search engine method, 182

AUTHORWARE PROFESSIONAL

The Premier Authoring Tool for Interactive Multimedia

MacWEEK praised Authorware Professional for its easy-to-use interface, *"The program's intuitive, icon-based paradigm allows for speedy design without scripting..."* Ben Long, MacWEEK, July 19, 1993

The ideal software tool for production of:
- Interactive Learning Applications (CBT)
- Kiosks
- Point of Sales Tools
- Digital Interactive Magazines
- Computer Based Reference Tools
- Interactive Books

Your First Step towards Creating Interactive CD ROM productions for Macintosh or Windows

Call Macromedia for the FREE Authorware Professional Working Model with its Comprehensive, 32 page User Guide!

1-800-945-9357

M MACROMEDIA

For more information, please turn the page

Authorware Professional
The Premier Authoring Tool for Interactive Multimedia on Macintosh and Windows

Authorware Professional is the premier authoring software for interactive multimedia applications. Its visual mapping approach allows non-technical courseware designers to build sophisticated multimedia applications without scripting. Authorware Professional is a cross-platform authoring software designed specifically for interactive multimedia application development.

Authorware Professional offers three important advantages for authoring and distributing interactive multimedia applications:

l Object Authoring allows users to focus on content and interactive design. An elegant iconic interface controls functional logic, making even the most complicated applications easy to author.

l Multiplatform architecture gives developers similar authoring environments and runtime distribution capabilities on both Macintosh and Windows.

l Multimedia tools provide the power to incorporate text, graphics, sound, animation, and digital and analog video which enhance the multimedia experience and greatly increase retention of the subject matter.

Features and Benefits

Extensive Interactivity:
Authorware Professional offers more interaction types than any other authoring software. Authors can create multimedia applications to any degree of complexity.

Media Manager:
Media Manager allows authors to store text, graphics, sound, and movies in libraries that can be referenced multiple times from one or many applications. The Media Manager greatly reduces the size of Authorware applications and speeds the authoring process.

Support for QuickTime, Video for Windows and Macromedia Director
QuickTime digital video, Video for Windows and interactive Director animations help authors develop applications which assist users with complex subjects, making applications more dynamic, exciting and effective.

Compatible Products

Graphics: Adobe Photoshop, Adobe Illustrator, Aldus Freehand, Aldus SuperPaint, Claris MacDraw Pro, Claris MacPaint, Macromedia MacroModel, Macromedia ModelShop II, Macromedia Swivel 3D Formats include: DIB, BMP, PCX, TIF, RLE, WMF, EPS, PICT, Paint

Animation: Macromedia Director (.MMM), Gold Disk Animation Works, Autodesk Animator, Animator Pro**Sound:** Macromedia SoundEdit and SoundEdit Pro files (on Windows, 3.1 compatible audio boards including Creative Labs Soundblaster Pro, IBM M-Audio, and Media Vision Pro Audio Spectrum)

Video Capture/Overlay: RasterOps ColorBoard 364, 24STV, 24XLTV, and MediaTime, Truevision NuVista Plus, VideoLogic DVA/4000, Truevision Bravado, IBM M-Motion, and more

Video Devices: NEC PC-VCR S98A; Panasonic TQ-2023F, TQ-2024F, TQ 2026, TQ 2027F; Pioneer LDV 2200, 4200/4200A, 6000/6000A and 8000; Sony LDP Series and more

CD ROM: All Macintosh compatible CD-ROM players and all Windows 3.1 compatible CD-ROM players

Authoring System Requirements

Recommended for Macintosh: SE with 4Mb RAM. Color authoring and Delivery, Minimum: MacII with 2Mb RAM (w/System 6.0.7), (4Mb RAM w/System 7.x). Recommended: 4 to 8 Mb RAM.

Recommended for Windows: 33+ MHZ 386 with 8Mb RAM, 16-color VGA (256-color with VGA+ card).

M MACROMEDIA

Macromedia, Inc.
600 Townsend
San Francisco, CA 94103

From Barron's Profiles Of American Colleges To Money Magazine And Harry's StoryDisc And Coloring Book, Laser Resources Inc. Is Committed To Bringing You Quality, Educational And Entertaining CD-ROMs.

Money Magazine - Money In The 90's includes the full text of all regular issues of Money Magazine from January 1990 through December 1993, plus the forecast issues and videos. Updated yearly, this disc provides you with solid, objective advice on investments, retiring early, saving or planning for your financial future. $49.95

Barron's Profiles of American Colleges with LRI's Multimedia College Supplement - A single disc features colorful maps and photographs of college and university campuses, tuition guidelines, videos and printable admissions applications for many participating schools. This CD-ROM makes access and retrieval easy for administrators, students and parents to use! $99.99

Harry's StoryDisc and Coloring Book - Captures 150 classic children's stories with more than 250 printable coloring book pages providing endless hours of quality entertainment for children. Includes such timeless tales as "Peter Pan," "Pinocchio," "Jungle Book" and "The Wizard of Oz". $59.95

Harry's Stories From Around The World - Second in a series of "Harry's" discs, this special collection features favorite folk stories from around the world, sure to delight children of many ages. Listening and reading skills are enhanced with classic tales from England, Hungary, Germany, France, Poland, Russia and Iceland. Also included are traditional Native American stories. $59.95

The Constitution - The Constitution of the United States on CD-ROM is a great educational tool. The disc includes life and times in early America leading up to the signing of the Constitution, a comprehensive description of all articles and amendments, and an in-depth explanation of the ways in which the Constitution has defined and influenced life in America. $59.95

The Declaration of Independence - Enjoy this tour of history. Read and listen as you uncover the details behind this momentous document that helped to forge a nation. $59.95

Earthworks - Journey to the center of this environmental CD-ROM that explores our planet Earth. Learn about the delicate balance that must be maintained for mankind to harmoniously co-exist with the planet and its precious resources. $59.95

World Video Chronicle - Watch the world go by with national and international news video highlights from 1990 to the present. Take a trip through time as you review history-making events displayed with original corresponding photographic imagery. $59.95

To Order Call
310.324.4444
(Fax 310.324.9999)
· · · · Or Write · · · ·
20620 S. Leapwood Ave., Bldg. F, Carson, CA 90746

The above discs are all available on Windows and MAC Multimedia platforms.

LASER RESOURCES' SUPERIOR PUBLISHING SERVICES BRING YOU THE LATEST IN CD-ROM TECHNOLOGY.

LRI is the resource to turn to for excellence in all facets of publishing services. As one of the pioneers in the CD-ROM industry, we've earned the reputation for being a hard-driving, superior-quality company.

We'd like to take this opportunity to thank Osborne/McGraw-Hill for choosing LRI to create the enclosed CD-ROM. Please note, this CD-ROM can run on both Windows and MAC Platforms.

DISTRIBUTION IS KEY TO OUR SUCCESS, AND YOURS.

Laser Resources Inc. is one of the few distributors in the world that is dedicated solely to the CD-ROM market. Uniquely customized software "bundling," or Value Added Reselling (VAR), has separated Laser Resources from its competitors—getting your software off the shelves, on the streets, and in the hands of your customers well ahead of your competition.

Developing marketing channels and focusing on applications for this thriving industry are just some of the ways that Laser Resources keeps on top of the market—always watchful for the latest technology to enhance your products.

Call Laser Resources for your next CD-ROM job or to find out more about our expanding network of Publishing and Distribution Services.

310-324-4444   Fax 310-324-9999

20620 S. Leapwood Ave., Bldg. F, Carson, CA 90746

INITIAL CAPS & HISTORIC ORNAMENTS

Aridi Computer Graphics CD-ROM contains all three volumes: *Initial Caps I*, *Initial Caps II*, and *Historic Ornaments, patterns and Frames*. That's 748 complete images (over 45 Megabytes) available in Black and white and in full color process (CMYK). These three volumes combine an assortment of Initial Caps font graphics and a selection of decorative art including full frames, ornaments, and patterns. These graphics hand drawn by a master designer, were inspired by tiles, old manuscripts, carved wood panels, fabrics, and other items from Europe during the middle ages and the Renaissance period.

The CD-ROM comes programed with both Macintosh and IBM/PC formats. You receive all the original images in multiple file formats. For Macintosh - EPS and 72 dpi PICT. for IBM/PC - EPS, PCX, and BMP.

TO ORDER PLEASE CONTACT

 ARIDI COMPUTER GRAPHICS   **1-800-755-6441**

5151 Beltline Rd, Suite 815 • Dallas, TX 75240 • (214)404-9171 • Fax (214)404-9172

Copyright © 1993 Aridi Computer Graphics, Inc. All rights reserved. Other brand and product names are trademarks of their respective holders.

Initial Caps 1

Initial Caps 2

CD-ROM SPECIAL OFFER $169
REGULAR RETAIL PRICE $249

Historic Ornaments 3

ARIDI COMPUTER GRAPHICS · HIGH QUALITY · HAND DRAWN ·
EPS FORMAT

TO ORDER CALL TOLL FREE
1-800-755-6441